P9-DMA-991
52 SHIVERTOWN RD.
NEW PALTZ, NEW YORK 12561

# Intelligence Applied

## UNDERSTANDING AND INCREASING
## YOUR INTELLECTUAL SKILLS

# Intelligence Applied

## UNDERSTANDING AND INCREASING YOUR INTELLECTUAL SKILLS

### Robert J. Sternberg

Yale University

Under the General Editorship of

### Jerome Kagan

Harvard University

**Harcourt Brace Jovanovich College Publishers**
Fort Worth   Philadelphia   San Diego
New York   Orlando   Austin   San Antonio
Toronto   Montreal   London   Sydney   Tokyo

*For Luis Alberto Machado, the first (but I hope not the last) Minister for the Development of Intelligence in Venezuela and in the world, and for his Adviser-General and right-hand man, José Dominguez Ortega, whose combined vision, dedication, and zeal made this book possible.*

Copyright © 1986 by Harcourt Brace Jovanovich, Inc.

All rights reserved. No part of this publication may be reproduced or transmitted in any form or by any means, electronic or mechanical, including photocopy, recording, or any information storage and retrieval system, without permission in writing from the publisher.

Requests for permission to make copies of any part of the work should be mailed to: Permissions, Harcourt Brace Jovanovich, Publishers, Orlando, Florida 32887.

ISBN: 0-15-541470-4

Library of Congress Catalog Card Number: 85-80086

Printed in the United States of America

COVER AND INTERIOR DESIGNED BY LOUIS NEIHEISEL, PTN.

# Preface

This book originated in a telephone call I received in 1980. The caller was Glenda Greenwald, currently editor of the *Human Intelligence Newsletter*, who was then representing Venezuela's newly appointed Minister for the Development of Intelligence, Luis Alberto Machado. Machado had heard about my research on intelligence and was interested in using it as the basis for a program to train intellectual skills in Venezuelan school-children. Our long-distance discussions resulted in the development of a proposal for two subprograms based on my componential subtheory of intelligence as it was formulated in 1980. Although Machado and his adviser, José Dominguez Ortega, were very interested in the proposal, there was a long delay before it was finally funded in January 1983 by El Dividendo Voluntario para la Comunidad.

That summer a Venezuelan college professor and consultant, Francisco Rivero, and a Venezuelan research assistant, Margarita Rodriguez-Lansberg, visited New Haven. After reviewing the materials we had prepared during the first eight months of the project, Dr. Rivero decided that they were too easy for the students who would be using them. Although the project had originally been intended for students in the early secondary-school years, arrangements had been made for the program to take place at the Metropolitan University of Caracas. However appropriate the project might have been for younger students, it would clearly be inappropriate for university students. Eight months into the project, therefore, we essentially had to begin again from scratch.

Starting over proved to be fortunate. From 1980 to 1983, my theorizing about intelligence had developed substantially. Now the proposed program not only was inappropriate for the students; it also no longer reflected my current thoughts on the matter. Dr. Rivero and I decided to base the new program on my current theory of intelligence—the triarchic theory—which subsumes the older componential subtheory. Since then, the program has been tested in two Venezuelan universities, and though the statistical data are not yet available, the "clinical" data are highly favorable.

The present program seeks not only to help people increase their intellectual skills but to help them understand these skills, as well. This book therefore addresses both the increasing and the understanding of intelligence. The material on understanding intelligence is a distillation and simplification of material in my recent book *Beyond IQ: A Triarchic Theory of Human Intelligence*. The training materials have never been published before, although many of them draw on materials I have used in my research.

The first part of this book contains background information: Chapter 1 describes and evaluates some previous theories of intelligence and programs to train intellectual skills. This chapter sets the stage for Chapter 2, which describes the triarchic theory of intelligence that motivates the present book. The second part of the book deals with the relation of intelligence to the internal world of the individual. What are the cognitive processes, strategies, and representations of information that enable us to think intelligently? The text explains what they are, how they can be improved, and how they can be applied to problems in academic and everyday life. The third part of the book deals with the relation of intelligence to experience. How do we deal with novel kinds of tasks and situations, and, once these tasks and situations are no longer novel, how can we learn to perform automatically when we encounter them? This part of the book deals with issues such as the nature of insight, mental speed, and how improving mental performance bears some resemblance to improving athletic performance. Chapter 8 deals with the application of intelligence to practical problems. How can we apply our mental processes to our everyday lives in the most efficient and effective way? This part of the book enables students to ensure that what they learn from the book stays with them when they leave the classroom. Finally, Chapter 9 deals with emotional and motivational blocks to the utilization of our intelligence. What kinds of emotional and motivational obstacles prevent us from fully using our intelligence, and how can we overcome these obstacles?

A number of features make this book unusual, even unique, among programs for training of intellectual skills. First, the program is based on a contemporary psychological theory that has extensive data to support it. Second, the book conceptualizes intelligence in a broad way; the range of cognitive skills addressed is much greater than in the typical program of this kind. Third, the book is written to motivate students, as well as teach them. Many practical examples are included, and the examples are drawn from many fields of endeavor. Moreover, the theory on which the program is based is described so that students will understand why the program can be useful to them and why they can expect to increase their intellectual skills during the course of the program. Fourth, the problems range from very abstract and test-like to very concrete and untest-like. This range is necessary in order to ensure that the students transfer their learning from one task and situation to the next. In order for this transfer to occur, a program must teach for transfer—which the present program does. It is unlike many other programs that rely solely on test-like problems to enhance students' intellectual skills. Fifth, the book contains an entire chapter on emotional and motivational blocks to the utiliza-

tion of intelligence. It does not matter how intelligent people are if they are unable to use their intelligence. This last chapter is intended to help students make full use of their developing intellectual skills.

The book is appropriate as a main text for either high-school or college level courses on critical thinking, improving thinking skills, improving intelligence, developing reasoning and problem skills, and the like. The book also can be used as a supplementary text in courses on study skills, thinking, intelligence, reasoning, problem solving, and other courses in which the aim is to teach students how to think.

Many people and institutions have contributed to making this book possible. First, I would like to thank Luis Alberto Machado and José Dominguez Ortega, to whom I have dedicated it. For five years they ran a unique institution in Venezuela, the Ministry for the Development of Intelligence. As a result of their efforts, the writing of this book and the experimental program based on it received funding. I would also like to thank El Dividendo Voluntario para la Comunidad for its generous funding of the Venezuela project. Francisco Rivero, my project coordinator in Venezuela, contributed many efforts on behalf of the project; Margarita Rodriguez-Lansberg helped me formulate much of the material in this book and cheered the project on even when I became discouraged by the delays. The officials and students of the Metropolitan University of Venezuela fully supported the project throughout its development. I am grateful as well to the Office of Naval Research, the Army Research Institute, and the Spencer Foundation, whose funding of my research on intelligence has made possible the theoretical and empirical development on which this book is based.

I would also like to thank Nilda Prichard for her typing of portions of the manuscript, and the following students and assistants whose research collaborations with me have provided some of the training materials included here: Barbara Conway, Janet Davidson, Louis Forster, Michael Gardner, Ann Kirkland, Robin Lampert, Diana Marr, Elizabeth Neuse, Susan Nolen-Hoeksema, Janet Powell, Margarita Rodriguez-Lansberg, Craig Smith, Larry Soriano, Rebecca Treiman, and Richard Wagner. I would like to thank all of those people in Venezuela and elsewhere who for five years provided the support that enabled the Ministry for the Development of Intelligence to flourish and carry on its unique experiment. Finally, I am grateful to Marcus Boggs, my acquisitions editor at Harcourt Brace Jovanovich, for his tremendous support throughout this project, and to Natalie Bowen for a superb job of editing.

**Robert J. Sternberg**

# Contents

# 5

## Knowledge-Acquisition Components   184

# 6

## Coping with Novelty   209

# 7

## Automatizing Information Processing   248

# 8

## Practical Intelligence   300

# 9

## Why Intelligent People Fail (Too Often)   338

# 1

# Views of Intelligence

I n order to understand the new theory of intelligence presented in this book and to use this theory to increase your own intelligence, you will find it useful to know something about the historical roots of this and other theories of intelligence. This chapter, therefore, will present a brief overview of the way psychologists and others have conceived of intelligence. Although, strictly speaking, you need not read this chapter to understand the rest of the book, it will give you an increased appreciation and understanding of the theory and intellectual exercises in subsequent chapters.

## The Definitional Approach to Intelligence

One way to seek to understand intelligence is simply to define it. We then use the definition as a basis for theorizing about intelligence, testing intelligence, and training intelligence. The nice feature of this approach is that it is simple: We need simply to find what intelligence is, and then proceed from there. The obvious shortcoming of the approach is that it is not always persuasive. It is one thing to define intelligence; it is another thing to get people to accept the definition.

We might think that just as a rose is a rose, a definition is a definition. This proposition turns out to be not quite true. In fact, two principal kinds of definitions of intelligence have been proposed—the operational definition and the "real" definition.

### Operational Definition

An *operational definition* attempts to define intelligence in terms of the way it is measured. Thus, an operational definition might define intelligence as

1

whatever it is that intelligence tests measure. We might think that no serious scientist would propose such a definition, or that if one did, no one would take it seriously. But precisely this definition of intelligence—as being whatever it is that intelligence tests measure—was proposed by a famous Harvard psychologist, E. G. Boring (1923). Moreover, Boring did not propose this definition as something merely suitable for scientific use. To the contrary, he suggested it in a popular magazine, the *New Republic*. We can see, therefore, that he was quite serious about having the general public accept the notion that psychologists had found the key to what intelligence is, and that the key was in their intelligence tests.

Even if Boring could sell the general public on such a definition, we might think that he would have little or no success in convincing scientists of it. Unfortunately, nothing could be further from the truth. Many scientists and educators alike have proceeded in their research and testing as though intelligence is nothing more and nothing less than what intelligence tests measure. Arthur Jensen (1969), a well-known advocate of the importance of heredity in intelligence, accepted this definition as a basis for his attempted demonstration in the *Harvard Educational Review* that group differences in intelligence can be understood as having a hereditary basis, and that as a result there is little hope for attempts to train people's intelligence. Other scientists have been less obvious and forthcoming in admitting their acceptance of the operational definition, but have proceeded to use it nevertheless. For example, when new tests of intelligence are proposed, their validity (that is, the extent to which they measure what they are supposed to measure) is usually assessed by relating scores on a new intelligence test to scores on older and more widely accepted tests. Thus, the older tests serve as the operational standard for the newer ones. To the extent that the new tests actually do measure anything new, they will be less related to the old tests and thus may be viewed as less valid than these older tests. Even experimental psychologists who attempt to study intelligence in the laboratory and to go beyond existing IQ-based notions of intelligence often validate their theories and new instruments against existing tests. Thus, they too become trapped into accepting the operational definition of intelligence. They may not be happy about doing so, but they do it nevertheless.

I have made no attempt above to hide my distaste for the operational definition of intelligence, which has two basic, interrelated problems. The first is that it is circular. Intelligence tests were originally devised in order to measure intelligence, not to define it. The designers of the tests based them on their own conceptions of intelligence and hoped that eventually the definition of intelligence would become more clear. They never intended for these tests actually to define intelligence. To the contrary, they believed that the tests could only make sense if they were based on some prior definition of intelligence. Thus, they were trying to have it both ways—the instruments that were supposed to be based on a definition of intelligence became the basis for such a definition.

The second problem with the operational definition of intelligence is that it seems to provide an ideal way to block further progress in understanding the nature of intelligence. If old, established tests are used as the primary or sole criterion against which new tests and conceptions of intelligence are to be assessed, then the new tests and conceptions will be viewed as valid only to the extent that they correspond to the old ones. There is no allowance for the possibility that the new tests or conceptions may actually be better than the older ones. The result is that we become locked into existing conceptions and measurement devices, whether they are any good or not. Existing tests of intelligence may well serve as one criterion against which to evaluate new tests and theories. It would be a pity, however, if they were to serve as the only criterion. Were this to happen, we would foreclose the possibility of ever learning more about the nature of human intelligence.

### *"Real" Definition*

According to the philosopher R. Robinson (1950), a *"real" definition* is one that seeks to tell us the true nature of the thing being defined. Such a definition goes beyond measurement and seeks to understand the underlying nature of intelligence. Perhaps the most common way of trying to find out just what intelligence is has been to ask experts in the field of intelligence to define it.

The most well-known example of this approach was the symposium that appeared in 1921 in the *Journal of Educational Psychology*. Fourteen experts gave their views on the nature of intelligence, with definitions involving activities such as the ability to carry on abstract thinking, the ability to learn to adjust oneself to the environment, the ability to adapt oneself adequately to relatively new situations in life, the capacity for knowledge, the amount of knowledge possessed, and the capacity to learn or to profit from experience. From one point of view, an examination of the full set of definitions seems to lead to the conclusion that there were as many definitions of intelligence as there were experts asked to define it. From another point of view, however, at least two themes seem to run through several of the definitions: the capacity to learn from experience and the capacity to adapt to one's environment. A view of intelligence accepted by many of these experts would seem to be one of intelligence as general adaptability to new problems and situations in life.

There have been other, more recent, definitions of intelligence that have been accepted by at least some people in the field. For example, David Wechsler (1958) defined intelligence as the global capacity of a person to act purposefully, to think rationally, and to deal effectively with his or her environment. Note the overlap between this definition and the composite of the definitions proposed in the 1921 symposium. George Ferguson (1956) has defined intelligence in terms of a person's ability to transfer his or her learning and accumulated experience from one situation to another. According to this definition, then, it is not just what we know that counts, but our ability to use this information in new kinds of situations that we confront in our lives. Again, this definition shows a striking degree of overlap with the consensus of the psychologists in the 1921 symposium.

Because definitions are such a subjective thing, we might think that there is simply no basis for judging one definition as either better or worse than another definition. This is not the case, however. For example, we saw that the operational definition of intelligence is a particularly unproductive one. I believe that Sir Cyril Burt's definition of intelligence is also an unproductive one. Burt (1940) defines intelligence as innate general cognitive ability. Some psychologists, such as Jensen, seem to accept a view of intelligence that is quite close to this one, but the definition seems problematical for at least two reasons. First, it assumes that intelligence is innate, that is, inherited. Although intelligence probably is at least partly inherited, the question of the degree to which it is heritable is an empirical one. Assuming that intelligence is innate essentially defines out of the concept of intelligence anything that may be environmentally controlled or developed. In this definition, then, Burt seems to assume what really ought to be proved. Second, the definition assumes that intelligence is exclusively cognitive. Although intelligence certainly draws upon a wide array of cognitive abilities, it seems at least possible that it may also involve other kinds of abilities, such as motivational ones. Again, Burt seems to be presupposing what instead ought to be proved.

In sum, then, the so-called real definition of intelligence can have some value if we look for commonality among various experts' definitions. When we do this, the abilities to learn from experience and to adapt to the environment seem to be essential ingredients of intelligence. However, we must be careful in accepting these definitions of intelligence. First, we have seen that a definition may end up presupposing what actually needs to be empirically demonstrated. Second, experts obviously disagree among themselves as to the definition of intelligence, and there is not even any guarantee that any of their definitions are correct. Thus, so-called real definitions of intelligence need to be interpreted with due caution.

## Theories of Intelligence

Just as there are different kinds of definitions, there are also different kinds of theories of intelligence. The theory that forms the basis of this book draws at least a little on each kind. Thus, it may be helpful to give a brief review of these theories.

### *Learning Theory*

Although we would think that there must be an intimate relation between learning and intelligence, psychologists studying learning have not been among the most active contributors to the literature on intelligence. Usually, they have preferred to study learning in its own right without touching on the topic of its relation to intelligence. One exception to this generalization was Edward Thorndike (1926, with Bregman, Cobb, and Woodyard), who wrote:

> The hypothesis which we present and shall defend asserts that in their deeper nature the higher forms of intellectual operation are identical with mere association or connection forming, depending upon the same sort of physiological connection but requiring *many more of them*. By the same arguments the person whose intellect is greater or higher or better than that of another person differs from him in the last analysis in having, not a new sort of physiological process, but simply a large number of connections of the ordinary sort.

In the learning theorist's view, then, all behavior—no matter how complex or "intelligent"—is seen as of a single type and our "intelligence" is seen as simply a function of the number and strength of stimulus-response connections we have formed and, perhaps, the rate at which we can form new ones.

Learning theorists have tended to emphasize the malleability and trainability of intelligence. This emphasis contrasts with that of many of the more avid adherents of intelligence tests, who have often, although by no means always, been more associated with hereditary points of view. Perhaps the most optimistic statement of what learning theory can do to mold a person's intellect and other skills was provided by John Watson (1930), who said, in one of the most well-known quotations of all psychology:

> Give me a dozen healthy infants, well-formed, and my own specified world to bring them up in and I'll guarantee to take any one at random and train him to become any type of specialist I might select—doctor, lawyer, artist, merchant-chief and, yes, even beggar-man and thief— regardless of his talents, penchants, tendencies, abilities, vocations, and race of his ancestors.

The main contributions of the learning-theory approach to intelligence seem to have been, first, its emphasis on the importance of learning in intelligence, and second, its optimism regarding the malleability and possible improvement of human intelligence. Thus, whether or not learning theorists were literally correct in what they said regarding the nature of intelligence, they appear to be correct in the spirit of what they had to say. I agree with them wholeheartedly that intelligence is a characteristic that can be increased and improved on, and that will be a main theme throughout this book.

### *Psychometric Theory*

Psychometric approaches to intelligence are those linked to the psychological measurement of intelligence. Such conceptions of intelligence have in common their reliance on individual differences among people as a basis for testing theories of intelligence, and in some cases as a stimulus to the formulation and revision of psychological theories. Psychometric researchers use techniques such as factor analysis to discover common patterns of individual differences across tests. These patterns are then hypothesized to derive from underlying sources of individual differences, namely, mental abilities.

As a simple example of such a factor analysis, consider five tests of mental abilities: vocabulary, number-series completions, general information, reading comprehension, and mathematical problem solving. Factor analysis would compute the degree of relationship (*correlation*) between each possible pair of the five tests. These correlations are expressed on a scale from $-1$ to $1$, where $-1$ means a perfect inverse relationship between scores on two tests, $0$ means no relationship between scores on two tests, and $1$ means a perfect positive relationship between scores on the two tests. For example, we would expect people's ability to do addition and subtraction problems to have a high positive relation. On the other hand, we would expect people's ability to do addition and to run quickly to have very little correlation. What factor analysis does is to cluster together those tests that tend to be more highly correlated. For example, factor analysis would probably group the vocabulary, general information, and reading comprehension tests in one cluster, and the number-series completion and mathematical problem-solving tests in another. Thus, observable performance on the five tests would be reduced to performance on two hypothesized underlying factors of mental ability, namely, verbal ability and quantitative ability. The idea in factor analysis, then, is to simplify a pattern of scores on a set of tests.

Psychometric theory and research seem to have evolved along three interrelated but distinguishable lines. These traditions, which convey rather different impressions of what intelligence is, can be traced back to Sir Francis Galton, Alfred Binet, and Charles Spearman.

**THE TRADITION OF SIR FRANCIS GALTON**    The publication of Charles Darwin's *Origin of Species* (1859) had a profound impact on many lines of scientific endeavor, among them the investigation of human intelligence. Darwin's book suggested that the capabilities of humans were in some sense continuous with those of lower animals and, hence, could be understood through scientific investigation of the kind that had been conducted on animals. There was also the intriguing possibility that in intelligence, as in physical characteristics, the development of intelligence in humans over the life span might in some way resemble the development of intelligence from lower to higher species.

Darwin's cousin, Sir Francis Galton, was probably the first to explore the implications of Darwin's book for the study of intelligence. Galton (1883) proposed two general qualities that distinguished the more gifted from the less gifted. The first was energy or the capacity for labor. The second was sensitivity to physical stimuli:

> The discriminative facility of idiots is curiously low; they hardly
> distinguish between heat and cold, and their sense of pain is so obtuse
> that some of the more idiotic seem hardly to know what it is. In their dull
> lives, such pain as can be excited in them may literally be accepted with a
> welcome surprise.

For seven years, between 1884 and 1890, Galton maintained an "anthropometric" laboratory at the South Kensington Museum in London where, for a small fee, visitors could have themselves measured on a variety of psychophysical tests, such as weight discrimination and pitch sensitivity.

James McKean Cattell brought many of Galton's ideas from England to the United States. As head of the psychology laboratory at Columbia University, Cattell was in a good position to publicize the psychophysical approach to the theory and measurement of intelligence. Cattell (1890) proposed a series of fifty psychophysical tests, such as dynamometer pressure (greatest possible squeeze of the hand), rate of arm movement over a distance of 50 centimeters, and the distance on the skin by which two points need to be separated for them to be felt separately. Underlying each was the assumption that physical tests measure mental ability. For example, Cattell claimed that "the greatest squeeze of the hand may be thought by many to be a purely physiological quantity. It is, however, impossible to separate bodily from mental energy."

The coup de grace for the Galtonian tradition—at least in its earliest forms—was administered by one of Cattell's own students. Clark Wissler (1901) investigated 21 psychophysical tests. His line of approach was correlational, the idea being to show that the various tests are fairly highly correlated and, thus, define some common entity (intelligence) that underlies all of them. Wissler's results were disappointing, however. He found the tests generally to be unrelated, and he concluded that his results "would lead us to doubt the existence of such a thing as general ability." However, psychologists did not give up hope of finding a construct of general intelligence, because an alternative approach was leading to greater success.

**THE TRADITION OF ALFRED BINET**    In 1904, the French Minister of Public Instruction formed a commission to study or create tests that would ensure that mentally defective children received an adequate education. The commission decided that no child suspected of retardation should be placed in a special class for the retarded without first being given an examination "from which it could be certified that because of the state of its intelligence, he was unable to profit, in an average measure, from the instruction given in ordinary schools." Alfred Binet, in collaboration with his colleague, Theophile Simon, devised tests to meet this placement need. Thus, whereas Galton's theory and research grew out of pure scientific concerns, Binet's grew out of practical educational concerns.

At the time, definitions for various degrees of subnormal intelligence lacked both precision and standardization, and personality and intellectual deficits were seen as being of the same ilk. Binet and Simon (1973) noted a case of one institutionalized child who seemed to be a victim of this state of confusion: "One child, called imbecile in the first certificate, is marked idiot in the second, feebleminded in the third, and degenerate in the fourth."

Binet and Simon's conception of intelligence and of how to measure it differed substantially from that of Galton and Cattell, whose tests they considered a waste of time. To Binet and Simon, the core of intelligence was

> judgment, otherwise called good sense, practical sense, initiative,
> the faculty of adapting oneself to circumstances. To judge well, to
> comprehend well, to reason well, these are the essential activities of
> intelligence. A person may be a moron or an imbecile if he is lacking in
> judgment: but with good judgment he can never be either. Indeed the rest
> of the intellectual faculties seem of little importance in comparison with
> judgment.

Binet cited the example of Helen Keller as someone of known extraordinary intelligence whose scores on psychophysical tests would be notably inferior, but who could be expected to perform at a very high level on tests of judgment.

According to Binet and Simon, intelligent thought is composed of three distinct elements: direction, adaptation, and criticism. *Direction* consists of knowing what has to be done and how to do it. When we need to add two numbers, for example, we give ourselves a series of instructions on how to proceed, and these instructions form the direction of thought. *Adaptation* refers to the selection and monitoring of our strategy during the course of performance. In solving a problem, we often have many paths to solutions, some of which will lead to better solutions and others to worse. Adaptive people tend to select better strategies, and they monitor their progress along the way to make sure that the strategy is leading where they want to be going. *Criticism* (or *control*) is our ability to criticize our own thoughts and actions— to know not only when we are doing well, but to be able to recognize when we are doing poorly, and to change our behavior in such a way as to improve our performance.

Because of his emphasis on test development, Binet has often been accused of being atheoretical in his approach to intelligence. The above discussion of Binet's views should make it clear that nothing could be further from the case. To the contrary, he and Simon conceived of intelligence in ways that were theoretically sophisticated and that resembled in content much of the most recent thinking regarding cognitive processing. Whatever the distinction between Galton's thinking and Binet's, it was not (as some would have it) that Galton was theoretically motivated and Binet was not. If anything, Binet had a more well-developed theory of the nature of intelligence. Instead, these scientists differed in the way they selected items for the tests with which they proposed to measure intelligence. Galton's test items were chosen to measure psychophysical abilities, but Galton did not attempt to validate his items. Binet's test items were more cognitive in nature, in that they measured the kinds of judgmental abilities that Binet considered to constitute intelligence. He also chose his items, however, to differentiate between performance of children of different ages or mental capacities as well as to correlate at a reasonably high level.

In its contemporary form, the Stanford-Binet Intelligence Scale starts with tests for children of age 2 and continues with tests up to the level of the intelligent adult. The scale was developed at Stanford University by Lewis Terman and Maud Merrill. Typical tests for older individuals include such things as vocabulary; induction, in which the experimenter makes a notch in an edge of some folded paper and asks subjects how many holes the paper will have when it is unfolded; reasoning, which requires solution of an arithmetic word problem; ingenuity, which requires individuals to indicate the series of steps that could be used to pour a given amount of water from one container to another; orientation, requiring reasoning about spatial direction; interpretation of proverbs; and reconciliation of opposites, which requires subjects to say in what ways two opposites are alike.

A second intelligence test in the tradition of Binet is one developed by David Wechsler (1958). The Wechsler Adult Intelligence Scale and the Stanford-Binet are the two individual tests that are most widely used in the United States and probably elsewhere. The Wechsler scale is based on

Wechsler's notion of intelligence as "the overall capacity of an individual to understand and cope with the world around him." Wechsler conceives of intelligence as a global entity in which no one particular ability is of crucial or overwhelming importance.

The Wechsler Adult Intelligence Scale is divided into two parts, a verbal part and a performance part. It yields a separate intelligence quotient (IQ) for each part, as well as a global score for the two parts combined. Like the Stanford-Binet, the tests must be individually administered and must consist only of those items appropriate to the age and ability of the subjects being tested. Examinees begin with items easier than those appropriate for their age and end with items difficult enough to result in repeated failure of solution.

The verbal part of the test includes subtests such as information, which requires the demonstration of knowledge about the world; similarities, which requires an indication of a way in which two different objects are alike; and arithmetic, which requires the solution of arithmetic word problems. The performance part of the test includes subtests such as picture completion, which requires recognition of a missing part in a picture of an object; picture arrangement, which requires rearrangement of a scrambled set of pictures into an order that tells a coherent story from beginning to end; and block design, which requires individuals to reproduce a picture of a design, constructed from a set of red, white, and half-red/half-white blocks, by actually building the design with physical blocks.

In sum, the tradition of Alfred Binet involves testing higher-order cognitive skills in order to assess a person's intelligence. The theories of Binet and Wechsler are extremely broad in their conceptualization of intelligence, and they are quite compatible with the conception of intelligence that motivates this book. Unfortunately, the tests are quite a bit narrower than the conceptions of intelligence that generated them, so that the scores derived from the tests reflect not so much the originators' conceptions of intelligence as a set of higher-order cognitive skills that are used in a variety of academic, and to some extent, other tasks.

**THE TRADITION OF CHARLES SPEARMAN** According to Charles Spearman (1927), originator of the factorial tradition, there are two kinds of factors in human intelligence: a general factor, which pervades all intellectual performances; and a set of specific factors, each of which is relevant to just one particular task. Spearman's belief that a single factor of intelligence was responsible for whatever was common in intellectual performance across tasks constituted what he believed to be a law of the "universal unity of the intellective function."

What was the actual psychological mechanism that gave rise to such a unity of intellective function—to what Spearman referred to as the $g$ (general) factor? Spearman considered a number of possible explanations, such as attention, will, plasticity of the nervous system, and the state of the blood, but he finally settled on an explanation in terms of mental energy. According to Spearman, the concept of mental energy originated with Aristotle, who defined energy as any actual manifestation of change. For Spearman, the energy was only a latent potential for such change. Thus, for Spearman but not for Aristotle, energy could be an entirely mental construct.

Godfrey Thomson (1939) proposed an alternative to Spearman's theory of mental energy, the theory of bonds. In this theory, the mind is conceived of as possessing an enormous number of bonds, including reflexes, habits, learned associations, and the like. Performance on any one task would bring to bear a large number of these bonds. Related tasks, such as those used in mental tests, would sample overlapping subsets of these bonds. A factor analysis of a set of tests might, therefore, give the appearance of a general factor, when in fact what was common to the tests was instead a multitude of overlapping bonds.

Not all psychometric theorists have accepted the notion of a general factor underlying intelligence. Louis Thurstone (1938) proposed a theory that tentatively identified seven primary mental abilities, which were identified through factor analysis. The mental abilities were verbal comprehension, number, memory, perceptual speed, space, verbal fluency, and inductive reasoning. These primary mental abilities were later used as a basis for the formulation of the Primary Mental Abilities Test. These tests, suitable for age levels ranging from those of children of kindergarten level through adults, measure the primary mental abilities in a paper-and-pencil, group-testing format. The contents of the test vary considerably across the age range covered by the test, but they vary only slightly in the abilities reported to be measured. For example, verbal comprehension is generally measured by tests of vocabulary, number by tests of arithmetic computation and reasoning, and inductive reasoning by number and letter series-completion problems.

As it happens, scores on factors representing the primary mental abilities are almost always correlated with each other. If the scores on these factors are themselves factor analyzed (in much the same way that task or test scores would be), a higher-order general factor emerges from the analysis. Before his death, Thurstone found himself with little choice but to concede the existence of a general factor. Not surprisingly, he believed this general factor to be of little importance and to be of second-order status only. Similarly, Spearman was eventually forced to concede the existence of group factors such as those identified by Thurstone. But Spearman believed that these group factors were of little importance.

J. P. Guilford has proposed an extension of Thurstone's theory that incorporates Thurstone's factors and adds many others as well. He splits the primary mental abilities and adds new ones, so that the total number of factors is increased from seven to 120. Guilford (1967) wrote that every mental task requires three elements: an operation, a content, and a product. Guilford pictured the relation among these three elements as that of a cube, with each of the elements—operations, contents, and products—representing a dimension of the cube. There are five kinds of operations: cognition, memory, divergent production, convergent production, and evaluation. There are six kinds of products: units, classes, relations, systems, transformations, and implications. Finally, there are four kinds of contents: figural, symbolic, semantic, and behavioral. Because the subcategories are independently defined, they can be multiplied, yielding 120 (5 × 6 × 4) different mental abilities. Each of these 120 abilities is represented by Guilford as a small cube embedded in the larger cube. Guilford and his associates have devised tests measuring many of these abilities. Cognition of figural relations, for example, is measured by tests such as figural analogies. Memory for semantic relations is measured by presenting subjects with series of relations, such as "Gold is more valuable than iron," and then testing the subjects' retention of these relations using a multiple-choice test.

More recently, theorists of intelligence such as Philip Vernon have proposed hierarchical models of mental ability. Vernon (1971) proposed a hierarchy with general intelligence at the top, verbal-educational and practical-mechanical abilities at the second level, and more specific abilities at lower levels.

What seems to be missing from most factorial theories of intelligence is any clear notion of the processes involved in intelligence. Cognitive theories of intelligence, which deal explicitly with such processes, will be considered in a later section.

### Piaget's Theory

Jean Piaget first entered the field of intellectual development when, working in Binet's laboratory, he became intrigued with children's *wrong* answers to Binet's intelligence test items. To understand intelligence, Piaget reasoned, the investigation must be twofold. First, as was done by Binet, we must look at the way a person acts on the environment—at a person's performance. But also, and here is where Piaget begins to part company with Binet, we must consider *why* the person performs as he or she does, taking account of the cognitive structure underlying the individual's actions. Through his repeated observation of children's performance and particularly of their errors in reasoning, Piaget concluded that there are coherent logical structures underlying children's thought but that these structures are different from those underlying adult thought. In the six decades that followed, Piaget focused his research on delineating what these cognitive structures might be at different stages of development and how they might evolve from one stage to the next.

Piaget believed that there were two interrelated aspects of intelligence: its function and its structure. A biologist by training, he saw the function of intelligence to be no different from the function of other biological activities, that is, adaptation. According to Piaget (1972), adaptation includes assimilating the environment to one's own structures (whether physiological or cognitive) and accommodating one's mental structures (again either physiological or cognitive) to encompass new aspects of the environment. According to Piaget, "A certain continuity exists . . . between intelligence and the purely biological process of morphogenesis and adaptation to the environment."

In Piaget's theory, the function of intelligence—adaptation—provides continuity with lower biological acts:

> Intelligence is thus only a generic term to indicate the superior forms of organization or equilibrium of cognitive structuring. . . . Intelligence . . . is essentially a system of living and acting operations.

Piaget rejected the sharp separation proposed by some between intelligent acts, on the one hand, and habits or reflexes, on the other. Instead, he preferred to speak of a continuum in which "behavior becomes more intelligent as the pathways between the subject and the object on which it acts cease to be simple and become progressively more complex."

Piaget further proposed that the internal organizational structure of intelligence and the way intelligence is manifested differ with age. It is obvious that an adult does not deal with the world in the same way as an infant. For example, the infant typically acts on its environment via sensorimotor structures and is thus limited to the apparent physical world. The adult, on the other hand, is capable of abstract thinking and is thus free to explore the world of possibility. Guided by his interest in the philosophy of knowledge and his observation of children's behavior, Piaget divided the intellectual development of the individual into discrete, qualitative stages. As the child progresses from one stage to the next, the cognitive structures of the preceding stage are reorganized and extended, through the child's own adaptive actions, to form the underlying structures of the next stage.

Piaget's description of the child's intellectual development depends on three core assumptions about the nature of this developmental process. First, four factors interact to bring about the development of the child. Three of these factors are the ones usually proposed: maturation, experience of the physical environment, and the influence of the social environment. To these three factors, however, Piaget added a fourth, which coordinates and guides the other three: equilibration, that is, the child's own self-regulatory processes. Thus, Piaget's theory centers on the assertion that children are active participants in the construction of their own intelligence.

Piaget's second assumption is that this intellectual development results in the appearance of developmental stages that follow an invariable sequential order. Each succeeding stage incorporates and extends the accomplishments of the preceding stage. Third, although the rate of development may vary across children, Piaget considered the stages themselves and their sequence to be universal.

In sum, Piaget's theory asserted that there is a single route of intellectual development that all humans follow, regardless of individual differences, although their progression along this route may be at different rates. Notice that Piaget did not share the interests of psychometric theorists in individual differences, and certainly did not use individual differences as the basis for formulating his theory of intelligence.

### Cognitive-Processing Theories

Cognitive-processing conceptions of intelligence seek to understand the ways in which people mentally represent and process information. Cognitive-processing researchers use techniques of data analysis such as computer simulation and mathematical modeling to discover patterns of data that suggest strategies of cognitive processing in tasks requiring the exercise of intelligence.

Cognitive research has often used the computer program as a metaphor for understanding how humans process information. The major distinguishing feature of the approach, however, is not its reliance on computer notions, but rather its concern with how information is processed during the performance of various kinds of tasks.

One of the earliest and most important scientists advocating a cognitive approach, F. C. Donders (1868), proposed that the time between a stimulus and a response can be represented as a sequence of successive processes, with each process beginning as soon as the previous one ends. The durations of these processes can be calculated through the use of a subtraction method, in which subjects solve each of two tasks proposed by the experimenter. Since these tasks differ only in that the more difficult task requires one more component process for its solution than the simpler task, the duration of the process can be computed by subtracting the time taken to solve the easier task from the time taken to solve the harder task. The subtraction method was popular for several decades but then came into disfavor because of the method's assumption of strict additivity—that is, it assumed that a given process could be inserted into, or deleted from, a task without somehow affecting the execution of other processes. This assumption seemed so unreasonable at the time that the method was shelved for about a century, until it was dusted off and used in modified form.

Although the subtraction method lay dormant, psychologists were still interested in information processing and the isolation of component processes. Perhaps surprisingly, one such psychologist was Charles Spearman, the highly influential psychometrician discussed previously. Spearman might also have been one of the most influential figures in a revival of the cognitive tradition, had the time been right. The time apparently was not right, however. Whereas Spearman's 1904 psychometric theory and methodology were eagerly adopted by workers in the laboratory and in the field, Spearman's later cognitive theory of 1923 was not, perhaps because there was no methodology yet available to provide an adequate test of the theory.

Spearman (1923) proposed three principles of cognition (which he might as easily have proposed as three fundamental *processes* of cognition) that he illustrated in the context of the solution of an analogy. The first principle, apprehension of experience, states that "any lived experience tends to evoke immediately a knowing of its characters and experiencer." In an analogy, such as LAWYER is to CLIENT as DOCTOR is to ————, apprehension of experience would correspond to the encoding of each analogy term, whereby the problem solver perceives each word and understands its meaning. The second principle, eduction of relations, states that "the mentally presenting of any two or more characters (simple or complex) tends to evoke immediately a knowing relation between them." In the sample analogy, eduction of relations would correspond to inferring the relation between LAWYER and CLIENT (a lawyer provides professional services to a client). The third principle, eduction of correlates, states that "the presenting of any character together with any relation tends to evoke immediately a knowing of the correlative character." In the sample analogy, eduction of correlates would correspond to the application of the rule previously inferred to generate an acceptable completion to the analogy: PATIENT.

Almost forty years later, two works appeared that revived the cognitive approach. One was by Newell, Shaw, and Simon (1958), the other by Miller, Galanter, and Pribram (1960). The goal of both programs of research was, as Miller and his colleagues put it, "to discover whether the cybernetic [computer-based] ideas have any relevance to psychology." Both groups of investigators concluded that they did have relevance and, moreover, that the computer could be a highly useful tool in psychological theorizing. Miller and his collaborators sought to understand human behavior in terms of "plans," that is, "any hierarchical process in the argument that can control the order in which a sequence of operations is to be performed." Critical for the cognitive approach was the authors' view that "a plan is, for an organism, essentially the same as a program for a computer." The authors did not wish to confuse matters, however, by failing to distinguish altogether between computer and human information processing:

> We are reasonably confident that "program" could be substituted everywhere for "plan" in the following pages. However, the reduction of plans to nothing but programs is still a scientific hypothesis and is still in need of further validation. For the present, therefore, it should be less confusing if we regard a computer program that simulates certain features of an organism's behavior as a theory about the organismic plan that generated the behavior.

The computer simulation method allowed cognitive psychologists to test theories of human information processing by comparing predictions generated by computer simulation to actual data collected from human subjects. In computer simulations, the researcher attempts to get the computer to mimic the cognitive processes that would be used by humans, if they were solving the problem at hand. Some investigators have preferred to test their theories by using quantitative models with mathematical parameters estimated directly from human data. Saul Sternberg (1969) proposed an "additive-factor" method that can do just that. This method is a substantial modification of the subtraction method proposed by Donders, and it avoids the restrictive assumptions of that method. In particular, it does not require the assumption that the experimenter can insert and delete stages of information processing into a task at will.

Whereas many psychometric theorists of intelligence have agreed that the factor is the fundamental unit of intellectual behavior, many cognitive theorists have agreed that the elementary information process—or the information-processing component, as it is sometimes called—is the fundamental unit. Cognitive theorists assume that all behavior of the human information-processing system is the result of combinations of these elementary processes, although they have disagreed as to exactly which processes are most important to understanding intelligence. Consider just a few of the theories that have been proposed regarding how information processing is related to intelligence, and also consider some of the experimental paradigms that have been used to test these theories.

A primary difference among cognitive theorists is in the level of cognitive functioning they emphasize in attempting to understand intelligence. At one extreme are the investigators who have proposed to understand intelligence in terms of sheer speed of information processing, and who have used the most simple tasks they could devise in order to measure pure speed uncontaminated by other variables. At the other extreme are the investigators who have studied very complex forms of problem solving, and who have de-emphasized or discounted speed of functioning in mental processing. In general, greater emphasis on speed of processing has been associated with investigators studying the simpler forms of information processing, whereas greater emphasis on accuracy and strategies in information processing has been associated with investigators studying the more complex forms of information processing.

**PURE SPEED**    Proponents of the notion that individual differences in intelligence can be traced back to individual differences in sheer speed of information processing have tended to use simple reaction-time and related tasks in order to make their point. In a simple *reaction-time* paradigm, the individual is required simply to make a single overt response as quickly as possible following the presentation of a stimulus. This paradigm has been widely used since the days of Galton as a measure of intelligence. Although Galton and Cattell, in the late nineteenth century, were strong supporters of the importance of sheer speed in intellectual functioning, the levels of correlation obtained between measures of simple reaction time and various standard measures of intelligence, none of which are perfect in themselves (such as IQ test scores and school grades), have been weak. There seems to be much more to intelligence than pure speed.

**CHOICE SPEED**    A slight complication of the above view is that intelligence derives not from simple speed of processing, but rather from speed in making choices or decisions to simple stimuli. In a typical *choice reaction-time* paradigm, the subject is presented with one of two or more possible stimuli, each requiring a different overt response. The subject has to choose the correct response as rapidly as possible following stimulus presentation. Correlations with psychometric measures of intelligence have been higher than those obtained for simple reaction time, but they are still relatively weak.

An interesting finding in the research of Jensen and others is that the correlation between choice reaction time and IQ tends to increase with the number of stimulus-response choices involved in the task. In other words, the larger the number of choices the subject has to make, and thus the more complex the choice reaction-time task, the more highly scores on this test correlate with measured intelligence.

**SPEED OF ACCESS**    In 1978, Earl Hunt proposed that individual differences in verbal intelligence may be understandable largely in terms of differences among individuals in *speed of access* to verbal information stored in long-term memory. According to Hunt, the more quickly people can access information, the more they can profit per unit time of presented information, hence the better they can perform on a variety of verbal tasks. With his colleagues C. Lunneborg and J. Lewis, Hunt (1975) initiated a paradigm for testing this theory that makes use of a letter-comparison task used by two psychologists, Posner and Mitchell (1967), in some of their research.

In this paradigm, subjects are presented with pairs of letters—such as AA, Aa, or Ab—that may be the same or different either physically or in name. For example, AA are the same both physically and in name; Aa are the same in name only; and Ab are the same neither in name nor in physical appearance. The subject's task is to indicate as rapidly as possible whether the two letters are a match: In one condition, people respond with respect to whether the letters are a *physical* match; in another condition, the same subjects respond with respect to whether the letters are a *name* match. The measure of interest is each person's average name-match time minus physical-match time. This measure is considered to be an index of the time it takes a person to access verbal information in long-term memory. Physical-match time is subtracted from name-match time in order to obtain a relatively pure measure of access time that is uncontaminated by sheer speed of responding. Thus, in contrast to those who study simple reaction time with particular interest in sheer speed of responding, Hunt and his colleagues do what they can to subtract out this element.

The lexical-access task yields a remarkably consistent picture with respect to its relation to measured intelligence: Correlations with scores on verbal IQ tests are typically weak to moderate. Thus, time to access verbal information in long-term memory seems to be related at some level to intellectual performance. But again, at best it is obviously only one contributor to individual differences in what standard psychometric intelligence tests measure.

**COMPONENTS OF REASONING AND PROBLEM SOLVING**    A number of investigators have emphasized the kinds of higher-order processing involved in reasoning and problem solving in their attempts to understand intelligence, among them Robert Glaser, James Pellegrino, Herbert Simon, and myself. Following in the tradition of Spearman's three principles of cognition, these investigators have sought to understand individual differences in intelligence in terms of differential processing of information in tasks such as analogies, series completions, and syllogisms. We will consider the two main emphases in this work—performance processes and executive processes.

Investigators seeking to understand intelligence in terms of *performance processes,* or *components*, seek to discover the processes people use in problem solving from the moment they first see a problem to the time they respond. Consider, for example, the widely studied analogy item. In a typical theory of analogical reasoning, completing an analogy item is broken down into component processes such as *inferring* the relation between the first two terms of the analogy and *applying* this inferred relation to the second half of the analogy. The basic idea is that individuals' skills in solving these problems derive from their ability to execute these processes. Moreover, the processes involved in analogy solution have been shown to be quite general across various kinds of inductive-reasoning problems. Thus, the components of information processing are of interest because they are not task-specific.

Investigators seeking to understand intelligence in terms of executive processes seek to discover the processes by which individuals plan, monitor, and evaluate their performance in reasoning and problem solving. The idea in this approach is not just to look at what individuals do in solving problems, but to look also at why and how they decide to do what they actually do.

Investigators using reasoning and problem-solving items have generally obtained higher correlations between scores on their tasks and psychometrically measured IQ scores than have investigators using some of the other approaches discussed above. Typically, correlations have been moderate to high.

To sum up, the various theoretical approaches seem, on the surface, to be quite different. Psychometric researchers seek to understand the *structure* of the mental abilities that constitute intelligence. Piaget sought to understand the *stages* in the development of intelligence. Cognitive researchers seek to understand the *processes* of intelligence. When we look at them in this way, we see that the approaches are not mutually incompatible—they do not so much give different answers to the same questions as they give different answers to different questions. For example, the psychometric researchers emphasize structural models whereas the cognitive researchers emphasize process models. In fact, the two kinds of models are complementary to each other. The factors of intelligence can be understood in terms of processes that enter into them. So, for example, if one has a factor of verbal ability, it is legitimate to ask what processes are responsible for individual differences in verbal ability. Or we might ask if certain processes tend to go together in intelligent performance in human beings. Factor analysis addresses this question. It conveniently organizes the processes of human intelligence into constellations of higher-order mental abilities. We need to understand intelligence from all these points of view. Which approach an investigator decides to take will be a function of the investigator's theoretical and methodological predispositions, as well as of the particular questions about intelligence that most interest that investigator.

The theory presented in this book draws on all these approaches, and others, as well, although it is probably most heavily influenced by the cognitive approach. However, it is not enough just to look at cognitive processing. To understand intelligence fully, we also need to understand how these cognitive processes operate in everyday life. In many respects, the theory of intelligence in this book is more complete than most of the theories discussed in this chapter. As you learn about the theory, you will see how it operates as you solve intellectual games and puzzles that illustrate various aspects of the theory and that may help you to sharpen your thinking skills.

## Attempts to Increase Intelligence

For most of this century, many psychologists studying intelligence testing were preoccupied with a single question: "How can we measure intelligence?" For several reasons, this preoccupation has turned out to be a grave mistake.

First, the concentration on measuring intelligence led psychologists to neglect the more important question, "What is intelligence?" It is scarcely surprising that intelligence tests did not improve much over the course of the years. Better tests could arise only from better ideas of what intelligence is, but curiously enough, few psychologists sought better tests through better understanding. Rather, their improvements resulted from small refinements of existing technology, but this technology was limited by the inadequacies of the minimal theory underlying it.

Second, the preoccupation with testing was based on certain assumptions, at least one of which—that intelligence is, for the most part, a fixed and immutable characteristic—was seriously in error. After all, if intelligence is constantly changing, or if it is even potentially changeable, what good could the tests really be? With scores changing all over the place, the tests' usefulness as measures that can rank-order individuals in a stable way over time would be seriously challenged.

Third, and most important, the preoccupation with testing and the assumption that intelligence is a fixed entity led to a neglect of two possibly more important and productive questions: "Can intelligence be trained, and if so, how?" This neglect was unfortunate, because the answer to the first question is yes. What this section will focus on is the second question: "How?" Consider two fairly representative examples of past programs which, like most existing programs, are both for children.

### Instrumental Enrichment

Instrumental Enrichment (IE), Reuven Feuerstein's well-known training program (1980), was originally designed for retarded children, but it has since been recognized by Feuerstein and others as valuable for upper-elementary and lower-secondary students at all levels of the intellectual spectrum. Based on Feuerstein's theory of intelligence, the IE program is intended to improve the cognitive functioning related to the input, elaboration, and output of information. Feuerstein has compiled a long list of cognitive deficiencies he believes his program can help to correct. Among them are (a) unplanned, impulsive, and unsystematic exploratory behavior; (b) impaired or nonexistent capacity for considering two sources of information at once, so that the child deals with data piecemeal rather than grouping and organizing facts; and (c) inadequacy in experiencing the existence of an actual problem and subsequently in defining it. Feuerstein's IE program is designed to correct these deficiencies and, at the same time, to increase the student's intrinsic motivation and feelings of personal competence and self-worth. ·

What are some of the characteristics of the Feuerstein program? Instrumental Enrichment does not attempt to teach either specific items of information or formal-operational, abstract thinking by means of a well-defined, structured knowledge base. To the contrary, it is as content-free as possible. Its materials or "instruments" each emphasize a particular cognitive function and its relationships to various cognitive deficiencies. Feuerstein defines an instrument as something by means of which something else is effected; hence, the student's performance on the materials is seen as a means to an end, rather than as an end in itself. Emphasis in analyzing IE performance is on processes rather than on products, so that the student's errors are viewed as a means of insight into how the student solves problems.

The IE program consists of thirteen different types of exercises, which are repeated in cycles throughout the program. Although the problems are abstract and "unworldly," instructors are required to bridge the gap between them and the real world as much as possible. The following samples of the kinds of materials in the program convey a sense of the types of activities in which students engage:

*1. Orientation of dots.*   The student is presented with a variety of two-dimensional arrays of dots and is asked to identify and outline, within each array, a set of geometric figures, such as squares, triangles, diamonds, and stars.

*2. Comparisons.*   In one form of comparison exercise, the student is shown a picture at the left of, say, two small apples that have no internal shading or coloring. The student is also shown two pictures at the right, in one of which the student might see a single apple, larger than the ones at the left, and fully shaded inside. In the other picture, the student might see three upside-down apples that are also larger than the two apples at the left. The student's task is to indicate, in each picture, which of the attributes of direction, number, color, form, and size differ between the picture at the left and each of the pictures at the right.

*3. Numerical progressions.*   In one kind of numerical progression problem, the student is given the first number in a sequence and a rule by which the sequence can be continued, for example, $+3$, $-1$. The student then has to generate the continuation of the sequence.

### Philosophy for Children

Philosophy for Children, Matthew Lipman's program (1980), is very different from the Feuerstein program. Yet it seeks to foster many of the same intellectual skills.

Philosophy for Children consists of a series of texts in which fictional children spend a considerable portion of their time thinking about thinking, and about ways in which better thinking can be distinguished from worse thinking. The keys to learning are identification and simulation: Lipman hopes that through reading the texts and participating in the classroom discussions and exercises that follow the readings, the students will identify with the characters and will simulate for themselves the kinds of thinking the children are shown to do. Like Feuerstein's program, Philosophy for Children is intended for upper-elementary and lower-secondary students, generally grades 5 through 8.

Lipman has listed 30 thinking skills that his program is intended to foster, a sampling of which includes the following:

*1. Concept development.*   In applying a concept to a specific set of cases, children should be able to identify those cases that are clearly within the boundaries and those that are clearly outside the boundaries. With the concept of "friendship," for example, children are asked questions such as whether people have to be of the same age to be friends, whether two people can be friends and still not much like each other, and whether it is possible for friends ever to lie to one another.

*2. Generalization.*    Given a set of facts, students should be able to note uniformities or regularities, and be able to generalize these regularities from given instances to similar ones. For example, children might be asked to consider generalizations that can be drawn from a set of given facts, such as "I get sick when I eat raspberries; I get sick when I eat strawberries; I get sick when I eat blackberries."

*3. Formulating cause-effect relationships.*    Students should be able to discern and construct formulations indicating relationships between causes and effects. For example, students might be given the statement "He threw the stone and broke the window," and then be asked whether the statement necessarily implies a cause-effect relationship.

As mentioned earlier, the skills trained through the Philosophy for Children program are conveyed through a series of stories about children. Consider, for example, the first chapter of *Harry Stottlemeier's Discovery*, the central book in the series. As the students read about the consequences of Harry's falling asleep in science class, they are introduced to a variety of thinking skills, such as the following:

*1. Problem formulation.*    Harry says, "All planets revolve about the sun, but not everything that revolves about the sun is a planet." He realizes he had been assuming that just because all planets revolve about the sun, everything that revolves about the sun must be a planet.

*2. Nonreversibility of logical "all" statements.*    Harry says, "An "all" sentence can't be reversed. If you put the last part of an "all" sentence first, it'll no longer be true." For example, he cannot convert "All model airplanes are toys" into "All toys are model airplanes."

*3. Reversibility of logical "no" statements.*    Lisa, a friend of Harry's, realizes that logical "no" statements can be reversed. "No submarines are kangaroos," for example, can be converted to "No kangaroos are submarines."

*4. Application of principles to real-life situations.*    Harry intervenes in a discussion between two adults, showing how a principle he had deduced earlier can be applied to falsify one of the adult's arguments.

Each chapter of each book in the program contains a number of "leading ideas." To continue with Chapter 1 of *Harry Stottlemeier's Discovery* as an example, the leading ideas include the process of inquiry, discovery and invention, the nature of thinking, the structure of logical statements, reversing subjects and predicates (conversion), identity statements, how the rule of conversion applies to sentences beginning with "no," using a rule in a practical situation, and truth. The teacher's manual provides a discussion plan and a series of exercises corresponding to each leading idea. For discovery and invention, for example, one of the exercises provides students with a list of items such as electricity, electric light bulbs, magnetism, magnets, television, and the Pacific Ocean; students are asked to classify each item as either a discovery or an invention, and then to justify their answer. Another exercise has students write a paragraph on a topic such as "My Greatest Discovery" or "What I'd Like to Invent."

The most notable similarity between the Lipman and Feuerstein programs is that both seek to train thinking skills. But given the basic similarity of goals, the differences between the actual programs are striking.

First, whereas Feuerstein's program minimizes the role of acquired knowledge and customary classroom content, Lipman's program maximizes such involvement. Although *Harry Stottlemeier's Discovery* is basically philosophical in tone, the subsequent books in the program—*Mark, Pixie, Suki,* and *Lisa*—each emphasize infusion of thinking skills into a different content area, such as the arts, social studies, ethics, and science.

Second, whereas the material in Feuerstein's program is highly abstract and contains only a minimum of words, the material in Lipman's program is conceptually abstract, but is presented through a wholly verbal text that deals with highly concrete situations.

Third, there is much less emphasis on class discussion and interchange in Feuerstein's program than in Lipman's. Similarly, the written exercises are less important in Lipman's program.

Fourth, Feuerstein's program was originally designed for retarded learners, although it has since been extended to children at most points along the continuum of intellectual ability. Lipman's program seems more oriented toward children of at least average ability, on a national scale of norms. Moreover, the reading will be a problem for children much below their grade level in reading skills.

## Conclusion

Do we really need intervention programs such as the two discussed in this chapter for training students in intellectual skills? The answer is clearly yes. During the last decade or so, we have witnessed an unprecedented decline in the intellectual skills of our schoolchildren, a decline shown in scores on tests such as the Scholastic Aptitude Test. College professors don't need SAT scores to be apprised of the decline, however; they can see it in the poorer class performance—and particularly in the poorer reading and writing—of their students. Perhaps intellectual skills could be better trained through existing curricula than they now are. But something in the system is not working, and programs such as those described here are exciting new developments for reversing the declines in intellectual performance we have witnessed in recent years.

To conclude, we not only *can* but *should* teach intelligence. Programs are now available that do an excellent, if incomplete, job of improving intellectual skills, but the vast majority of students are not now being exposed to these programs. Indeed, the heavy content of traditional curricula barely allows room for such training. For this reason I and others believe the time has come to supplement standard curricula with training in intellectual skills. Psychologists can certainly continue to test intelligence, but they would provide more of a service to people by developing their intelligence than by merely measuring it.

# 2

# The Triarchic Theory of Human Intelligence

The theory of human intelligence presented in this book provides a broader basis for understanding intelligence than do many, if not all, of the theories considered in Chapter 1. The theory is called *triarchic* because it consists of three parts: The first part relates intelligence to the internal world of the individual, specifying the mental mechanisms that lead to more intelligent or less intelligent behavior. This part of the theory specifies three kinds of mental processes that are instrumental in planning what things to do, learning how to do the things, and actually doing them. The second part of the theory specifies at what point in a person's experience with handling tasks or situations intelligence is most critically involved. In particular, this part of the theory emphasizes the roles of dealing with novelty and of automatizing mental processing in intelligence. The third part of the theory relates intelligence to the external world of the individual, specifying three kinds of acts—environmental adaptation, environmental selection, and environmental shaping—that characterize intelligent behavior in the everyday world. This part of the theory thus emphasizes the role of environmental contact in determining what constitutes intelligent behavior in a given milieu.

The first part of the theory, which specifies the mental mechanisms of intelligent behavior, is universal: Although individuals may differ in what mental mechanisms they apply to a given task or situation, the potential set of mental mechanisms underlying intelligence is claimed to be the same across all individuals, social classes, and cultural groups. The second part of the theory is universal with respect to the relevance of novelty and automatization to intelligence, but relative with respect to when a given task or situation is novel or in the process of becoming automatized for a given individual or sociocultural group. In other words, a task that is quite familiar to Americans might be quite unfamiliar to Africans, or vice versa. The third part of the theory is universal with respect to the importance of environmental adaptation, selection, and shaping to survival and fit in different environmental contexts, but relative with respect to just what behaviors constitute adaptation, selection, and shaping within different environments. For example, what is adaptive in one country might not be particularly adaptive in another, and might be grossly maladaptive in a third. Thus, the contents of behavior that are appropriate can very widely from one environment to another.

In short, then, parts of the theory are culturally universal, and parts are culturally relative. When people ask whether intelligence is the same thing from one culture to another or even from one individual to another, they are asking too simplistic a question. The most complex but appropriate question is, "What aspects of intelligence are universal and what aspects of intelligence are relative with respect to individuals and groups?" The triarchic theory addresses and attempts to answer this question.

## Components of Intelligence

The first part of the triarchic theory specifies the internal mental mechanisms that are responsible for intelligent behavior. These mental mechanisms are referred to as information-processing components. A *component* is a mental process that may translate a sensory input into a mental representation, transform one mental representation into another, or translate a mental representation into a motor output. Components perform three basic kinds of functions: *Metacomponents* are higher-order processes used in planning, monitoring, and evaluating performance of a task. *Performance components* are processes used in the execution of a task. *Knowledge-acquisition components* are processes used in learning new things. It is essential to understand the nature of these components, because they form the mental bases for the other parts of the theory, that is, for dealing with novel kinds of tasks and situations, for automatizing performance, and for adapting to, shaping, and selecting environments.

### Metacomponents

The *metacomponents* are "executive" processes, in that they essentially tell the other kinds of components what to do. They also receive feedback from the other kinds of components as to how things are going in problem solving or task performance. They are responsible for figuring out how to do a particular task or set of tasks, and then for making sure that the task or tasks are done correctly. I strongly emphasize the role of metacomponents in intelligence. Not all theorists of intelligence share this view, however. A concrete instance of this difference in opinion is with respect to the view I and some others have toward speed of mental functioning.

The assumption that "smart is fast" permeates North American society. Interestingly, this assumption is by no means universal. For example, it is not prevalent in most parts of South America. When North Americans refer to someone as "quick," they are endowing that person with one of the primary attributes of what they perceive an intelligent person to be. The pervasiveness of this assumption can be seen in a recent study of people's conceptions of intelligence, in which Americans were asked to list behaviors characteristic of intelligent persons (Sternberg et al., 1981). Answers such as "learns rapidly," "acts quickly," "talks quickly," and "makes judgments quickly," were common. It is not only the average person who believes that speed is so important to intelligence: Several prominent contemporary theorists of intelligence, such as Arthur Jensen and Earl Hunt, base their theories of intelligence in large part on individual differences in the speed with which people process information.

The assumption that more intelligent people think and act more quickly also underlies the overwhelming majority of intelligence tests. It is rare to find a group test that is not timed, or a timed test that virtually everyone can finish at a comfortable rate of problem solving. I would argue that this assumption is a gross overgeneralization: It is true for some people and for some mental operations, but not for all people or all mental operations. What is critical is not speed per se, but speed *selection*—knowing when to perform at what rate, and being able to think and act rapidly or slowly depending on the task or situational demands. Thus, it is resource allocation, a metacomponential function, that is central to general intelligence.

Converging kinds of evidence support this view that resource allocation rather than speed per se is critical to intelligence. Some of this evidence comes simply from our everyday experiences in the world. We all know people who take their time in doing things, but do them extremely well. And it is common knowledge that snap judgments are often poor judgments. Indeed, in the 1981 study my colleagues and I did on people's conceptions of intelligence, "does not make snap judgments" was listed as an important attribute of intelligent performance. Moreover, there are theoretical reasons for believing that to be quick is not always to be smart. In a classic but little-known book on the nature of intelligence, Louis Thurstone (1924) proposed that a critical element of intelligent performance is the ability to withhold rapid, instinctive responses, and to substitute for them more rational, well-thought-out responses. According to this view, the instinctive responses a person makes to problems are often not the best ones for solving those problems. The ability to inhibit acting upon these responses and to consider better responses is critical for high-quality task performance. More recently, David Stenhouse (1973) has arrived at the same conclusion as Thurstone via a comparative analysis of intelligence across different species. Interestingly, his conclusion appears to have been arrived at wholly independently of Thurstone's. Stenhouse appears to have been unaware of Thurstone's book.

A number of findings from psychological research—both my own and others'—undermine the validity of the view that to be smart is always to be fast. First, it is well known that, in general, a *reflective* rather than an *impulsive* cognitive style in problem solving is associated with more intelligent problem-solving performance. Jumping into problems without adequate reflection is likely to lead to false starts and erroneous conclusions. Yet timed tests often force a person to solve problems impulsively. It is often claimed that the strict timing of such tests merely mirrors the requirements of highly pressured and productive societies. But most of us seem to encounter few significant problems in work or personal life that demand only the 5 to 50 seconds allowed for a typical problem on a standardized test. Of course, some people, such as air traffic controllers, must make consequential split-second decisions as an integral part of their everyday lives. But such people seem to be the exception rather than the rule.

Second, in a 1981 study of planning behavior in problem solving, I found that more intelligent people tend to spend relatively more time than do less intelligent people on global (higher-order) planning, and relatively less time on local (lower-order) planning. In contrast, less intelligent people emphasize local rather than global planning. The point is that what matters is not total time spent, but how the time is distributed across the various kinds of planning. Although for the problems we used (complex forms of analogies), quicker problem solving was associated, on the average, with higher intelligence, looking simply at total time masked the inverse relation in the amounts of time spent on the two kinds of planning.

Third, in studies of reasoning in children and adults, we have found that although greater intelligence is associated with more rapid execution of most performance components, problem encoding is a notable exception to this trend (Sternberg and Rifkin, 1979). The more intelligent person tends to spend relatively more time encoding the terms of a problem, presumably in order to facilitate subsequent operations on these encodings. When I first arrived at Yale University, for example, I arranged the books on my shelf in what was pretty much a random order. Whenever anyone wanted to borrow a book or when I needed one, I had to look through my titles before I finally happened on the one I was looking for. Finally, I got fed up with this disorganization and decided to alphabetize the books by title. In effect, I was devoting additional time to encoding the titles of the books in a way that would make them more easily retrievable when I or other people needed them. Now, when I need a book, I can find it much more rapidly because of the additional time I spent in encoding the book titles. Of course, lending libraries operate on a similar principle.

Finally, in a study of metacomponential processes in reading, R. K. Wagner and I (1983) found that although faster readers, on the average, tended to have higher comprehension and to score higher on a variety of kinds of tests, simply looking at overall reading time masked important differences between more and less skilled readers. In the study, which involved reading standard texts of the kinds found in newspapers and books, we found that relative to less skilled readers, more skilled readers tended to allocate relatively more time to reading passages for which they would be tested in greater detail, and relatively less time to reading passages for which they would be tested in lesser detail.

Obviously, it would be foolish to argue that speed is never important. For example, in driving a car, slow reflexes or thinking can result in an accident that otherwise might have been averted. In many other situations, too, speed is essential. But many if not most of the consequential tasks people face in their lives do not require problem solving or decision making at split-second speed. Instead, they require intelligent allocations of time for the various problems at hand. Ideally, intelligence tests would stress allocation of time rather than sheer speed in solving various kinds of problems. Thus, the meta-component of resource allocation is a critical one in intelligence.

## Performance Components

*Performance components* are used in the execution of various strategies for solving problems. Whereas metacomponents decide what to do, performance components actually do it. The performance components are probably the ones that are best measured by existing intelligence tests.

The number of performance components that people might use in solving all the tasks that could possibly confront them is without doubt extremely large. If our goal were to identify them all, we could probably spend several lifetimes at the task. Fortunately, certain performance components are more important than others. For example, studies of mental test performance have shown that one set of components—those of inductive reasoning, such as inferring and applying relations—are quite general across many of the items typically found in intelligence tests. In other words, a handful of performance components accounts for performance on many of the tasks found on intelligence tests. Thus, to the extent people wish to improve their scores on such tests, they need not identify and improve large numbers of components. They can concentrate on just a few of them, as we will later in this book.

It is important to realize that people can use different performance components to solve a given task. Consider a syllogistic reasoning task, for example, such as "John is taller than Mary. Mary is taller than Jane. Who is tallest?" In solving problems such as this, some people use a primarily linguistic strategy for solving the problem, representing information about the individual in terms of verbal propositions. Other people tend to solve the problem spatially, representing information about the problem in terms of a mental image that interrelates the three people in the problem. But most individuals use a combination of linguistic and spatial strategies to solve the problem. The point is that a given individual could achieve a given score on a syllogistic-reasoning test through different combinations of performance components. Simply assigning a person a score in terms of number correct or time taken to solve the problem tells virtually nothing about the kinds of mental processes that the person used to solve the problem.

Separation of the performance components used in solving problems is critically important for diagnosis and remediation of problem-solving performance. Consider a concrete example of why this is so. Suppose that a group of children or adults is given a test requiring reasoning by analogy. A typical problem on such a test might be VENEZUELA : SPANISH :: BRAZIL : (a. ENGLISH, b. PORTUGUESE, c. FRENCH, d. GERMAN). In a typical testing situation, people would solve a large number of analogies such as this one, and the measure of their reasoning ability would be their total number correct on the test. There is a problem with the logic of scoring the analogies test in this way, however. Consider a person who is a very competent reasoner, but who is reading-disabled. In other words, the person has no trouble reasoning about relations, but has considerable trouble in encoding the terms of the problem upon which he or she must reason. The reading-disabled people may have great difficulty in obtaining a high score on an analogies test, especially if it is timed, merely because they read the terms slowly and with great difficulty. But the low score does not reflect difficulties in reasoning, but rather difficulties in encoding the terms of the analogical reasoning problem. Other persons might get problems wrong simply because they lack knowledge. In other words, merely providing a total score can camouflage rather than elucidate a person's strengths and weaknesses. It is for this reason that it is useful to break scores down into their underlying performance and other components.

### Knowledge-Acquisition Components

*Knowledge-acquisition components* are processes used in learning. It has long been known that the ability to learn is an essential part of intelligence, although performance on trivial kinds of learning tasks, such as memorizing nonsense syllables, is not particularly related to intelligence. It is meaningful rather than trivial learning that is important to intellectual ability.

The emphasis this book places on knowledge-acquisition components contrasts with certain other views regarding what should be emphasized in intelligence. Most of the major intelligence tests currently in use measure intelligence as previous years' achievement. What is an intelligence test for children of a given age would be an achievement test for children a few years younger. In some test items, like vocabulary, the achievement orientation is obvious. In others, it is disguised, as, for example, in verbal analogies. Note that the reasoning in the verbal analogy used as an example above requires substantial knowledge. The person solving it has to know in advance that most people in Venezuela speak Spanish and that most people in Brazil speak Portuguese. But virtually all tests commonly used for the assessment of intelligence place heavy achievement demands on the people tested.

The emphasis on knowledge is consistent with some current views of differences in expert-versus-beginner performance that stress the role of knowledge. For example, William Chase and Herbert Simon found in 1973 that a major distinction between expert and beginning chess players was not in the processes they used to play chess, but in the knowledge they brought to chess playing. Similar results have emerged in studies of expert-versus-nonexpert solvers of physics problems. And indeed, there can be no doubt that differences in knowledge are critical to differences in performance between more and less skilled individuals in a variety of domains. But surely the critical question for a theorist of intelligence to ask is how these differences in knowledge came to be. Certainly, just sheer differences in amounts of experience are not perfectly correlated with levels of expertise. Many people play the piano for many years, but do not become concert-level pianists; chess buffs do not all become grand masters, no matter how often they play. And simply reading a lot does not guarantee a high vocabulary. What seems to be critical is not sheer amount of experience, but rather, what one has been able to learn from that experience. According to this view, then, individual differences in knowledge-acquisition components have priority over individual differences in knowledge. To understand what makes people more expert at certain things, we must understand first how current individual differences in knowledge evolve from individual differrences in the acquisition of that knowledge.

Consider, for example, vocabulary. It is well known that vocabulary is one of the best predictors, if not the single best predictor of overall IQ score. Yet vocabulary tests are clearly achievement tests. Can the underlying ability tapped by vocabulary tests be measured without presenting people with what is essentially an achievement test?

There is reason to believe that vocabulary is such a good predictor of intelligence because it indirectly measures people's ability to acquire information in context. Most vocabulary is learned in an everyday context rather than through direct instruction. Thus, new words are usually encountered for the first time (and subsequently) in textbooks, novels, newspapers, lectures, and the like. More intelligent people are better able to use surrounding contexts to figure out the words' meanings. As the years go by, the better "decontextualizers" acquire the larger vocabularies. Because so much learning, including vocabulary learning, is contextually determined, people's ability to use context to add to their knowledge base is an important skill in intelligent behavior. Later in the book, you will receive instruction in how better to use context to increase your vocabulary.

To conclude, an important aspect of intelligence is the set of mental mechanisms or components that are used in learning how to solve problems, in deciding what strategy or strategies to use in solving these problems, and in actually solving the problems. The first part of the triarchic theory of intelligence specifies in some detail what these mental mechanisms are. (The bibliography at the end of this book contains references to works by myself and others that describe in more detail the components of intelligence, and the evidence that has been amassed to test theories regarding the nature of these components.) But a theory of mental mechanisms is not enough to account for intelligence, completely. To understand why, suppose you are at a restaurant and are trying to decide what to order for lunch. Such a decision requires complex componential processing. You need to decide among alternative possible meals, balancing off what you would like with what you can afford. You may also need to make decisions regarding each of several parts of a given meal. Thus, deciding on and ordering a meal can be full of information-processing components. Yet individual differences in people's abilities to decide on and order meals are not particularly indicative of individual differences in their levels of intelligence. Thus, a theory that specified only mental mechanisms would seem to be missing something in terms of specifying just what intelligence is. Let us turn now to a consideration of other aspects of intelligence.

# Experience and Intelligence

According to the triarchic theory, there are two facets of a person's experience with tasks or situations that are particularly critical to intelligent behavior. These facets are the ability to deal with novel kinds of tasks and situational demands, and the ability to automatize information processing.

## *Ability to Deal with Novelty*

The idea that intelligence involves the ability to deal with novelty is itself far from novel, having been proposed by a number of recent investigators, such as Raymond Cattell (1971), John Horn (1979), Kjell Raaheim (1974) and Richard Snow (1979), among others. In a 1981 article, I proposed that intelligence involves not merely the ability to learn and reason with new concepts but the ability to learn and reason with new *kinds* of concepts. Intelligence is not so much the ability to learn or think within familiar conceptual systems as it is the ability to learn and think within new conceptual systems, which can then be brought to bear upon already existing knowledge.

It is important to note that task novelty is not the only criterion in assessing the usefulness of a task for measuring intelligence. An appropriate task should be novel, but not totally outside a person's past experience. If the task is too novel, then the person will not have any past experience to bring to bear on it, and as a result, the task will simply be outside the person's range of comprehension. Calculus, for example, would be a highly novel field of endeavor for most 5-year-olds. But the calculus tasks would be so far outside their range of experience that such tasks would be worthless for the assessment of their intelligence.

Novelty can be a function of the situation in which tasks are presented as well as of the tasks themselves. The idea is that people's intelligence is best shown not in run-of-the-mill situations that are encountered regularly in everyday life, but rather in extraordinary situations that challenge people's ability to cope with the environment to which they must adapt. We all know people who perform well when confronted with tasks presented in a familiar milieu, but who fall apart when presented with similar or even identical tasks in an unfamiliar context. For example, a person who performs well in his or her everyday environment might find it difficult to perform the same tasks if under intense pressure to get them done. In general, some people can perform well only in situations that are highly favorable to their getting their work done. When the environment is less supportive, the quality of their performance is greatly reduced. It is for this reason that performance in one stage of life is often not accurately predictive of performance in another stage of life. For example, I have found that the performance of my graduate students during the time they are in graduate school is only moderately predictive of their performance when they get out of graduate school and take jobs. In graduate school, as in a home setting, they were enmeshed in a highly supportive and nurturant environment. But when they get jobs, they often confront harsh, unfamiliar environments, in which they receive nowhere near the level of support they had received in graduate school. As a result, only some of the students who succeeded in graduate school are able to succeed in their jobs. In sum, then, the ability to deal with novel tasks and situations is an important aspect of intelligence.

The ability to deal with novelty is illustrated particularly well by the processes of *insight*. According to a theory formulated by Janet Davidson and myself (1984), insights are of three kinds: selective encoding, selective combination, and selective comparison.

*Selective encoding* involves distinguishing irrelevant from relevant information in one's field of experience. We are all barraged with much more information than we can possibly handle. An important task confronting each of us is to select the information that is important for our purposes, and to filter out the information that is not important. Selective encoding is the process by which this is done. Consider, for example, a particularly significant example of selective encoding in science, the unusual means by which Sir Alexander Fleming discovered penicillin. Fleming was performing an experiment that involved growing bacteria in a petri dish, which is a little glass or plastic dish that contains a gelatin in which bacteria grow easily. Unfortunately, from some points of view, the culture was spoiled: A mold grew within the culture and killed the bacteria. A lesser scientist would have bemoaned the failure of the experiment and promised to do a better job next time. Fleming, however, noticed that the mold had killed the bacteria, and thereby provided the basis for his discovery of the important antibiotic, penicillin.

Insights of *selective combination* involve taking selectively encoded information and combining it in a novel but productive way. Often, it is not enough just to identify the important information for solving a problem. One must also figure out how to put it together. Consider a famous example of what might be called a selective-combination insight, the formulation of the theory of evolution. The information upon which Darwin drew to formulate this theory had been available to him and others for a long time. What had eluded Darwin and his contemporaries was how this information could be combined so as to account for observed changes in species. Darwin finally saw how to combine the available information, and thus was born his theory of natural selection.

Insights of *selective comparison* involve novel relating of new information to old information. Creative analogies fall into the domain of selective comparison. In important problems, we almost always need to bring old knowledge to bear upon the solution of new problems, and to relate new knowledge to old knowledge. Insights of selective comparison are the basis for this relating. A famous example of an insight of selective comparison is Kekulé's discovery of the structure of the benzene ring. Kekulé had been seeking this structure for some time, but without success. One night, he dreamed that he was watching a snake dancing around and around. Finally, the snake bit its tail. When Kekulé arose, he realized that the image of the snake biting its tail formed the geometric shape for the structure of the benzene ring.

To sum up, the ability to deal with novelty is a crucial one in intelligence, and one of several ways to measure it is through the assessment of insightful problem solving. The processes of selective encoding, selective combination, and selective comparison form three of many bases for dealing with novel or nonentrenched kinds of tasks and situations.

### *Ability to Automatize Information Processing*

Many kinds of tasks requiring complex information processing seem so intricate that it is a wonder we can perform them at all. Consider reading, for example. The number and complexity of operations involved in reading is staggering, and what is more staggering is the rate at which these operations are performed. Performance of tasks as complex as reading would seem to be possible only because a substantial proportion of the operations required are *automatized*—that is, done without conscious thought—and thus require minimal mental effort. Deficiencies in reading have been theorized to result in large part from failures in automatization of operations.

The proposal being made here is that complex verbal, mathematical, and other tasks can feasibly be executed only because many of the operations involved in their performance have been automatized. Failure to automatize such operations, whether fully or in part, results in a breakdown of information processing and hence less intelligent task performance. Intellectual operations that can be performed smoothly and automatically by more intelligent individuals are performed only haltingly and under conscious control by less intelligent individuals. In sum, more able people can automatize information processing unusually efficiently and effectively.

### *Relationship Between the Two Abilities*

For many (but probably not all) kinds of tasks, the ability to deal with novelty and to automatize information processing may occur along an experiential continuum. When people first encounter a task or kind of situation, ability to deal with novelty comes into play. More intelligent people will more rapidly and fully be able to cope with the novel demand being made on them. For example, on their first day in a foreign country, tourists almost always have to make various kinds of adjustments to the demands of an unfamiliar culture. Their intelligence is called into play in dealing with these unusual demands. The fewer the resources that must be devoted to processing the novelty of a given task or situation, the more the resources that are left over to automatize performance; conversely, more efficient automatization of performance leaves additional processing resources for dealing with novel tasks and situations. In the example of the foreign country, the less attention tourists must devote to handling new kinds of stimulation, the more attention they have left over for dealing with the complexities that confront them. Thus, it is easier for an American who speaks only English to change money in England than in France, because the individual does not have to cope, in England, with a new language as well as with a new currency.

As a result, novelty and automatization trade off with each other, and the more efficient the person is at the one, the more the resources that are left over for the other. As experience with the kind of task or situation increases, novelty decreases, and the task or situation will become less appropriate in its measure of intelligence from the standpoint of processing the novelty. However, after some amount of practice with the task or in the situation, automatization skills may come into play, in which case the task will start to become a more appropriate measure of automatization skill.

### *Implications for Designing*
### *Tests That Measure Intelligence*

The experiential view suggests one reason why it is so exceedingly difficult to compare levels of intelligence fairly across members of different sociocultural groups. Even if a given test requires the same components of performance for members of the various groups, it is extremely unlikely to be equivalent for the groups in terms of its novelty and the degree to which performance has been automatized prior to the examinees' taking the test. Consider, for example, nonverbal reasoning tests, requiring skills such as analogy solution, matrix completion, and the like. Research has shown that differences between members of various sociocultural groups are actually greater on these tests than they are on the verbal tests that the nonverbal tests were designed to replace. But the nonverbal tests, contrary to the claims that have often been made for them, are *not* culture-fair, and they are certainly not culture-free. Individuals who have been brought up in a test-taking culture are likely to have had much more experience with these kinds of items than are individuals not brought up in such a culture. Thus, the test items will be less novel and performance on them more automatized for members of the standard U.S. culture than for its nonmembers. Even if the processes of solution are the same, the degrees of novelty and automatization will be different, and hence the tests will not be measuring the same thing across populations. As useful as the tests may be for within-group comparisons, between-group comparisons may be deceptive and unfair. A fair comparison between groups would require comparable degrees of novelty and automatization of test items as well as comparable processes and strategies.

In sum, behavior involves intelligence particularly when it draws on adaptation to novelty and automatization of performance. It is not enough merely to specify a set of processes involved in intelligence. Consider, again, selecting lunch from a menu at a restaurant. Such a selection process involves a wide variety of components of various kinds. For example, we need to decide what meal to eat, whether or not to have dessert, and if we are to have dessert, whether we should order less of a main course or skip the appetizer, and so on. Yet, even though the task of deciding on a meal may be full of components of cognition, it does not seem to be a particularly good index of individual differences in intelligence. The reason is that this task involves neither novelty nor the development of automatization. It is at a region in the experiential continuum that is just not very interesting from the standpoint of individual differences in intelligence.

## The Context of Intelligence

The triarchic theory defines intelligence in context as *mental activity involved in purposive adaptation to, shaping of, and selection of real-world environments relevant to one's life*. Consider just what this definition means.

I define intelligence in terms of mental activity underlying behavior in real-world environments that are *relevant* to one's life. We could not legitimately assess the intelligence of an African Pygmy by placing a Pygmy in a North American culture and using North American tests, unless it were relevant to test the Pygmy for survival in a North American culture and we wished to assess the Pygmy's intelligence for this culture (as, for example, if the Pygmy happened to live in our culture and had to adapt to it). Similarly, a North American's intelligence cannot legitimately be assessed in terms of his or her adaptation to Pygmy society unless adaptation to that society were relevant to the person's life. Moreover, intelligence is *purposive*. It is directed toward goals, however vague or subconscious these goals may be.

## Adaptation

Intelligence involves *adaptation* to one's environment. Indeed, definitions of intelligence have traditionally viewed it in terms of adaptation to the environment, but intelligence tests usually do not measure or account for adaptive skills. Consider some examples.

Seymour Sarason, a colleague of mine at Yale, once described to me his first job experience. His job was to administer a standardized intelligence test to students at an institution for the retarded. In those days, the students were essentially confined. When Sarason arrived on the scene, he found himself with nothing to do. A number of students had just planned and successfully executed an escape from the school. Eventually, they were rounded up and brought back to Sarason for testing. Sarason gave them the Porteus Mazes Test, a standard intelligence test that is particularly appropriate for retarded individuals. To his chagrin, the students for the most part were not able to solve even the first problem correctly. It became obvious to him, as perhaps it does to you now, that whatever it is the test measures, it was not the mental skills involved in the successful planning, although only partially successful implementation, of the escape. Clearly, some kind of intelligence not measured by the test was involved in the planning of the break.

Another relevant example comes from Robert Edgerton's book *The Cloak of Competence* (1967). In this book, Edgerton describes the lives of retarded persons released from institutional settings. In particular, he describes some of the adaptive strategies such people use to make their lives easier. For example, one strategy used by a man who could not tell time was to wear a watch that did not work. In the street he would then look at his watch, pretend to notice that it did not tell the correct time, and then say to a stranger something like, "Excuse me, but I notice my watch isn't working. Could you tell me the correct time?" Again, the ingenuity involved in the broken-watch maneuver implies some form of intelligence. At the same time, we could not call such a man highly intelligent, if only because his inability to tell time is a fact that must be considered in its own right.

Adaptive requirements can differ widely from one culture to another, so that attempts to impose an intelligence test on a new culture can result in a charade. Consider, for example, a salient difference between the U.S. and Venezuelan cultures. In the United States, time is of the essence, and speed is considered an extremely important part of everyday life. Meetings start on time, classes start on time, appointments start on time. Although lateness is tolerated in some settings, such as parties, the normal expectation is for people to be prompt. Indeed, at one of the meetings at which I recounted this anecdote, the moderator of the meeting attempted to start the meeting early—a full five minutes before it was scheduled to begin.

Venezuelans and members of many other cultures, including those of South America, Africa, and others, do not place the same premium on time, nor do they even seem to have the same notions about it. This fact was illustrated to me quite dramatically when I went to a meeting on the nature of intelligence held in Venezuela. The meeting was scheduled to begin at 8:00 A.M. on the first day. I was miffed, because I had arrived tired and had no great desire to wake up for an 8:00 meeting, but I arrived there on time, as did four other people, the only North Americans attending the meeting. Only the North Americans seem to have even considered the possibility that the meeting would start on time. In fact, it did not start until around 9:30, a full hour and a half after it had been scheduled to begin. This tardiness in starting meetings, as well as in other aspects of everyday life, is rife throughout Venezuela as well as other cultures. To be on time for meetings or appointments can actually be maladaptive, in that the chances are that there are other things one would rather do than sit around and wait for the meeting to begin. To North Americans, perhaps, this endemic lateness would seem to be maladaptive or even unintelligent. However, in Venezuela, it is quite adaptive and the only sensible way to behave there. In fact, I asked a Venezuelan about this matter, and she readily admitted that Venezuelans tend to be late. However, she also noted that once they start, Venezuelans are fully ready to engage in the task at hand and are less likely than North Americans to take time out for coffee breaks or idle conversation. And indeed, in the United States, one often finds that even if meetings do start on time, there is a substantial lag until people are really geared up for the meeting, and the starting time is often followed rather soon by coffee or other breaks. As a member of the U.S. culture, I wouldn't want it any other way, but the point is that what may be adaptive varies from one culture to another.

Differences in what is considered adaptive behavior in various cultures can be seen in the domain of intelligence testing as well as in everyday life. A particularly noteworthy instance of this fact derives from an anecdote told by Joe Glick. Glick and his colleagues (Cole et al., 1971) were studying the cognitive performance of members of the Kpelle tribe in Nigeria. One of the tasks they used was a sorting task, in which the subjects were given cards with either words or pictures on them and asked to sort the items in a sensible way.

According to U.S. standards, the intelligent and developmentally more advanced way of sorting is by taxonomic category. In other words, given a list of, say, fruits, animals, and vehicles of conveyance, the intelligent way of sorting is considered to be in terms of these categories. Indeed, in Piaget's theory as well, use of taxonomic categorization is considered more advanced than use of other kinds of categorization, such as functional categorization. The same principle applies to defining words. So, for example, on the Stanford-Binet and the Wechsler Intelligence Tests, more credit is given for higher-order, taxonomic definitions than is given for functional definitions. If asked to define *car*, the subject is given more credit for the definition "a vehicle of conveyance" than for a definition such as "uses gas" or "rides along streets." In defining as well as sorting words, the more intelligent behavior is considered to be the taxonomic rather than the functional organization of information.

When Glick asked the Kpelle to sort, he found that the adults uniformly preferred a functional sorting to a taxonomic one. A less able investigator would have stopped there and simply concluded that the Kpelle are less intelligent than are people in the United States. Indeed, it is a common finding in cross-cultural research that members of other cultures perform less well on standard kinds of intelligence tests than do members of the U.S. culture. But Glick did not stop there. Rather, he persisted in trying to get the Kpelle to sort taxonomically. At first, he was unsuccessful. Finally, in desperation, he asked them to sort the way stupid people would, and then the Kpelle had no difficulty at all in sorting taxonomically. The point is that their conception of what constituted an intelligent basis for this sorting differed from the standard U.S. one. What was adaptive in their culture and what is adaptive in the U.S. were quite different. Thus, the standard test was not measuring adaptation relative to Kpelle norms, but relative to U.S. norms.

### Environmental Selection

As we have seen, adaptation is an important part of intelligent behavior as it occurs in context. However, contextually appropriate intelligence does not stop with adaptation. There may be instances in which, in a sense, it is actually maladaptive to be adaptive. For example, our values may not correspond to the values of the environment we are in—perhaps a business where the values are too cutthroat for our taste, or perhaps a larger setting, such as a country. For example, it would be hard to argue that, during the Nazi period, adaptation was clearly the intelligent course of action for Germans and other citizens. Similarly, we may find that our interests are not well represented by our environment—perhaps an utterly boring job that offers us no challenge. In such a case, it is not necessarily intelligent to adapt to the demands of that particular job. The point is that there are instances in which the more contextually intelligent thing to do may be to *de*select the environment we are in and to *re*select a different environment, a process that can be referred to as *environmental selection*. Such a process may involve leaving one job for another, one spouse for another, or one country for another.

Knowing when to quit is every bit as important as knowing when to persist. For example, in science, researchers inevitably encounter any number of dead ends that are unfruitful for further research. Scientists can waste years of their careers attempting to follow up on these dead ends. This is a no-win strategy. The intelligent scientist, as well as the intelligent person in any other field of endeavor, has to know when to quit as well as when to start.

Consider how environmental selection can operate in the career choices of individuals, and particularly of seemingly gifted individuals. A rather poignant set of real-world examples is provided by Ruth Feldman in *Whatever Happened to the Quiz Kids?* (1982). The Quiz Kids—on both radio and, later, television—were selected for a number of intellectual and personal traits. All or almost all of them had exceptionally high IQs, typically well over 140 and in some cases in excess of 200. Yet Feldman's book shows how much less distinguished the Quiz Kids' later lives have been than their earlier lives—in many cases, even by their own standards. There are undoubtedly any number of reasons for this lesser later success, including so-called regression effects, by which extreme performance earlier on tends to be followed by less extreme performance later on. But what is striking in biography after biography is that the Quiz Kids who were most successful were those who found what they were good at and were interested in, and then pursued it relentlessly. The less successful ones had difficulty finding any one thing that interested them, and a number of them floundered while trying to find a niche for themselves.

### Environmental Shaping

Intelligence also involves mental activity in *shaping* the environment, a tactic we use when our attempts to adapt to a given environment fail, or when it is impractical, inadmissible, or premature to select a new environment. For example, we may be committed by religious beliefs to the permanence of marriage, and therefore see divorce as an unrealistic alternative. In such a case, we may attempt to reshape our environment so as to improve the fit between ourself and the environment. The marital partner may attempt to restructure the marriage; the employee may try to convince the boss to see or do things differently; the citizen may try to change the government, through either violent or nonviolent means. In each case, however, they attempt to change the environment so as to improve their fit to the environment, rather than merely trying to adapt to what is already there.

What this means is that there may be no one set of behaviors that is "intelligent" for everyone, in that people can adjust to their environment in different ways. Whereas the components of intelligent behavior are very likely universal, their use in the construction of environmentally appropriate behavior is likely to vary not only across groups, but across individuals. What does seem to be common among people who master their environments is the ability to capitalize on their strengths and to compensate for their weaknesses. Successful people are able not only to adapt well to their environments, but actually to modify the environments they are in so as to maximize the goodness of fit between the environment and their adaptive skills.

What is it, for example, that distinguishes the "stars" in any given field of endeavor from all the rest? Of course, this question is broad enough to be the topic of a book, and many books have in fact been written on the topic. But for our present purpose, the distinguishing characteristics we should note are (a) at least one very well-developed skill, and (b) an extraordinary ability to capitalize on that skill or skills in one's work. For example, if you were to generate a short list of stars in your own environment, the chances are that they do not share any single ability, as traditionally defined. Rather, each has a talent or set of talents that they make the most of in their work. At the same time, they minimize the significance of skills in which they are deficient, either by delegating tasks requiring those skills to others or by structuring their tasks in such a way that those skills are not required. My own list of stars, for example, includes a person with extraordinary spatial visualization skills, a person with a talent for coming up with the counterintuitive but true, and a person who has an extraordinary sense of where events are leading. These three particular persons (and others on my list) share little in terms of what sets them apart, aside from at least one extraordinary talent on which they capitalize fully in their work. Although they are also highly intelligent in the traditional sense, so are many others who never reach the height of accomplishment.

## Conclusion

To sum up, this chapter has briefly outlined a triarchic theory of intelligence. The theory comprises three "subtheories": a componential subtheory, which relates intelligence to the internal world of the individual; an experiential subtheory, which relates intelligence to both the external and the internal worlds of the individual; and a contextual subtheory, which relates intelligence to the external world of the individual. The componential subtheory specifies the mental mechanisms responsible for the planning, execution, and evaluation of intelligent behavior. The experiential subtheory expands on this definition by regarding as most relevant to the demonstration of intelligence, behavior that involves either adjustment to novelty, automatization of information processing, or both. The contextual subtheory defines intelligent behavior as involving purposive adaptation to, selection of, and shaping of real-world environments relevant to one's life.

An important issue concerns the combination rule for the abilities specified by the three subtheories. How does the intelligence of a person who is average in the abilities specified by all three subtheories compare to the intelligence of a person who is gifted in some abilities but low in others? Or what can be said of the intelligence of a person whose environmental opportunities are so restricted that he or she is unable to adapt to, shape, or select the environment? There seems little point in specifying any combination rule at all, in that no single index of intelligence is likely to be very useful. Different individuals may be more or less intelligent through different patterns of abilities. In the first case above, the two individuals are quite different in their patterns of abilities, and an overall index will hide this fact. In the second case, it may not be possible to obtain any meaningful measurement at all from the person's functioning in his or her environment. Consider, as further examples, the comparison between (a) a person who is very adept at componential functioning and thus likely to score well on standard IQ tests, but who is lacking in insight, or more generally, in the ability to cope well with novel kinds of tasks or situations versus (b) a person who is very insightful but not particularly adept at test-like componential operations. The first person might come across to people as smart but not terribly creative, the second as creative but not terribly smart. Although it might well be possible to obtain some average score on componential abilities and abilities to deal with novel tasks and situations, such a composite would obscure the critical differences between the functioning of the two individuals. Or consider a person who is both componentially adept and insightful, but who makes little effort to fit into the environment in which he or she lives. Certainly some overall average that hides the person's academic intelligence in a combined index that is reduced because of reduced adaptive skills would not be very meaningful. The point to be made, then, is that intelligence is not a single thing: It comprises a very wide array of cognitive and other skills. Our goal in theory, research, and measurement ought to be to define what these skills are and to learn how best to assess and possibly to train them, not to figure out a way to combine them into a single, but possibly meaningless number.

Where does this theory leave us with regard to existing intelligence tests? No existing test measures all or even most of the skills that have been discussed in this chapter. Indeed, to the extent that intelligence comprises somewhat different skills for different people, there is no one, wholly appropriate test. Whereas it might be possible to construct tests of componential skills that would apply to quite broad ranges of individuals, tests of skills involved in attaining contextual fit would almost certainly apply to fewer people. The ideal instrument for assessing intelligence would probably be one that combines measurements of different kinds that together take into account the considerations above. No one measurement or combination of measurements would yield a definitive IQ, because any one instrument can work only for some people some of the time. Moreover, it is unclear that any single index can do justice to the variety of skills that constitute the basis for the triarchic theory of intelligence. A single index would be more likely to obscure than to elucidate a person's levels and patterns of abilities. Which instruments work for which people will be variable across people within and between sociocultural groups. The best we can hope for is a battery of assessments that would enable us to learn more about intelligence than any one kind of assessment could tell.

Given the fallibility of present tests, should we stop using tests altogether? No, because used judiciously, test scores generally provide some incremental validity over other types of assessment. Moreover, right now we lack alternatives—conventional intelligence tests are about all we have to serve as a standard for intelligent performance. What is important is that the tests be used judiciously and prudently. Otherwise, their use is worse than their non-use. There is an allure to exact numbers. An IQ score of 119, an SAT score of 580, a mental-abilities score in the 74th percentile—all sound very precise. Indeed, social psychologists have found that people tend to weigh accurate-sounding information highly, almost without regard to its validity. But the appearance of precision is not substitute for the fact of validity. Indeed, a test may be precise in its measurements, but not of whatever it is that distinguishes the more from the less intelligent.

Few people are willing to admit that they are entranced by test scores. When they hear the results of experiments showing that people overvalue precise-sounding information of low validity, they tend to think of these results as applying to others. When I worked one summer at the Psychological Corporation, distributor of the Miller Analogies Test (a widely used test for graduate admissions and financial-aid decisions), we heard what I considered then, and still consider, an amazing story: A teachers college in Mississippi required a score of 25 on the Miller test for admission. The use of this cutoff was questionable, to say the least, in that 25 represents a chance score on this test. A promising student was admitted to the college despite a sub-25 Miller score, and went through the program with distinction. When it came time for the student to receive a diploma, she was informed that the diploma would be withheld until she could take the test and receive a score of at least 25. Consider the logic here: The predictor had somehow come to surpass the criteria in importance! The test had become an end rather than a means.

I told this pathetic story to a large meeting of teachers of the gifted, showing them how bad things could be. Afterward, a teacher came up to me and told me an essentially identical story (except for a higher cutoff score) as it pertained to her own quite reputable university.

That this kind of thinking is not limited to isolated cases is shown by the fact that I've encountered personally, and heard about innumerable times, similar experiences at major universities. Consider, for example, the cases of applicants to graduate (and often, undergraduate) programs with stellar credentials except for marginal test scores. In my experience, these applicants receive a "full and open discussion" of their credentials, and then they are rejected. Often, admissions decision makers know in their heart, right from the beginning of the discussion, that the decision will be negative, so that the discussion seems more an alleviation of their feelings of guilt at going with test scores than anything else. These negative decisions are particularly frustrating when the applicants have shown excellent competence at the criterion task (in my profession, psychological research) and yet are rejected on the basis of test scores that are at best highly imperfect predictors of performance.

When the means becomes the end—when people forget which is the criterion and which the predictor—then the test becomes more important than the performance it is supposed to predict. When criterion information is unavailable or scanty, test scores can serve a very useful function; people who might otherwise be denied admission to programs on the basis of inadequate evidence may be admitted because their test scores show them capable of high-level performance. But when criterion information is available, the tests may be superfluous, or even counterproductive. The criterion information in these cases should receive the lion's share of attention in making decisions about future performance.

In sum, intelligence tests as they now exist work for some people some of the time; but they do not work for other people much of the time. Moreover, the people for whom they do not work are often the same ones, again and again. Applied conservatively and with full respect for all the available information, tests can be of some use. Misapplied or overused, they are worse than nothing.

In the next section of this book, you will encounter a variety of exercises for increasing your intellectual skills along the lines suggested by all three subtheories of the triarchic theory. There exist many sets of exercises for improving one's intelligence, but they tend to be limited to a narrow definition of intellect. The exercises in this book cover the broad range of cognitive and other skills specified by the triarchic theory of human intelligence.

# 3

# Metacomponents

A colleague of mine was about to take a trip to California. He had his plane reservation all set. In order to get to the airport in New York City, he was to take a limousine from New Haven, Connecticut. My colleague woke up late; concerned that he would miss the limousine and therefore the plane, he rushed to get ready to leave. Because the limousine makes stops along the way to the airport, and thus takes a while to reach the airport, it was necessary to get to the limousine terminal well in advance of the plane's departure. He packed quickly, realizing that he was probably forgetting some of the things he would need for the trip. But he had no time to reflect on what he would and would not need. After he had packed, he jumped into his car and rushed over to the limousine terminal. Because he was traveling during the morning rush hour, his progress in driving to the limousine terminal was slow. To make things worse, he seemed to hit every red light, and there was construction on one of the roads, slowing down traffic. He arrived at the limousine terminal just as the limousine was pulling out. My colleague was extremely agitated that he had missed the limousine, but saw nothing he could do. The next limousine would not leave for another hour, and it would arrive at the airport too late for him to make the airplane. He waited for that limousine anyway, even though he did miss his plane and had to take the next one out.

This anecdote provides an almost classic example of poor planning, which in this instance led to a failure to accomplish a goal. Had it not been for a string of poor planning decisions, the colleague easily could have made his

41

plane. First, he could have packed the night before his departure, so that he would not have to spend his time in the morning rushing to get his things together. Second, he could have set an alarm clock or been more careful to arise on time so that he would not have been rushed and risked missing his limousine. Third, he could have planned out a route to the limousine terminal that would minimize the number of traffic lights and the amount of traffic, and would avoid road construction. Fourth, when he missed his limousine, he could have considered other possibilities than merely waiting for the next limousine. For example, he might have driven rapidly to the first limousine stop and picked up the limousine there. Or he could have driven to the airport and parked there. Although this would have added some minor expense to the cost of the trip, he could have made his plane. Finally, he could have checked into the possibility of a commuter flight from New Haven to the New York airport. There was, in fact, such a flight that he could have taken that would have gotten him to the airport on time.

This anecdote illustrates the importance of planning and decision making in everyday intelligence. Good planning and decision making, as well as accurate evaluation of one's actions, can lead to a variety of positive and satisfying outcomes. Poor planning and decision making, or the failure adequately to evaluate one's course of action, can lead to dissatisfaction and a string of negative outcomes. What is sometimes referred to as "executive information processing" proves to be an important part of everyone's intelligence.

As you'll remember from Chapter 2, this book calls the executive processes people use in planning, monitoring, and evaluating their problem solving and performance *metacomponents*. Metacomponents are an essential ingredient of intelligence, and any effort to improve our intelligence must necessarily involve metacomponential skills. What are these skills? This chapter presents some of the most important ones.

# Defining the Nature of a Problem
## *Examples*

Consider the anecdote above about my colleague missing his plane. He could have made his plane had he redefined the problem facing him. From beginning to end, he defined his problem as one of reaching the limousine terminal in time for him to take a limousine to the airport. Had he redefined the problem as one of obtaining suitable transportation to reach the *airport* so that he could make his plane, he might have considered transportation alternatives other than the limousine. But by considering only the limousine, he lost the opportunity to arrive on time.

Another even more commonplace example of the pitfalls of inadequate definition of the nature of the problem derives from Shirley Heath's account of life in "Roadville," a town in the Piedmont Carolinas of the United States. Heath (1983) describes how the residents of the town often find themselves, like many others, without sufficient money to make ends meet. When they find themselves with inadequate funds, they view their problem as one of finding more money in order to pay their bills. Often they will look for second and even third jobs in order to obtain the needed funds. Curiously, they seem not to consider the possibility of reducing their spending, and thereby decreasing their need for funds. Thus, they define their problem as one of insufficient funds rather than as one of overspending. By redefining their problem, they could achieve their goal of making ends meet without overtaxing themselves.

The unhappy consequences of suboptimal definition of a problem can be seen in the political arena as well as in private life. In 1972, a group of men broke into the Democratic National Committee headquarters at the Watergate complex in Washington, D.C. To this day, it is not known exactly why the break-in took place. When members of the Nixon administration started receiving details regarding the break-in, they viewed their problem as one of containing and covering up the situation as much as possible. As more and more information about the break-in leaked out, the members of the Nixon political team made increasingly futile efforts to prevent disclosure of unsavory facts. Eventually, the cover-up became considerably more of a problem than even the break-in had been. By defining their problem as one of covering up the break-in rather than as one of providing full disclosure in a minimally harmful way, the campaign committee seriously reduced the credibility of the Nixon administration and Nixon eventually found himself obliged to resign.

The effects of inadequate definition of problems can be seen strikingly in some psychological investigations. For example, in one investigation I did with my collaborator, Bathsheva Rifkin (1979), we asked children in grades 2, 4, and 6, as well as college students, to solve pictorial analogies. In these analogy problems, items were presented in the form A is to B as C is to $D_1$ or $D_2$, where $D_1$ and $D_2$ are two alternative answer options. We were interested in how many analogies children at the different grade levels could solve correctly.

We encountered an unwelcome surprise when we attempted to score the test booklets of some of the second-graders. Rather than circling either the first or the second of the two answer options, as the instructions had indicated they should, some of these children had circled either the first term or the second term (A or B) of the analogy. At first, this strategy seemed to make no sense at all, and we had no idea why these children had circled one of the first two terms rather than one of the answer options. We soon found out. The children in the experiment were elementary-school students at a Jewish day school. At this school, instruction was typically in English in the morning and in Hebrew in the afternoon. As a result, the children were accustomed to reading in a left-to-right fashion in the morning, and in a right-to-left fashion in the afternoon. What some of these children had done was inappropriately to transfer their right-to-left reading behavior to the analogy problem, which, in fact, had been administered during the afternoon. In other words, they had defined the problem in a way that was appropriate to their usual afternoon activity—reading Hebrew—but in a way that was inappropriate for the analogy-solving activity.

### Improving Your Definition of the Nature of a Problem

You can do several things to improve the ways in which you define problems. When you are confronted with a problem that you are having difficulty solving, consider the following strategies that may help you to redefine the problem in a more nearly optimal way:

*1. Reread or reconsider the question.*    In certain kinds of problems, such as mathematical word problems, you'll be given some background information and then asked a question that requires you to use this background information in order to reach a solution to the problem. If you misread the question, you will often find it impossible to solve the problem, or even if a solution is reached, it is to a problem other than the one that was posed. It is therefore important to make sure that the problem you are attempting to solve is in fact the problem that is being posed. In other words, it is important to make sure that the question being answered is the same as the question being asked.

*2. Simplify your goals.*    Sometimes, you may set certain goals for yourself or others that prove difficult to meet. You may then try harder or make others try harder in an attempt to reach the goals. Sometimes this strategy works, and the problem can therefore be solved. At other times, however, the strategy fails: You find yourself simply unable to meet the goals, or you find that others cannot reach the goals you have set for them. In such instances, consider whether you can simplify the goals to make them attainable. Often, you can substitute an attainable goal with little or no loss in terms of the ultimate outcome. Sometimes, arriving at a lesser goal can make you aware of ways in which the more difficult goal can be reached.

*3. Redefine your goals.*    Sometimes, instead of setting a more modest goal for yourself, you need only to change the goal to make it more appropriate for what you wish to accomplish. In such instances, you need to define the problem in a way that leads toward this redefined goal.

### Exercises

Some of the classical problems in the psychological literature are difficult because people tend to misdefine their nature. These problems highlight the importance of correctly defining a problem to intelligent performance. Consider three such problems.

**THE NINE-DOT PROBLEM**    Figure 3-1 contains nine dots arrayed three by three. The "nine-dot problem" is simply stated:

**Your task is to connect all nine dots with a set of line segments. You must never lift your pencil off the page, and you must not use more than four lines. See if you can connect the nine dots with a series of line segments without ever taking your pencil off the page. After you have tried the problem, only then look at the solution (Figure 3-17) at the end of the chapter. Do not read on until you have tried the problem.**

---

**FIGURE 3-1**

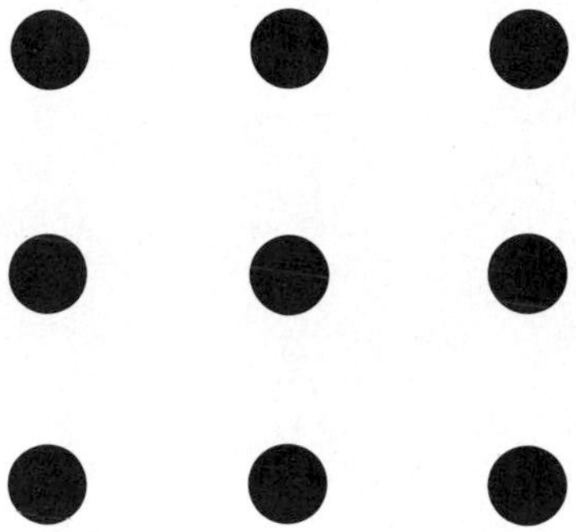

---

---

As you can now see, the nine-dot problem can be solved. However, people find it extremely difficult to arrive at the solution, and most never do, no matter how hard they try. An examination of the solution reveals why. Most people assume that the lines must be kept within the confines of the square formed by the nine dots. They do not allow their solution to extend beyond the boundaries of the dots, even though there is nothing in the problem that even suggests this constraint. Nevertheless, most people presuppose that it exists. The problem cannot be solved with four lines restricted to the interior of the figure. In other words, by placing an unnecessary and unwarranted constraint on themselves, people make the problem insoluble. This problem provides a classic example of how defining a problem in a nonoptimal way can reduce, and in this case eliminate, the chances of finding a solution to the problem. Unfortunately, people do this all the time, as the nine-dot problem shows. Of course, simply knowing that you can go outside the borders does not solve the nine-dot problem; to the contrary, it still remains a challenge. The point is, though, that until you accept the possibility of going outside the borders, the problem is not even soluble. The lesson for you to learn is that you should not place constraints on your solution that are neither inherent in nor implied by the problem.

**THE MONK PROBLEM**

A monk wishes to pursue study and contemplation in a retreat at the top of a mountain. The monk starts climbing the mountain at 7:00 A.M. and arrives at the top of the mountain at 5:00 P.M. of the same day. During the course

## FIGURE 3-2

of his ascent, he travels at variable speeds, and takes a break for lunch. He spends the evening in study and contemplation. The next day, the monk starts his descent at 7:00 A.M. again, along the same route. Normally, his descent would be faster than his ascent, but because he is tired and afraid of tripping and hurting himself, he descends the mountain slowly, not arriving at the bottom until 5:00 P.M. of the day after he started his ascent. Figure 3-2 shows the monk's route. The question is this: Must there be a point on the mountain that the monk passes at exactly the same time of day on the two successive days of his ascent and descent? If so, provide a plausible demonstration that this is the case. If not, show why this need not necessarily be the case. Do not read on until you have finished your attempt to solve the monk problem. Only then check the solution (Figure 3-18) at the end of the chapter.

In fact, it is necessarily the case that the monk must pass through exactly the same point (or altitude) on the mountain at corresponding times on the days of his ascent and descent. The solution shows why this must be the case. The problem becomes much easier to conceptualize if rather than imagining the same monk climbing the mountain one day and going down the mountain the next, you imagine two different monks, one ascending and the other descending the mountain on the same day. You may assume that the monks start and finish at the same time, although this assumption is not necessary for solution of the problem. Note that in this redefinition of the problem, the monk's descent on the second day is reconceptualized as a different monk's descent on the same day as the first monk's ascent. This reconceptualization does not change the nature of or solution to the problem, but only makes it easier to see what that solution is. Note how, if there were two monks, their paths of ascent and descent would necessarily cross each other. The point at which the two lines of ascent and descent cross each other is the point at which the original monk's paths of ascent and descent must "cross each other" at the same time of day. In terms of the reconceptualization of the problem, it is at this point that the two monks meet. Obviously, their meeting must be in a given place at a given time. The redefinition of the problem simply makes it easier to see how it must be the case that at some point the original monk will be at a given point at a given time of day on the two consecutive days.

The monk problem is not insoluble in its original form. The argument that the monk's paths of ascent and descent must reach a given point at a given time on the two consecutive days can be made without the suggested reconceptualization of the problem. However, redefining the problem in the way suggested makes the problem much easier to solve. This problem provides an example of how redefining a problem can make the solution easier. The redefinition highlights the critical feature of the solution to the problem.

**THE HATRACK PROBLEM**

The hatrack problem is a construction problem in which a person is required to build a structure sufficiently stable to support a man's hat and overcoat using only two sticks (one, $1'' \times 2'' \times 60''$, the other, $1'' \times 2'' \times 43''$) and a $2''$ C-clamp. The opening of the clamp is wide enough so that both sticks can be inserted and held together securely when the clamp is tightened. The room is $12'3'' \times 13'5''$. The ceiling is $8'$ high, but two beams jut down from the ceiling about $1'$, dividing the room into thirds.

Study Figure 3-3 on the next page and try to solve this problem before reading on or checking the solution (Figure 3-19) at the end of the chapter.

The solution shows that the hatrack can be constructed by wedging together the two poles against the floor and the ceiling by means of the C-clamp. The C-clamp is used as a hook on which to hang the hat and coat. Most people have a great deal of trouble solving this problem. There are any number of reasons for this, some of which will not be considered until later. But a major reason for this difficulty is that they focus on the materials found in the room and never conceive of the possibility of using the floor and the ceiling as part of their solution. By failing to consider this possibility, they eliminate their chance of solving the problem. Notice that there is nothing in the problem that precludes use of the floor and the ceiling. Once again, we see how people artificially restrict the range of possibilities for their problem solutions. They place constraints into their solution that are neither contained in nor even implied by the problem. By redefining the problem to allow use of the floor and ceiling, people can readily solve the hatrack problem.

FIGURE 3-3

People have great difficulty solving all three of these problems. One might think that the difficulty is due to the perversity of psychologists in thinking of difficult problems for people to solve. However, there are many problems in our everyday lives that we fail to solve or solve in a nonoptimal way because of our inadequate definition of the nature of the problem.

## Selecting the Components
## or Steps Needed to Solve a Problem
### Examples

Anyone who has ever bought a house or rented an apartment knows the great difficulty people often confront in deciding which house to buy or which apartment to rent. At first, it may seem like a simple matter of finding our dream house or dream apartment. Unfortunately, we rarely find the house or apartment of our dreams. Even if we were able to find such a house or apartment, the chances are that its price would put it beyond reach. As a result, we have to start making compromises and trade-offs in an attempt to decide which of several options is the best one. Typically, none of the houses or apartments will seem quite right. They will vary in quality on many dimensions, and what these dimensions are will probably not even be clear at first. Unless we find some systematic way of deciding among the options, we may be overwhelmed by the difficulty involved in choosing the best place in which to live. How would you go about solving the problem of choosing the best house or apartment?

What can at first seem like an insoluble problem can become a soluble one if you decide on a set of criteria for evaluating places to live, and a set of weights for evaluating the criteria. For example, you might first decide what features are important to you in selecting a house or apartment. Such features might include the overall size of the place, its location, its price, its proximity to your school or place of work, its condition, the amount of closet space, and so on. The important thing is that the list contain each of the criteria that is of some importance to you in making your decision. Another person might produce a different list, of course.

Once you have decided on the set of criteria, you need to decide on a set of weights to assign to each of those criteria. These weights indicate how important each of the criteria is in making the final decision. For example, you might decide to use a 5-point scale, where 1 represents a low weight and 5 a high weight. On this scale, you might decide, for instance, that size of the place is very important (5), whereas condition of the place is not so important (2), because you can always improve it. With these criteria for making a decision and these weights to use in assessing the criteria, you have gone a long way toward arriving at a solution to the problem. Still other steps remain to be taken, and these will be considered below.

Let's move to another example. Any number of things in life may cause depression. These include the loss of a friend or loved one, poor grades in school, a move to a new location, loneliness, disappointment with our social life, and so on. The first problem we face when we are depressed is recognizing that fact. This recognition falls under the domain of defining the nature of the problem. But recognizing that we are depressed is obviously not sufficient for relieving the depression. Very often, people remain depressed because they either fail to face the fact that they are depressed, or because once they have faced this fact, they do not construct a systematic plan for doing something about it. Suppose you recognized yourself as depressed. What might you do?

A first step might be to ask yourself why you are feeling depressed. You might choose to make a list of things that are not going quite right in your life, and ask yourself which, if any, of these things might be the source of your depression. Such a list might also give you a clue as to how to get rid of your depression. For example, if you find yourself depressed because of a non-existent social life, you might decide to start attending social events. If you are unaware of what events there are that you could attend, you might check the newspaper or ask people for suggestions in this regard. If you find yourself depressed because of low grades in a college course, you might decide upon a plan of action for improving your grades. This plan would consist of a series of steps designed to raise your performance in the courses that are giving you trouble. Regardless of the source of depression, the important thing would be to decide on a plan for alleviating whatever it is that is causing you to feel blue.

The importance of choosing an appropriate set of steps for problem solution can be seen in the international as well as in the personal domain. For example, the problem of mutual arms reduction across nations is largely (although not exclusively) a matter of finding a set of appropriate steps for accomplishing the reduction. The greatest difficulty arms negotiators seem to face is finding a set of steps for reduction that is mutually agreeable to all parties. If only such steps could be found, the negotiators would be a long way toward solving their problem.

Sometimes, people are unable to solve problems because they do not have the means to do so. A striking example of this can be seen in the attempts by children of different ages to solve analogies. It has often been found that very young children have great difficulty with analogy problems. The great epistemologist Jean Piaget (1972) even suggested that children are virtually unable to solve analogies before around the age of 11 or 12. Why do young children have so much difficulty in solving analogies? Research by a number of investigators indicates that young children are unable to conceive of second-order relations—that is, relations between relations. Consider, for example, the analogy LAWYER is to CLIENT as DOCTOR is to (a) MEDICINE, (b) PATIENT. A number of steps are needed to solve this analogy. But the single step that seems to present an insurmountable problem for young children is that of "mapping" the higher-order relations between LAWYER and CLIENT on the one hand, and DOCTOR and PATIENT on the other. Notice that the essence of analogy is the relation between these two relations. In both cases, a professional renders services to an individual. In one case, the services are legal, in the other case, medical. Thus, although the lower-order relations are not the same (one involves legal services and the other medical services), there is a higher-order relation between the two kinds of services. Children under about age 11 are unable to see this higher-order relation. In effect, the step of "mapping" seems to be unavailable to them.

It is important in this and other cases to distinguish between the notions of *availability* and *accessibility* of problem-solving components. Sometimes, people simply lack the mental or physical means to solve a problem. Thus, the ability to map second-order relations is apparently unavailable to young children. At other times, however, the components to the solution may be available, but relatively inaccessible. In other words, an individual is able to perform a certain step, but does not realize its applicability.

Consider, for example, how you would go about memorizing the following list of words: BOOK, TABLE, CHAIR, NEWSPAPER, SOFA, MAGAZINE, NOVEL, DESK, POEM, BED, PAMPHLET. People usually use two basic strategies in memorizing such a list. In the first strategy, called "rehearsal," they simply repeat the words to themselves over and over again in the order given. The second strategy is called "category clustering." In this particular list, the words tend to fall into two general categories: pieces of furniture and things to read. A list is usually more easily recallable if the words are mentally clustered by content categories. Rehearsal and category clustering both improve long-term recall of lists of words, and these two strategies are *available* to almost everyone. However, Earl Butterfield and John Belmont (1977) have found that mentally retarded individuals do not tend to use these strategies spontaneously. If they are explicitly told to use them, then, in fact, they will. In other words, their problem is not one of strategy availability; rather, it is one of strategy accessibility. The strategies simply are not *accessible* to these individuals. They have to be reminded again and again of the applicability of rehearsal and clustering to the recall task.

### Improving Your Selection of Task Components

There are several things you can keep in mind that will facilitate your choosing the steps or components needed to solve the problem.

*1. Choose steps that are the right size for solving the problem, that is, steps that are neither too small nor too large.*   One of the biggest difficulties people face in solving problems is that of choosing steps that are the wrong size. If the steps are too large, people simply find themselves unable to solve the problem. In effect, they have bitten off more than they can chew. But choosing steps that are too small can result in extremely long problem-solving processes and the frustration that goes with them. You will usually want to solve a problem in as little time as possible, and choosing very small steps can thwart your attainment of this goal.

*2. Make the first step an easy one.*   People often find that the hardest step to take in solving a problem or in accomplishing a task is the first one. They have difficulty getting started. This difficulty may derive from their inability to see how to start the problem, or it may result from their difficulty in getting the momentum to start problem solving or task performance. For example, graduate students have a notoriously hard time getting their Ph.D. dissertations started. They tend to find smaller, less important tasks to fill their time, and to put off starting the more important but seemingly infinitely larger task. At a more mundane level, people often put off the more difficult chores they have to do around the house, doing the easier ones first. For example, our basement desperately needs to be cleaned, but cleaning it seems like a Herculean task. I have therefore managed to find other chores to do around the house for weeks on end, putting off the inevitable cleaning of the basement that I know most needs to be done. By making the first step an easy one to get the task started, people can often acquire the momentum they need to complete the task.

*3. Consider alternative steps to solution before choosing any one set of steps.*   In his famous book *Administrative Behavior* (1957), Herbert Simon described a strategy frequently used by people in solving problems. In this strategy, called "satisficing," people choose the first minimally acceptable course of action, rather than considering all the available options and only then settling on the optimal course of action. Clearly a suboptimal strategy, "satisficing" is an easy strategy to avoid. Before settling on a suboptimal set of steps for solution just because it happened to be the first one you thought of, consider other alternatives.

### Exercises

1.  Suppose you have been admitted to three different colleges. Your selection of college will determine a great deal about what the next four

years of your life will be like. List some of the steps you would take in order to help you decide among colleges and choose the best one.

2. You are in a foreign country where you don't speak the language. You have a bad headache and serious digestive trouble. You realize you need a doctor. What steps might you take (a) to convey to an inhabitant of the country that you need a doctor and (b) to convey to the inhabitant what your symptoms are?

3. One of the most serious issues facing the world today is nuclear arms reduction. A major problem is that the countries involved seem to have trouble deciding on a series of steps that will result in mutual arms reduction. What steps could a pair of countries take in order to realize a reduction in their armaments?

## Selecting a Strategy for Ordering Components of Problem Solving

When solving a problem of any kind, it is not sufficient merely to select the information-processing components that will best, or even satisfactorily, solve the problem. You must also combine these components into a workable strategy for problem solution. Two major issues arise when combining a set of components or steps of problem solution.

First, you must decide in what order to execute the components or steps. For example, in solving a mathematical word problem, it is not enough to know that solution of the problem requires a multiplication, a subtraction, and a division. You must know the order in which these steps need to be performed, as the order of step execution usually affects the solution to the problem. Indeed, one well-known test for understanding mathematical concepts, the Stanford Achievement Test, asks examinees the operations that need to be performed for each mathematics problem and the order in which they should be performed. Consider a very simple example:

Joe gave a storekeeper $1.00 for two apples. The apples cost 35¢ apiece. How much change did Joe receive?

This problem can be solved by a multiplication and a subtraction. But in what *order* are these operations executed? If the operations are not done in proper order [$1.00 − (2 × 35¢)], the problem will be solved incorrectly. The multiplication must be done first.

### Improving Your Selection of a Strategy

There are some steps you can take in order to improve your selection of a strategy in problem solving. Some of these steps are listed below.

1. *Be sure you consider the full problem.*    Problem solvers often make errors because they believe they have solved the problem before they have

actually finished. Their answer to the problem is thus only an answer to a subproblem of the full problem. Test item writers are aware of this tendency, and often create distractors (wrong answers) that are plausible by virtue of their being subproblem solutions. The problem solver solves part of the problem, sees the solution he or she has reached as one of the answer options, and quickly selects it. Unfortunately, the solver did not complete all of the steps necessary to solve the full problem. Research on problem solving has shown that these partial solutions are one of the primary sources of error in problem solving. For example, my research has shown that in solving analogies, younger children tend to be poorer than older children in large part because they did not consider all of the available attributes or answer options of the problem. Moreover, adults who make errors on analogy problems frequently do so because they have not considered the terms of the problems fully enough. So make sure that you consider the full problem before offering or choosing a solution.

2. *Don't immediately assume the "obvious."*   Another frequent source of error in problem solving occurs when the problem solver assumes the "obvious" but the obvious turns out to be wrong. Such assumptions can take various forms. For example, sometimes a problem appears to be a case of a certain kind of familiar problem, whereas in fact it is not a case of this familiar kind of problem at all. Other times, the problem solver simply makes assumptions that are unjustified. We saw, for example, in the nine-dot problem how the assumption that one must stay within the borders of the nine dots makes the problem impossible to solve. Other assumptions can relate specifically to the issue of ordering the steps of a problem. For example, solvers often assume that they should work forward in solving a problem. However, it is often easier to work backward—that is, to start with a solution, and then attempt to generate the premises of the problem. Backward problem solving often works particularly well in logical and mathematical proofs. Similarly, people often assume that they should start with the premises and work directly toward the conclusion. But sometimes problems that are unmanageable when solved as wholes become easier when broken down into a series of subproblems. The problem solver formulates a series of subgoals, and rather than trying to reach the final goal directly, tries to reach each of the sequence of subgoals. Accomplishment of each of the subgoals then leads to solution of the whole problem.

Consider, for example, the problem above on mutual arms reduction. If our goal was the elimination of all nuclear weapons, we might be quite frustrated in ever reaching this goal, because the steps toward reduction are just too many and too complicated. With such a goal, the problem will almost certainly be solved only through the judicious selection of subgoals. For example, a first step might be the freezing of production of new nuclear weapons. This subgoal will obviously not result in a reduction of weapons, much less an elimination of all weapons, but it would seem to be a reasonable first subgoal toward the final goal of eliminating nuclear weapons. A second subgoal might be the elimination of certain kinds of nuclear weapons, or the removal of such weapons from certain locations.

The point, then, is that achieving a very difficult goal may be possible only if we are willing to work toward this goal through the selection of subgoals. Assuming that we should directly seek the final goal is almost certainly a mistake.

*3. Make sure your sequencing of steps follows a natural or logical order toward the goal you wish to reach.*    Often, solvers choose a sequence of steps for solving a problem, and then attempt to order the steps in a way that will reach the solver's ultimate goal of solution. Before actually carrying out the steps, make sure that the ordering you have selected is the most natural or most logical one for the given problem, and that none of the steps assumes information that, given your ordering, will not be attained until later. Consider, for example, the case of my friend who needed a bookcase for his office. We decided to go looking together at the local stores. It was not until we had gotten to the first store and seen the selection available that my friend realized he had failed to measure the space into which the bookcase was to fit. He had been all ready to select among different styles of bookcases before addressing the prior question of the size of bookcase that he could fit into the available space.

### Exercises

**SEARCHING THE FIELD**    Consider the following problem, which is a variant of a kind of problem found on standardized intelligence tests.

**Figure 3-4 shows an irregularly shaped field. Somewhere in that field is a valuable gold coin. Your problem is to set up a strategy of search so that in systematically walking through the field, you will find that gold coin. Show by drawing lines with your pencil the systematic search strategy you might use that would guarantee your finding the gold coin.**

The critical element for solution of this problem is that the search strategy be ordered and systematic. Random roaming around the field or unsystematic attempts to look at different parts are unlikely to yield the gold coin. A variant of this problem is found in everyday life when one misplaces something in the home. For example, I frequently lose my glasses and then have to search my house for them. Anyone who has searched for the car keys in his or her house knows the importance of setting up a systematic, ordered strategy for search. Random wandering around the house or apartment can lead to multiple looks in a given place where one has already looked, and no looks in other places that may very well have keys. Anyone who has been through this experience can remember with chagrin looking several times in one spot and not finding the missing keys, but then failing to look in another spot that has them.

**PERMUTATION PROBLEMS**    A related problem in which setting up a systematic order of steps is crucial is the permutation problem used by Piaget and others as a measure of formal-operational (advanced) reasoning. This kind of reasoning is usually identified with children who are at least 12 or so years of age and with adults, although the large majority of these children and

**FIGURE 3-4**

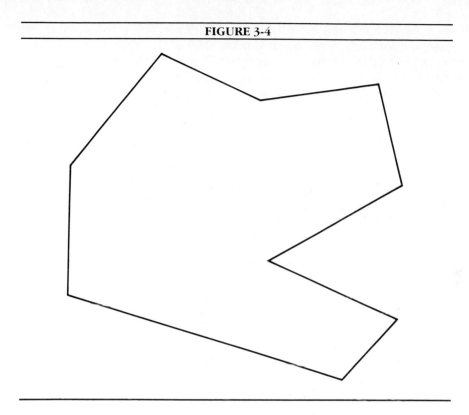

adults seem not to be fully formal in their reasoning. Thus, your ability to solve this particular problem may give you an indication of just how capable you are in formal reasoning. If you do not solve the problem in the way that typifies formal reasoners, you will in a few minutes, showing the ease with which improvement in intellectual skills can sometimes be obtained.

**Here are four letters: A, B, C, D. Provide a listing of all the possible permutations (orders) in which these four letters can be written. (For example, A, B, C, D is one permutation and D, C, B, A is another.)**

This problem can be either quite easy or quite difficult, depending on the strategy used to solve it. If you simply attempt to solve it in an unsystematic fashion, the chances of your listing all of the possible permutations are probably quite slim. However, if you set up a systematic strategy, ordering your listing of the permutations in a systematic way, you will easily be able to list them all. In fact, when this item is used as a measure of formal operations, the important thing the examiner looks for is not so much the number of permutations listed as the strategy that is used to generate these permutations. In other words, the ordering of steps is the critical feature that the examiner looks for in scoring performance on this problem.

In order to achieve a solution, the first thing that is useful to know is the number of possible permutations. This knowledge will enable you to check to make sure that you have listed them all. There is a simple formula for computing the number of possible permutations. This formula makes use of the idea of a factorial, which is represented as an exclamation point (!) after the number for which the factorial is being sought. In this case, because there are four letters for which we are seeking all possible permutations, the expression is 4!. The value of 4! is equal to the number of possible permutations. This expression is solved by taking the number after which the exclamation point appears and then multiplying it by each of the natural numbers that is less than that number down to 1. In this case, one would multiply $4 \times 3 \times 2 \times 1$, attaining a product of 24, the number of possible permutations.

Now that we know there are 24 possible permutations, we have to list them. A systematic way of obtaining the entire list is to hold one letter constant and to vary subsequent letters systematically, repeating the procedure for each letter. For the present example, this strategy would yield:

1.  A   B   C   D
2.  A   B   D   C
3.  A   C   B   D
4.  A   C   D   B
5.  A   D   B   C
6.  A   D   C   B

Note how the first letter, A, is held constant in each of these six permutations and variation is done from the right end moving toward the left. In other words, first the last two letters, C and D, are interchanged with each other, and only then is the third-to-last place interchanged. As a result, there are six permutations with the letter A appearing first, and two permutations each with B, C, and D, in the second position. Because there are 24 possible permutations, we know that we must be one-quarter of the way through the entire list. As all of these permutations have had A in their first position, we know we must be on the right track, because now we need to generate six permutations with each of B, C, and D in the first position. The rest of the list of permutations is:

7.  B   A   C   D
8.  B   A   D   C
9.  B   C   A   D
10.  B   C   D   A
11.  B   D   A   C
12.  B   D   C   A
13.  C   A   B   D
14.  C   A   D   B
15.  C   B   A   D
16.  C   B   D   A
17.  C   D   A   B
18.  C   D   B   A
19.  D   A   B   C

20.  D   A   C   B
21.  D   B   A   C
22.  D   B   C   A
23.  D   C   A   B
24.  D   C   B   A

Here are two more permutation problems you can try on your own: H, N, Q, T, and 4, 7, 9, 11. See if you can list all possible permutations of these sets of letters and numbers.

**MISSIONARIES AND CANNIBALS PROBLEM**   One of the most famous problems requiring careful ordering of steps is the so-called Missionaries and Cannibals problem, which has been in the problem-solving folklore for many years and has also been studied extensively by psychologists. Try to solve the problem, which goes like this:

Three missionaries and three cannibals are on a river bank. The missionaries and cannibals need to cross over to the other side of the river. They have for this purpose a small rowboat that will hold just two people. There is one problem, however. If the number of cannibals on either river bank exceeds the number of missionaries, the cannibals will eat the missionaries. How can all six get across to the other side of the river in a way that guarantees that they all arrive there alive and uneaten?

You will find the solution (Figure 3-20) to the Missionaries and Cannibals problem at the end of the chapter. The solution contains several noteworthy features. First, the problem can be solved in a minimum of eleven steps, including the first and the last steps. Second, the solution is essentially linear in nature. At all but two steps along the solution path, the only error that can be made is to go directly backward in the solution. In other words, there are only two possible moves, the last one to have been made and the next one that can be made. At two steps, there are two possible forward-moving responses, but both of these lead toward the correct answer. Thus, again, the only error possible is returning to a previous state in the solution of the problem. A secondary problem is making an illegal move—that is, a move that is not permitted according to the terms of the problem. An example of an illegal move would be one that resulted in more than two individuals in the boat. You might wonder, given the essentially linear nature of the solution path, why or how people have trouble solving this kind of problem at all. The biggest problems they seem to have, according to those who have studied the problem, are (a) inadvertently moving backward, (b) making illegal moves, and (c) not realizing the nature of the next legal move.

If you are now ready for a somewhat more difficult challenge in terms of ordering the steps of the Missionaries and Cannibals problem, then try the Missionaries and Cannibals problem again, except with five missionaries and five cannibals. Again, your task is to get all of the missionaries and cannibals from one bank of the river to the other, and no more than three individuals are allowed in the boat at any one time. Moreover, once again, you must never allow it to happen that there are more cannibals than missionaries on either bank or in the boat, as in this case the cannibals would eat the missionaries.

This problem is quite a bit more difficult than the earlier version because the solution is no longer linear. Try the problem before checking the solution (Figure 3-21) at the end of the chapter. As you can see from the figure, many more moves are legal, but some lead to dead ends.

Herbert Simon and Stephen Reed (1976) have done some research in order to find out the strategies people actually use in solving the Missionaries and Cannibals problem when there are five missionaries and five cannibals to be transported across the river. Their research has indicated that people seeking to solve this problem use either of two strategies or a combination of these two strategies. The first strategy, a *balance* strategy, results in the problem solver selecting the move that balances the number of missionaries with the number of cannibals on each side of the river. This strategy makes sense because the problem solver is seeking to avoid a situation where the number of cannibals is greater than the number of missionaries on either side of the river. The second strategy, a *means–ends* strategy, selects moves that maximize the number of persons across the river (odd-numbered moves) and minimize the number of persons on the initial side of the river (even-numbered moves). At some steps along the paths to solution, these two strategies yield the same move. At other steps, they do not. Both strategies assume that problem solvers will make only legal moves and that they will test for previous moves so as not to go back to an earlier state of problem solving. Interestingly, a pure means–ends strategy will result in the problem being solved in eleven moves, whereas a pure balance strategy will result in the problem never being solved at all! Instead, a pure balance strategy will result in the problem solver getting stuck in an "infinite loop." Simon and Reed hypothesized, and their results confirmed, that what problem solvers tend to do is to start off problem solving with a balance strategy, and later shift to a means–ends strategy. Problem solvers differ in the exact point during problem solving at which they switch from one strategy to the other.

**WATER-JUG PROBLEM**    A related kind of problem, which also requires a carefully ordered sequence of steps, is the water-jug problem. Water-jug problems are found on the Stanford-Binet and on other intelligence tests. Here is an example of the water-jug problem:

A mother sends her boy to the river in order to measure out 3 quarts of water. The mother gives her son a 7-quart bucket and a 4-quart bucket. How can the son measure out exactly 3 quarts of water using nothing but these two buckets and not guessing as to the amount of water that he brings home? Try to solve this problem before reading on.

This is a simple example of a water-jug problem. To solve the problem, the son merely needs to fill the 7-quart bucket first and pour the water into the 4-quart bucket. He is now left with 3 quarts of water in the 7-quart bucket.

Consider now a slightly harder water-jug problem:

**A circus owner sends one of his clowns to bring back from a nearby river 7 gallons of water to give to the elephants. He gives the clown a 5-gallon bucket and a 3-gallon bucket and tells him to bring back exactly 7 gallons of water. How can the clown measure out exactly 7 gallons of water using nothing but these two buckets and not guessing at the amount?**

This problem is a bit more difficult. First, the clown needs to fill the 5-gallon bucket. Next, he must pour the water into the 3-gallon bucket. Having done this, he throws the 3 gallons back into the river. He now takes the 2 gallons left in the 5-gallon bucket and pours them into the 3-gallon bucket. By filling the 5-gallon bucket again, he will now have 5 gallons in that bucket and 2 gallons in the other bucket, for a total of 7 gallons.

Of course, there are "water-jug" problems that do not make use of either jugs or water. Such problems, which are identical in form to the water-jug problem but which make use of different entities in the problem statements, are called "problem isomorphs." Although they are parallel in form to the original problems, research by John Hayes and Herbert Simon (1976), among others, has shown that problem isomorphs are sometimes easier and sometimes harder than the original problem. In other words, changing the content of a problem can change its difficulty, even if the form of the problem remains unchanged. So consider a problem isomorph for the water-jug problem:

**A cook needs 1 gram of salt to season a special meat he is cooking. When he opens the drawer to get a measuring spoon, he finds out that he has only an 11-gram measuring spoon and a 4-gram measuring spoon. How can the cook measure out exactly 1 gram of salt using nothing but these two spoons and not guessing at the amount?**

What the cook needs to do is to fill the 4-gram measuring spoon first and pour the salt into the 11-gram measuring spoon. Then, he needs to repeat this procedure two more times. The third time, he will be able to pour only 3 of the 4 grams into the 11-gram spoon. He will be left with 1 gram of salt on the 4-gram spoon. Now consider a similar problem:

**With a 5-minute hourglass and a 9-minute hourglass, what is the quickest way to time a 13-minute steak?**

One strategy for solving this problem is to start both hourglasses and the steak together. After the 5-minute hourglass runs out, turn it over. When the 9-minute hourglass runs out, turn over the 5-minute hourglass. It will run for 4 minutes, yielding a total time of 13 minutes.

The type of problem characterized in this section can be made somewhat more difficult by including three rather than two water jugs, hourglasses, or whatever. Consider, for example, this problem:

You have three jugs—A, B, and C. Jug A has a capacity of 8 quarts, Jug B has a capacity of 5 quarts, and Jug C has a capacity of 3 quarts. Initially, Jug A is full, but the two smaller jugs are empty. How can you divide the contents of the largest jug evenly between the largest and middle-sized jugs—that is, between Jugs A and B?

This problem is quite a bit harder than the problem that has preceded it. See if you can solve it, then check the solution (Figure 3-22) at the end of the chapter. As shown in the figure, you pour 3 quarts from Jug A into Jug C, and then pour Jug C into Jug B. Pour 3 more quarts from Jug A into Jug C. Now pour 2 quarts from Jug C into Jug B, filling Jug B (5 quarts). One quart is left in Jug C. Empty Jug B into Jug A; then pour the 1 quart from Jug C into Jug B. Fill Jug C again from Jug A. Finally, empty Jug C into Jug B.

**THE TOWER OF HANOI AND ITS VARIATIONS**    One of the most famous problems in the problem-solving literature is the Tower of Hanoi problem. In this problem, the solver is presented with three sticks and a set of discs mounted on the first of those sticks. The discs are of unequal sizes, and they are mounted so that the largest one is on the bottom, the next largest one is immediately above that, and so on until the top of the pile, which contains the smallest disc. The number of discs varies from one version of the problem to another. The idea is to transfer all of the discs from the first stick to the third stick, using the middle stick for intermediate steps of problem solving. In transferring the discs, the solver is never allowed to place a larger disc on top of a smaller disc. A picture of a typical Tower of Hanoi puzzle is shown in Figure 3-5.

Because this book does not come with a set of discs and sticks, it is necessary to use isomorphs to the Tower of Hanoi problem in order to give you a chance to solve problems of this type. Consider the following isomorph, studied by John Hayes and Herbert Simon (1976):

Three five-handed extraterrestrial monsters were holding three crystal globes. Because of the quantum-mechanical peculiarities of their neighborhood, both monsters and globes come in exactly three sizes with no others permitted: small, medium, and large. The medium-sized monster was holding the small globe; the small monster was holding the large globe; and the large monster was holding the medium-sized globe. Since this situation offended their keenly developed sense of symmetry, they proceeded to transfer globes from one monster to another so that each monster would have a globe proportionate to his own size. Monster etiquette complicated the solution of the problem since it requires: (a) that only one globe be transferred at a time; (b) that if a monster is holding two

## FIGURE 3-5

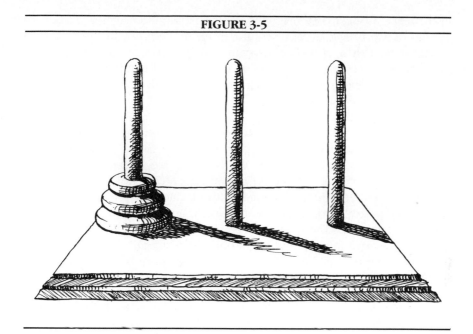

globes, only the larger of the two may be transferred; and (c) that a globe may not be transferred to a monster who is holding a larger globe. By what sequence of transfers could the monsters have solved this problem?

Try to solve the problem before checking the solution (Figure 3-23) at the end of the chapter.

In this section, we have seen different instances in which the metacomponent of deciding upon an order for performance components may be exercised. As you have seen, a wide variety of problems require careful ordering of steps to solution. In each of the kinds of problems in this section, the hardest part of the problem is not actually coming up with the steps, but deciding on the order in which the steps should be taken. Other kinds of problems, of course, are more or less difficult for other reasons. Let us now consider problems whose difficulty derives largely from how to represent them mentally.

## Selecting
## a Mental Representation
## for Information

An important part of many kinds of problem solving is the way or ways that information is represented mentally. Such a mental representation might be in the form of a pictorial image, a set of propositions, an algebraic equation, or yet some other format. Problems that could be solved easily using one form of mental representation are often solved only with difficulty or not at all using another. Sometimes, you will need to supplement your mental representation with an external representation of information. So, for example, in solving a mathematics problem, you may find it helpful to draw a diagram or to set up a series of equations that represent the terms of the problem. Such external diagrams can then facilitate your problem solving, especially the way in which you proceed to represent information about the problem in your head. Psychologists studying mental representations have learned some interesting things about them.

## Examples

One psychologist studying mental representations, Patricia Linville (1982), has looked at the relation between the way in which we represent information about other people and our stereotypes about and prejudices toward these people. One of her most interesting findings is that simple mental representations tend to lead toward extreme judgments about people, whether favorable or unfavorable. The converse also holds: Extreme judgments tend to imply simple representations about people. For example, she has found that prejudices toward members of certain groups tend to be accompanied by simple mental representations about the members of those groups. This finding makes sense, because almost inevitably, a complex representation simply will not support the prejudice. This finding gives credence to the view that one of the best ways to fight prejudice is through fighting ignorance—the more we know about the members of any group, the less likely it is that we'll be prejudiced toward them.

Linville has also discovered a connection between simplicity of mental representations about unfavorable events and depression following those events. People who become depressed after a particular event, such as the loss of a love, tend to view that event in very simple terms. As the complexity of their view increases, their tendency to be depressed about the event decreases. This finding gives credence to Aaron Beck's notion (1976) that depression is at least partly cognitive in nature, and that a way to fight depression is to teach people to reason realistically and logically about the event or events leading to the depressive state.

Another instance in which proper representation can facilitate problem solving is in major decisions we face in our lives, such as the decision of whether to buy a car, whether to undergo surgery, what college to attend, and so on. In trying to make such decisions, we often find ourselves overwhelmed by the available information, and at a loss to know just what to do with it. Because the extent of the information exceeds the capacities of our working memories to hold it all at one time, we can only deal with limited aspects of the decision at one time, and we sometimes find ourselves going over the same information again and again, but not really making progress in evaluating the wealth of information available that might facilitate the decision making. At one time, psychologists accepted a notion of a completely rational person, who would take all the information and weigh it accurately. They later came to realize that such a procedure in decision making is the exception rather than the rule. Herbert Simon, for example, proposed that people "satisfice" rather than maximize when presented with a decision to be made. People "satisfice" when they take the first minimally acceptable choice that occurs to them, rather than considering all of the possible choices and then selecting the optimal ones. It is as if the mental load is too great to consider all possible alternatives and all possible reasons for these alternatives, so people simply fail to consider most of the alternatives and most of the possible reasons for them. Again, inadequately representing the information about the problem leads to a suboptimal decision.

In another area, I have also found that the way in which people represent information can critically affect their problem-solving abilities. In collaboration with Bathsheva Rifkin (1979), I presented children of roughly 7, 9, 11, and 18 years of age picture analogies that required the children to see various kinds of relations between the pictures. One of the more striking findings from the study was that the mental representations of the children for the pictures changed with increasing age. The youngest children tended to represent information about the pictures "separably"—that is, they encoded each of the attributes of the pictures separately, retaining separate representations for each of these attributes in their heads. In contrast, the older children tended to represent information about the pictures "integrally"—that is, although they may have encoded the pictures separately, they integrated the pictures when mentally representing and storing them in the head. The advantage of the integral representation for the pictures is that it consumes less working-memory space. Because they "chunked" the information more efficiently, the older children were able to hold more information in their heads, and to process this information more efficiently. Other studies of children's encoding strategies and working-memory capacities, such as ones by Micheline Chi (1978), have also tended to suggest that younger children differ from older ones not in the number of "slots" in their working memory, but rather in the amount of information they can pack into each of these slots because of their greater efficiency of encoding presented information.

In other studies, it has been found that people of the same age will often solve cognitive problems differently, depending on their particular pattern of abilities. An important theme running throughout this book is that intelligent people, and hence effective problem solvers, tend to be people who capitalize on their strengths and compensate for their weaknesses in solving problems. Thus, it is important for you to know what your strengths and weaknesses are. In the realm of mental representation of information, for example, some people tend to be better at representing information spatially, or in the form of mental images; other people tend to be better at representing the same information linguistically, or in the form of sentences or propositions. Consider, for example, the so-called sentence-picture comparison problem. In this fairly simple problem, solvers are asked to compare the contents of a sentence to the contents of a picture, and then to say whether or not they match. For example, they might be presented with the sentence, "Star is below plus," and then with the picture $\overset{*}{+}$. In this particular case, the content of the sentence and the picture do not match, so the answer is "no." Another example of the problem is "Star is not below plus," $\overset{*}{+}$. In this somewhat harder example, the correct answer is "yes." Colin MacLeod, Nancy Mathews, and Earl Hunt (1978) studied people's strategies for solving this kind of sentence-picture comparison problem. In their article, they reported that people use either of two primary strategies for solving these problems. One strategy entails representing information from the sentence verbally. The solver takes the sentence and summarizes its content in the form of a propositional string, such as [star above plus]. In the other strategy, the solver represents information from the sentence spatially. In this strategy, the solver converts the verbal information into an image, and then compares this image to the picture that is presented. MacLeod and his colleagues found that whether people represented information linguistically or spatially was in part a function of their respective ability levels in these two domains. People who were "more verbal" were more likely to represent information linguistically; people who were "more spatial" were more likely to represent information spatially. Thus, they were adopting the mental representation that most suited their own patterns of ability.

Unfortunately, people do not always use the mental representation that is most suited to their patterns of abilities. In a study of linear syllogistic reasoning (that is, reasoning for problems such as "John is taller than Pete. Pete is taller than Sam. Who is shortest?"), for example, Evelyn Weil and I found in 1980 that although there exist both linguistic and spatial strategies for problem solution, as well as a strategy that combines linguistic and spatial elements, people do not tend to select the strategy that is most suited to their pattern of abilities. Perhaps because of the greater complexity of these problems relative to the sentence-picture comparison problems, the optimal strategy is less obvious. Indeed, in these problems, people are usually not initially aware of the availability of alternative strategies. Thus, use of better mental representations could facilitate their problem solving.

### Improving Your Selection of a Mental Representation

There are some steps you can take to help you better mentally represent problems. Here are some of them:

*1. Know your pattern of abilities.*    Sometimes, problems can be solved in alternative ways. For example, the sentence-picture comparison problems described earlier can be solved using either a spatial or a propositional (linguistic) mental representation. Knowing your pattern of abilities can help you choose which kind of representation is optimal for you. If you are better at spatial tasks than at linguistic tasks, you may well be better off choosing a spatial mental representation. Conversely, if you tend to be better at linguistic tasks, you may be better off selecting a linguistic representation. If you are equally adept at both kinds of tasks, than you may choose either option, depending on the particular problem, or else choose a mixed strategy that employs both spatial and linguistic elements. The point is that if you know your pattern of abilities, you are in a better position to use the kind of mental representation that you will find most convenient.

Consider a concrete example of how important knowledge of one's pattern of abilities can be. I teach several statistics courses that involve fairly complicated kinds of statistical techniques, several of which can be understood geometrically, algebraically, or both, although ultimately the two kinds of representations of information are equivalent. I teach the conceptual bases for the techniques both ways, and I find quite a bit of diversity in which route students choose. If my students know where their pattern of abilities lies, it is easier for them to capitalize on this information to facilitate learning of these complicated statistical techniques.

*2. Use multiple representations whenever possible.*    In problems where multiple representations for information are possible, it often helps to use at least two of these representations. If you know you are better at representing information one way than another, then you can designate one of the representations as primary and the other as secondary. The advantage to using multiple representations is that even if they are formally equivalent, they may not be equivalent psychologically. Sometimes, you can see aspects of a problem when representing it one way that are not obvious when you represent the problem another way. Using multiple forms of representation potentially helps you recognize more aspects of the nature of the problem. For example, drawing a diagram often helps you solve a problem algebraically, even though the diagram is strictly geometric.

Sometimes the problem is not one of multiple *forms* of representation but of multiple representations of a given form. Consider, again, the problem of mutual arms reduction or elimination. One of the major difficulties in achieving any progress at all toward this goal has been the inability or unwillingness of two major powers, the United States and the Soviet Union, to see things from each other's point of view. When each side attempts to solve the problem from its own point of view, the attempt invariably fails, because solution of the problem is dependent on mutual steps toward reduction, which in turn are dependent on mutual understanding. In international relations, in general, problems are often difficult to solve because of the inability or unwillingness of one side to see the other side's point of view. The same is true, of course, in smaller-scale relations, such as marriage. Many married couples have repeated disagreements, which may lead to separation or divorce, largely because they are unable or unwilling to put themselves in each other's shoes. In problems between individuals or groups, satisfactory solutions almost inevitably depend on each party's being able to represent information in the way that the other party does. Experience has shown that such mutual understanding is not easy to come by.

*3. Use external representation.*    Many complicated problems can become much simpler if you do not rely totally on mental representations of the problem. Consider a linear syllogism, in which properties of various people or objects are compared. The problem is much simpler to solve if you draw a little diagram representing the relations among people or objects. Suppose, for example, you are told "John is not as tall as Pete. Sam is not as tall as John. Who is shortest?" The solution is much easier to come by if you array the three individuals in a vertical linear ordering expressing their relative heights. The point, then, is to use external representations of information wherever possible in order to reduce the load on your internal processing capacities.

**FIGURE 3-6**

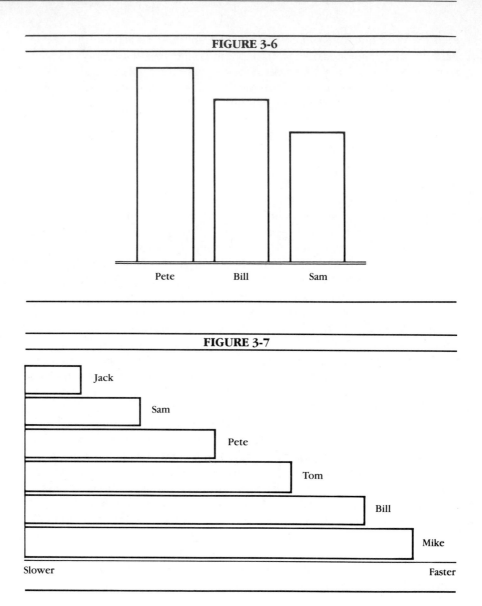

**FIGURE 3-7**

### Exercises

1.  Pete is faster than Bill. Sam is slower than Bill. Who is slowest?

This rather simple problem is a straightforward illustration of how a spatial representation for information—whether mental or external—can help in your solution of a problem. The easiest way to solve this problem is simply to construct a vertical linear array and to place the individuals in the array, as in Figure 3-6.

2.  Bill is faster than Tom. Pete is faster than Sam. Pete is slower than Tom. Bill is slower than Mike. Sam is faster than Jack. Who is fastest?

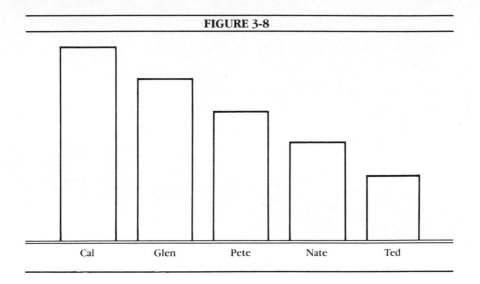

**FIGURE 3-8**

Again, the easiest way to solve this problem is through the use of a linear array. In this case, however, you need to accommodate six individuals on the array rather than just three. In this problem, the relation between individuals is one of speed rather than height. It is probably still easiest to represent the individuals in terms of a vertical linear array, with the "fastest" pole at the top of the array and the "slowest" pole at the bottom of the array. However, you may also choose to use a horizontal linear array, placing either "faster" or "slower" at the left or right sides of the array, respectively. One correct solution is shown in Figure 3-7.

3.  **Glen is older than Pete but not as old as Cal. Cal is older than both Pete and Nate. Nate is younger than Pete but older than Ted. Who is youngest?**

This problem is similar to the others, except that each sentence contains two relations between individuals rather than just one. Again, however, the problem can be solved via a simple linear ordering, as in Figure 3-8.

4.  **Three men—Henry, Louis, and Pete—differ in their levels of wealth. The last names of these three men are Toliver, Gray, and Masters, but not necessarily in that order. Louis is not as wealthy as Henry. Pete is wealthier than Louis but not as wealthy as Henry. Toliver is wealthier than Gray. Masters is not as wealthy as Gray. What is the full name of the least wealthy individual?**

This problem requires two spatial arrays, one of which relates the first names to each other, the other the last names. The problem can then be solved by correctly linking up the corresponding first and last names. The solution appears in Figure 3-9.

FIGURE 3-9

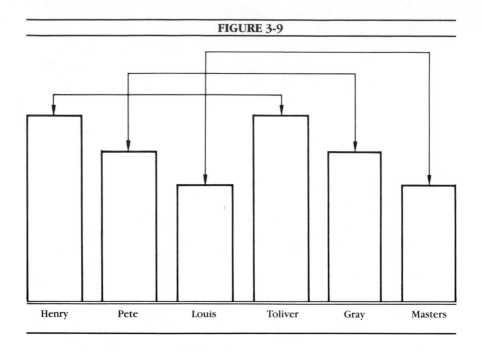

| Henry | Pete | Louis | Toliver | Gray | Masters |

FIGURE 3-10

|  | MARBLES | BASEBALL CARDS |
|---|---|---|
| Tom | $(2 + 4) = 6$ | $(6 [\# \text{ marbles}] + 4) = 10$ |
| Dick | 2 | $(2 [\# \text{ marbles}] \times 2) = 4$ |
| Harry | $(13 - [6 + 2]) = 5$ | $(10 + 2) = 12$ |

5.  Three boys—Tom, Dick and Harry—have among them 13 marbles and twice as many baseball cards. Tom has 4 more baseball cards than marbles. Dick's 2 marbles are 4 fewer than Tom's, and Dick has twice as many baseball cards as he has marbles. Harry has 2 more baseball cards than does Tom. How many marbles does Harry have?

The easiest way to solve this problem is through the construction of a table listing Tom, Dick, and Harry as three rows down and marbles and baseball cards as two columns across. As you are given information, you should place it in the table. As this problem is a bit more difficult than the ones that have preceded it, Figure 3-10 goes through each of the steps

**FIGURE 3-11**

|         | French          | Italian | Chinese |
|---------|-----------------|---------|---------|
| Ellen   | 2               | 0       | 2       |
| Marty   | 1               | 0       | 3       |
| Sue     | $(16 - 11) = 5$ | 2       | 1       |

**FIGURE 3-12**

|        | Sam | Louise | Dave |
|--------|-----|--------|------|
| Joan   | X   | X      |      |
| Patty  |     |        | X    |
| Sandy  |     |        |      |

6. Ellen, Marty, and Sue are interested in cooking. Among them they own a total of 16 cookbooks. Of Ellen's 4 books, half are French but none are Italian. Marty owns the same number of books as Ellen, but owns only half as many French cookbooks as does Ellen, and the same number of Italian cookbooks as does Ellen. Sue owns only 1 Chinese cookbook, but the same number of Italian cookbooks as Ellen owns Chinese cookbooks. How many French cookbooks does Sue own?

This problem, like the preceding one, is best solved by setting up a table. The table might have the names arrayed as rows down the left side of the table and the kinds of cookbooks as columns arrayed across the top. Again, you must enter the information in the problem in order to figure out the solution. Figure 3-11 shows the complete table and the correct answer.

7. Three women—Joan, Patty, and Sandy—have among them three children—Sam, Louise, and Dave. Sam likes to play with Patty's son. Sandy occasionally baby-sits for Joan's children. Who is Louise's mother?

This problem is solved by creating a table listing Joan, Patty, and Sandy in three rows and Sam, Louise, and Dave in three columns. The full soution appears in Figure 3-12.

## FIGURE 3-13

|  | Su | M | Tu | W | Th | F | Sa |
|---|---|---|---|---|---|---|---|
| Doctor |  |  |  |  |  | X | X |
| Restaurant | X | X |  |  |  |  |  |
| Golf |  |  |  |  |  |  |  |
| Movies |  |  |  | X | X |  |  |

8.  One day last week, I went to the doctor, ate lunch at a restaurant, played golf, and went to the movies in the evening. On Wednesday they only show a matinee, but they do show evening movies all the other days except Thursday. The doctor does not have office hours on Friday or Saturday, and the restaurant is closed on Monday. On Sundays, I have a policy of always cooking all my own meals. On what day of the week did I go to the doctor, eat lunch at the restaurant, play golf, and go to the movies?

This problem, like the ones preceding it, is most easily solved by making a table. You may either array the four activities as four separate rows and the seven days of the week as seven separate columns, or you may simply choose to cross out days of the week as they are excluded. The latter procedure is the simpler, and probably the more efficient one. The solution appears in Figure 3-13.

9.  Janet, Barbara, and Elaine are a housewife, lawyer, and physicist, although not necessarily in that order. Janet lives next door to the housewife. Barbara is the physicist's best friend. Elaine once wanted to be a lawyer but decided against it. Janet has seen Barbara within the last two days, but has not seen the physicist. Indicate the respective occupations of Janet, Barbara, and Elaine.

This problem, like the last two, is best worked out by creating a table. The table might have Janet, Barbara, and Elaine as rows, and housewife, lawyer, and physicist as columns. Figure 3-14 shows the solution.

10.  A marketing company is doing a survey of a limited number of people who own General Motor cars. In their survey, they phone 1,500 people who own Chevys, 1,200 people who own Buicks, 800 people who own Oldsmobiles, 50 people who own both Chevys and Buicks, 20 people who own both Buicks and Oldsmobiles, and 30 people who own both Chevys and Oldsmobiles. What is the total number of people phoned by the marketing company? (Note that the owners of particular types of cars, such as Chevys, may also be owners of second cars. In other words, the figure for

**FIGURE 3-14**

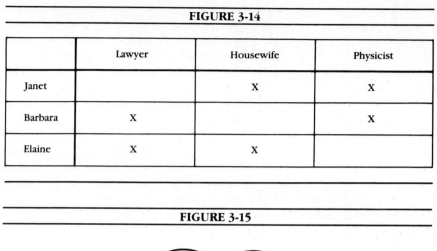

|         | Lawyer | Housewife | Physicist |
|---------|--------|-----------|-----------|
| Janet   |        | X         | X         |
| Barbara | X      |           | X         |
| Elaine  | X      | X         |           |

**FIGURE 3-15**

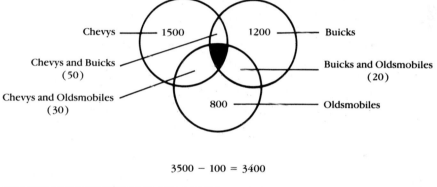

Chevys —— 1500        1200 —— Buicks

Chevys and Buicks
(50)

Chevys and Oldsmobiles
(30)

Buicks and Oldsmobiles
(20)

800 —— Oldsmobiles

$$3500 - 100 = 3400$$

the ownership of a single kind of car includes within it the number of individuals owning that kind of car or that plus another kind of car.)

This problem is most easily solved by creating a diagram with overlapping circles representing the numbers of people owning each possible combination of cars, as in Figure 3-15.

## Allocating Your Resources

Perhaps no metacomponent is more important to successful problem solving, and even successful living in general, than the metacomponent involved in resource allocation. People are constantly making decisions about resource allocation that have significant and even profound effects on their lives.

### *Examples*

Consider the plight of a typical college freshman, who has been used to a routine that she established in high school. But this routine no longer applies. Not only is the student likely to have more work than she has ever encountered before, but she is often faced by a dazzling array of possibilities for extracurricular involvement: participation in sports, participation in dramatic activities, going to movies, dating classmates, working on the college newspaper, and so on. There just doesn't seem to be enough time to do everything she would like to do. For this reason, new college students usually need to rearrange their schedules and their styles of living. The way in which they allocate their time can have a substantial effect on their success in college, no matter how "success" is defined. For instance, many first-year students who run into academic trouble do so because they did not budget a sufficient amount of time for academic work.

Now consider the student who is taking a scholastic aptitude test. Such tests usually do not allot sufficient time for the student to solve every problem carefully and to his complete satisfaction. As a result, he finds himself having to allocate his time in a way that will maximize his score. Test-wise students learn certain strategies for budgeting their time effectively: skipping over difficult items and coming back to them later, saving very time-consuming problems for later, and not spending too much time on a problem in which initial attempts fail to lead to a solution. By efficiently allocating their time during a test, they can substantially increase their score on that test. Notice that although such a test is not designed to measure the metacomponent of resource allocation directly, by imposing a time limit it is likely to measure this metacomponent indirectly.

Resource allocation continues to be important beyond the student years. A difficult decision many adults face is that of how to allocate their time among their family, friends, and work. Many of us find that although the demands upon our time are different from those that we faced in our student days, they are nonetheless equally or even more pressing. A poignant ballad by the late folksinger Harry Chapin, "The Cat's in the Cradle," highlights this dilemma. As a boy grew up, his father never found much time to spend with him. In later years, when the father wanted to spend time with his grown-up son, the son had become too busy. The father realizes that his son is merely emulating him, and is now refusing to spend with him the time that the father had refused to spend with his son with they were both younger.

Earl Hunt, Marcy Lansman, and others have studied resource allocation within the context of a dual-task paradigm. Participants in their experiments are asked to solve a difficult primary task (such as a matrix reasoning test) at the same time that they are asked to solve a secondary, usually simpler, task (such as a probe reaction-time task). The idea is that while the participants are solving the primary task, a visual or auditory signal may appear, and the participants must press a button as quickly as possible. Thus, although they allocate most of their mental-processing resources to the difficult primary task, they nevertheless have to allocate at least some of their processing resources to the simpler secondary task. Hunt and Lansman (1982) have found that more intelligent individuals are better able to allocate their attentional resources and to divide their attention between the two tasks effectively.

Barbara Hayes-Roth and her colleagues have been studying allocation of resources in planning for a number of years. They are particularly interested in what makes a person a good planner. Consider, for example, the problem of performing a number of errands on a single journey. Often you have only limited time to perform the errands, and the order in which you do them needs to reflect both the importance of each errand and the locations of the places in which the errands can be performed. Hayes-Roth has studied how individuals go about handling this type of planning situation. With Sarah Goldin (1980), she has found that (a) good planners tend to spend relatively more time on higher-level planning (or metaplanning) than do poorer planners, especially taking into account the importance of each of the errands and the proximity of the various places in which the errands can be performed; (b) good planners exhibit more attentional flexibility than do poor planners; and (c) good planners make more use of knowledge about the outside world (for example, when stores open and close) in their planning than do poor planners.

### Improving Your Allocation of Resources

As the above examples imply, there are a number of steps you can take to improve your allocation of mental and physical resources. Here are some of those steps:

1. *Be willing to spend relatively large amounts of time on high-level planning.*    Both my own results and those of Goldin and Hayes-Roth show the importance of a person's willingness to spend large amounts of time on high-level planning. Notice the use of the term *willingness* here. Many people who could be better planners aren't because they are simply unwilling to spend the time it takes to be a good planner. They impulsively jump into tasks before they are ready to perform them, with the result that they do not perform the tasks as effectively and efficiently as they otherwise might have. As a result, they often have to go back and make up for the time they should have spent on planning. Thus, when you are confronted with a new problem, it is important for you to spend the time needed to plan a strategy that will maximize performance on the task.

2. *Make full use of your prior knowledge in planning and in allocating your resources.*    Although people differ greatly in the amount of knowledge that they bring to a task, they differ at least as greatly in the extent to which they bring whatever knowledge they have to bear upon that task. Your allocation of resources will be much more effective if you use all of the information you have available in order to plan and allocate time effectively. For example, in planning a strategy for doing errands, mentally visualizing the various paths you may have to traverse in order to do the errands constitutes a sensible and effective use of prior knowledge. If you have in your mind even a vague image of the geographical layout of the paths you will have to traverse, then use it in planning your errands or tasks.

3. *Be flexible and willing to change your plans and allocations of resources.*    As we all know, even the best-laid plans can go astray. It is therefore important that you keep in mind the possibility of plans going awry, and maintain flexibility in implementing your plans. If a given strategy or allocation of resources does not succeed, then you must be ready to

change to another plan or set other priorities for resource allocation. For example, one of the most damaging strategies in taking a test is that of spending too long on a given problem. Occasionally, you may find that a problem you had thought you could solve in a reasonable amount of time is taking much longer than you had anticipated. Just as you have to know when and how to start a problem, you also have to know when and how to stop. Sometimes the best decision is just to give up and to move on. Similarly, in other kinds of situations, you may follow a path that turns out to be a dead end. For example, you may choose a topic for a term paper and later find that there is little reference material on this topic, or that the ideas for the term paper just aren't coming to mind. Persevering in that choice of topic may result in a frustrating experience and a poor grade on the paper. The point is that it is just as important for you to know when to change your allocation of resources as it is to know how to allocate them initially.

*4. Be on the lookout for new kinds of resources.*    People often come to take for granted the resources they have available for accomplishing a given task and close their eyes to the possibility that new resources will improve their performance of the task. For many years, for example, I wrote my papers directly on a typewriter. I would write each page and then revise it as many times as needed until I got the page just the way I wanted it. The result was a fairly polished first draft, but also a lot of wasted paper, as I would do each page over and over again in an attempt to make it approach final form. When personal computers entered the scene, I was reluctant to switch over from my typewriter. I had become so used to a particular style of writing that I could not imagine that any other style would suit me better. After repeated urgings from my colleagues, I eventually decided to try writing with a word-processing program on a microcomputer. To my surprise, I found that the speed with which I could write a paper increased at least twofold. The reason was that all the changes I needed to make on a given page could be made without starting the whole page over from scratch. Formerly, if I wanted to insert a new sentence in the middle of a page, I had to retype the whole page. Under the new system, I could simply insert the sentence and go on. We all have our own examples of blindness to new possibilities for resources that could improve our performance. Try your best to be open to new possibilities as they arise.

## *Exercises*

1.  Think of the major categories that you might use to represent the kinds of activities you do during your waking hours. Such categories might include study time, eating time, recreational times of various sorts, and so on. Estimate the number of hours you spent on each of these types of activities during the past week. Then calculate the percentage of total time spent on each of these activities. Draw a pie (circle) graph representing your allocation of time among these various activities. Each piece of the pie should be proportional to the percentage of time you spent on the activity it represents. Now draw a pie graph representing the way in which you

would ideally like to allocate your time among these activities. Compare the two graphs, and consider how you might be able to make your actual distribution of time correspond more closely to your ideal distribution of time.

Use the street grid of San Pedro in Figure 3-16 to help you solve the following two exercises.

2.  You are going to France this afternoon. There are some things you need to get in town before you go back home. You have to go to one of the local banks ( 20 or 86 ) to buy some travelers' checks. Your finest jacket was eaten by moths so you need to buy a new one to wear on your trip ( 39 or 59 ). As you are going on a student exchange program, you want to buy a present at a gift store ( 100 or 31 ) for the family you are staying with. This family has a farm with a stable and a swimming pool, so you want to get a bathing suit and riding boots either at the sports supplies store ( 75 ) or in one of the department stores ( 26 or 64 ). Your mother suggested you buy a French phrase book ( 48 ) to help you over the language barrier even though your French is very fluent. You have a book from the library that is due in two days, and you want to return it before you leave ( 68 ). Finally, you have to pick up your sister at her swimming lesson ( 57 ) and take the subway ( 34 or 104 ) home.

It is now 9:30 A.M. You just took a final exam at the University ( 25 ), and you need to be home by 1:00 P.M. to finish packing. You have to do your errands by foot. It takes 15 minutes to cross the town by foot in either direction. You probably won't be able to do everything but do the best you can.

3.  This afternoon you will be quite busy. At 5:30 P.M. you have to pick up your husband at the telephone company ( 8 ) and go back home together but before that you have lots of chores to do.

Before 4:00 P.M. ( closing time ), you have to pick up your new car at the car dealer ( 42 ). Then, you have to take it to the gas station ( 2 ) and park it in a parking lot ( 23 ) to do your errands by foot.

You want to go to the health spa ( 19 ) to do some exercising for at least one hour. You need a baby-sitter for tomorrow and you know that at the fire station ( 63 ) you can get a list of names from a friendly fireman. You want to buy some records at the record store ( 46 ). Tomorrow is your son's birthday so you want to buy him a bicycle either in the bicycle shop ( 93 ) or in either of the department stores ( 26 or 64 ). Because you are changing the curtains in your living room, you need to buy some fabric at the fabrics store ( 66 ) and get some curtain rods at the hardware store ( 29 or 82 ).

It is 2:30 P.M. You are standing at the subway station at El Saman Street ( 34 ). You have to do your errands by foot. It takes 15 minutes to cross the town by foot in either direction. You probably won't be able to do everything but do the best you can.

**FIGURE 3-16**

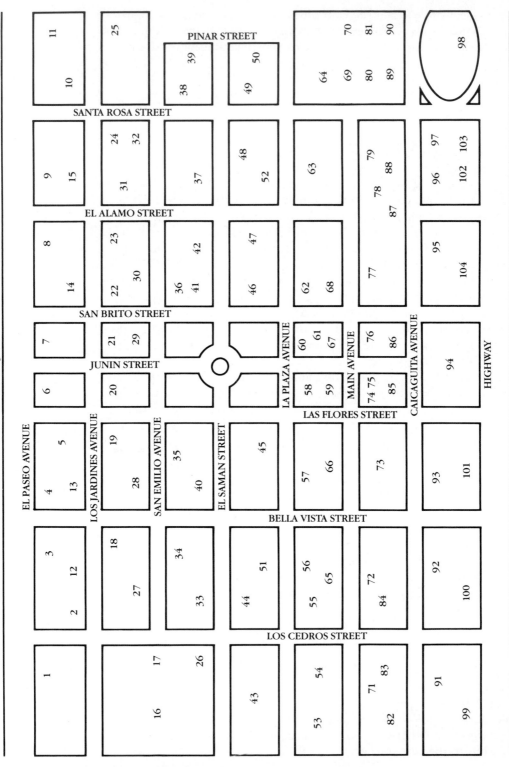

Now consider how your solutions to exercises 2 and 3 might have changed if you had decided that certain errands were more important than others. In such a case, you would take into account priority as well as location of each errand.

4.  A subtest occasionally found on intelligence tests measures a skill called word fluency. In this kind of subtest, you are often asked to think of as many words as you can beginning with a certain letter in a fixed amount of time. For example, you might be asked to think of all the words you can beginning with the letter *y* in four minutes. People frequently try to solve this kind of problem without any particular strategy, simply writing down whatever words come to mind. However, it is possible to improve one's performance on this kind of task by spending the time in advance to think up a systematic strategy. Think up a systematic strategy for performing this kind of test. Then give yourself four minutes exactly to think of as many words as you can that begin with the letter *d*. Did your strategy contribute to your effective performance on this task?

5.  Another kind of subtest frequently found on intelligence tests is the anagram. In anagram problems, you are presented with scrambled words. Your task is to rearrange the letters of each word so as to form an intact word. Usually, the total number of possible rearrangements is staggeringly large. You thus need to formulate strategies that will enable you to look at only a subset of the possible rearrangements. Below are five anagrams. Think first about what kinds of strategies you can use so that you will not have to list all possible rearrangements of the letters. Then use these strategies, plus whatever other new strategies you can think of, to facilitate your solution of the anagrams. The answers are at the bottom of the page, but do not look until you have tried to unscramble the words.

(a)  T–N–K–H–G–I

(b)  H–U–L–A–G

(c)  P–T–T–M–E

(d)  E–R–H–O–S*

6.  Imagine you are in charge of allocating funds for various charities whose goal is to fight different diseases, such as heart disease, cancer, and tuberculosis. These charities both support research on the various diseases and also help those who are suffering from the diseases. You have $500,000. What considerations would you use in deciding how much money to allocate to the various charities? For example, two possible considerations are the number of people who suffer from the disease and the mortality rate for the disease. Once you have decided on the considerations you would use in deciding among charities, decide upon how much you would weigh each of these considerations in allocating funds.

---

*The answers are (a) *knight*, (b) *laugh*, (c) *tempt*, and (d) *horse* or *shore*.

7.  You are the campaign manager for a senatorial candidate, and have $100,000 to spend on a political campaign. On what activities should you spend these funds, and how much money should you allocate to each activity? (Some possible examples of activities are fund-raising events, newspaper advertisements, television spots, and the like.)

8.  You are a top-level business executive, and have to decide whether to begin mass production of a new product, the "widget." Before mass marketing the widget, you need to decide how well it will sell. The product is designed to reduce household electrical consumption. What kinds of tests might you perform to decide how successful the widget will be before you actually spend money to mass-produce it?

## Solution Monitoring

In problem solving, many of the most important decisions are made at the beginning—the decision as to the nature of the problem, the decision as to what processes to use, the decision as to how to represent information, and so on. You may often make the wrong decisions for any number of reasons. For one thing, you may have misread the terms of the problem; for another, you may have selected a strategy that, although capable of solving the problem, will solve it only slowly or with great difficulty. It is important for you as a problem solver to realize that your initial decisions are not irrevocable. To the contrary, you should view them as tentative and be prepared to change them as the need arises. It is one thing to make an incorrect decision at the start of problem solving; it is another to persist in that decision, either because you are unaware of the means to change it or because you are unwilling to change it.

### Examples

Careful monitoring of the solution process might have or should have led to a change in strategy in any number of decisions at any level. For example, the experience of the United States in Vietnam was an instance in which virtually no matter how the situation was monitored, indications were that our involvement was a mistake, or at least not accomplishing the end it was supposed to accomplish. Yet it took the United States many years to withdraw. A number of factors impelled continued involvement, such as national pride, the desire to meet a commitment to another government, and so on. However, it became clear to almost everyone in the United States that whatever the reason for staying, the reasons for leaving outweighed them.

A second example of solution monitoring occurs in our everyday interactions with others, and especially interactions involving high stakes, such as job interviews. During such conversations, we are almost continually receiving feedback, which is sometimes subtle, about the kind of impression we are making. Some of this feedback may be verbal; the rest of it is nonverbal. Careful monitoring of this feedback and acting on it increases the probability of our attaining the goals set out for that conversation, whatever they may be.

Indeed, whole books have been written about how to interpret nonverbal signals during the course of a conversation.

In my own work, I frequently have to give presentations to diverse audiences. Before giving any talk, I now ask my sponsors about the composition of the audience, including questions such as the number of people expected, their level of background in psychology, their interests, and their reason for coming to hear me speak. I then attempt to tailor my presentation so as to meet the needs and background of the audience. Occasionally, I make a misjudgment. However, I try to recognize this misjudgment early during the talk rather than after the talk is over. When I become aware that a talk is not going over well, I try to change it as much as possible to suit the audience better. Obviously, there is less I can do in the middle of a talk than before it starts, but it is often not too late to make some changes in the middle that will make at least a modest success out of what otherwise might have been a failure. Thus, as a speaker, I see my job as partially one of monitoring audience reaction.

The same monitoring applies to a teaching situation. Talented teachers try to stay aware of whether their students are understanding and are interested in the material presented. If understanding or interest is waning, good teachers attempt to figure out why, and then correct their presentation so as to increase either its comprehensibility, its interest, or both.

What kinds of cues are useful in determining whether an audience is with the speaker, whether it is an audience of professionals or an audience of students? The kinds of things I look for are eye contact, absence of side conversations that are obviously irrelevant to the material presented, audience or class questions that show mental engagement with the material, and facial expressions showing interest in the material.

Here are a few more examples of solution monitoring, which is important in various phases of everyone's life.

Many of us, at one time or another, seek some kind of therapeutic intervention, whether physical or psychological. During the course of the therapy, we can observe whether things are improving. If they are not, we ought to consider getting out of therapy, or at least switching therapists. Without doubt, any number of people go to a therapist for years without any noticeable sign of improvement, yet fail to consider the possibility that the time has come either to discontinue the therapy or to find another kind of therapy.

A second example of the need to monitor is in enrollment in book clubs, record clubs, and so on. Such clubs often have highly attractive initial offers designed to get people to join. One wonders how the clubs can afford such offers. One of the things they bank on is that people's inertia will prevent them from quitting, even if they are dissatisfied with the products or level of service they are receiving. Many clubs will automatically send a book or record every month unless the club member tells them not to. The strategy here is that most people simply will not bother to return the postcard indicating lack of desire for the product. Similarly, the clubs often offer to refund money spent on a purchase if the purchase is mailed back. Here, they bank on the fact that wrapping up a book or a record and sending it back is enough of an inconvenience to prevent many people from bothering to do it.

A third example of the need for solution monitoring is in choice of stores, such as supermarkets. Many people decide on a supermarket for any of several reasons, and then continue to patronize it over the years. Often, they do not continue to monitor whether the quality of the products at that supermarket is superior to that at other local supermarkets, or whether the prices are lower. In other words, once the decision is made to patronize a certain store, the decision is not often enough and actively enough reconsidered. The result can be wasted money or unnecessary dissatisfaction with the products purchased.

The need for solution monitoring can be shown in psychological research as well as in everyday experience. One striking example of solution monitoring can be seen in children's reading of text. Ellen Markman (1979) has presented children with reading passages in which there are flagrant self-contradictions. In other words, material later in the passage contradicts material earlier in the passage. Astonishingly, the children often fail to notice these contradictions. Their monitoring of their reading comprehension is apparently inadequate, with the result that they are unable to see the contradiction in the paragraph. Adults are not immune to this problem, either.

The point of all these examples is a simple one: The decision-making process in problem solving does not end once the initial decisions have been made and solution of the problem proper has begun. Rather, decision making must continue throughout the solution of the problem until the solver is wholly satisfied with the solution.

### *Improving Your Solution Monitoring*

There are several steps you can take to improve your solution monitoring in problem solving. Here are some of these steps:

1. *Be aware of the need for solution monitoring, and act upon this need.* The most important step you can take is simply to be aware of the need to monitor your solution strategies, and then to act upon this awareness. Many people simply fail to monitor their problem-solving strategies, or even if they do monitor them, they do nothing with the feedback they obtain. The most important step you can take is to be alert for the need to change your strategy or your representation of the problem, and then to act.

2. *Beware of "justification of effort."*   You also need to be aware of what social psychologists call "justification of effort," which they have found is a powerful force in human thought and action. Once people have invested a substantial amount of time or other resources in a given course of action, they seek reasons to justify this investment. The greater the investment, the harder it is to write it off. Many people, for example, have suffered heavy losses in the stock market because they were unwilling to recognize that a once-attractive stock has ceased to be attractive, and may actually now be a poor investment. Similarly, people in intimate relationships often recognize that the relationship is no longer succeeding, but fail to withdraw because

they feel they have invested so much time and emotional energy in the relationship.

The same problem, of course, confronts business executives every day. When a new product is introduced, an enormous investment often goes into the production and marketing of that product. No matter how adequate the initial marketing tests are, a product initially believed to be successful may fail, or a product that was once successful may no longer be selling. A tough decision business executives face is that of discontinuing the product. Despite their enormous investment in the product's continued existence, the correct decision is often to withdraw it from the market.

In a similar vein, scientists often have to recognize that problems they are pursuing, or methods they are using to solve those problems, are dead ends. Many a scientific career has been wasted because the scientist was unable or unwilling to recognize that the time had come to move on to a different problem or methodology for research. Being a good scientist requires not only knowing which problems to pursue and how to pursue them, but also knowing when to give up gracefully and to proceed to something else.

*3. Avoid impulsiveness in solution monitoring.*    Sometimes, in problem solving, you will realize that something is wrong and that some course of action needs to be taken to correct whatever problem has arisen. For example, in taking a test, re-solving a mathematics problem may yield a new answer. Avoid the tendency immediately to withdraw from your first path or solution and to jump at the second. It is always possible that it is your solution monitoring rather than your initial solution that is in error. Indeed, studies of behavior on multiple-choice tests have shown that the conventional wisdom regarding erasures is correct: When a first answer is erased and a new one put in its place, the first answer is often right and the new answer wrong.

Of course, you should not avoid monitoring solutions altogether. You should recognize, however, that the solution-monitoring process, like the original problem-solving process, is susceptible to error, so that you need to take care in your response to the results of the monitoring process. Cautiousness in solution monitoring has become particularly important in the computer age. Often, in computer programming and text editing, people discover errors in their programming or writing. With a computer, they can very easily delete an entire file containing a great deal of information, only to regret it later on, when they realize that the deleted material was actually satisfactory after all, or that at least parts of it were usable.

*4. Be open to, but evaluative of, external feedback.*    People receive external feedback on their problem solving from a variety of sources. This external feedback can be helpful to you in your problem-solving monitoring. Others may pick up errors in problem solving that you fail to pick up yourself. However, it is important to evaluate external feedback just as carefully as you evaluate your own internal feedback. You need to consider the probable reliability of the source of the feedback and the usefulness of the feedback. All of us are familiar with the situation in which we receive feedback from someone who knows less about the problem than we do.

Such feedback is not necessarily worthless, but its source needs to be considered. Another possibility is that you will receive accurate feedback, but find that it is in unusable form. For example, a suggestion to solve a difficult problem via a computer is not useful if you have no computer available. In sum, be receptive to, but critical of, external feedback. Most importantly, avoid defensiveness in receiving such feedback. Defensiveness inevitably works against high-quality problem solutions. First, it will blind you to recognizing the problems in your solutions. Second, it discourages others from even giving feedback. If others realize that you will react defensively, they may be reluctant to comment on your performance, with the result that they withhold feedback that would have been helpful.

5. *Actively seek external feedback.*    Often, people are surprised by the lack of feedback they receive for their efforts. For example, partners in marriage frequently feel that they have very little idea of what their spouse thinks of them. Junior executives vying for promotion sometimes feel that they have little idea either of their superiors' opinions of them or what their chances for promotions are. The point of all this is that people are often willing to give feedback, but only if they are asked. In each of these situations, the problem of lack of external information might quickly be solved by requesting the feedback that is not coming spontaneously.

### Exercises

1. Consider a real-life problem that you have solved in the past month. How might more adequate monitoring of your solution processes have improved your solution of the problem?

2. You are in a job interview and concerned that you make the best impression possible. During the course of the interview, you find yourself monitoring both your own behavior and that of the interviewer in order to determine how well the interview is going. What kinds of signs might you look for in the interviewer's behavior to get some indication of the interviewer's opinion of you?

3. In negotiations for mutual arms reduction, probably the most difficult problem the negotiating parties face is one of monitoring the decisions made regarding reduction of arms. What kinds of steps might be taken to monitor each side once steps for mutual arms reduction have been agreed upon?

4. Government officials and economists are constantly monitoring the success of governmental economic programs. What kinds of monitoring would you do in order to determine whether or not a given economic program is a success?

5. Marriages often break down because the individuals involved fail to monitor the quality of their relationship, or if they do monitor it, are not alert to signs of a breakdown. What kinds of signs should one look for that indicate a marriage is faltering, and what constructive steps might be taken in response to the realization that any of these signs indicates trouble?

6. Earlier in this chapter, you solved several versions of the Missionaries and Cannibals problem. This is a problem in which monitoring your solution processes can greatly increase the speed with which you attain a solution. What kinds of monitoring should you do in order to improve your performance on this problem?

7. One of the primary purposes of this book is to effect an improvement in its readers' intellectual skills. How could you or your instructor go about monitoring—both formally and informally—whether this goal is being met?

8. One of the most important questions scientists in a given field face is whether their research is progressing, and at a larger level, whether there is progress in the particular field of science in which they are working. What are some of the signs that a field is progressing, and what are some of the signs that it is stagnant?

---

**FIGURE 3-17**

---

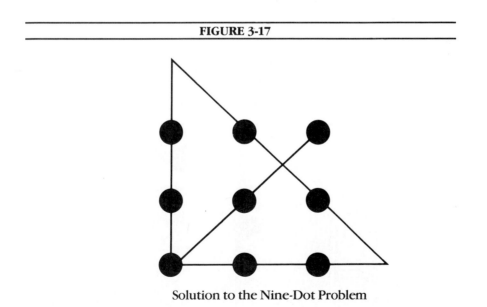

Solution to the Nine-Dot Problem

---

**FIGURE 3-18**

Solution to the Monk Problem

**FIGURE 3-19**

Solution to the Hatrack Problem

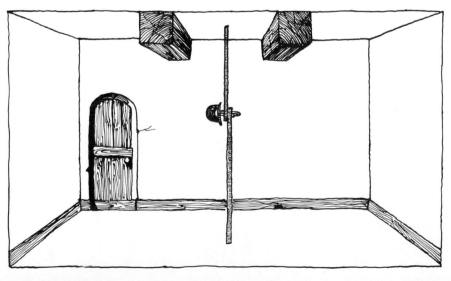

**FIGURE 3-20**

## Solution to the Three Missionaries and Three Cannibals Problem

M—Missionaries    C—Cannibals

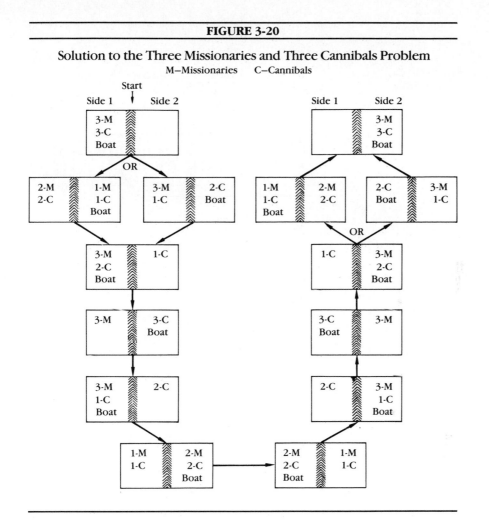

**FIGURE 3-21**

## Solution to the Five Missionaries and Five Cannibals Problem

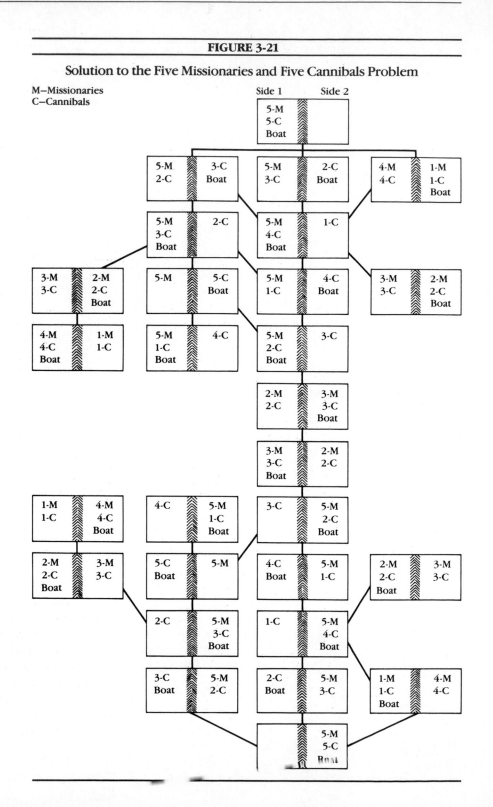

M—Missionaries
C—Cannibals

## FIGURE 3-22

### Solution to the Three-Jug Problem

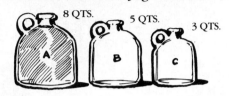

1.

2.

3.

4.

5.

6.

7.

8.

## FIGURE 3-23

### Solution to the Monster-Globe Problem

| 1. | M | L | S |
|---|---|---|---|
| | s | m | l |

| 2. | M | L | S |
|---|---|---|---|
| | s | l & m | – |

| 3. | M | L | S |
|---|---|---|---|
| | – | l & m | s |

| 4. | M | L | S |
|---|---|---|---|
| | – | m | l & s |

| 5. | M | L | S |
|---|---|---|---|
| | | m | – | l & s |

| 6. | M | L | S |
|---|---|---|---|
| | | m | l | s |

# 4

# Performance Components

**W**hereas people use metacomponents to plan, monitor, and evaluate their course of action during problem solving, they use *performance components* to do the actual problem solving. We might view metacomponents as the executives in a business operation, and performance components as the workers taking the lead or instructions of the executive. Metacomponents and performance components must work together. Metacomponents alone are inadequate for solving a problem because they make the decisions about what to do, but do not actually do it. Performance components alone are inadequate for solving problems because they execute a problem-solving strategy, but they do not decide what strategy to use in the first place. Thus, problem solving requires both metacomponents and performance components for its successful completion.

The number of performance components used in problem solving is quite large. Which performance components are used in solving a problem depends largely on the kind of problem and the content of that particular problem. So, for example, a mathematical problem is likely to require performance components quite different from those involved in solving a verbal problem. It would be impossible and undesirable to attempt to list and describe all of the possible performance components here. Instead, we will concentrate on those performance components that research has shown to be most important in both academic and everyday problem solving.

## Encoding

*Encoding* is the process by which people perceive the terms of a problem and access information stored in long-term memory that may be relevant to problem solution. A good encoding of a problem can often go a long way toward

**FIGURE 4-1**

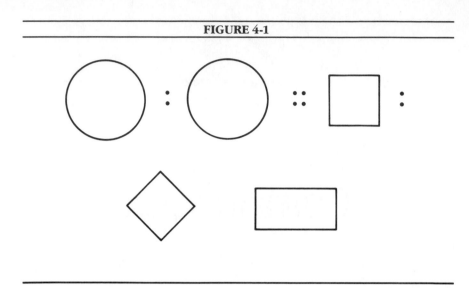

solving the problem; conversely, a poor encoding can often guarantee that the problem will not be solved. Consider the verbal analogy WASHING-TON : ONE :: LINCOLN : (a) FIVE, (b) FIFTEEN, (c) TWENTY, (d) TWENTY-FIVE. Many people find this analogy challenging not because the reasoning involved is difficult and not because the vocabulary is hard, but rather because they fail to encode the proper attributes for the analogy terms that will lead to a correct solution. Most frequently, people think of George Washington as the first U.S. president, and so they look for the number corresponding to the ordinal position of Lincoln as president. As it turns out, Lincoln was the sixteenth president, and so there is no option that will satisfy that encoding. The correct solution is FIVE, because Washington's portrait appears on a one-dollar bill, and Lincoln's portrait appears on a five-dollar bill. Notice how, in this analogy, a relatively full encoding of possible attributes of Washington and Lincoln is necessary for a correct solution to the problem.

Consider another example of how encoding can be important in the solution of a problem, in this case, the nonverbal, or figural, analogy shown in Figure 4-1.

In this analogy, the first two terms appear to be exactly the same; both are simply circles. The third term is a square, and the two options for fourth terms are a diamond and a rectangle. At first glance, neither of these two options appears to be correct or even plausible. After all, we have understandably encoded the first two terms of the analogy as being identical. However, if we now consider the possibility that the second circle represents a 45-degree rotation with respect to the first circle, it is possible to re-encode the second term as a rotated version of the first term. In this case, the second term would still look like the first term, but it would be a rotated version of it. It is now possible to select the diamond as the correct answer, as it is a 45-degree rotated version of the square. The important point to notice in this problem is that an initial encoding is not necessarily the final encoding. It is sometimes necessary to re-encode terms to attain an encoding that may not be obvious, but that is the most appropriate one for the given problem.

## Inference and Inferential Fallacies

If we were to select one performance component as most important of all, we might well select *inference* as that component. Inference is the discovery of one or more relations between objects or events. For example, if you hear that a friend is in the hospital, you are likely to infer that the friend is either ill or injured. Nothing in what you heard may have directly stated this. It is possible, for example, that the friend is merely visiting someone in the hospital or has taken a job in the hospital. But unless you have evidence to the contrary, you are quite likely to infer that there is a problem and to become concerned.

### *Kinds of Inferences*

Inferences can be of many different kinds, and there also exist many different classification schemes for analyzing the various kinds of inferences. The classification scheme described here is one that I have used for classifying the kinds of inferences between pairs of words that can be used on the Miller Analogies Test, a high-level test used for graduate selection and placement purposes. Remember that this scheme applies to inferences between pairs of words. Other schemes would be needed for inferences between pairs of pictures or between various kinds of events. Some of the latter kinds of inferences are discussed later in this book.

*1. Similarity.* Relationships are between synonyms or words that are nearly the same in meaning. An example is HAPPY : GLAD. These two words are synonyms. Think of two or three other pairs of words that have a similarity relation between them.

*2. Contrast.* Relationships are between antonyms or words that are nearly the opposite in meaning. An example of a contrast relation is WET : DRY. These two words are antonyms. Think of two or three other contrasts.

*3. Predication.* Terms are related by a verb or verbal relationship. One term describes something about the other term. Some of the possibilities are: A is caused by B; A makes B; A rides on B; A eats B; A is a source of B; A induces B; A studies B; A is made of B; A uses B. An example of a predication relation is AUTOMOBILE : ROAD. An AUTOMOBILE rides on a ROAD. Another example of predication with a rather different kind of relation is DOG : BARKS. A DOG performs the action of BARKING. Think of two or three other examples of predication relations.

*4. Subordination.* Relations are those in which an object A is a type of B. An example of a subordination relation is TROUT : FISH. Think of two or three other subordination relations.

5. *Coordination.*    The two terms are a single type of thing, that is, they are members of the same category. An example of a coordination relation is LETTUCE : CABBAGE. In this case, both terms are vegetables. Think of two or three other coordination relations.

6. *Superordination.*    Relations are those in which A is a category in which B falls. An example of a superordination relation is BIRD : ROBIN. In this case, BIRD is a category into which ROBIN falls. Think of two or three other superordination relations.

7. *Completion.*    In this case, each term is part of a complete expression. An example of a completion relation is SAN : JOSE. In this case, the two words form a single unit, giving the names either of a saint or of a city, depending on point of view and context. Think of two or three other completions.

8. *Part–Whole.*    In these relations, A is a part of B. An example of a part–whole relation is DAY : WEEK. In this case, a DAY is a part (one-seventh) of a WEEK. Think of two or three other part–whole relations.

9. *Whole–Part.*    In these relations, B is a part of A. An example of a whole–part relation is PIE : SLICE. A PIE is a whole of which a SLICE is a part. Think of two or three other whole–part relations.

10. *Equality.*    These relations involve mathematical or logical equivalence. An example is TWO-FIFTHS : FORTY PERCENT. TWO-FIFTHS and FORTY PERCENT are equivalent amounts. Think of two or three other equality relations.

11. *Negation.*    Negation relations involve logical or mathematical negations. An example is EQUAL : UNEQUAL. In this case, all relationships between numbers can be covered by these two terms, which are mathematical negations of each other. Another example is TRUE : FALSE. Think of two or three other negation relations.

12. *Word Relations.*    These inferences involve grammatical relations between words. An example is EAT : ATE. In this case, ATE is the past tense of EAT. Think of two or three more word-relation inferences.

13. *Nonsemantic Relations.*    In these relations, words are related to each other in a way that involves properties other than the semantic properties of the words. An example of such a relation is EAT : MEET. In this case, the words happen to rhyme. Another kind of nonsemantic relation involves the letters in the word, for example, PAT : TAP. In this case, PAT is TAP spelled backward.

Although these relations may seem quite straightforward and obvious, their importance arises not only in recognizing kinds of inferences, but in solving more complex kinds of problems that require inferences as part of their solution, for example, analogies. An analogy that may be obscure can become easier once you recognize the inferential relation on which it is based.

Below is a list of 25 pairs of words. Your task is to write next to each pair of words how the two words are related to each other and then to classify the pair of words in terms of the thirteen categories of relations just presented. The answer key appears at the end of the problem set.

| Word Pair | Relation | Classification |
|---|---|---|
| 1. COVER : BOOK | | |
| 2. RUE : CHEW | | |
| 3. AIRPLANE : FLY | | |
| 4. DAFFODIL : LILAC | | |
| 5. EMPTY SET : NULL SET | | |
| 6. CLUE : HINT | | |
| 7. LAID : DIAL | | |
| 8. EARLY : LATE | | |
| 9. LADDER : RUNG | | |
| 10. NEGATIVE : NONNEGATIVE | | |
| 11. BETTER : BEST | | |
| 12. HUMAN : MAMMAL | | |
| 13. NEW : ORLEANS | | |
| 14. STAR : DWARF | | |
| 15. CARPENTER : HAMMER | | |
| 16. X OR Y : NOT X AND NOT Y | | |
| 17. CIRCLE : SEMICIRCLE | | |
| 18. PLATE : FREIGHT | | |
| 19. FURNITURE : CHAIR | | |
| 20. MELIORATE : IMPROVE | | |
| 21. STICK : STUCK | | |
| 22. HEAVENLY : HELLISH | | |
| 23. FINGER : HAND | | |
| 24. SQUARE ROOT OF 64 : $2^3$ | | |
| 25. CLUB : WEAPON | | |

---

### ANSWERS TO INFERENCE PAIR PROBLEMS

| *Relation* | *Classification* |
|---|---|
| 1. A cover is a part of a book. | Part–Whole |
| 2. *Rue* and *chew* rhyme. | Nonsemantic Relation |
| 3. An airplane flies for its means of locomotion. | Predication |
| 4. A daffodil and a lilac are both kinds of flowers. | Coordination |
| 5. The empty set and the null set are mathematically equivalent. | Equality |
| 6. *Clue* and *hint* are synonymous. | Similarity |
| 7. *Dial* is *laid* spelled backwards. | Nonsemantic Relation |
| 8. *Early* and *late* are antonyms. | Contrast |
| 9. A ladder is composed in part of rungs. | Whole–Part |
| 10. All real numbers that are not negative are nonnegative. | Negation |
| 11. *Better* is the comparative form, and *best* the superlative form, of *good*. | Word Relation |
| 12. A human is a kind of mammal. | Subordination |
| 13. New Orleans is a city. | Completion |
| 14. A dwarf is a kind of star. | Superordination |
| 15. A carpenter uses a hammer. | Predication |
| 16. The logical negation of *X or Y* is *Not X and Not Y*. | Negation |
| 17. A circle can be divided into two semicircles. | Whole–Part |
| 18. *Plate* and *freight* rhyme. | Nonsemantic Relation |
| 19. One kind of furniture is a chair. | Superordination |
| 20. *Meliorate* and *improve* are synonyms. | Similarity |
| 21. *Stuck* is the past tense of *stick*. | Word Relation |
| 22. *Heavenly* and *hellish* are antonyms. | Contrast |
| 23. A finger is part of a hand. | Part–Whole |
| 24. The square root of 64 and $2^3$ both equal 8. | Equality |
| 25. A club is a kind of weapon. | Subordination |

---

## Inferential Fallacies

Although people make inferences all the time, not all of these inferences are correct or justified by the data. Philosophers and semanticists, as well as psychologists, have attempted to classify and study the various kinds of fallacious inferences that people can make. The classification described here is by no means the only one or even necessarily the best one, but Susan Nolen-Hoeksema and I (1983) have found it useful in understanding the kinds of fallacies people commit in their everyday reasoning behavior. This list is based on the work of both philosophers such as Irving Copi (1978) and psychologists such as Amos Tversky and Daniel Kahneman (1974), Ellen Langer (1978), and Aaron Beck (1976).

*1. Representativeness.*    Sometimes we believe that the cause of some event must resemble that event. For example, a great event must have a great cause. When we decide that two or more things or events are related simply because they resemble each other, we have committed the fallacy of representativeness. Consider an example of the representativeness fallacy:

> Robert had a date to go to dinner with an actress, after watching a performance of the play in which she had the lead role. However, Robert sent a note back to the actress after the play, saying, "Your were so believable in your acting of that murder scene that I don't feel safe going out with you."

In this particular instance, Robert assumes that the actress's behavior in the play was representative of her behavior outside the play setting. But in this case, he has no logical basis for assuming that the actress's behavior in the play will represent her behavior outside the acting situation.

Here is an example of someone committing the fallacy of representativeness. Can you say why this scenario exemplifies the commission of this fallacy?

> Senator Charles was announcing the winners of the "Golden Fleece" Award for the biggest rip-off of taxpayers in 1981. Senator Charles said, "I bestow the 'Golden Fleece' Award upon Professor Dudley for his government-funded study of the nature of romantic love. As you may remember, we recently reviewed a study of the nature of romantic love, and it was absolutely worthless. Clearly, this study will be, too."

Can you think of an example of the representativeness fallacy that has applied to your own life or the lives of your friends?

*2. Irrelevant Conclusion.* We commit the fallacy of irrelevant conclusion when our conclusion is irrelevant to the line of reasoning that led to it. Consider an example of this fallacy:

> Joni is retiring from work. Her pension will be small, and her retired husband has little income. She told her husband she wants a convertible for Christmas. Her husband asked her why she thought she should get a convertible for Christmas, when they couldn't afford it. Joni replied, "I deserve a convertible because I am about to retire."

Notice that Joni has created a cause–effect relationship that exists only in her head. At least from the standpoint of her husband and most others, her retirement in and of itself does not merit a new car, no matter how many other reasons there might be to get her one.

Here is another example of the commission of the fallacy of irrelevant conclusion. Can you say why this little scenario exemplifies this fallacy?

> Joseph was the prosecuting attorney in a case in which the defendant had been accused of murdering his mother. To assert the defendant's guilt, Joseph argued, "Murder is a horrible thing to do. But to murder one's own mother deserves even swifter and harsher punishment."

Can you think of an example of the fallacy of irrelevant conclusion either in your own life or in the lives of your friends?

*3. Division.*   We commit the fallacy of division when we assume that what is true of the whole is necessarily true of each individual part of the whole. Consider this example of the fallacy of division:

**Mr. and Mrs. Smith were discussing their daughter's latest boyfriend. Mrs. Smith told Mr. Smith that this young man was a Republican who was presently working for the Republican caucus in the Congress. Mr. Smith commented, "Well, if he's a dedicated Republican, that means he isn't a liberal, at least."**

Mr. Smith is assuming that because most or all of the Republicans he knows are not liberals, his daughter's boyfriend also will not be a liberal. However, the fact of the boyfriend's being a dedicated Republican in no way guarantees that he is not a liberal. To the contrary, a number of Republicans are, in fact, liberals.

Here is another example of the fallacy of division. Can you say why this particular fallacy applies in this case?

**Juanita and William were introduced at a party. William learned that Juanita lives and works in Washington, D.C. He said, "If you work in Washington, D.C., you must be a politician."**

Can you think of any examples of the fallacy of division that apply either in your own life or in the lives of people you know?

*4. Labeling.*   To attach some label to yourself or to others is a distorted thought process when the label is unjustified by the circumstances, or when the label is inappropriately used as a reason for behavior or lack of behavior. Consider an example of unjustified labeling:

**Harriet was on a 1,200 calorie-per-day diet, which included no sweets. One day, Harriet succumbed to temptation and ate an entire quart of ice cream. Harriet thought, "How disgusting of me to eat a quart of ice cream. I am a pig."**

Harriet has committed the fallacy of labeling because she has overreacted to her own weakness in succumbing to temptation. In fact, it is quite typical for people on low-calorie diets to succumb occasionally. By labeling herself a pig as a result of such failure to resist temptation, in fact, the chances are increased that she will not continue with the diet because of the low self-image she has assigned to herself.

Here is another example of someone committing the fallacy of labeling. Can you say why this fallacy applies in this instance?

Henry was a farmer's son from an obscure town in the Midwest. At college, Henry fell in love with the richest, most popular, most beautiful woman on campus. Henry often said to himself, "If only I weren't a hick farmer, then I'd have a chance with that beautiful, sophisticated woman."

Can you think of an example of labeling as it applies in your own life or that of others?

*5. Hasty Generalization.*    We commit the fallacy of hasty generalization by considering only exceptional cases and quickly generalizing from those cases to a rule that actually fits only those exceptions. Here is an example of a hasty generalization:

After she finished college, Cleo went for her first interview for a job. In the interview, the interviewer told her that her academic work looked quite good, but that her resumé showed a lack of experience in the professional field, and that, therefore, his company couldn't hire her. Cleo went home thinking, "If that company won't hire me without my having experience, no company will."

In this instance, Cleo is rushing to the generalization that just because she wasn't hired by one company, no other company will hire her either. In fact, such generalizations are typical of individuals who are on the job market and have an unsuccessful initial interview. Often, their hasty generalizations lead these people to become discouraged too early, and to stop looking for a job prematurely.

Here is an example of another hasty generalization. What is the fallacy, and why is it a hasty generalization?

Bill and a friend were discussing the governor of their state. Bill said, "The governor is a total failure because his economic programs actually have done damage to the state's economy."

Can you think of an example of a hasty generalization you have recently made?

*6. Skill, Not Chance.*    In situations in which an outcome is controlled entirely and always by chance, it is fallacious to assume that any skill on the part of an agent is involved in the outcome. Consider an example of this fallacy:

Joey had been practicing flipping coins for several days. His mother finally asked him why he was practicing. Joey explained, "I want to get into the *Guinness Book of World Records* as the person who can make a coin flip come up heads every time."

Of course, Joey's practicing will have no influence on how often the coin comes up heads.

Here is another example of this fallacy. Can you spot the problem?

> **Nancy put quarters into a slot machine until she had lost her ten-dollar roll. She was considering whether or not to buy more quarters from the casino office. She thought to herself, "I am sure that if I can get enough practice with this darn machine I'll eventually be able to start getting some more money out of it."**

Can you think of any instances in which you committed this fallacy?

*7. Personalization.*    If you see yourself as the cause of some event for which you were not primarily responsible, you have committed the fallacy of distorted personalization. Taking personally a statement that is not directed toward you is also an inappropriate personalization. Consider an example of a personalization:

> **Bernard's mother was recently committed to a psychiatric institution. Unfortunately, her family had a history of such commitment. When Bernard's father asked him how he felt about this, Bernard said, "Well, I am sure that I put Mom in there. What's worse, I'm sure that she knows that I am to blame."**

In this example, Bernard personalizes the cause of an event for which, most likely, he was not responsible.

Here is another example of a personalization. Can you say why this particular fallacy applies in this instance?

> **Janet's first-grader came home one day with a note from his teacher that said that the child was doing poorly in school. Janet said to herself, "I am a terrible mother because my child is doing so badly at school."**

Can you think of any examples of personalizations that you or others have committed in the recent past?

*8. Appeal to Authority.*    The pattern of the fallacy of appeal to authority is to argue that a claim is true because Authority X supports it. An argument that appeals to authority is a fallacy whenever that authority is not suitable to give evidence. Consider an example of this fallacy:

> **Congress is presently trying to decide whether it has a right to take a legal stand on when a human life begins. During congressional debates on the matter, one representative was heard to say, "If the medical world, the religions, and all the philosophies cannot agree on when a human life begins, then it is the responsibility of the Congress to make that decision."**

In this example, Congress is clearly in no better position, and may well be in a worse position, to make the decision regarding when human life begins than doctors, clergy, or philosophers.

Can you spot the appeal to authority in the example below?

Marvin was being interviewed by the admissions board of the law school he wished to attend the next year. One of the board members asked Marvin why he thought he would make a good lawyer. Marvin replied, "Well, my father is a plumber, but he always wanted to be a lawyer. He's always told me I'd make a good lawyer, and I respect his opinion in this matter."

Have you experienced any appeals to authority when people have tried to convince you of the validity of certain of their arguments?

9. *Magnification/Minimization.*   People sometimes magnify their negative characteristics or their mistakes. People also sometimes minimize their positive characteristics or accomplishments. In such cases, they are illogically evaluating the situation by magnification or minimization. Here is an example of this fallacy:

Small College could not afford to hire another professor to teach 20th-century literature, so they asked Professor Short, whose expertise was in 18th-century literature, to teach 20th-century literature. Professor Short said, "Well, given that I'm one of the world's greatest experts on 18th-century literature, I have no doubt that I could teach the 20th-century literature course just as well as I could teach the 18th-century literature course, which is perfectly."

In this instance, Professor Short may or may not be exaggerating his expertise in 18th-century literature, but he is almost certainly exaggerating his ability to teach the 20th-century literature course.

Here is another example of a person's committing the magnification/minimization fallacy. Can you see why?

Marion was congratulating Donna on Donna's recently winning the prize for the best senior project in her department. Donna responded sincerely, "Oh, winning a prize means absolutely nothing. It has no value to me or to anyone else."

Can you think of any instances in which you have magnified or minimized a situation, thereby distorting your perception of it?

10. *Composition.*   We commit the fallacy of composition when we reason that what is true of parts of a whole is necessarily true of the whole itself. Consider an example of the fallacy of composition:

When forming his panel of advisers, the newly elected governor chose the best person for each advisory position. The governor bragged to the press, "I'll have the most effective, efficient advisory panel any governor could have, because I have the best people on my panel."

In this instance, the governor is assuming that even if it is the case that everyone on his committee is maximally effective and efficient, this effectiveness and efficiency will carry over to the panel as a whole. However, even if each adviser works well individually, there is no guarantee that the individuals will work well collectively. They may, in fact, spend all their time arguing.

Here is another example of the fallacy of composition. Can you spot the fallacy?

Jill went to Warren's apartment for a cocktail before they were to go out to dinner. Warren asked Jill if she would like beer or wine. Jill said, "Well, I like beer and wine equally well and really can't decide between them now, so why don't you put both beer and wine into my glass?"

Can you think of any examples where you or others have committed the fallacy of composition, thereby distoring your inference processes?

*11. "Should" Statement.*    "I must do this," "I should feel that," and "They should do this" are examples of "should" statements. Such statements are irrational when they are used as the sole reason for behavior. Consider an example of the irrational use of a "should" statement:

Cecil sat his teenage son down for a talk. Cecil told his son, "Everyone in our family is a success. You must be a success and carry on the family tradition."

This vignette provides a typical example of the use of "should" statements, and also illustrates how children often have unrealistic expectations for themselves simply because of their parents' unrealistic expectations.

Here is another example of the commission of this fallacy. Can you spot it?

Part of Gordon's duties as manager of a small apartment building was to shovel the snow from the front walk. One morning Gordon woke up with a fever and a horrible cold. He looked out the window and saw that five inches of snow had fallen the night before. Gordon thought, "With this cold it would be crazy for me to go out and shovel snow but it has to be done, so here I go."

Can you think of any examples of how your own use of "should" statements has impelled you to do things that you really should not have done?

*12. False Cause.* An event occurs and a cause for that event is sought. If the mere fact of coincidence or temporal succession is used to identify the cause, the fallacy of false cause has been committed. Consider an example of the fallacy of false cause in action:

**Jenny and Mark went into a restaurant at about 6:00 P.M., dressed rather casually. Although the restaurant was only about half full, the hostess seated Jenny and Mark in an obscure corner table near the kitchen. Jenny remarked to Mark, "She certainly doesn't want us seen in this restaurant, the way we're dressed. That's why she sat us in the corner."**

In this instance, Jenny is assuming that it is her and Mark's clothing that has resulted in their being seated in an obscure corner. It is possible, of course, that Jenny is correct. However, there are other possible reasons why they might have been placed in an obscure corner, for example, the possibility that all the other tables were reserved or that the hostess simply had not given much thought to where she would seat them.

Here is another example of this fallacy. Can you see why this fallacy applies in this instance?

**Buck worked in a large office. He had applied for a promotion, but a woman was promoted instead of Buck. Buck said to himself, "It's obvious that the woman was promoted instead of me just because she is a woman."**

Can you think of any instances in which you have assigned false causes in order to rationalize a sequence of events?

*13. Invalid Disjunction.* If only two solutions to a question or situation are considered when there are actually more than two solutions that should be considered, and you believe that these are the only two solutions that could possibly be relevant to the question or situation at hand, you have committed the fallacy of invalid disjunction. Here is an example of a commission of this fallacy:

**The curriculum committee wanted to give Professor Potts another two classes to teach per year. Professor Potts much preferred to do research rather than to teach. She told the committee, "I can teach or I can do research. Take your pick."**

In this instance, Professor Potts has set up an invalid disjunction. She is assuming that she can do either teaching or research, but not both.

Here is another example of an invalid disjunction. Can you spot it?

**Bob wanted to go to law school, but only at Clearview University. Thus, Bob applied only to Clearview University, thinking, "If I don't get into Clearview University, I might as well not go to law school at all."**

Can you think of any instances in which people have used invalid disjunctions to their detriment?

*14. Availability.*   People commit the fallacy of availability when they accept the first explanation or an early explanation that comes to mind for an event without considering other, less obvious or readily available explanations. Consider an example of the fallacy of availability:

**Stewart owned a restaurant where he employed 25 people. One day he noticed money missing from the cash register. Just after he noticed the missing money, he noticed Frank, one of his employees, walking away from the area of the cash register with a puzzled expression on his face. Stewart shouted, "Frank, you stole money from the cash register."**

In this instance, Stewart concludes that Frank stole the money from the cash register because Frank had the misfortune to be the first possible culprit who came to Stewart's mind. Stewart has no real evidence of Frank's guilt, but jumps to an unwarranted conclusion because Frank happens to be readily available in Stewart's mind.

Consider another example of the fallacy of availability:

**As Dawn and Barry took their seats for the symphony concert, they noticed that two children were sitting with their parents a couple of rows behind them. During the concert, Dawn and Barry could hear paper rustling behind them several times. Dawn whispered to Barry, "Those kids sitting behind us must be the ones who are rustling paper during the quiet points of the music!"**

Can you think of any instances in which you or others have committed the fallacy of availability, thereby failing to exclude other alternative explanations for a problem being confronted?

*15. Argumentum ad Populum.*   The reasoning behind argumentum ad populum is, "If everyone else thinks this way, it must be right." Consider an example of an argumentum ad populum:

**A state assemblyman, when asked why he went along with the new governor's social policies, replied, "The governor was elected by a large majority of the popular vote. Thus, it seems to me that the governor must know what she's doing."**

A majority vote in no way guarantees that elected officials know what they are doing.

Here is another example of an argumentum ad populum. Can you see why?

Jackie's dad asked her why she wanted a computer for Christmas. Jackie replied, "I want a computer because all my friends are getting them, and they sure know what they are doing."

Can you think of other examples of this kind of fallacy?

*16. Argument from Ignorance.* This fallacy is committed whenever it is argued that something is true simply because it has not been proven false, or that it is false simply because it has not been proven true. Here is an example of an argument from ignorance:

The last paragraph of the experimental report stated that despite elaborate experimental design and statistical procedures, Bexit's model had not been proven. Sally thought, "I really thought this model was the correct one, but it's failed to be proven in this study, so I guess it is not the correct one."

Sally jumped to the conclusion that because the model had not been found to be correct in this one instance, it must be false. In science, however, as well as in other aspects of life, one failure to prove something to be true does not provide conclusive evidence that it is false.

Here is another example of an argument from ignorance. Can you spot it?

On Halloween night, Nate told his roommate, Sam, that he believed in ghosts. Sam told Nate, "You must be kidding." Nate replied, "Well, no one can prove to me that ghosts don't exist, so I believe in them."

Can you give any examples of your own of arguments from ignorance that you have heard?

*17. Mental Filter.* A person using a mental filter picks out one small aspect of a situation, often a negative aspect, and focuses on that one small aspect so that the "bigger picture" is distorted. It is as though all incoming events are perceived through a filter cast by that small aspect of the situation. Consider an example of the use of a mental filter:

Peg wanted to lose 20 pounds by Christmas vacation. The day before she was to leave for Christmas vacation, she weighed herself, and found that she was 5 pounds short of her 20-pound goal. Peg told her roommate, "I am really mad at myself for losing only 15 pounds, and not the full 20 pounds that I wanted to lose!"

In this example, Peg's obsession with losing the full 20 pounds prevents her from appreciating the 15 pounds that she has lost.

Here is another example of the use of a mental filter. Can you spot it?

Walt asked Harriet why she refused to subscribe to the local newspaper, since it was the only source of local news and she had expressed to him such a great interest in local news. Harriet replied, "I hate newspapers that have comics sections, and even though I would like to learn about the local news, I refuse to read the newspaper because it has a comics section."

Can you think of a situation in which your own use of a mental filter has distorted your reasoning?

*18. Emotional Reasoning.*   If we use our emotions or feelings as tangible evidence of a truth, then we are using emotional reasoning. "This is true because I feel it is true," is the paradigm of emotional reasoning. Here is an example of the use of emotional reasoning:

Alice had a paper that was not yet completed but that was due in two days. She considered working on the paper Tuesday evening after dinner, but instead she picked up the newspaper and lay down on the couch, thinking, "I'm not really in the mood to work tonight, so I wouldn't get anything done anyway."

In this instance, Alice did not feel like working, so she jumped to the conclusion that therefore she would get nothing done. She did not even attempt to get something done, so she had no way of knowing whether once she started working she might not find that she could, in fact, make progress on the paper.

Here is another example of the use of emotional reasoning. Can you see why?

Jeremy went to his girl friend's house one evening only to find her very angry at him, for some reason unknown to him. He asked her what he had done to make her angry, and she replied, "I don't remember what you did. But I know I'm mad, so you must have done something."

Can you think of any examples of your own or others' use of emotional reasoning?

*19. Argumentum ad Hominem.*   In this type of fallacious reasoning, aspects of a person's character, lifestyle, race, religion, sex, and so on, are submitted as evidence for a conclusion, even when these circumstances are irrelevant to the situation being examined. The argument is against the person rather than against the person's position on a matter. Here is an example of an argumentum ad hominem.

Mr. George picked up a new book on the history of the United States. He read in the "About the Author" portion of the flap that the author of the book was 24 years old. Mr. George put the book down, commenting "No one 24 years old can write knowledgeably about their country's history."

Mr. George concludes that the author's age precludes her from writing a decent history. In fact, the book might be quite good. Mr. George has no way of knowing without reading it or reviews of it but instead chooses to focus on a characteristic of the author in making his judgment about the book.

Here is another example of an argumentum ad hominem. Can you see why it is an instance of this kind of fallacy?

**Two women were testifying in a court case. One woman, who was a hairdresser, claimed she saw the defendant leaving the scene of the crime. The other woman, who was a prostitute, claimed that the defendant was with her during the time that the crime happened. One of the jurors thought, "I'll take the word of a hairdresser over the word of a prostitute any day."**

Can you think of an example of an argumentum ad hominem, perhaps in the political domain?

It is important to note that these 19 types of fallacies do not form an exhaustive list of possible reasoning fallacies, nor are they mutually exclusive. A given example of fallacious reasoning can often involve more than one kind of fallacy, or can be classified as exemplifying more than one. The important thing is to be aware of the kinds of fallacies people can commit, both in formulating your own reasoning and in evaluating the reasoning of others.

## Practice in Detecting Fallacies

Following are 25 vignettes presenting examples of everyday reasoning. Some of them involve fallacies, others do not. For each vignette, first determine whether the reasoning is valid or fallacious, and if it is fallacious, try to characterize the nature of the fallacy. Remember that there is often no unique characterization of a fallacy; hence, there may be more than one correct answer. Answers appear after the problems.

1.  **Jerry was fixing the first meal he and his new wife would eat in their new house. He wanted it to be a very special meal, but he accidentally charred the steaks black, although he and his wife liked steaks rare. Jerry said, "I never do anything right!"**

2.  **Some factory workers were sitting together at lunch discussing the dangerous working conditions at the factory. One worker commented that there wasn't much they could do about the conditions. Kay replied, "We may just be factory workers, but that doesn't mean we can't fight for our rights!"**

3.  **Chris refused to eat his peas, because, he explained, they were green. When Jack questioned this reason for disliking peas, Chris explained, "My mother always made me eat a lot of green vegetables, and I came to dislike having green things at meals."**

4. Nina was having a very hard time writing a paper based on some library research she had done. Her roommate was surprised that Nina was having trouble writing, because Nina had said she found some great sources in the library for her paper. Nina commented, "Even if I have the best possible references on this subject, the paper won't be particularly good unless I can tie them all together well."

5. Josh and Sandy were discussing the Reds and the Blues, two baseball teams. Sandy asked Josh why he thought the Reds had a better chance of winning the pennant this year than the Blues. Josh replied, "Every man on the Reds is better than every man on the Blues, so the Reds must be the better team."

6. As a senior in high school, Jeff won a scholarship to a good college. Jeff had never intended to go to college. He wanted to work with his hands as a carpenter. But Jeff thought, "I really ought to take this opportunity to have a free college education, even if I never intended and don't really want to go to college."

7. The mayor of Kayville was recently asked why he thought violence on the streets had diminished since he was elected last year. He replied, "My administration promised to be tough on criminals. We obviously intend to keep that promise, and the criminals are backing off."

8. Adam's father was tried and convicted for embezzling funds from a charity for which he had worked. Adam does not want to go to his high school anymore because, he says, "Everyone at school knows about Dad's crime, and I am sure that they will think I am a crook, too."

9. Peter asked his girl friend, Sarah, why she refused to go to a party with him. Sarah said, "I have a cold sore on my lip! I'm not going to any party looking like a disgusting freak!"

10. A medical researcher, Carol, had been taking hormone samples from thirty patients who had cancer of the liver. In three of the patients, she noticed unusually high concentrations of the hormone DNG. She reported to her supervisor, "I think I've found a significant link between DNG and liver cancer, based on this evidence from three cancer patients."

11. Tony and Leo were ambassadors from two different countries that often had political confrontations with each other. Although Tony and Leo often met on opposite sides of the negotiation table, they were good friends. When asked about this friendship, they said, "There is no reason we cannot be good friends even though we must argue with each other on behalf of our countries."

12.   Ivan was in a car wreck last month, in which he was hurt only slightly. Now, he refuses to ride in a car, saying, "I was almost killed once. I'm not going to get into a car ever again."

13.   Sheila was home on vacation from college. She knew her grandmother wanted to see her, but she did not enjoy visiting her grandmother, who was a constant complainer, and besides, she had to finish a term paper. But Sheila thought, "I should want to go to see my grandmother."

14.   Mike voted for the underdog candidate in the mayoral campaign. His father asked Mike why he had voted this way. Mike replied, "This candidate has never won an election in which he's run. I thought it was his turn, so I voted for him."

15.   Josh was getting dressed to go out to dinner with a woman he liked a great deal. His mother suggested he wear his beige silk shirt. He declined, saying, "I wore that shirt the last time I went out with my former girl friend. She didn't like that shirt, and as a result, I never saw her again. I'm certainly not going to wear it again tonight."

16.   Janice, a senior in high school, had consulted her vocational counselor and her math teacher for suggestions regarding colleges to which she should apply as a prospective math major. Janice thought, "My vocational counselor knows of math programs in general, and my math teacher can assess the merits of particular math programs, so I should consult them both."

17.   Troy had been quite overweight most of his life. He finally lost a good deal of weight, and his friend was congratulating him on his weight loss. Troy commented, "Even though I lost weight, I still think of myself as a fat person, and I probably always will."

18.   Sally was planning a trip to Las Vegas. She particularly liked the dice-throwing games, and was anxious to win enough by gambling to pay for her trip. A month before her trip, she began practicing throwing dice, thinking, "If I practice with the dice, I'll have a better chance of winning."

19.   The professor asked Beth why she took all summer to do a term paper that had been due in May. Beth answered, "Well, did you want me to hand in my paper in May or to do a good job?"

20.   Carol had eaten caviar once, several years ago. She did not like the taste of caviar at all then. At a party she attended recently, Carol was offered a cracker with caviar on it. Carol thought, "Well, just because I didn't like caviar when I tried it a few years ago does not mean that I won't like it if I try it now."

21. Wayne was the organizer of a large conference for dentists. Everything seemed to be going smoothly at the conference. On the second day of the conference, Wayne overheard two dentists talking. One told the other that he thought the conference was extremely boring this year. Wayne thought, "It makes me feel pretty terrible to hear criticism from the speakers I brought to this conference."

22. Three-year-old Jimmy loves broccoli. Jimmy's mother claims that "Jimmy loves broccoli because I ate a lot of broccoli while I was pregnant with him."

23. Mark knew that the winner of the international chess championships was often a Russian. A Russian family moved in next door to Mark's house. Mark went next door one day, thinking, "If they are Russian, they can teach me how to play chess."

24. Twin brothers, Terry and Jerry, had both received their Ph.D.'s in their respective fields. Terry had received his from a prestigious university, and Jerry had received his from a modest state university in their hometown. Jerry said to his wife one day, "I always feel inferior to Terry because he received his degree at a prestigious university and I didn't."

25. Beth, a movie star, refused to go to a photography session for her newest movie. When asked by her exasperated agent why, Beth answered, "Darling, I don't feel beautiful today. And if I don't feel beautiful, I don't look beautiful."

---

### ANSWERS TO INFERENTIAL-FALLACY PROBLEMS

Keep in mind that there are other possible classifications for these fallacies. The important thing is for you to become aware of the kinds of fallacies people can commit, and of how to stop them in your own reasoning and in the reasoning of others.

| | |
|---|---|
| 1. Fallacious. Hasty generalization. | 14. Fallacious. Irrelevant conclusion. |
| 2. Valid. | 15. Fallacious. False cause. |
| 3. Fallacious. Irrelevant conclusion. | 16. Valid. |
| 4. Valid. | 17. Fallacious. Labeling. |
| 5. Fallacious. Composition. | 18. Fallacious. Skill, not chance. |
| 6. Fallacious. "Should" statement. | 19. Fallacious. Invalid disjunction. |
| 7. Fallacious. False cause. | 20. Valid. |
| 8. Fallacious. Personalization. | 21. Fallacious. Personalization. |
| 9. Fallacious. Magnification/minimization. | 22. Fallacious. Representativeness. |
| 10. Fallacious. Hasty generalization. | 23. Fallacious. Division. |
| 11. Valid. | 24. Fallacious. Magnification/minimization. |
| 12. Fallacious. Hasty generalization. | 25. Fallacious. Emotional reasoning. |
| 13. Fallacious. "Should" statement. | |

# Mapping

*Mapping* is the recognition of a higher-order relation between two lower-order relations. Thus, it is related to, but nevertheless different from, inference, which is the recognition of a relation between two terms or single items. For example, recognizing the relation between GRAY and ELEPHANT requires an inference. Recognizing the relation between GRAY and ELEPHANT, on the one hand, and BROWN and GRIZZLY BEAR, on the other hand, requires mapping.

Psychological research has shown that performing inferences is easier than performing mappings, on the average, and that the ability to perform inferences develops earlier in children than the ability to perform mappings. For example, Bathsheva Rifkin and I (1979) showed that whereas children solving analogies can perform inferences as young as the second grade, or roughly 7 years of age (the lowest age level tested), children cannot map relations until, at earliest, roughly the fourth grade (or 9 years of age). In Jean Piaget's well-known theory of cognitive development, the ability to map second-order relations is a hallmark of entrance into what Piaget calls the "formal-operational period," which begins at roughly 11 or 12 years of age. The ability to infer relations, however, begins much earlier, probably as early as 4 years of age.

Mapping is essential to the solution of most kinds of analogies. Indeed, we might argue that mapping forms the essence of an analogy, in that analogical reasoning and problem solving require us to see the second-order relation between two lower-order relations. Consider a sample analogy, such as GRAPES is to WINE as BARLEY is to BEER. The essence of the analogy is the recognition that grapes are used to make wine just as barley is used to make beer.

Following are 25 sets of pairs of terms, as would be found in *verbal* analogies. See if you can figure out the second-order relation that relates the first two terms to the second two terms. Thus, in the above example, the relation would have been one of the first item, either GRAPES or BARLEY, being used as a basis for making the second item, either WINE or BEER. Note that the first-order relations must be inferred before the second-order relations can be mapped, and that the first-order relations can be classified according to the inferential scheme described earlier in the chapter. Note also that the inferences and mappings required by verbal items can often require substantial knowledge as well as an ability to reason well. Answers appear after the problems.

| First Relation | Second Relation | Relation Between Relations |
|---|---|---|
| 1. CHECK : PROBABLE | CASH : CERTAIN | _____ |
| 2. IRISH : SETTER | LABRADOR : RETRIEVER | _____ |
| 3. MORNING STAR : VENUS | EVENING STAR : VENUS | _____ |
| 4. SHORTEST : DECEMBER | LONGEST : JUNE | _____ |
| 5. VANILLA : BEAN | TEA : LEAF | _____ |
| 6. NOON : EVE | 12:21 : 10:01 | _____ |

7.  STEP : STAIRCASE          RUNG : LADDER            _____

8.  OCHER : YELLOW            LAVENDER : PURPLE        _____

9.  STOP : POTS               STOOL : LOOTS            _____

10. UNICORN : SINGLE          DUET : BICYCLE           _____

11. CLUB : LOWEST             SPADE : HIGHEST          _____

12. VITAMIN C : LEMON         VITAMIN A : LIVER        _____

13. PACIFIC : OCEAN           JUPITER : PLANET         _____

14. ELECT : SELECT            TIE : STY                _____

15. SHIRT : WEAR              BLOODY MARY : DRINK      _____

16. APRIL : 30                FEBRUARY : 28            _____

17. COMPARATIVE : BETTER      SUPERLATIVE : BEST       _____

18. OTHELLO : JEALOUS         HAMLET : REFLECTIVE      _____

19. SKIRMISH : BATTLE         DRIZZLE : RAINFALL       _____

20. GERIATRICS : OLD AGE      PEDIATRICS : INFANCY     _____

21. DOVE : PEACE              HAWK : WAR               _____

22. GONDOLA : CANAL           TRAIN : TRACK            _____

23. EGYPT : PHARAOH           ROMAN EMPIRE : EMPEROR   _____

24. NEAPOLITAN : ITALY        MUSCOVITE : USSR         _____

25. ATOM : MOLECULE           CELL : ORGANISM          _____

## ANSWERS TO VERBAL MAPPING PROBLEMS

1. A check has probable value in a financial transaction (in that it is not certain to clear). Cash has a certain value. Thus, the two first-order relations pertain to the likelihood of value that the first item has in a financial transaction.
2. An Irish Setter and a Labrador Retriever are both kinds of dogs. Thus, both first-order relations specify names of dogs.
3. The morning star is a name for Venus, as is the evening star. Thus, both first-order relations specify names for Venus.
4. The shortest day of the year occurs in December. The longest day of the year occurs in June. Thus, each first-order relation specifies the length of day in a critical month of the year.
5. Vanilla comes from a bean, whereas tea comes from a leaf. Thus, the two first-order relations specify the origin of the first item in each relation.
6. *Noon* and *eve* are both palindromes (that is, what they spell is the same both forward and backward). Similarly, 12:21 and 10:01 are both numerical palindromes. Thus, each first-order relation specifies a palindrome.

7. A step is a part of a staircase, just as a rung is part of a ladder. Thus, each first-order relation is a part-whole relation.

8. Ocher is a shade of yellow, whereas lavender is a shade of purple. Thus, each first-order relation specifies the shade one color is of another.

9. "Pots" is "stop" spelled backward. Similarly, "loots" is "stool" spelled backward. Thus, in each pair, the second word is the first word spelled backward.

10. A unicorn and a single both refer to one of something. A duet and a bicycle both refer to two of something. Thus, the two elements in each pair both refer to number.

11. In certain games of cards, such as bridge, the suit of clubs is the lowest, whereas the suit of spades is the highest. Thus, each first-order relation relates a suit to its rank order.

12. A lemon is an excellent source of vitamin C, whereas liver is an excellent source of vitamin A. Thus, each first-order relation relates a vitamin to a particularly good source of that vitamin.

13. The Pacific is an ocean, whereas Jupiter is a planet. Thus, each first-order relation is one of set membership (subordination).

14. "Select" sounds the sames as "elect" except for its initial "S" sound. "Sty" sounds the same as "tie" except for its initial "S." Thus, each first-order relation involves placing an "S" sound before the first term of the pair.

15. One wears a shirt whereas one drinks a Bloody Mary. Thus, each first-order relation specifies a predication of the second term to the first.

16. April has 30 days, whereas February has 28. Thus, each first-order relation specifies the number of days in a month.

17. "Better" is the comparative degree of "good," whereas "best" is the superlative degree. Thus, each first-order relation specifies the given degree of the word "good."

18. In the Shakespearean plays named, Othello was noteworthy for his tendency to be jealous, whereas Hamlet was noteworthy for his tendency to be reflective. Thus, each first-order relation specifies a particularly salient trait of a Shakespearean protagonist.

19. A skirmish is a small battle, whereas a drizzle is a small rainfall. Thus, each first-order relation specifies at the left a scaled-down version of what is stated at the right.

20. Geriatrics is a medical specialty dealing with old age, whereas pediatrics is a medical specialty dealing with infancy. Thus, each first-order relation specifies a medical specialty dealing with a certain age group.

21. A dove is a symbol of peace, whereas a hawk is a symbol of war. Thus, each first-order relation specifies an animal symbol of a given state.

22. A gondola travels on a canal, whereas a train travels on a track. Thus, each first-order relation specifies a means of conveyance.

23. In ancient times, a Pharaoh ruled Egypt whereas an Emperor ruled the Roman Empire. Thus, each first-order relation pertains to the kind of ruler an ancient state had.

24. A Neapolitan is from Italy (Naples). A Muscovite is from the USSR (Moscow). Thus, each first-order relation specifies the country of origin of a person from a particular city.

25. Atoms combine to form a molecule. Cells combine to form an organism. Thus, each first-order relation specifies a part-whole relationship.

# Application

This process involves applying a relation that has been previously inferred. For example, in the simple analogy LAWYER : CLIENT :: DOCTOR : _____, you must first *infer* the relation between LAWYER and CLIENT, *map* this relation to the new domain headed by DOCTOR, and then *apply* the relation so as to generate the best possible completion, namely, PATIENT. Sometimes, instead of being asked to generate the correct response, you will be asked to choose the correct response from several answer options. So, for example, the sample analogy might have read LAWYER : CLIENT :: DOCTOR : (a) MEDICINE, (b) NURSE, (c) PATIENT, (d) M.D.

# Justification

Justification is necessary when none of the available answer options for a problem seems to be quite correct, and your task becomes that of choosing the best, although imperfect, answer option. In problems requiring justification, you must use even more than the usual degree of discrimination. Consider, for example, the analogy LAWYER : CLIENT :: DOCTOR : (a) MEDICINE, (b) SICK PERSON. In this analogy, the better of the two answer options is clearly SICK PERSON. However, this answer option seems to be imperfect. PATIENT would probably be a better completion to the analogy. Thus, in this example, we had to choose the better of the two answer options, but we recognize that this answer option, although better, is not necessarily the one that ideally fits the analogy.

## Practice Problems Using
## Performance Components
### Analogies

Analogies can be expressed via verbal or via figural (geometric) content. In the case of figural analogies, the problem solver's task is the same as in verbal analogies, except that the possible relations are different. (See the section on *Inference* for a description of verbal relations.) Thus, the same mental processes of encoding, inference, mapping, application, and justification are necessary, yet the stimulus is different. Typically, geometric analogies involve additions, deletions, and transformations of geometric figures or portions of such figures, and the problem solver's task is to figure out what these additions, deletions, and transformations are.

Consider, for example, the figural analogy in Figure 4-2a. In this analogy, there are three terms (or *givens*) in the stem and four answer options. Your task is to figure out which answer option best completes the analogy. In the first term of the analogy, two sets of two parallel lines intersect at right angles. In the second term of the analogy, two single lines intersect at right angles. What has been done to the first figure in order to arrive at the second figure? You can probably *infer* that the relation between the first term and the second term is one of deletion. Two of the perpendicular lines have been deleted from the first figure in order to create the second figure. One therefore needs to *map* this deletion relation to the second half of the analogy. The third term

# FIGURE 4-2

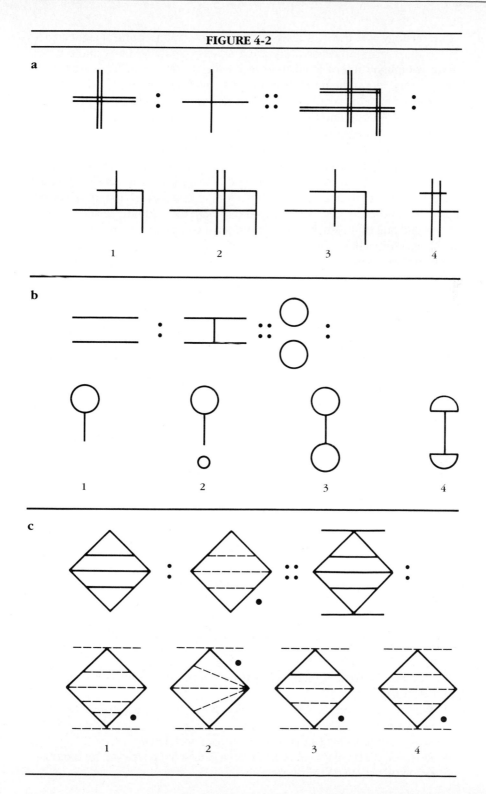

of the analogy also involves a set of parallel lines intersecting at right angles. In this third term, however, there are four sets of parallel lines, and they are more complexly interrelated than in the first term. In order to *apply* the relation inferred in the first half of the analogy, what you must do is to delete one from each of the set of parallel lines. Doing this generates the third of the four answer options, and this answer option is the correct one.

Now look at the second sample analogy (Figure 4-2b). The first term involves two horizontal parallel lines. The second term seems to involve the same two parallel lines plus a perpendicular line connecting the two parallel lines extending from the top line to the bottom line. The relation you are likely to *infer* in this analogy is one of addition of a part. That part, of course, is the perpendicular line. So you'll need to *map* the addition relation over to the second half of the analogy. The third term contains two empty circles that are situated one above the other. You will now need to *apply* the relation you inferred above. The best answer option is the one with the two empty circles connected by a line, as in the first half of the analogy.

Now consider a third sample analogy (Figure 4-2c). In this analogy, the first term involves a diamond with three horizontal lines within its borders. The three horizontal lines divide the diamond into four segments. In the second term, the diamond appears again and so do the horizontal lines. But in the second figure, the horizontal lines have become broken rather than solid lines. A relation to be *inferred* is thus one of transformation. The solid lines have been transformed into broken lines. Moreover, a dot has been added. This relation now needs to be *mapped* to the second half of the analogy. The third term of the analogy involves the same diamond, except with additional horizontal lines at the top and the bottom of the diamond. *Applying* the relation inferred above, which completion do you find best satisfies the transformation inference? The answer is (4), the only completion that has five broken horizontal lines.

You have thus seen three sample analogies, one involving *deletion* in the relation between the first two terms, one involving *addition* in the relation between the first two terms, and one involving *transformation* (as well as addition) in the relation between the first two terms. Below are 40 verbal and 30 more figural analogies for you to solve, all of which involve various combinations of addition, deletion, and transformation in the relations between terms. Answers appear after the problems.

---

### *VERBAL ANALOGIES*

1. CANDLE : TALLOW :: TIRE : (a) AUTOMOBILE, (b) ROUND, (c) RUBBER, (d) HOLLOW.
2. SPOUSE : HUSBAND :: SIBLING : (a) FATHER, (b) UNCLE, (c) BROTHER, (d) SON.
3. 480% : 4.8 :: 3.6% : (a) .0036, (b) .036, (c) .36, (d) 3.6
4. EINSTEIN : RELATIVITY :: DARWIN : (a) GRAVITY, (b) PLANETARY ORBITS, (c) EVOLUTION, (d) MAGNETISM.

5. SONATA : COMPOSER :: LITHOGRAPH : (a) PHYSICIST, (b) ARTIST, (c) SCULPTOR, (d) AUTHOR.

6. MISDEMEANOR : CRIME :: PECCADILLO : (a) STUTTER, (b) PRETENSE, (c) AMNESIA, (d) SIN.

7. STUBBORN : MULE :: FICKLE : (a) CHAMELEON, (b) SALAMANDER, (c) TADPOLE, (d) FROG.

8. FEEL : ANESTHESIA :: SEE : (a) EYEBALL, (b) EYES, (c) GLASSES, (d) BLINDNESS.

9. CORPORAL : BEAT :: CAPITAL : (a) STUN, (b) MAIM, (c) KILL, (d) SHOCK.

10. WATER : ICE :: RAIN : (a) CYCLONE, (b) SNOW, (c) HAIL, (d) DRY ICE.

11. STENCIL : LETTERS :: COMPASS : (a) KIND, (b) DIRECTION, (c) NORTHWEST, (d) CIRCLE.

12. LEGISLATOR : LOBBYIST :: JURY : (a) LAWYER, (b) JUDGE, (c) COURT STENOGRAPHER, (d) FOREMAN.

13. TRAP : PART :: RAT : (a) GOOD-BYE, (b) WHOLE, (c) BAIT, (d) TAR.

14. EMERALD : MINE :: PEARL : (a) OYSTER, (b) CLAM, (c) MINE, (d) RIVER.

15. AIR : VACUUM :: COLOR : (a) CHROMA, (b) VIOLET, (c) RAINBOW, (d) BLACK.

16. OLD : MAID :: TWENTY : (a) ONE, (b) NINE, (c) SIXTY, (d) ONE HUNDRED.

17. XL : LX :: CC : (a) CCC, (b) CD, (c) DC, (d) CM.

18. CONE : MEGAPHONE :: TORNADO : (a) FUNNEL, (b) CLOUD, (c) HURRICANE, (d) SPHERE.

19. ACTUAL : VIRTUAL :: IN FACT : (a) IN CAUSE, (b) IN TIME, (c) IN TRUTH, (d) IN EFFECT.

20. CANINE : DOG :: EQUINE : (a) COW, (b) GOAT, (c) HORSE, (d) PIG.

21. COLT : HORSE :: LAMB : (a) GOAT, (b) SHEEP, (c) MULE, (d) COW.

22. COWARDLY : GLOOMY :: YELLOW : (a) BLUE, (b) WHITE, (c) GREEN, (d) RED.

23. RAINCOAT : RAIN :: FOXHOLE : (a) FOXES, (b) GUNFIRE, (c) DISCOVER, (d) EARTHQUAKES.

24. OWL : FOOLISH :: LION : (a) TIMID, (b) LARGE, (c) WISE, (d) TEMPERAMENTAL.

25. BALD : HAIR :: ALBINO : (a) HEIGHT, (b) PAIN, (c) SIGHT, (d) PIGMENT.

26. GREEK : GREEK :: ROMAN : (a) INDO-EUROPEAN, (b) LATIN, (c) MEDITERRANEAN, (d) ROMANSH.

27. BUDDHISM : NIRVANA :: CHRISTIANITY : (a) JESUS, (b) HELL, (c) HEAVEN, (d) SATAN.

28. DIMINISH : AUGMENT :: INCREDIBLE : (a) BELIEVABLE, (b) WRONG, (c) FANCIFUL, (d) HUMOROUS.

29. PARTICIPLE : WALKING :: INFINITIVE : (a) HAVING EATEN, (b) TO SLEEP, (c) HAS TRIED, (d) TO THE STORE.

30. HOUND : BLOOD :: DOG : (a) SHEEP, (b) PLASMA, (c) VULTURE, (d) HARASS.

31. HEAVY-FOOTED : PLODDING :: HEAVY-HANDED : (a) UNCOORDINATED, (b) TACTLESS, (c) STRONG, (d) COORDINATED.

32. LION : EAGLE :: SPHINX : (a) PTERODACTYL, (b) DODO, (c) VULTURE, (d) PHOENIX.

33. DISLIKE : HATE :: RESPECT : (a) LOVE, (b) PROTECT, (c) REVERE, (d) OBEY.

34. BEND : PLIABLE :: BREAK : (a) BRITTLE, (b) TRANSPARENT, (c) OPAQUE, (d) FLEXIBLE.

35. CAN : MAY :: ABILITY : (a) ACHIEVEMENT, (b) PERMISSION, (c) MONTH, (d) DESIRE.

36. FIRE : ASBESTOS :: WATER : (a) VINYL, (b) AIR, (c) COTTON, (d) FAUCET.

37. PAIR : COUPLE :: PARE : (a) SEVERAL, (b) ONE, (c) PEAR, (d) PRUNE.

38. ROCKET : ROCK :: JACKET : (a) COAT, (b) CLOTH, (c) JACK, (d) WASP.

39. FAMINE : FOOD :: DROUGHT : (a) DESERT, (b) THIRST, (c) RAIN, (d) CROPS.

40. LEGISLATOR : MAKES :: POLICEMAN : (a) INTERPRETS, (b) ENFORCES, (c) BREAKS, (d) ENACTS.

---

### ANSWERS TO VERBAL ANALOGY PROBLEMS

1. (c). A candle is frequently made of tallow. A tire is frequently made of rubber.
2. (c). A husband is a spouse. A brother is a sibling.
3. (b). 480% is equal to 4.8. 3.6% is equal to .036.
4. (c). Albert Einstein was primarily responsible for relativity theory. Charles Darwin was primarily responsible for the theory of evolution.
5. (b). A sonata is the creation of a composer. A lithograph is the creation of an artist.
6. (d). A misdemeanor is a minor crime. A peccadillo is a minor sin.
7. (a). A mule is reputed to be stubborn. A chameleon is reputed to be fickle.
8. (d). Anesthesia is a state in which one does not feel. Blindness is a state in which one does not see.
9. (c). In corporal punishment, a person is beaten. In capital punishment, a person is killed.
10. (c). When water is frozen, it becomes ice. When rain is frozen, it becomes hail.
11. (d). A stencil is used to draw letters. A compass is used to draw a circle.
12. (a). The job of a lobbyist is to persuade a legislator. The job of a lawyer is to persuade a jury.
13. (d). *Part* is *trap* spelled backward. *Tar* is *rat* spelled backwards.
14. (a). Emeralds are found in mines. Pearls are found in oysters.
15. (d). A vacuum is the absence of air. Black is the absence of color.
16. (a). Old Maid and Twenty-One are both names of card games.
17. (a). 40 : 60 :: 200 : 300. This problem makes use of Roman numerals.
18. (a). A cone and a megaphone have roughly the same shape, as do a tornado and a funnel.
19. (d). *Actual* means in fact. *Virtual* means in effect.
20. (c). *Canine* means doglike. *Equine* means horselike.
21. (b). A lamb is a young sheep. A colt is a young horse.
22. (a). A cowardly person is often referred to as "yellow." A person who feels gloomy is often referred to as "blue."
23. (b). A raincoat provides protection from rain. A foxhole provides protection from gunfire.
24. (a). An owl is reputed to be wise, which is the opposite of foolish. A lion is reputed to be bold, which is the opposite of timid.
25. (d). A bald person lacks hair. An albino lacks pigment.
26. (b). The ancient Greeks spoke Greek. The ancient Romans spoke Latin.

27. (c). The concept of heaven in Christianity is analogous to that of Nirvana in Buddhism.
28. (a). *Diminish* and *augment* are antonyms, as are *incredible* and *believable*.
29. (b). *Walking* is a participle. *To sleep* is an infinitive.
30. (a). A bloodhound and a sheep dog are both types of dogs.
31. (b). Someone who is heavy-footed is plodding. Someone who is heavy-handed is tactless.
32. (d). A lion and an eagle are both real animals. A sphinx and a phoenix are both mythological animals.
33. (c). To hate someone is to dislike them a great deal. To revere someone is to respect them a great deal.
34. (a). A pliable object will easily bend, whereas a brittle object will easily break.
35. (b). When someone can do something, they are able to do it. When someone may do something, they have permission to do it.
36. (a). Asbestos is fireproof. Vinyl is waterproof.
37. (d). A pair is a couple. To pare is to prune.
38. (c). *Rocket* is *rock* with an *et* at the end. *Jacket* is *jack* with an *et* at the end.
39. (c). A famine is caused by a lack of food. A drought is caused by a lack of rain.
40. (b). A legislator makes the laws. A policeman enforces them.

## FIGURE 4-3

### Figural Analogies

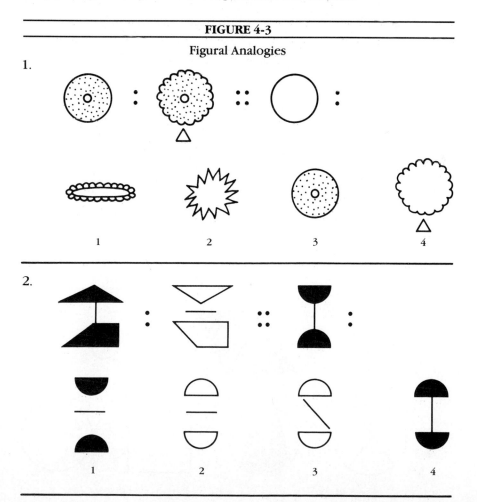

# FIGURE 4-3 continued

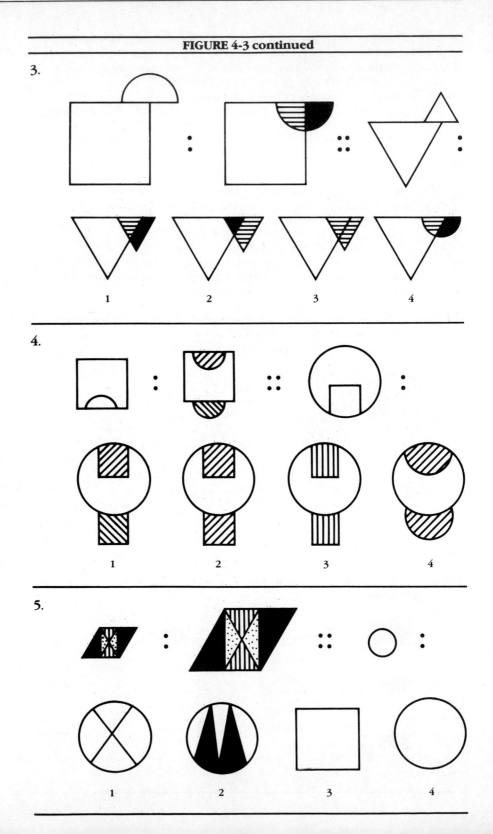

## FIGURE 4-3 continued

6.

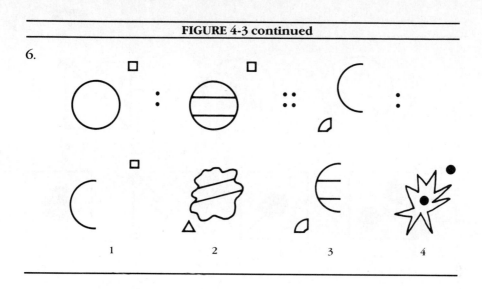

7.

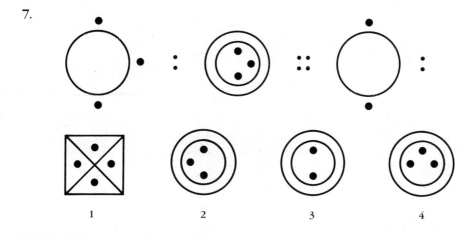

8.

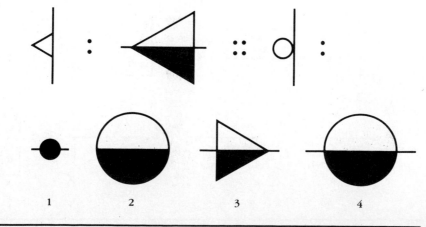

**FIGURE 4-3 continued**

9.

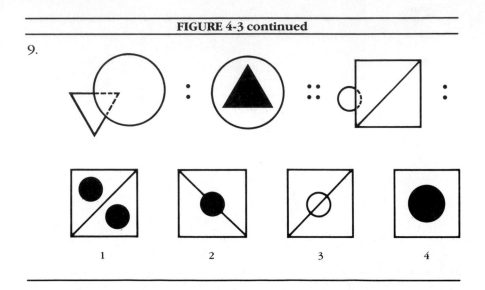

10.

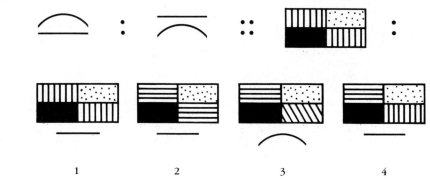

11.

**FIGURE 4-3 continued**

12.

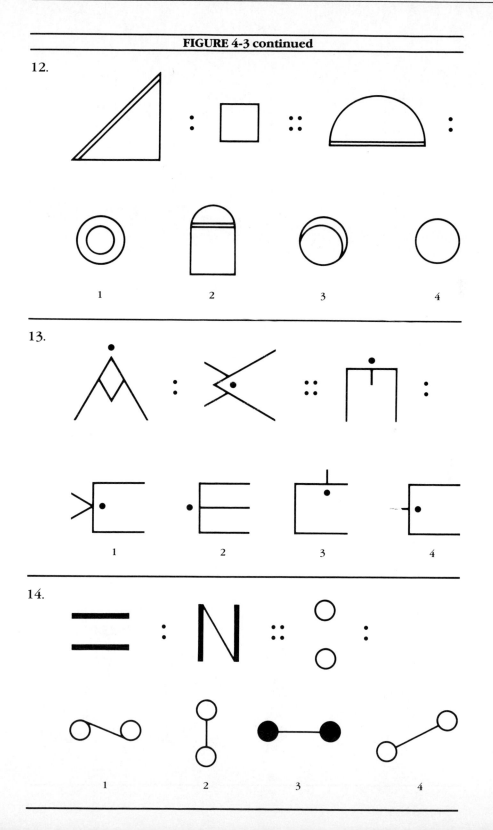

13.

14.

## FIGURE 4-3 continued

15.

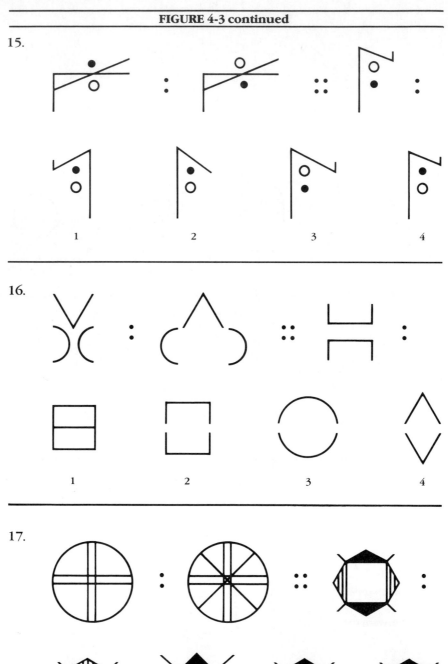

16.

17.

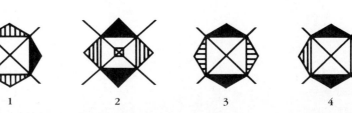

## FIGURE 4-3 continued

18.

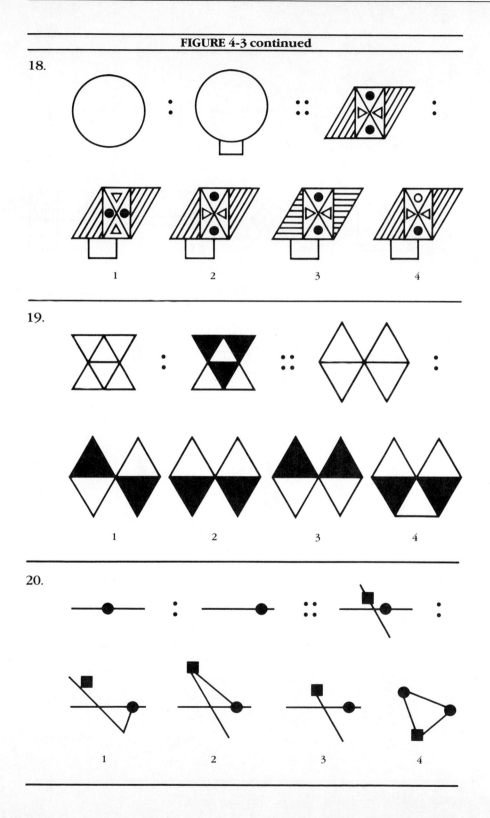

19.

20.

## FIGURE 4-3 continued

21.

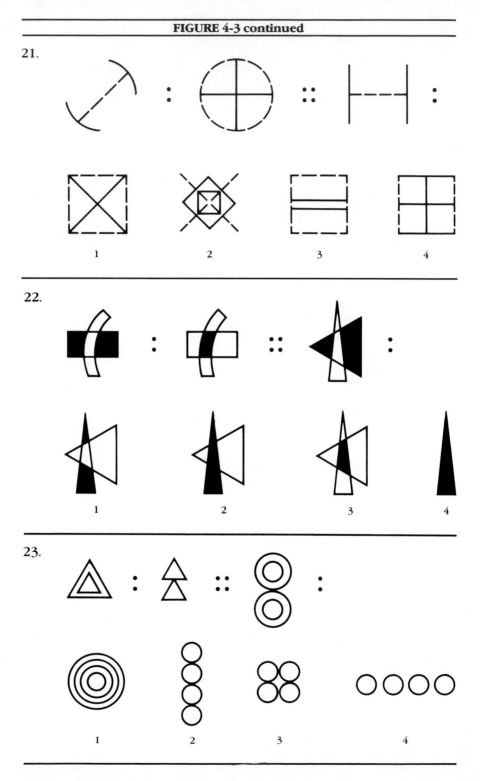

22.

23.

## FIGURE 4-3 continued

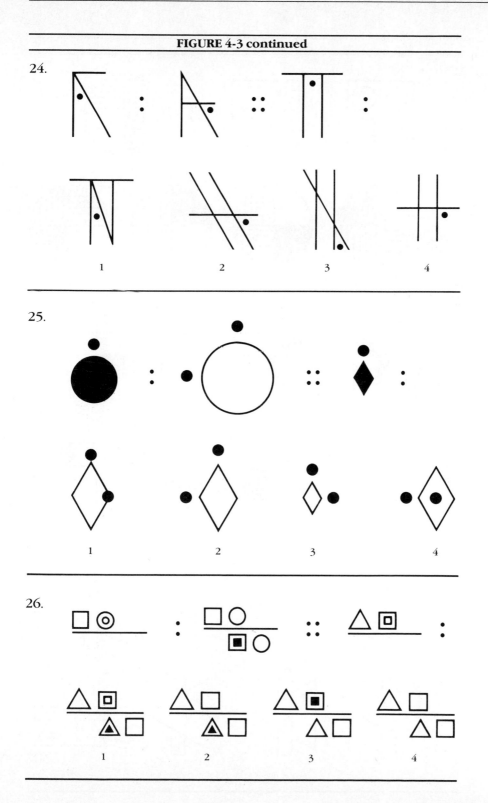

**FIGURE 4-3 continued**

27.

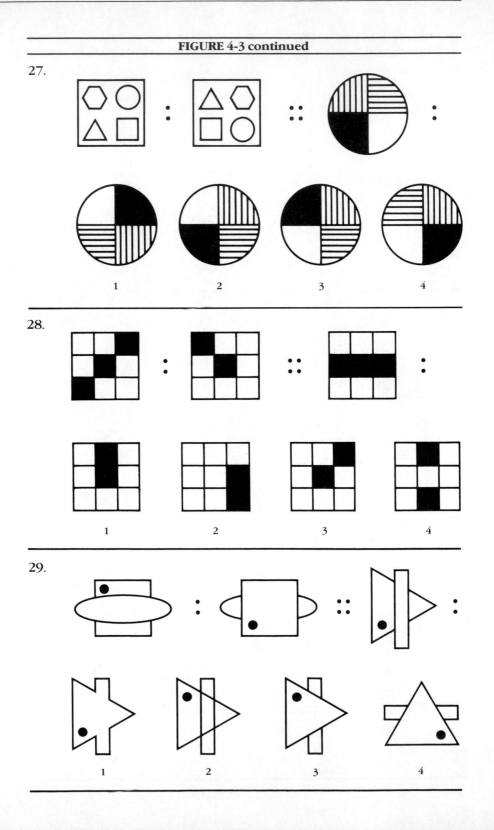

28.

29.

## FIGURE 4-3 continued

30.

---

## ANSWERS TO FIGURAL ANALOGY PROBLEMS (FIGURE 4-3)

| | | | | | |
|---|---|---|---|---|---|
| 1. 4 | 6. 3 | 11. 3 | 16. 2 | 21. 1 | 26. 2 |
| 2. 2 | 7. 3 | 12. 4 | 17. 4 | 22. 3 | 27. 3 |
| 3. 1 | 8. 4 | 13. 4 | 18. 2 | 23. 2 | 28. 1 |
| 4. 1 | 9. 2 | 14. 1 | 19. 2 | 24. 4 | 29. 3 |
| 5. 4 | 10. 1 | 15. 4 | 20. 3 | 25. 2 | 30. 4 |

### Series Completions

The performance components of inference, mapping, application, and justification apply to other kinds of inductive reasoning problems besides analogies. One of the most frequently encountered kinds of such problems are series completion problems. In these problems, the solver is usually given some terms that form a series of some kind, and the task is to complete the series. Consider, for example, this simple series completion problem: 2, 5, 8, —. In this problem, you must *encode* the terms, then *infer* the relation between each successive pair of numbers, and then *apply* this relation to generate a correct completion, namely 11. Note that mapping is not needed in this form of series completion, because all the terms are within a single domain. It is possible, however, to create complex series completion problems where mapping is required. Suppose, instead, that the problem had read: 2, 5, 8, 11: 4, —. In this case, the inferred relation is the same as before, namely, +3. However, before applying this relation, you must *map* it to a new numerical domain, one starting with the number 4. *Applying* the +3 relation thus produces an answer of 7 in this form of the problem.

Series completion problems, like analogies, can involve words or figures. Consider the following series completion problem: LIE, KNEEL, STAND : HIGH, (a) TALL, (b) HIGHER. In this problem, the relation to be *inferred* is one of progressively greater vertical height. This relation needs to be *mapped* to the term HIGH and then applied so as to yield a correct answer. If HIGHER is not perceived as an ideal answer option, then *justification* is required to recognize this answer option as better than TALL. Note that the performance components used to solve an analogy are here being applied to a series completion problem. The form of the problem is somewhat different from the form of the analogy, but the mental operations are practically identical. The main difference is that instead of having to infer the relation between only two terms, you must infer successive relations between each adjacent pair of three terms. Thus, in the sample, you need to infer first the relation between LIE and KNEEL, and second the relation between KNEEL and STAND.

Here are 40 sample verbal series completions that require you to use the performance components of inference, mapping, application, and justification, followed by 30 sample figural series completions. Answers follow the problems.

## VERBAL SERIES COMPLETIONS

1. BABY, TODDLER, CHILD  :  SEEDLING, (a) LEAF, (b) BRANCH, (c) TREE, (d) BARK.
2. HEAD, NECK, WRIST  :  BRACELET, (a) ARTIST, (b) SHOULDER, (c) TOE, (d) RING.
3. BURNT, WELL-DONE, MEDIUM  :  PINK, (a) RED, (b) BLACK, (c) GRAY, (d) WHITE.
4. EYE, JAY, KAY  :  TEA, (a) LAY, (b) SEA, (c) YOU, (d) COFFEE.
5. CHERRY, ORANGE, GRAPEFRUIT  :  BASEBALL, (a) NEEDLE, (b) GOLF BALL, (c) FOOTBALL, (d) VOLLEYBALL.
6. CITY, COUNTY, STATE  :  PROVINCE, (a) COUNTRY, (b) LORE, (c) TOWN, (d) GOVERNMENT.
7. ARID, DRY, DAMP  :  WET, (a) SOAKING, (b) SPEAKING, (c) MOIST, (d) DESERT.
8. CANTALOUPE, MELON, FRUIT  :  VEGETABLE, (a) MINERAL, (b) FOOD, (c) LETTUCE, (d) LEMON.
9. GREAT GRANDFATHER, GRANDFATHER, FATHER  :  MOTHER, (a) GRANDDAUGHTER, (b) DAUGHTER, (c) GRANDMOTHER, (d) CHILD.
10. CONCEPTION, BIRTH, MARRIAGE  :  23, (a) 0, (b) 10, (c) 352, (d) 82.
11. ROCKET, JET, PROPELLER PLANE  :  TORTOISE, (a) CHEETAH, (b) HARE, (c) ANT, (d) MARSUPIAL.
12. RHODE ISLAND, CONNECTICUT, NEBRASKA  :  GERMANY, (a) CANADA, (b) ALASKA, (c) MONACO, (d) BERLIN.
13. TABLE OF CONTENTS, INTRODUCTION, CONCLUSION  :  EPILOGUE, (a) INK, (b) PROLOGUE, (c) PLOT, (d) INDEX.
14. LOITERING, SMUGGLING, KIDNAPPING  :  LIFE IMPRISONMENT, (a) MURDER, (b) ELECTRIC CHAIR, (c) DETENTION, (d) CRIME.
15. ANIMAL, VERTEBRATE, MAMMAL  :  REPTILE, (a) PIG, (b) BIRD, (c) SNAKE, (d) FROG.
16. PLAY, ACT, SCENE  :  BOOK, (a) CHAPTER, (b) LIBRARY, (c) NOVEL, (d) AUTHOR.
17. ZERO, ONE, TWO  :  CIRCLE, (a) CUBE, (b) ELLIPSE, (c) SPHERE, (d) ROUND.
18. 4, 3, 2  :  CHESS, (a) BRIDGE, (b) PAWN, (c) SOLITAIRE, (d) GAME.
19. SPRING, SUMMER, FALL  :  JACKET, (a) DRESS, (b) COAT, (c) WOOL, (d) BOOTS.

20. CONSERVATIVE, MODERATE, LIBERAL : PROGRESSIVE, (a) POLITICAL, (b) REACTIONARY, (c) DEMOCRATIC, (d) RADICAL.

21. ANCIENT, MEDIEVAL, RENAISSANCE : CANDLE, (a) LIGHT BULB, (b) ELECTRICITY, (c) SUN, (d) TALLOW.

22. EIGHTH, QUARTER, HALF : DOUBLE, (a) TRIPLE, (b) QUADRUPLE, (c) NOTHING, (d) FRACTIONAL.

23. TRUNK, SUITCASE, HANDBAG : PITCHER, (a) CUP, (b) WATER, (c) LITER, (d) AQUARIUM.

24. VILLAGE, TOWN, CITY : CARACAS, (a) NEW YORK, (b) VENEZUELA, (c) HAMLET, (d) OXFORD.

25. ENGAGED, MARRIED, SEPARATED : BIRTH, (a) BABY, (b) LIFE, (c) CONCEPTION, (d) DEATH.

26. MATCH, PENCIL, BROOMSTICK : NEEDLE, (a) WIG, (b) HAYSTACK, (c) SWORD, (d) AUTOMOBILE.

27. IMPOSSIBLE, UNLIKELY, POSSIBLE : MAYBE, (a) NEVER, (b) YES, (c) UNCERTAIN, (d) UNKNOWN.

28. HEALTHY, SICK, DYING : HOSPITAL, (a) OFFICE, (b) GRAVEYARD, (c) DUST, (d) OLD AGE HOME.

29. ALERT, FATIGUED, DROWSY : YAWN, (a) ASLEEP, (b) LAUGH, (c) SIGH, (d) SNORE.

30. MEASURE, MIX, BAKE : EAT, (a) DIGEST, (b) STOVE, (c) COOL, (d) PAN.

31. ANTARCTICA, SOUTH AMERICA, CENTRAL AMERICA : MEXICO, (a) CHILE, (b) GUATEMALA, (c) GREENLAND, (d) WASHINGTON, D.C.

32. ONLY CHILD, TWINS, TRIPLETS : TRICYCLE, (a) BICYCLE, (b) CAR, (c) UNICYCLE, (d) ICE SKATES.

33. FRIEND, GIRL FRIEND, FIANCÉE : MISS, (a) MRS., (b) HIT, (c) WIFE, (d) MOTHER.

34. PLOW, PLANT, HARVEST : GRAIN, (a) MOLECULE, (b) FLOUR, (c) SEED, (d) WHEAT.

35. A, E, I : EYE, (a) SEE, (b) O, (c) OH, (d) EAR.

36. 100%, .75, 1/2 : 3/6, (a) WHOLE, (b) ONE-EIGHTH, (c) .4, (d) 1/4.

37. DESPISE, DISLIKE, LIKE : GOOD, (a) EVIL, (b) EXCELLENT, (c) BETTER, (d) ADMIRE.

38. BACH, BEETHOVEN, GERSHWIN : VAN GOGH, (a) PICASSO, (b) MICHELANGELO, (c) SHOSTAKOVICH, (d) REMBRANDT.

39. ALL, MANY, FEW : SEVERAL, (a) EARLY, (b) NONE, (c) FEW, (d) NUMEROUS.

40. EINSTEIN, NEWTON, PYTHAGORAS : CHAUCER, (a) SATAN, (b) HEMINGWAY, (c) GALILEO, (d) HOMER.

---

## ANSWERS TO VERBAL SERIES COMPLETION PROBLEMS

1. (c). A baby, as it grows older, becomes a toddler and then a child; a seedling becomes a tree.

2. (d). Parts of the body moving down and outward are the head, neck, and wrist; jewelry to be worn on the body, moving outward, are a bracelet and a ring.

3. (a). Successively lesser degrees of cooking meat are burnt, well-done, medium. Red meat is still less cooked than pink meat.

4 (c). These words are pronounced the same as the successive letters of the alphabet, I, J, and K; similarly, tea is pronounced like the letter T and you is pronounced like the successive letter, U.

5. (d). These round fruits are successively larger in size; a volleyball has the same spherical shape as a baseball, but is larger in size.

6. (a). A city, county, and state are units of government of successively greater size; a province and a country are units of government, also of successively greater size.

7. (a). Arid, dry, and damp are degrees of dampness that increase in amounts of moisture; wet and soaking are also increasing degrees of dampness in amounts of moisture.

8. (b). A cantaloupe is a kind of melon and a melon is a kind of fruit; a vegetable is a kind of food.

9. (b). A great grandfather, grandfather, and father are successive generations; a mother and a daughter are also successive generations.

10. (d). Conception, birth, and marriage for people occur at successively later ages; 23 and 82 are successively later ages for people. (352 is an implausible age, although older than 23!)

11. (c). A rocket, jet, and propeller plane are successively slower in their movements; an ant is slower in movement than a tortoise.

12. (a). Rhode Island, Connecticut, and Nebraska are successively larger states; Canada is a larger country than Germany.

13. (d). The table of contents, introduction, and conclusion come successively later in a book; the index comes later than the epilogue.

14. (b). Loitering, smuggling, and kidnapping are successively more serious crimes; life imprisonment and the electric chair are successively more serious punishments.

15. (c). A mammal is a type of vertebrate, which is a type of animal; a snake is a kind of reptile.

16. (a). A play, act, and scene are successively smaller units of drama; a book and a chapter are successively smaller units of prose.

17. (c). Zero, one, and two are successively greater numbers of dimensions; a sphere is a circle expanded into a successively greater number of dimensions (from 2 to 3).

18. (c). 4, 3, and 2 are successively smaller numbers of players; chess and solitaire are played by successively smaller numbers of players (2 and 1).

19. (b). Spring, summer, and fall are successive seasons; a jacket and a coat are worn in successive seasons (often, autumn and winter).

20. (d). A conservative, moderate, and liberal are successively further left on the political spectrum; a progressive and a radical are also successively further left.

21. (a). Ancient, medieval, and Renaissance times are successively more modern; a light bulb is a more modern form of lighting than a candle.

22. (b). Eighth, quarter, and half are, successively, twice as large as each other; quadruple is twice as large as double.

23. (a). A trunk, suitcase, and handbag hold successively less content; a cup holds less content than a pitcher.

24. (a). A village, town, and city are successively larger units of urban populations; Caracas and New York are successively larger cities.

25. (d). Engaged, married, and separated refer to successive potential events in the course of life; birth and death are also successive events in life.

26. (c). A match, pencil, and broomstick are successively longer straight objects; a sword is a longer straight object than a needle.

27. (b). Impossible, unlikely, and possible refer to increasing probabilities of occurrence; yes represents a higher probability of assent than maybe.

28. (b). Healthy, sick, and dying refer to three successively lesser states of health; a hospital and a graveyard refer to locations of persons in successively lesser states of health.

29. (d). Alert, fatigued, and drowsy refer to successively lower states of arousal; a yawn and a snore are oral outputs from successively lower states of arousal (tiredness and sleep).

30. (a). In making a cake, one first measures, then mixes, then bakes. Later on, one first eats and then digests the cake.

31. (c). Antarctica, South America, and Central America are geographic areas successively in the northward direction; Mexico and Greenland are geographic areas successively in the northward direction.

32. (b). An only child, twins, and triplets refer to successively increasing numbers of items, in this case, siblings; a tricycle and a car have successively increasing numbers of items, in this case, wheels.

33. (a). Friend, girl friend, and fiancée refer to successive states in a heterosexual interpersonal relationship; Miss and Mrs. also refer to successive states in a heterosexual interpersonal relationship.

34. (b). In farming, one first plows, then plants, and then harvests; similarly, in milling, one first has grain and then flour.

35. (c). A, E, and I are successive vowels; eye and oh are words sounding the same as the names of successive vowels.

36. (d). 100%, .75, and 1/2 are quantities that successively decrease by 1/4; 3/6 and 1/4 are also quantities that successively decrease by 1/4.

37. (c). Despise, dislike, and like refer to increasingly favorable dispositions toward someone; good and better are also increasingly favorable dispositions.

38. (a). Bach, Beethoven, and Gershwin were successively later composers; Van Gogh and Picasso were successively later artists.

39. (b). All, many, and few refer to successively lesser amounts; several and none also refer to successively lesser amounts.

40. (d). Einstein, Newton, and Pythagoras were successively less recent scientists; Chaucer and Homer were successively less recent authors.

---

## FIGURE 4-4

### Figural Series Completions

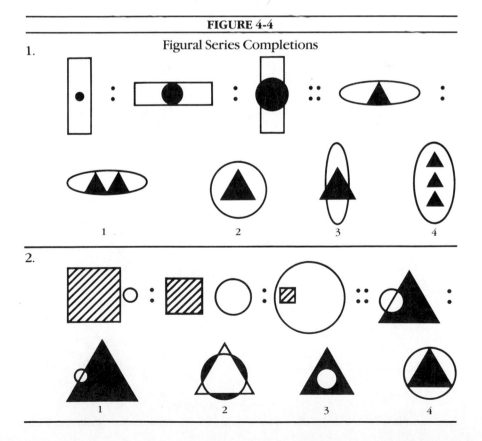

**FIGURE 4-4 continued**

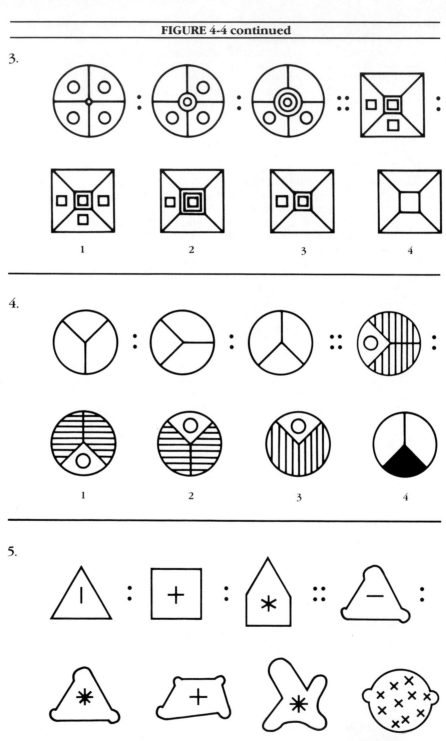

## FIGURE 4-4 continued

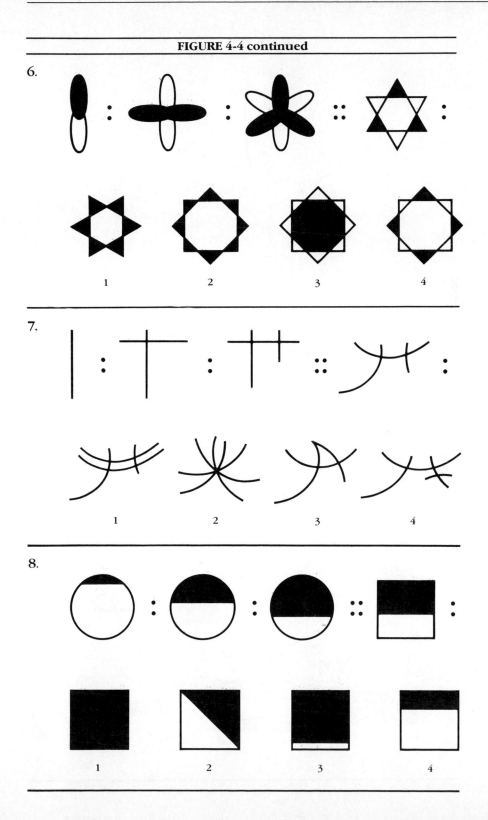

## FIGURE 4-4 continued

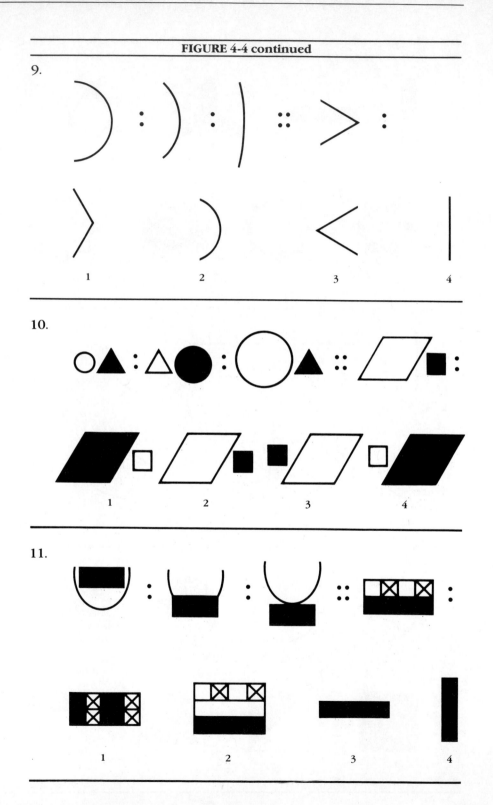

## FIGURE 4-4 continued

12.

13.

14.

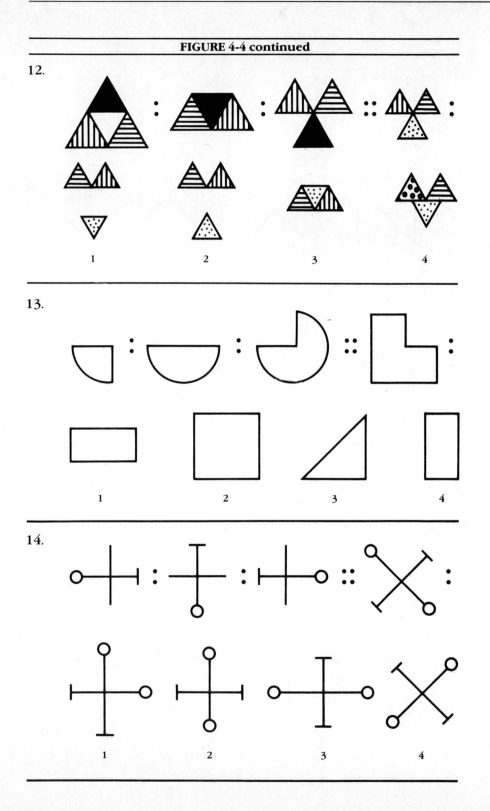

## FIGURE 4-4 continued

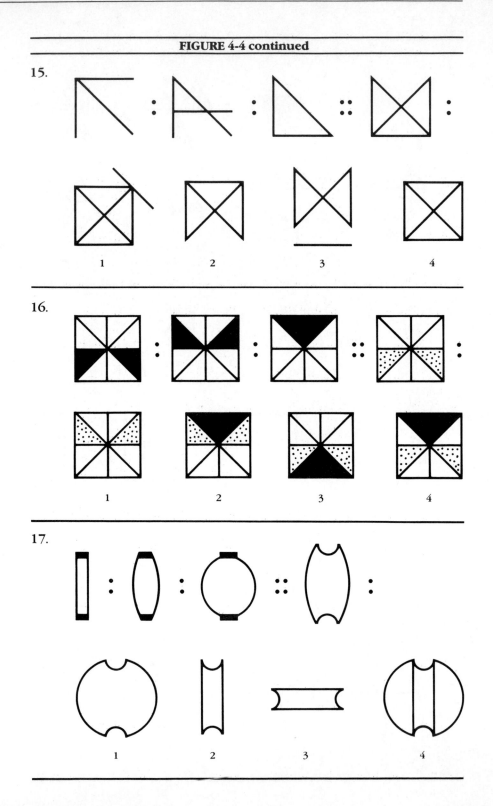

15.

16.

17.

## FIGURE 4-4 continued

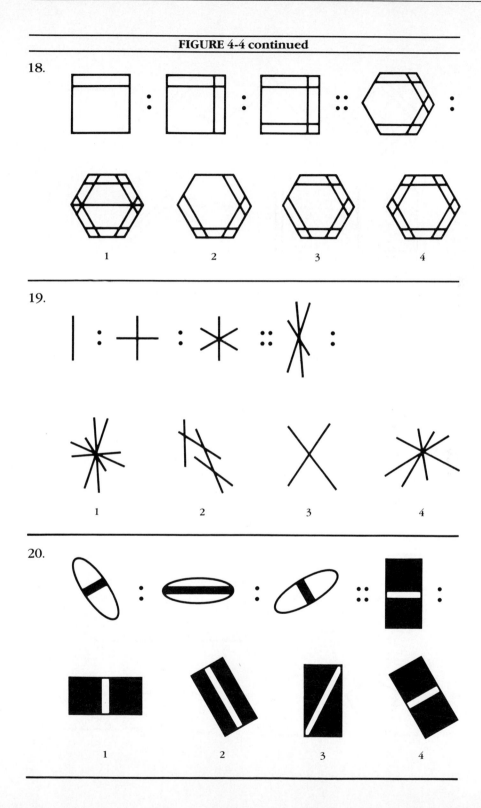

**FIGURE 4-4 continued**

21.

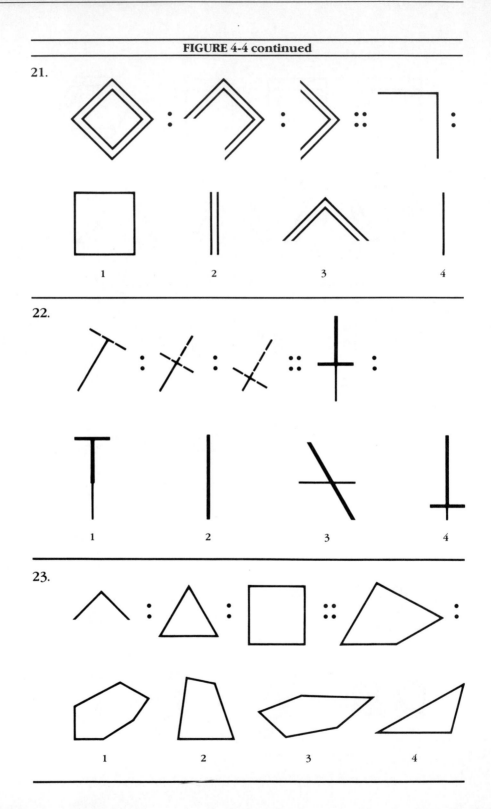

22.

23.

## FIGURE 4-4 continued

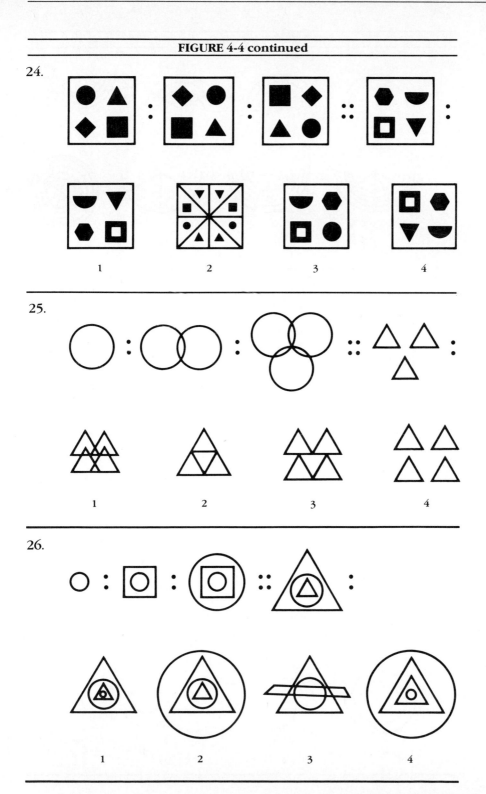

**FIGURE 4-4 continued**

27.

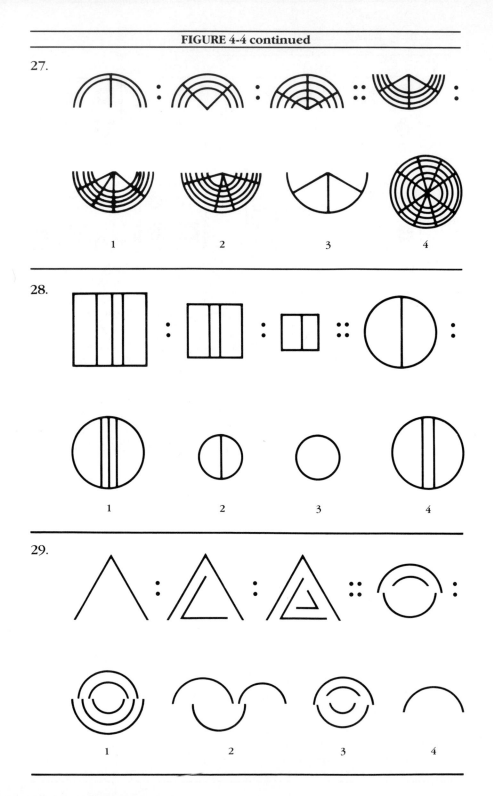

## FIGURE 4-4 continued

30.

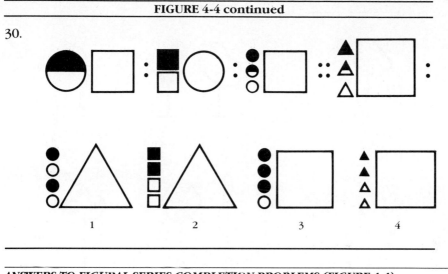

---

### ANSWERS TO FIGURAL SERIES COMPLETION PROBLEMS (FIGURE 4-4)

| | | | | | |
|---|---|---|---|---|---|
| 1. 3 | 6. 4 | 11. 2 | 16. 1 | 21. 4 | 26. 2 |
| 2. 4 | 7. 4 | 12. 1 | 17. 1 | 22. 4 | 27. 1 |
| 3. 2 | 8. 3 | 13. 2 | 18. 3 | 23. 3 | 28. 3 |
| 4. 1 | 9. 1 | 14. 4 | 19. 4 | 24. 4 | 29. 3 |
| 5. 2 | 10. 4 | 15. 3 | 20. 2 | 25. 1 | 30. 2 |

## Classifications

*Classification* problems require essentially the same set of performance components as analogy and series completion problems. Like analogies and series completions, classification problems can come in a variety of forms. One form consists of a set of terms, one of which does not belong with the others. The solver's task is to figure out which term does not belong with the others. For example, in the problem PESO, POUND, DOLLAR, CURRENCY, RUPEE, the word CURRENCY does not fit with the others, because it is a superordinate term with respect to the other terms. A peso, a pound, a dollar, and a rupee are all units of currency. Another form of classification problem consists of a set of terms followed by a set of answer options, for example, LION, DOG, GIRAFFE, FOX, (a) BIRD, (b) WHALE, (c) TUNA, (d) WASP. Here, the task is to figure out which of the answer options belongs with the original set of terms. The best response to this problem is WHALE, because it is the only one among the answer options that, like all the terms originally given, is a mammal.

Another format sometimes used in understanding and solving classification problems is somewhat different from these. This form consists of four sets of two terms each. Preceding the four sets of terms is a single term appearing by itself. The solver's task if to indicate with which of the four sets of two terms the single term should appear. In the example, SECRET (a) VISIBLE, OBVIOUS; (b) HIDDEN, CONCEALED; (c) SILENT, QUIET; (d) LIKELY, PROBABLE, the correct an-

## FIGURE 4-5

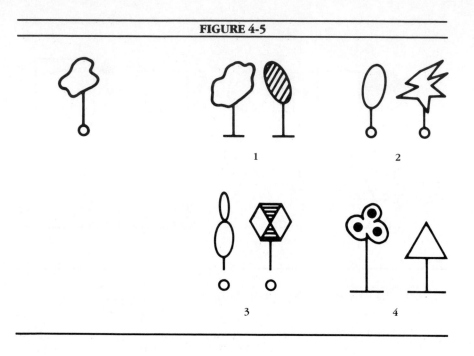

swer is (b). The performance components used to solve such problems are much the same as those used to solve analogies and series completions, although they are applied in a slightly different way. First, you must *encode* the terms. Next, you must *infer* the relation between each of the two terms in each pair. For example, VISIBLE and OBVIOUS both refer to things being easy to see or to understand. HIDDEN and CONCEALED both refer to things being difficult to see or understand. Next, you must *map* the higher-order difference or differences between the pairs of lower-order relations inferred. You need to map these differences because you will use them as the bases for deciding in which of the four categories the single word belongs. Finally, you need to *apply* what you have learned in order to determine in which category the single word belongs. In this case, applying what you have learned leads you to classify SECRET with the second set of terms.

The same performance components apply to figural classification problems. Consider, for example, the classification problem in Figure 4-5. First, you must *encode* the terms of the problem. Next, you must *infer* what is common to each of the pairs of two terms. In this example, what seems to be common is that they have a vertical line extending down from a shape, and an object at the bottom. What differentiates the four sets of figures? Apparently, it is the set of shapes at the top and the objects at the bottom. The differences must be *mapped*. Now look at the single term. It has a shape with a single region at the top and a circle at the bottom. *Application* reveals that it belongs with the second pair of terms (2). Notice that although the content is different, the performance components used to solve the problem are the same as those used with verbal content.

Following are 40 verbal and 30 nonverbal classification problems. Use the performance components of encoding, inference, mapping, and application to solve these problems. In some instances, the single word or picture will not seem to fit particularly well with either the terms at the left or the terms at the right. In these instances, you must use the performance components of *justification* in order to decide which of the four classes of terms provide the best, although not ideal, fit.

## VERBAL CLASSIFICATION PROBLEMS

In each of the following problems, a single word is followed by four pairs of words. Your task is to decide with which of the four pairs of words the single word most appropriately belongs, and then to choose this pair as the correct answer. Answers appear after the problems.

1. MAGAZINE (a) LECTURE, SERMON; (b) BOOK, LETTER; (c) AUTHOR, NOVELIST; (d) WORD, SENTENCE.
2. BLACK (a) GRAY, WHITE; (b) YELLOW, PURPLE; (c) COLOR, CHROMATIC; (d) DARK, OPAQUE.
3. PASTE (a) SCISSORS, KNIFE; (b) ADHESIVE, CONNECTOR; (c) PAPER, CARDBOARD; (d) GLUE, TAPE.
4. CORNEA (a) EYEBROW, EYELASH; (b) PUPIL, IRIS; (c) EYE, EAR; (d) VISION, SIGHT.
5. GOLD (a) DIAMOND, RUBY; (b) SAPPHIRE, TURQUOISE; (c) SILVER, PLATINUM; (d) MONEY, CURRENCY.
6. KNEE (a) LEG, ARM; (b) FINGER, TOE; (c) THIGH, FOREARM; (d) ELBOW, HIP.
7. GOOSE (a) CHICKEN, DUCK; (b) HAWK, CANARY; (c) EGG, OFFSPRING; (d) BIRD, OMNIVORE.
8. TRUNK (a) TABLE, COUNTER; (b) ELEPHANT, SUITCASE; (c) CHEST, CABINET; (d) BREATHING, DRINKING.
9. POLE (a) GOLF BALL, MARBLE; (b) PENCIL, ROD; (c) VAULTER, JUMPER; (d) NORTH, SOUTH.
10. APPLE JUICE (a) LEMONADE, ICED TEA; (b) ROOT BEER, GINGER ALE; (c) WINE, BEER; (d) MACINTOSH, DELICIOUS.
11. FLOUNDER (a) FROG, TOAD; (b) HESITATE, DELIBERATE ON; (c) GOLDFISH, GUPPIE; (d) TROUT, BASS.
12. GREENLAND (a) FRANCE, GERMANY; (b) ITALY, GREECE; (c) CUBA, ENGLAND; (d) ICELAND, GERMANY.
13. SUN (a) DAFFODIL, LEMON; (b) TOMATO, SHERRY; (c) LETTUCE, LIME; (d) NIGHT, LIMOUSINE.
14. LIKELY (a) DEFINITE, CERTAIN; (b) IMPOSSIBLE, UNDOABLE; (c) POSSIBLE, PROBABLE; (d) LIKABLE, FRIENDLY.

15. SMALLPOX (a) CANCER, LEUKEMIA; (b) INFLUENZA, COLD; (c) BOTULISM, PTOMAINE; (d) POLIO, DIPHTHERIA.

16. UNCLE (a) GRANDMOTHER, GRANDSON; (b) FATHER, DAUGHTER; (c) AUNT, NEPHEW; (d) BROTHER, SISTER.

17. SHARK (a) TRUCK, TAXI; (b) FERRY, TUGBOAT; (c) JET, HELICOPTER; (d) SATELLITE, ROCKET SHIP.

18. STREAM (a) LAKE, POND; (b) OCEAN, SEA; (c) RIVER, BROOK; (d) PUDDLE, POOL.

19. CONTRIBUTE (a) DONATE, GIVE; (b) LEASE, SELL; (c) BUY, RENT; (d) INVEST, SPECULATE.

20. ASSAULT (a) THEFT, ARSON; (b) KIDNAPPING, MURDER; (c) PERJURY, CONTEMPT; (d) HANG, ELECTROCUTE.

21. ORANGE (a) PEAR, APPLE; (b) GRAPE, KUMQUAT; (c) CANTALOUPE, HONEYDEW; (d) LEMON, GRAPEFRUIT.

22. FRENCH (a) GERMAN, SWEDISH; (b) RUSSIAN, SERBO-CROATIAN; (c) SPANISH, ITALIAN; (d) LATIN, GREEK.

23. BULL (a) DOE, MARE; (b) CAMEL, HORSE; (c) STALLION, ROOSTER; (d) COW, GOAT.

24. CIRCLE (a) TRIANGLE, SQUARE; (b) SPHERE, PYRAMID; (c) POINT, LINE; (d) ELLIPSE, POLYGON.

25. CABIN (a) MANSION, CASTLE; (b) HUT, BUNGALOW; (c) TENT, WIGWAM; (d) HIVE, NEST.

26. PALMISTRY (a) CHEMISTRY, GEOLOGY; (b) ASTROLOGY, PHRENOLOGY; (c) ALCHEMY, MAGIC; (d) SOCIOLOGY, PSYCHOLOGY.

27. PAUL (a) HERMAN, JEFFREY; (b) ABIGAIL, MARGARET; (c) ROBERT, ALEXANDER; (d) PETER, FRANCIS.

28. ALUMINUM (a) BRASS, PEWTER; (b) URANIUM, RADIUM; (c) LEAD, COPPER; (d) BAUXITE, PYRITE.

29. BACON (a) CHEESE, BUTTER; (b) HAMBURGER, STEAK; (c) PORT, BEEF; (d) FRANKFURTER, SAUSAGE.

30. HIS (a) MY, ITS; (b) OUR, THEIR; (c) YOU, HE; (d) US, THEM.

31. WOULD (a) CAN, WILL; (b) MIGHT, COULD; (c) MAY, SHOULD; (d) WON'T, CAN'T.

32. APRIL (a) TUESDAY, SATURDAY; (b) JANUARY, AUGUST; (c) SPRING, SEASON; (d) JUNE, SEPTEMBER.

33. HUMID (a) HOT, COLD; (b) CLIMATE, WEATHER; (c) DRY, DAMP; (d) WINDY, STILL.

34. STONE (a) BRICK, WOOD; (b) FEATHER, PAPER; (c) ROCK, CAVE; (d) SCULPTURE, MOSAIC.

35. PROTON (a) ELECTRON, NEUTRON; (b) ATOM, MOLECULE; (c) POSITRON, NUCLEON; (d) QUARK, CHARM.

36. DIAMOND (a) RHINESTONE, COAL; (b) PEARL, AMBER; (c) COAL, ANTHRACITE; (d) EMERALD, RUBY.

37. LOBSTER (a) PEANUT BUTTER, FILET MIGNON; (b) TUNA, CAVIAR; (c) CRAB, MUSSEL; (d) THERMIDOR, LANGOSTINO.

38. COW (a) MAN, KANGAROO; (b) ROBIN, BLUEBIRD; (c) CAT, ELEPHANT; (d) WORM, SNAKE.

39. LINOLEUM (a) CARPET, RUG; (b) FLOOR, CEILING; (c) MUG, CUP; (d) ACETATE, VINYL.

40. KING (a) FIREFIGHTER, POLICEMAN; (b) EMPEROR, MONARCH; (c) DUKE, PRINCE; (d) EARL, DUCHESS.

## ANSWERS TO VERBAL CLASSIFICATION PROBLEMS

1.  (b).  A book and a letter, like a magazine, are written forms of communication.
2.  (a).  Gray and white, like black, are achromatic shadings.
3.  (d).  Glue and tape, like paste, are used to fasten things together.
4.  (b).  The pupil and the iris, like the cornea, are parts of the eyeball.
5.  (c).  Silver and platinum, like gold, are precious metals.
6.  (d).  The elbow and the hip, like the knee, are joints.
7.  (a).  A chicken and a duck, like a goose, are forms of poultry.
8.  (c).  A chest and a cabinet, like a trunk, are storage containers.
9.  (b).  A pencil and a rod, like a pole, are basically cylindrical in shape.
10. (a).  Lemonade and iced tea, like apple juice, are noncarbonated beverages.
11. (d).  Trout and bass, like flounder, are kinds of fish.
12. (c).  Cuba and England, like Greenland, are islands.
13. (a).  A daffodil and a lemon, like the sun, are generally yellow in color.
14. (c).  The words *possible* and *probable*, like the word *likely*, are adjectives referring to probability where the probability is neither zero nor one.
15. (d).  Polio and diphtheria, like smallpox, are bacterial infections.
16. (c).  An aunt, a nephew, and an uncle are collateral relatives.
17. (b).  A ferry and a tugboat, like a shark, move in water.
18. (c).  A river and a brook, like a stream, are continuously flowing bodies of water.
19. (a).  To donate and to give, like to contribute, are ways of handing over resources of one kind or another.
20. (b).  Kidnapping and murder, like assault, are crimes against persons.
21. (d).  A lemon and a grapefruit, like an orange, are citrus fruits.
22. (c).  Spanish and Italian, like French, are modern romance languages.
23. (c).  A stallion and a rooster, like a bull, are male animals.
24. (d).  An ellipse and a polygon, like a circle, are completely enclosed continous curves.
25. (b).  A hut and a bungalow, like a cabin, are modest, permanently placed, forms of dwelling.
26. (b).  Astrology and phrenology, like palmistry, are pseudosciences devoted to understanding human beings and their potential futures.
27. (d).  Peter and Francis, like Paul, were saints in certain Christian religions.
28. (c).  Lead and copper, like aluminum, are metals (but not alloys).
29. (d).  A frankfurter and a sausage, like bacon, are usually made from pork.
30. (a).  My and its, like his, are singular possessive adjectives.
31. (b).  *Might* and *could*, like *would*, are auxiliary verbs used to express conditionality.
32. (d).  June and September, like April, are months which each have thirty days.
33. (c).  Dry and damp, like humid, refer to levels of moisture in the air.
34. (a).  Brick and wood, like stone, can be used to construct a house.
35. (a).  An electron and a neutron, like a proton, are basic particles constituting an atom.
36. (d).  An emerald and a ruby, like a diamond, are precious gems.
37. (c).  A crab and a mussel, like a lobster, are shellfish.

38. (c). A cat and an elephant, like a cow, are animals whose locomotion depends on four legs.
39. (a). A carpet and a rug, like linoleum, can be used as surfaces for floors.
40. (b). An emperor and a monarch, like a king, can be male rulers over a kingdom or empire.

---

### FIGURE 4-6

### Figural Classifications

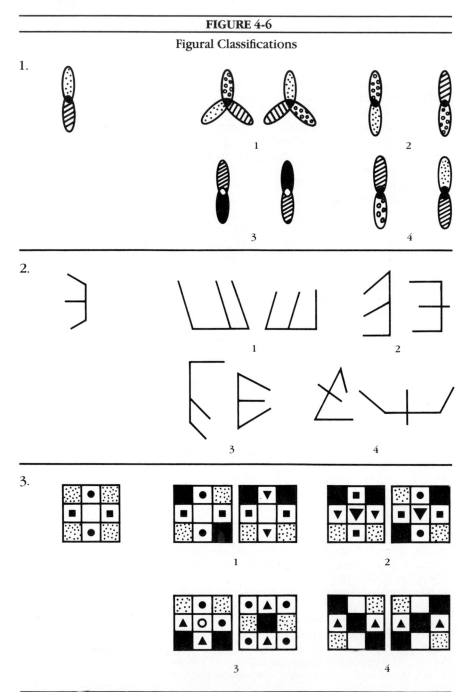

## FIGURE 4-6 continued

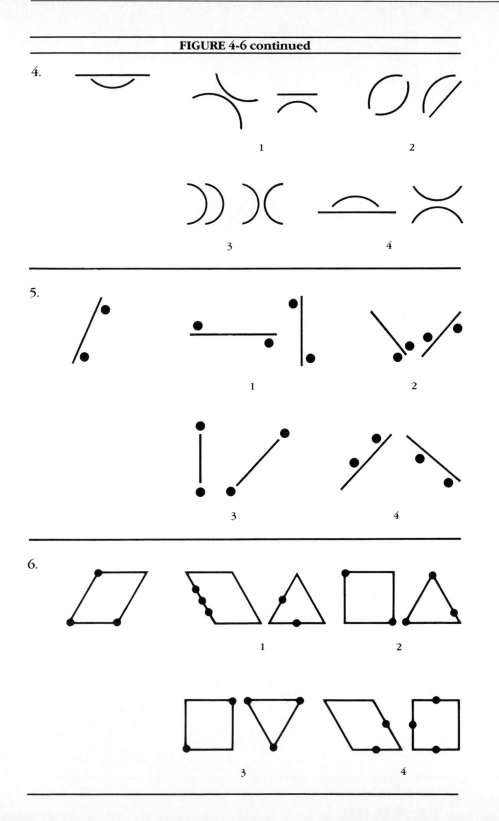

## FIGURE 4-6 continued

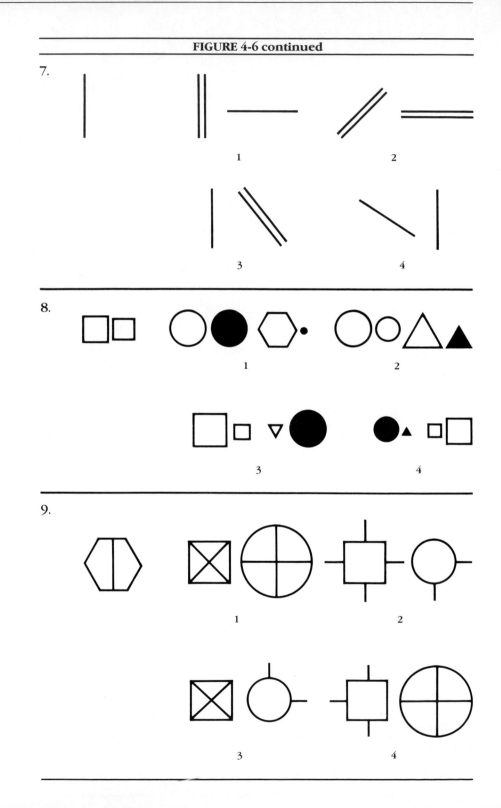

## FIGURE 4-6 continued

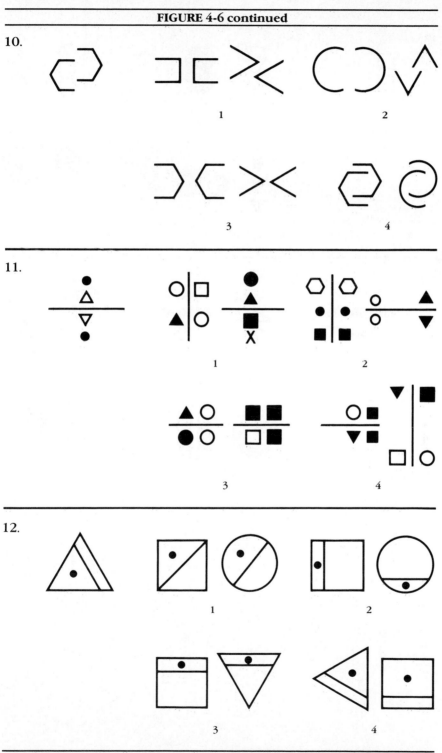

## FIGURE 4-6 continued

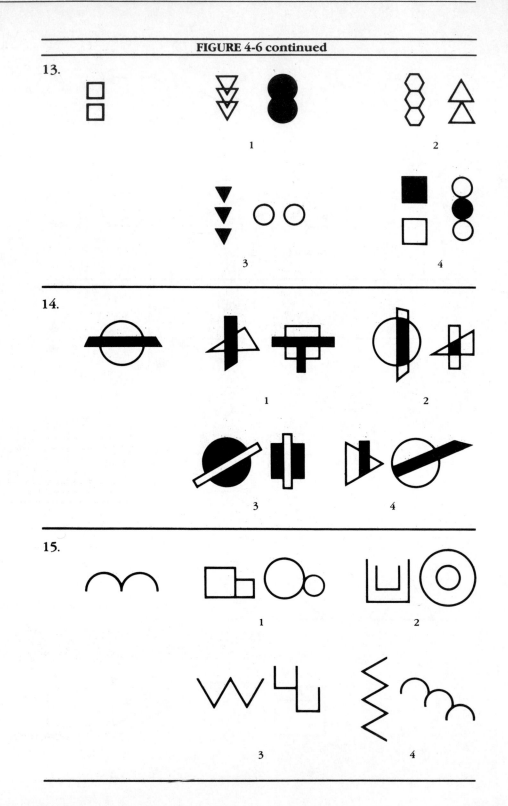

13.

1

2

3

4

14.

1

2

3

4

15.

1

2

3

4

## FIGURE 4-6 continued

16.

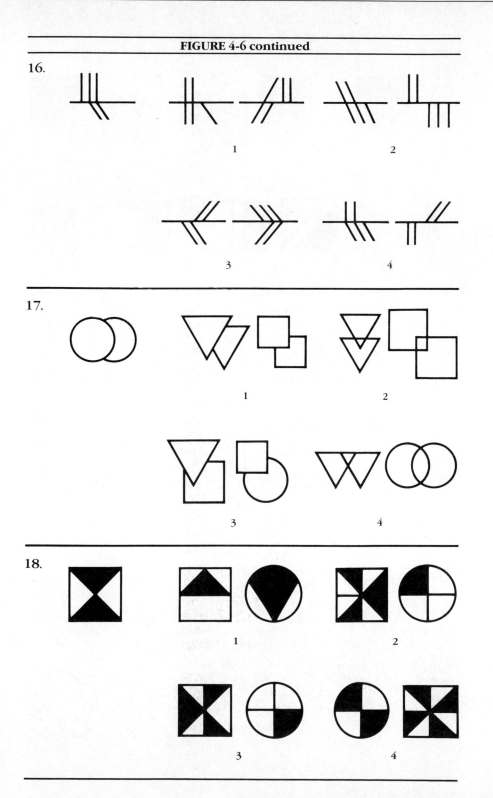

1

2

3

4

17.

1

2

3

4

18.

1

2

3

4

**FIGURE 4-6 continued**

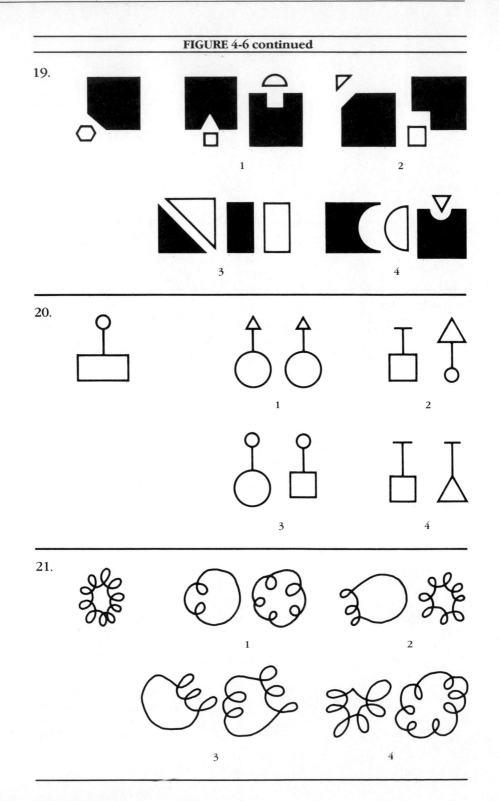

19.

20.

21.

## FIGURE 4-6 continued

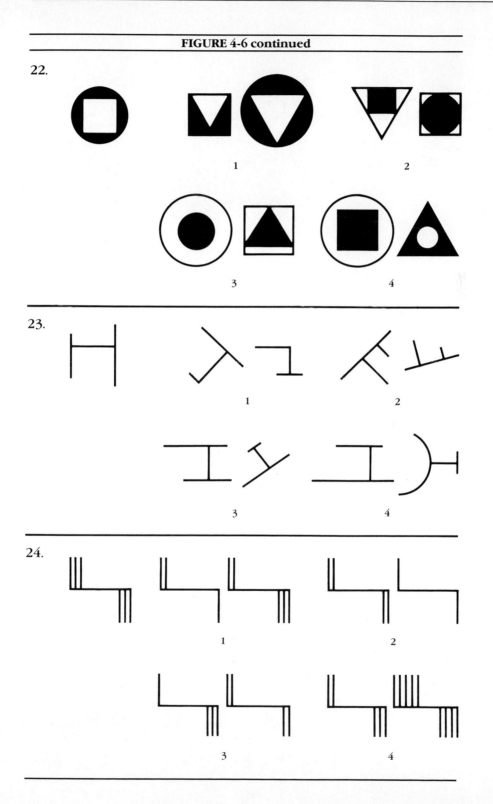

22.

1    2

3    4

23.

1    2

3    4

24.

1    2

3    4

**FIGURE 4-6 continued**

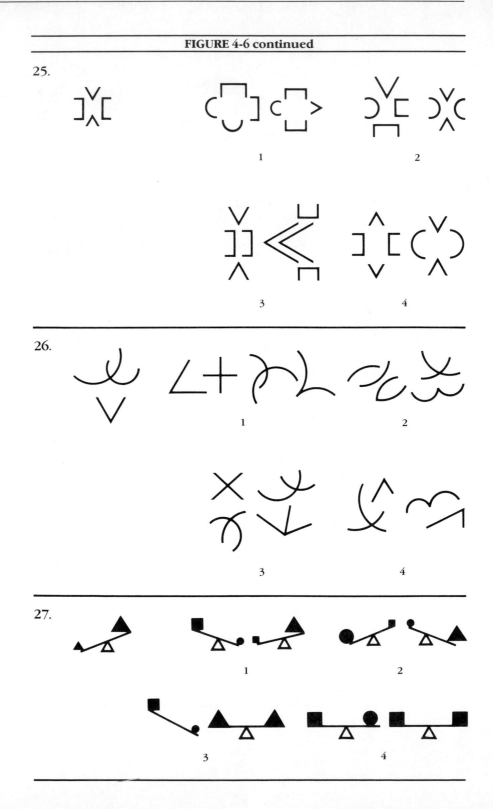

**FIGURE 4-6 continued**

28.

29.

30.

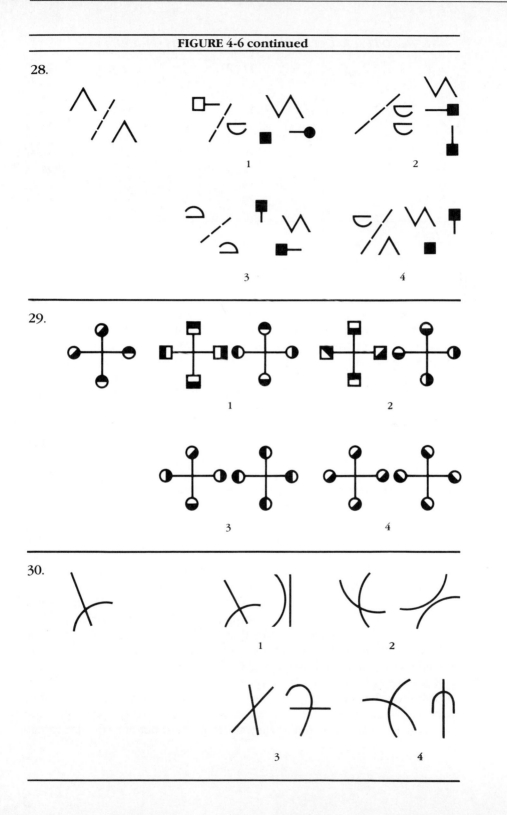

---

### ANSWERS TO FIGURAL CLASSIFICATION PROBLEMS (FIGURE 4-6)

| | | |
|---|---|---|
| 1.  2 | 11.  2 | 21.  2 |
| 2.  3 | 12.  4 | 22.  1 |
| 3.  1 | 13.  3 | 23.  3 |
| 4.  2 | 14.  1 | 24.  2 |
| 5.  4 | 15.  3 | 25.  2 |
| 6.  3 | 16.  4 | 26.  4 |
| 7.  4 | 17.  1 | 27.  1 |
| 8.  4 | 18.  4 | 28.  3 |
| 9.  1 | 19.  1 | 29.  2 |
| 10.  2 | 20.  3 | 30.  1 |

---

### Matrix Problems

Another kind of inductive-reasoning problem that combines elements of analogy, series completion, and classification problems is the *matrix* problem. In a matrix problem, there are typically nine small squares, or cells, embedded in one large square. In each of the small squares is a figural design that is part of several patterns. The patterns go horizontally across the matrix and vertically down the matrix. Usually, one of the cells of the matrix is blank, most typically, the cell at the lower right. The solver's task is to figure out what figural design ought to go in the empty cell in order to finish the various patterns—that is, what figure will complete the horizontal and vertical patterns of which it is a part. Matrix problems are particularly good but often difficult tests of general intelligence: indeed, one of the most famous intelligence tests of all time, the Raven Progressive Matrices, is composed exclusively of matrix problems.

Figure 4-7 contains some sample matrix problems for you to try. The first one is worked out for you. In the first sample problem, only things unique to the two uppermost or leftmost boxes in each column or row are added. Things common to the two boxes are dropped. In column 1, the top and bottom triangles are unique to the two boxes, A and D. (They appear in one box, but not in the other.) So they are added together in G. The right triangle is common in both (A and D) so it is dropped from G. In column 2, the left and right triangles are unique to boxes B and E; therefore, they both appear in box H. In column 3, the top and bottom triangles, as well as the left and right triangles, are unique in boxes C and F; therefore, they appear in I. Does this rule also work in an horizontal direction? Yes. If you take row 1, you will see that the top, left, and right triangles are unique in boxes A and B, so they appear in C. Now try the other rows on your own. In "unique addition," you do not have to add from left to right or from top to bottom; you also can go from right to left and from bottom to top. Do these matrices on your own. Some of them follow the "unique addition" rule; others follow other rules.

Notice that there is a sense in which these problems are two-dimensional series problems. In choosing the correct element for the empty lower-right cell, you need to choose the element that correctly completes each of the horizontal and vertical series simultaneously. Answers to these matrix problems appear after the problems.

---

### FIGURE 4-7

**Sample Problem**              **Matrices**

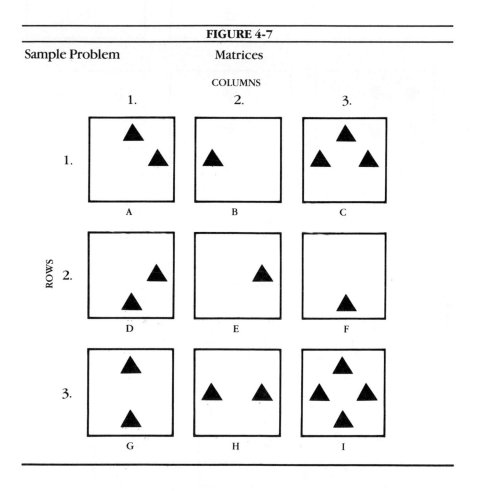

Figure 4-7 continues on next page

## FIGURE 4-7 continued

1.

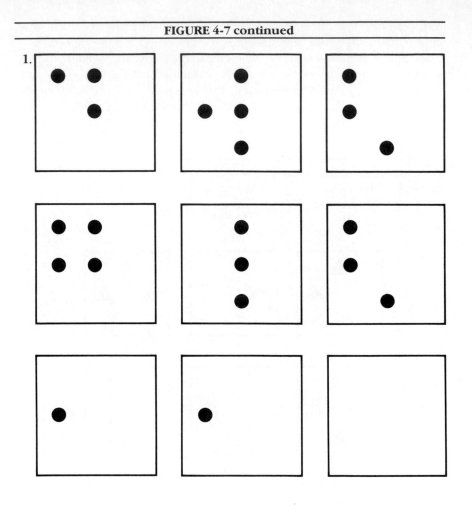

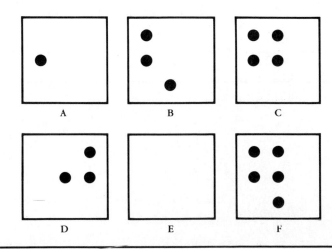

## FIGURE 4-7 continued

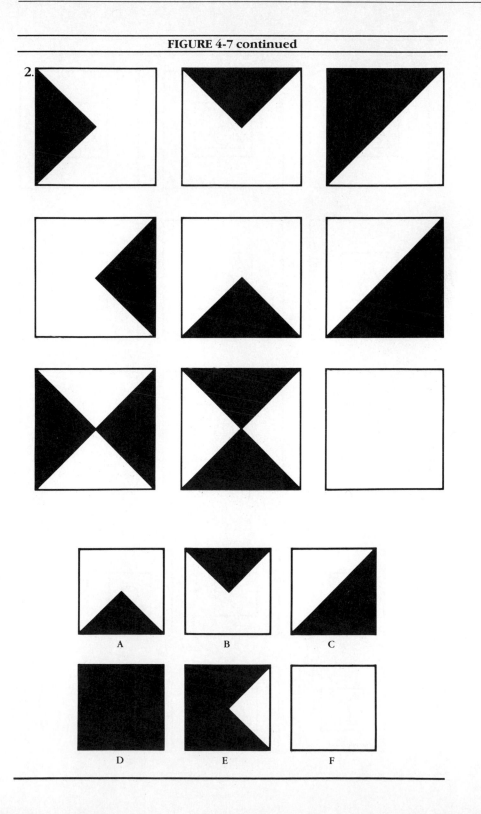

## FIGURE 4-7 continued

3.

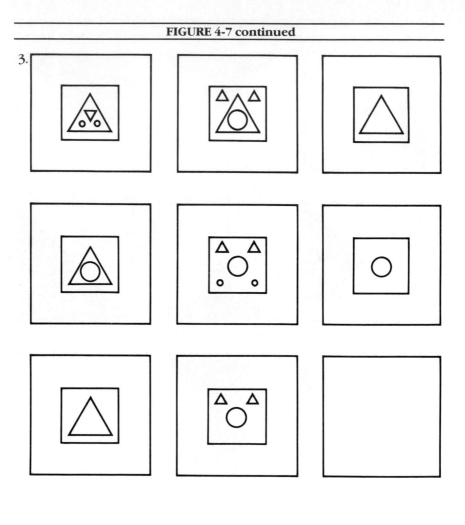

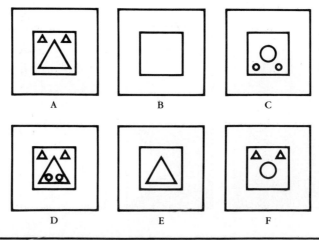

## FIGURE 4-7 continued

4.

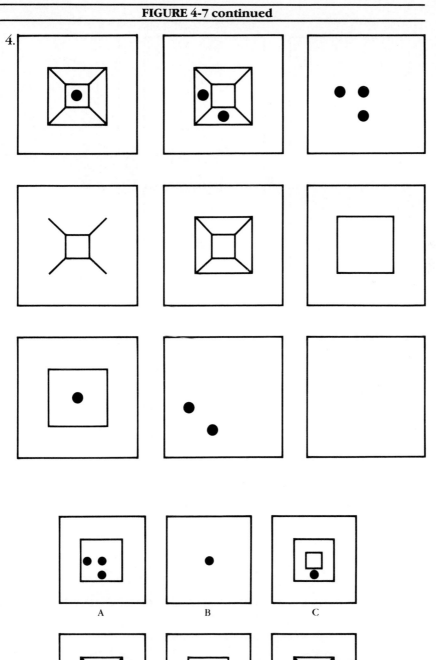

A          B          C

D          E          F

## FIGURE 4-7 continued

5.

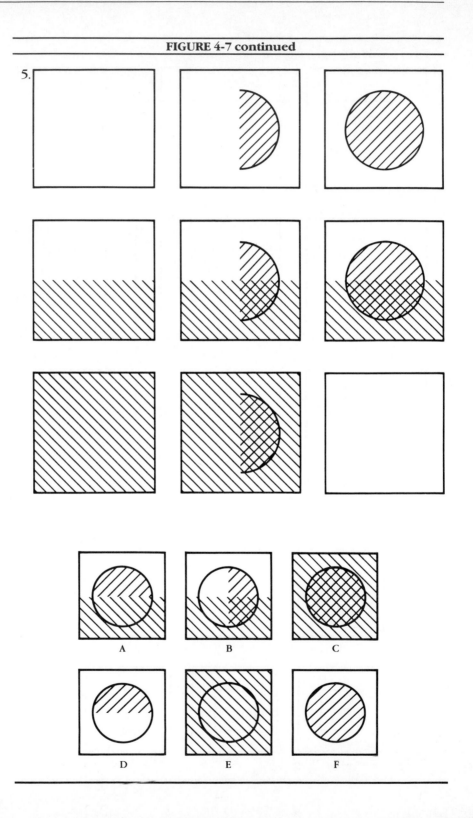

## FIGURE 4-7 continued

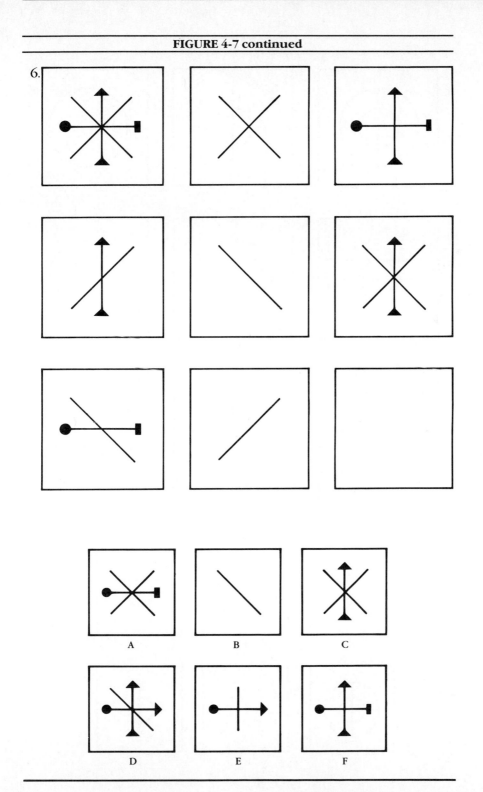

## FIGURE 4-7 continued

7.

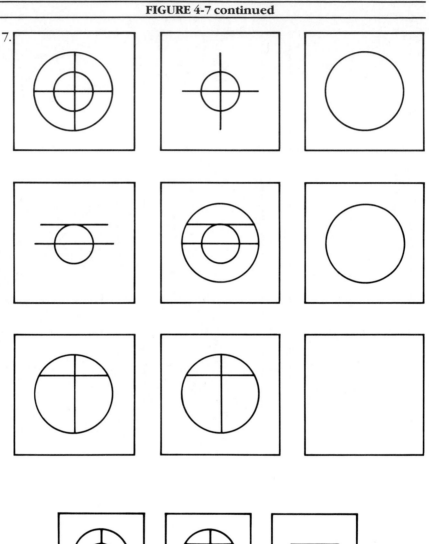

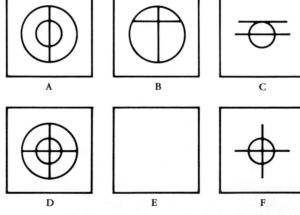

## FIGURE 4-7 continued

8.

## FIGURE 4-7 continued

9.

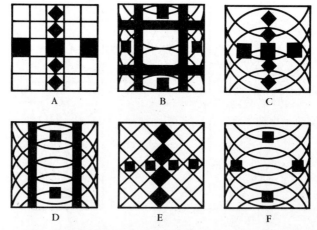

## FIGURE 4-7 continued

10.

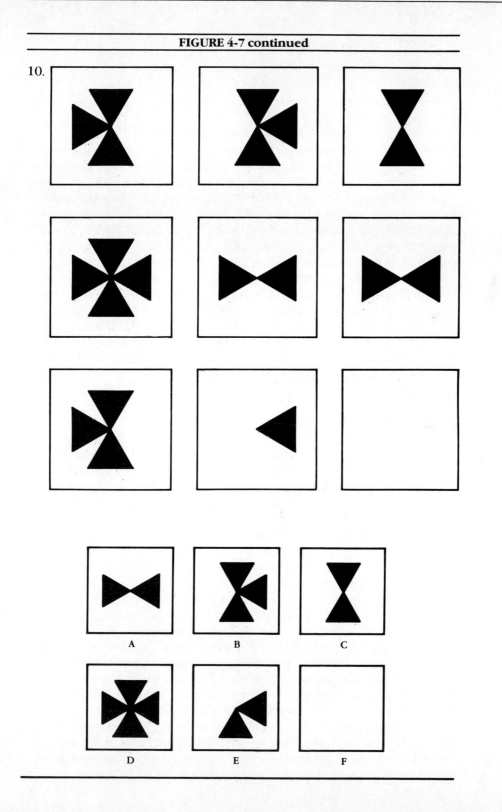

---

### ANSWERS TO MATRIX PROBLEMS (FIGURE 4-7)

| 1. E | 3. B | 5. C | 7. E | 9. C |
|------|------|------|------|------|
| 2. D | 4. A | 6. A | 8. F | 10. F |

---

## Practical Reasoning Problems

The analogy, series completion, classification, and matrix problems described above are among the problem types most frequently found on intelligence tests because such problems have been found to be exceptionally good measures of intelligence, by psychometric standards. In other words, scores on these problems tend to correlate very highly with scores on a variety of kinds of intelligence tests, and with achievement test scores and academic performance. However, these kinds of problems are, in a sense, quite esoteric. Few people encounter straightforward analogy, series completion, classification, or matrix problems in either their everyday personal lives or their occupational settings. Yet, our goal in training intellectual skills is for the skills to generalize beyond esoteric problems to the kinds of reasoning that people need in everyday life. The problems presented in this section give you an opportunity to engage in such generalization. These problems require you to *encode* information, *infer* relations, and *apply* these relations to new situations. The two kinds of problems presented here are legal and clinical reasoning problems.

### LEGAL REASONING PROBLEMS

In legal reasoning, a lawyer, a judge, or a client has to consider, among other things, principles of law and the facts of the case. One of the most difficult problems the legal reasoner confronts is that of figuring out which principles of law are relevant to the case, and which facts of the case have legal implications. For example, thousands of principles of law might be relevant to any given case, and it is often difficult to figure out which particular principles are relevant in a given instance. Moreover, the number of facts relating to a given case can be extremely large, but only a small proportion of these facts have legal consequences. A frustration often faced by participants in legal embroilments is that the facts of the case that are relevant from a legal standpoint are often not those that seem most relevant from a personal standpoint. For example, settlements of lawsuits sometimes hinge on what appear to the plaintiff in the suit to be minor technicalities rather than the major injustices that the plaintiff may believe that he or she has suffered. In the legal reasoning problems presented below, you are asked to engage in legal reasoning, albeit in a simplified form. The principles and cases with which you will be presented are in some respects similar to the kinds of principles and cases that are found on the Law School Admission Test (LSAT).

In each of the cases below, you will be presented with a brief story describing a legal proceeding, followed by some principles of law, some facts extracted from the case, and a choice of two outcomes for the legal proceeding. First, you need to *infer* which principle of law from among those given is most relevant to this particular case. You should indicate which of these principles you have chosen. Second, you need to (selectively) *encode* which fact this principle most directly bears upon. You should again indicate your response. Finally, you need to *apply* the selective principle to the chosen fact in order to decide the outcome of the case. You should again indicate your response, here communicating what you believe to be the correct outcome for this particular case. Although, of course, the reasoning you will be required to do here is a gross simplification of the kind of reasoning lawyers and judges have to do in an actual case, it will give you the flavor of what is required in legal reasoning, and particularly of how the performance components of induction can be applied in a real-world setting.

Below are 10 legal reasoning problems. Read each case carefully; then solve the problems on your own, inferring principles, encoding facts, and applying the principles to the facts so as to obtain a legal outcome for the case. In each problem, choose the one principle and the one fact that are critical to solving the case, and then solve it. Use only the information in each problem. Please keep in mind that the principles given below, as well as the facts of the particular cases, are imaginary, even though the kind of reasoning you need to apply is not. Answers are at the end of the problem set.

*Problem 1.* On May 1, Dillenger Industries sent a letter to Ecolo Engineering offering to buy Ecolo's new anti-smog device. The letter offered to pay Ecolo $200,000 for the rights to the device. It requested that Ecolo submit its acceptance by letter.

Ecolo's president, Harold Koffer, phoned Dillenger on May 3 and indicated interest in discussing the offer further. After some discussion, he said that he intended to reply affirmatively to Dillenger's original offer in a letter of confirmation.

On May 8, Koffer sent a letter of acceptance to Dillenger but requested that Dillenger pay $225,000. When Dillenger received the letter (May 10), he phoned Koffer and asked him to wait a few days so that he could raise the extra money. The next day (May 11), Koffer phoned Dillenger and informed him that he had sold the device to General Filters instead. Dillenger brought suit against Ecolo for breach of contract. Will Dillenger win?

---

**PRINCIPLES**

1.  In order for a contract to be legally enforceable, the services to be performed under the contract must be legal under the law of the place where the contract is to be performed.
2.  In order to form a contract, there must be an offer and an acceptance. Acceptance is an expression of assent to the terms of the offer made by the accepter in a manner requested by the offerer.

**FACTS**

1.  Dillenger made an offer to Ecolo Industries requesting reply by letter.

2. Koffer indicated interest in the offer.
3. Koffer's letter of acceptance changed the terms of Dillenger's original offer.
4. Koffer sold the device to General Filters instead of to Dillenger.

**OUTCOMES**
1. Dillenger will win.
2. Dillenger will lose.

---

*Problem 2.* Captain Taylor was hired under a contract to command an ocean-going ship belonging to Mr. Mayer. The ship was to sail from San Francisco to Manila and back. While in Manila, Taylor had a fight with the first mate, and he resigned his command. A new captain was appointed. However, because the radio had been knocked out in a storm, notice of this change was not communicated to Mayer. Taylor helped the new captain on the trip back to San Francisco. The ship arrived safely. No damages had resulted from the change of command.

When the ship arrived in San Francisco, Mayer learned the above facts. He paid Taylor for his services as captain up to the time he quit, but he refused to pay him for his services in helping get the vessel home. Taylor sued Mayer to recover wages for his services on the return trip. Will Taylor win?

---

**PRINCIPLES**
1. A man is not required to pay for that which he has had no opportunity of rejecting. Under circumstances where there is no opportunity of rejecting, acquiescence cannot be presumed to arise from silence.
2. If one of two parties to a contract breaks the obligation which the contract imposes and the other party is injured owing to the break, then the injured party has the right of action for damages.

**FACTS**
1. Taylor voluntarily resigned his command.
2. Mayer did not learn of Taylor's resignation until the ship arrived home.
3. Taylor helped the new captain on the return trip.
4. The ship arrived safely in San Francisco.

**OUTCOMES**
1. Taylor will win.
2. Taylor will lose.

---

*Problem 3.* Harris Co. was a U.S. department store, and Ross-Jones Co. was an English manufacturing firm. The two firms entered into a written agreement spelling out in detail arrangements for carrying out their business with each other. Under the agreement, the English firm was to accept as binding or reject as not binding orders from Harris Co. promptly following receipt of each order, and was to make deliveries during the following six-month period. The agreement also stated that "this memo is not written as a formal or legal agreement and shall not be subject to legal jurisdiction in the law courts of either the United States or England."

A dispute arose between the parties, and the English firm terminated the agreement without giving reasonable notice. They refused to deliver certain orders then outstanding that they had already accepted. Harris Co. sued Ross-Jones Co. to recover damages from the nondelivery of goods that were to have been delivered during the following six-month period. Will Harris Co. win?

## PRINCIPLES

1. A written agreement is not a legally binding contract unless both parties intended to enter into legal obligations and communicated these intentions to each other.
2. Orders accepted under a written agreement become legally binding contracts upon acceptance.

## FACTS

1. Harris Co. and Ross-Jones Co. entered into a written agreement.
2. The parties did not intend for the agreement to be a legal contract.
3. Ross-Jones Co. terminated the agreement without giving reasonable notice.
4. Ross-Jones Co. refused to deliver orders which they had accepted as binding according to the written agreement.

## OUTCOMES

1. Harris Co. will win.
2. Harris Co. will lose.

*Problem 4.* Mrs. Brown wanted to buy two vacation houses at a beach resort. She intended to use one for her family and to give the second to her married son and his family.

Mrs. Brown found a suitable house for her own family and signed a written binder with the owner, Mr. James, to purchase the house. Under the binder, Mrs. Brown agreed to take title within 30 days, at which time she would pay the balance of the $15,000 price. She paid $2,000 in signing the binder, leaving a balance of $13,000. She also agreed to sign a full-length contract-of-purchase within 90 days. A copy of the contract with all the essential terms of their agreement clearly stated therein was attached to the binder.

Mrs. Brown found another house suitable for her son about one block from the James house. This house was owned by Mrs. Hanks. She signed a binder which stated that the parties contemplated a sale of the Hanks property to Mrs. Brown "subject to the terms of a contract being arranged." Mrs. Brown paid $10 to Mrs. Hanks for signing the binder. The parties did not begin to arrange the contract at this meeting.

A few days later it developed that Mr. James was anxious to complete the sale of his home to Mrs. Brown, but Mrs. Hanks was not willing to sell her property at a reasonable price. Mrs. Brown took legal action against Mrs. Hanks to force her to sell her property in accordance with their binder. Will Mrs. Brown win?

---

**PRINCIPLES**

1. An acceptance of an offer by signing a binder with an attached copy of the contract containing all the essential terms of the agreement constitutes a complete, enforceable contract.
2. An agreement to try to arrange terms for a contract is merely an expression of willingness to negotiate and is not an enforceable contract.

**FACTS**

1. Mrs. Brown signed a binder with Mr. James to purchase his house.
2. The binder for the James house included a copy of the contract.
3. Mrs. Brown signed a binder with Mrs. Hanks to purchase her house.
4. The binder for the Hanks house stated that the parties contemplated a sale of the Hanks property to Mrs. Brown subject to the terms of a contract to be arranged later.

**OUTCOMES**

1. Mrs. Brown will win.
2. Mrs. Brown will lose.

---

*Problem 5.* The manager of ABC Jewelry Co. suspected one of his employees, Miss Jones, of taking a valuable ring from the display case. On the night of June 24, the manager sent one of his friends, who was experienced in the repossession of merchandise, to Miss Jones's apartment. He knocked on the door, and when she opened it he said, "I want you." In the room the repossessor demanded the ring, but on discovering that the ring Miss Jones was carrying in her pocketbook was not the missing ring, he left.

On June 25th, the manager called Miss Jones into his office. Behind closed doors, the manager and a private detective charged her with theft and threatened to send her to jail if she did not sign a statement admitting the theft. Miss Jones said she was quitting the firm and asked permission to make a telephone call. The request to use the phone was denied, and she was subjected to continued restraint and high-pressure questioning.

Miss Jones later sued the repossessor and the ABC Jewelry Co. for damages resulting from false imprisonment in her apartment on the night of June 24. Will Miss Jones win?

## PRINCIPLES

1. Force and threats used to restrain freedom of action and to keep a person in a place against his or her will constitute false imprisonment, and a person so restrained can recover damages.
2. Although inquiry after stolen property may affect a suspect unpleasantly, as long as the subject's freedom of action is in no way restrained, such inquiry does not constitute false imprisonment.

## FACTS

1. On the night of June 24, the repossessor knocked on Miss Jones's door and demanded the ring, saying "I want you."
2. The repossessor did not restrain Miss Jones in her apartment against her will.
3. On June 25th, the manager restrained Miss Jones in his office while questioning her.
4. The manager did not permit Miss Jones to make a phone call.

## OUTCOMES

1. Miss Jones will win.
2. Miss Jones will lose.

*Problem 6.* Mr. Peters owned an apartment building near the county airport. Some airplanes flew over the building at low altitudes, while others flew over at higher altitudes. One day Mr. Peters erected a tall television antenna on top of his building. A low-flying plane owned by Air Mideast hit the antenna with its wingtip, causing some damage to both the plane and the antenna.

Mr. Peters brought suit against Air Mideast for the damage to his property. Will Mr. Peters win?

## PRINCIPLES

1. A landowner who in no way contributes to the injury of an uninvited trespasser is not liable to that trespasser.
2. The owner of land has the exclusive right to as much of the space above it as may be actually occupied and used by him and necessarily incident to such occupation and use, and anyone passing through such space without the owner's consent is a trespasser. The owner may recover damages for such trespass.

## FACTS

1. Mr. Peters erected a television antenna on top of the apartment building that he owned, and a plane hit the antenna.

2. Airplanes had previously flown in the area occupied by the antenna.
3. The antenna was very tall.
4. The plane was damaged when it hit the antenna.

**OUTCOMES**
1. Mr. Peters will win.
2. Mr. Peters will lose.

---

*Problem 7.* Mr. Yankin agreed to sell Mr. Wheeler "100 eggs for $50." He intended 100 dozen, while Mr. Wheeler intended 100 crates. Later, Mr. Yankin agreed to sell Mr. Wheeler butter at 30 cents per pound, but Mr. Yankin really meant to say 40 cents per pound.

On delivering the 100 dozen eggs, Yankin found that Wheeler expected 100 crates of eggs. Yankin got mad and refused to sell any eggs at all to Wheeler. Wheeler sued Yankin to force him to sell 100 crates of eggs for $50. Will Wheeler win?

---

**PRINCIPLES**
1. Parties to an agreement are bound by what each states and not what each means.
2. Mutual mistakes by both parties to an agreement regarding quantity might or would prevent a meeting of the minds, and without a meeting of the minds there is no legally enforceable obligation.

**FACTS**
1. Yankin and Wheeler agreed on a contract for eggs.
2. Yankin and Wheeler had different interpretations of the quantity of eggs to be sold.
3. Yankin agreed to sell Wheeler butter at a certain price.
4. Yankin meant to sell the butter at a different price.

**OUTCOMES**
1. Wheeler will win.
2. Wheeler will lose.

---

*Problem 8.* Mr. Watson and Mr. Parson signed articles of co-partnership under which each was to receive 50 percent of the profits for the total operations of the partnership. It was further specified that Watson would have primary direction of the warehouse and that Parson would have primary direction of the shoreline installations. At the time of making the written agreement, there was some talk about Watson's receiving 60 percent of the profit and Parson 40 percent because Watson had superior experience. Later, Watson sued Parson to secure 60 percent of the profits. Will Watson win?

**PRINCIPLES**

1. A written instrument cannot be changed by oral evidence because written agreements are more definite than oral ones and the usefulness of written instruments cannot be impaired by such oral contradiction.
2. Oral evidence can be introduced in a trial to explain ambiguities and technical terms so that the written agreement may be enforced as intended by the parties when the agreement was made.

**FACTS**

1. According to the written agreement, Watson and Parson were each to receive 50 percent of the profits.
2. According to the written agreement, Watson would have primary direction of the warehouse.
3. According to the written agreement, Parson would have primary direction of the shoreline installations.
4. Watson had more experience than Parson.

**OUTCOMES**

1. Watson will win.
2. Watson will lose.

---

*Problem 9.* Smith, an art dealer, sold a valuable oil painting to Johnson. Johnson had no way to get the painting home at that time, and so told Smith to leave the painting on the wall of the store. He said that he would pick it up that evening.

Two hours later Nielson entered Smith's shop and a clerk sold the same painting to Nielson without realizing that Smith had previously sold it to Johnson. Johnson returned that evening and found the painting missing. He sued Nielson to recover the painting. Will Johnson win?

---

**PRINCIPLES**

1. If a seller of goods retains possession following the initial sale to one party, and later he or his agent sells the goods to a second party, then the seller shall be liable for damages to the wronged first purchaser.
2. If a buyer temporarily leaves goods he buys in the seller's possession and the seller or his agent resells these goods to an innocent subsequent purchaser, the subsequent purchaser who has possession of the goods has the better claim of title.

**FACTS**

1. The painting in question was valuable and irreplaceable.
2. Smith sold the painting to Johnson.
3. Johnson had no means of getting the painting home at the time he bought it.
4. Johnson left the painting in Smith's store, and a clerk unknowingly sold it to Nielson.

**OUTCOMES**
1.  Johnson will win.
2.  Johnson will lose.

---

*Problem 10.* Mr. Padd brought some new ballpoint pens to his wealthy friend Mr. Crass, with a pad of "blank" paper on which to test the pens. Unknown to Crass, Padd had prepared two negotiable promissory notes on two of the pages of the writing pad in such a way as not to be readily noticeable. Crass told Padd he would appreciate a gift of a couple of the pens, and Padd asked Crass to try the pens on the pad of "blank" paper to be sure they worked well. Padd flipped the pages for Crass to test the pen, but Padd was careful to conceal the two pages containing the promissory notes so that Crass could see only the blank bottom portions when he signed his name. Padd kept one of the notes for $100 and sold the other to Mr. Crown, who did not know of the deception. Crown presented the note to Crass, and Crass refused to pay. Crown sued Crass to recover the amount of the note. Will Crown win?

---

**PRINCIPLES**
1.  A person who acquires a negotiable note in good faith may recover the amount thereof from the maker.
2.  A person who has been guilty of fraud and deception in having a maker execute a negotiable note cannot recover on it from the maker.

**FACTS**
1.  Padd fraudulently had Crass sign two promissory notes.
2.  Padd kept one note.
3.  Padd sold the other note to Crown.
4.  Crown did not know of Padd's deception when he bought the note.

**OUTCOMES**
1.  Crown will win.
2.  Crown will lose.

---

*ANSWERS TO LEGAL REASONING PROBLEMS*

| Principles | Facts | Outcomes |
|---|---|---|
| 1. 2 | 3 | 2 |
| 2. 1 | 2 | 2 |
| 3. 2 | 4 | 1 |
| 4. 2 | 4 | 2 |
| 5. 2 | 2 | 2 |
| 6. 2 | 1 | 1 |

| | | |
|---|---|---|
| 7. 2 | 2 | 2 |
| 8. 1 | 1 | 2 |
| 9. 2 | 4 | 2 |
| 10. 1 | 4 | 1 |

## CLINICAL REASONING PROBLEMS

People often think of lawyers and doctors as being similar in little other than their professional status and income. However, there are striking similarities in the kinds of reasoning they need to do on the job. Medical diagnosis problems are in many respects similar to legal reasoning problems. The problems presented below will require you to make clinical inferences for a test that is often used in psychiatric diagnosis, the Rorschach Inkblots Test. Though the principles given below, as well as the facts of the particular cases, are imaginary, the kind of reasoning you need to apply is not.

In each hypothetical case, you will receive a protocol of a patient (that is, the patient's response to the presentation of an inkblot, where the patient's task is to describe what he or she sees in the inkblot). You will also be presented with some principles of interpretation for the Rorschach test, some facts summarized from the entire protocol, and some alternative diagnoses. Your task will be first to *infer* which principle is most relevant for making a clinical diagnosis in this case, second, to (selectively) *encode* the fact to which this principle most directly applies, and third, to *apply* the principle to the fragment in order to select the correct diagnosis. In reality, of course, a clinician would not make a diagnosis based on the application of a principle of test scoring to a single response. As with the above legal reasoning problems, this task represents a gross simplification of the reasoning in which professionals must engage. Nevertheless, it gives you some idea of the kind of reasoning in which clinicians must engage when making their clinical diagnoses. Note that the structure of these problems is parallel to the structure of the legal reasoning problems. As noted above, for all the difference in contents, the inductive reasoning processes required for clinical diagnosis are quite similar to those required for legal reasoning.

Below are 10 clinical diagnosis problems. Choose the relevant principle and the relevant fact, and then make your diagnosis. Solutions to the problems appear after the problems. To repeat: *All principles and responses are imaginary.*

*Problem 1.* "Well I see the whole blot as a big bat. It has two antennae, and it's flapping its wings. I guess it uses its radar to fly around. Oh, now it looks like the bat is turning into something else. Yes, I see two angels, one on each side of the card. They have big wings. And in the middle there's a woman. She has her hands up. There's those little blobs that look like hands at the top. She's raising her hands up to Heaven, you see, because the angels are taking her to Heaven." *Diagnose:* High intelligence or not.

**PRINCIPLES**

1. Responses in which adjacent areas of the blot are combined in a meaningful way indicate high intelligence.
2. When a subject gives two or more responses that are vague or lacking in detail, low intelligence is indicated.

**FACTS**

1. The subject gives two responses to the card.
2. The first response is a bat.
3. The second response is two angels and a woman.
4. The angels are carrying the woman to Heaven.

**OUTCOMES**

1. The subject has high intelligence.
2. The subject does not have high intelligence.

*Problem 2.* "I see a demon. Oh, there are his eyes (pointing to the triangular white areas). I think he's staring at me. . . . There is his nose (pointing to the pointed black area at the bottom), and his two pointed ears at the sides. . . . That demon looks really mean. He looks ready to strike. His fangs are out. His nose is smelling out the enemy." *Diagnose:* Paranoid or not.

**PRINCIPLES**

1. When the subject treats the card as having personal content, paranoia is indicated.
2. When the subject sees aggressive movement taking place, paranoia is counterindicated.

**FACTS**

1. The demon is staring at the subject.
2. The demon has triangular white eyes.
3. The demon is ready to strike.
4. The demon is mean.

**OUTCOMES**

1. The subject is paranoid.
2. The subject is not paranoid.

*Problem 3.* "It's a bat . . . No it's not; it turned into a cockroach. In the middle of the card, there's the cockroach. That cockroach is really dirty, like the ones crawling around my sink at home. Wait, now it became a butterfly. Yes, I know what it is—it's a butterfly. The bat metamorphosed into a butterfly because the cockroach bit him. That cockroach is really mean and dirty." *Diagnose:* Brain damage or not.

### PRINCIPLES
1. Shifting responses coupled with inability to recall previous responses indicate brain damage.
2. Illogical use of cause and effect relationships counterindicates brain damage.

### FACTS
1. The subject sees three different animals in the card.
2. Each animal is seen to be turning into the next one.
3. The bat changed into a butterfly because the cockroach bit it.
4. The cockroach is dirty.

### OUTCOMES
1. The subject has no brain damage.
2. The subject has brain damage.

*Problem 4.* "It's an angel—looks like he's conducting an orchestra or something. But he doesn't have a head. Those two pincer-like things at the top, those are the hands conducting. And you can see the wings out at the sides. The part in the middle is the body, and down there are his feet." *Diagnose:* High intelligence or not.

### PRINCIPLES
1. A response that uses all parts of the blot indicates high intelligence.
2. A response that includes movement over a large area of the blot indicates low intelligence.

### FACTS
1. The angel's body is in the middle of the card, its wings are at the sides, and its hands are at the top.
2. The angel is moving its hands.
3. The angel lacks a head.
4. The angel is male.

### OUTCOMES
1. The subject has high intelligence.
2. The subject has low intelligence.

*Problem 5.* "It's two witches with big black cloaks. It must be Halloween. They're dancing around, and their cloaks are blowing in the breeze. It's Halloween night. They each have a rabbit. The rabbits are just sitting there in midair." *Diagnose:* Introverted or not.

---

**PRINCIPLES**
1. When both human and animal figures are seen, but only the animals are moving, introversion is indicated.
2. If the subject locates the scene he or she sees in the blot in a specific time or place, introversion is counterindicated.

**FACTS**
1. The subject sees human and animal figures.
2. The rabbits are floating in the air.
3. The witches are dancing.
4. It is Halloween night.

**OUTCOMES**
1. The subject is introverted.
2. The subject is not introverted.

---

*Problem 6.* "Well, at the top there's the two black clouds. And the pointed thing is a rocket. It seems to be shooting up into the clouds. And in the middle there's a big white hole. There's some black dirt all around the hole." *Diagnose:* Impulsive or not.

---

**PRINCIPLES**
1. Use of enclosed white areas indicates lack of impulsiveness.
2. Use of color terms indicates impulsiveness.

**FACTS**
1. The two blobs at the top are black clouds.
2. The pointed shape near the top is a rocket.
3. The white area in the middle is a hole.
4. The black circular area is dirt.

**OUTCOMES**
1. The subject is impulsive.
2. The subject is not impulsive.

---

*Problem 7.* "It's a fur muff. In the middle is where you put your hands. I think it's made out of lamb's fur . . . it looks white and fluffy. My sister has a muff like that. But what are those two blobs at the top? That might be the ends of her scarf dangling down. She has a pretty scarf that goes with her muff." *Diagnose:* Suicidal tendencies or not.

**PRINCIPLES**
1. Suicidal tendencies are present if and only if texture and dark colors are used in combination.
2. If the subject uses texture on one side of the blot only, suicidal tendencies are indicated.

**FACTS**
1. The subject sees the muff.
2. The muff is white and fluffy.
3. The muff is like the subject's sister's.
4. The muff is made of lamb's fur.

**OUTCOMES**
1. The subject has suicidal tendencies.
2. The subject does not have suicidal tendencies.

---

*Problem 8.* "Hmm . . . I don't know what this card is supposed to be. Oh yes, in the middle, the pointed thing is a carrot. Actually, it's two carrots next to each other. I can't see anything else. Oh . . . I do see a stomach. Yes, there's a big hole where all the stomach is digesting the carrot." *Diagnose:* Compulsive or not.

**PRINCIPLES**
1. Hesitation in responding indicates compulsiveness.
2. Anatomical content in the initial response indicates compulsiveness.

**FACTS**
1. The subject first sees two carrots.
2. The subject then sees a stomach.
3. The subject pauses frequently in responding.
4. The subject attempts to integrate the two responses.

**OUTCOMES**
1. The subject is compulsive.
2. The subject is not compulsive.

---

*Problem 9.* "It's some clouds in the sky. They look like storm clouds; they're big black clouds. I see the drops of rain coming down at the bottom.

Oh, now I see something else. It's two people facing each other. They seem to be sitting down. It looks like they're playing patty-cake with each other. See, they're holding their hands up." *Diagnose:* Psychopathic or not.

---

**PRINCIPLES**
1. If intact human bodies are seen, psychopathy is not present.
2. If humans are perceived as performing actions not usually performed by humans, psychopathy is indicated.

**FACTS**
1. The subject sees two different things in the blot.
2. The first response is clouds.
3. The second response is two people.
4. The people are playing patty-cake.

**OUTCOMES**
1. The subject is not psychopathic.
2. The subject is psychopathic.

---

*Problem 10.* "It's two magicians facing each other. They have just made a bow tie appear, and it's floating in the air between them. On the sides I see two rabbits. The magicians made the rabbits appear just a while ago, and they're floating in the air, too. Now the magicians are leaning toward each other and are pulling open a hat or something. I think something might come out of the hat." *Diagnose:* Schizophrenic or not.

---

**PRINCIPLES**
1. If the figures on either side of the blot are in a helping relationship, schizophrenia is not present.
2. If animate beings are seen to be falling, schizophrenia is indicated.

**FACTS**
1. The magicians are both pulling open a hat.
2. The magicians have produced a bow tie and two rabbits.
3. The bow tie and rabbits are floating in the air.
4. The magicians are facing each other.

**OUTCOMES**
1. The subject is not schizophrenic.
2. The subject is schizophrenic.

## ANSWERS TO CLINICAL REASONING PROBLEMS

| Principles | Facts | Outcomes |
| --- | --- | --- |
| 1.  1 | 4 | 1 |
| 2.  1 | 1 | 1 |
| 3.  2 | 3 | 1 |
| 4.  1 | 1 | 1 |
| 5.  2 | 4 | 2 |
| 6.  1 | 3 | 2 |
| 7.  1 | 2 | 2 |
| 8.  1 | 3 | 1 |
| 9.  1 | 3 | 1 |
| 10.  1 | 1 | 1 |

# 5

# Knowledge-Acquisition Components

It is often said that the chief thing separating humankind from other animal life is our ability to learn and use language. By any standard, this ability is impressive. With only minor flaws, we regularly use a grammatical system that to this day linguists and psychologists do not fully understand. We apply this grammatical system to vocabularies that, for adults, are usually estimated to exceed 50,000 words; for educated adults, they may exceed 70,000 or 80,000 words. The prodigious size of people's vocabularies becomes even more amazing when we consider that only a very small proportion of these words were ever directly taught. In our early school years, we are probably more likely to have formal instruction in spelling than in vocabulary, and the vocabulary that is directly taught is apt to be the vocabulary that is most likely to be forgotten. However we acquire the tens of thousands of words in our vocabulary, it is clearly not primarily on the basis of direct instruction.

The skills we use to acquire our vocabularies would seem to be critical as building blocks of our intelligence. Psychologists have found vocabulary to be one of the best single indicators, if not the very best indicator, of a person's overall level of intelligence. The importance of vocabulary to the measurement of intelligence is shown by the fact that the two major individual scales of intelligence—the Stanford-Binet and the Wechsler—each contain vocabulary items as a centerpiece, and by the fact that many group-administered tests of intelligence also contain vocabulary items. Clearly, if people wish to understand and increase their intelligence, then they would want to understand the bases for vocabulary acquisition and then work on improving their vocabulary-acquisition skills.

The thesis advanced here, and one believed by many other psychologists as well, is that people learn the meanings of most words as they encounter the words *in context*. In many instances, people may not even be fully aware of acquiring the new words' meanings. Suppose, for example, you were reading a book or a magazine, and encountered a word that you either did not know or were only vaguely familiar with. At this point, you might consult a dictionary, but it is at least as likely that a dictionary would not be readily accessible, or that you would be too lazy or busy to go about finding one. In such instances, you might endeavor to figure out the meaning of the word through the use of the context surrounding the word. Quite often, the surrounding context provides a wealth of information about the word in question. This chapter will focus on developing your skills in finding and using such contextual information.

In order to improve your verbal decontextualization ability, you need to improve three kinds of skills: (a) learning the processes that govern the activities required to figure out the meanings of unknown words, (b) learning the kinds of information (or cues) to which these processes apply, and (c) learning the variables that make the task of word decontextualization more or less difficult. Let us turn now to each of these three kinds of skills.

## The Processes of Knowledge Acquisition

In learning the meanings of new words embedded in context, the reader has to separate helpful and relevant information in context from extraneous material that is irrelevant to or may actually get in the way of learning the words' meanings. Moreover, the reader must combine the selected information into a meaningful whole, using past information about the nature of words as a guide. Deciding what things would be useful for defining a new word and deciding what to do with these useful things once they are isolated are processes that are guided by the use of old information. The reader constantly seeks to connect the context of the unknown word to something with which he or she is familiar. Thus, we see that processing the available information requires three distinct operations: (a) locating relevant information in context, (b) combining this information into a meaningful whole, and (c) interrelating this information to what the reader already knows. These processes will be referred to from now on as selective encoding, selective combination, and selective comparison, respectively.

### Selective Encoding

*Selective encoding* involves sifting out relevant from irrelevant information. When you encounter an unfamiliar word in context, cues relevant to deciphering its meaning are embedded within large amounts of unhelpful or possibly even misleading information. You must separate the wheat from the chaff by sifting out the relevant cues. Most readers selectively encode information without even being aware that they are doing it. By becoming more aware of this process, you are in a better position to improve your use of it.

When you encounter an unfamiliar word, imagine the word to be the center of a network of information. In the sentence where the unknown word occurs, seek out cues concerning its meaning. Then expand your systematic search, checking the sentences surrounding the sentence containing the unknown word.

Consider the brief passage in Box 5-1.* Even in this rather obvious example, there is much information to weed out. For instance, in order to figure out the meaning of the word *macropodida*, we need not know that the man in the passage was on a business trip, that he was tired, or that he squinted in the bright sunlight. Although such information may be quite relevant to the story as a whole, it is entirely irrelevant to our purpose of figuring out the meaning of the unknown word.

---

**BOX 5-1**

He first saw a *macropodida* during a trip to Australia. He had just arrived from a business trip to India, and he was exhausted. Looking out at the plain, he saw a *macropodida* hop across it. It was a typical marsupial. While he watched, the animal pranced to and fro, intermittently stopping to chew on the surrounding plants. Squinting because of the bright sunlight, he noticed a young *macropodida* securely fastened in an opening in front of the mother.

---

In the first sentence, there are two important cues: (1) the man *saw* a macropodida, so macropodidae must be visually perceptible, and (2) the man saw the macropodida in Australia, so that macropodidae must be found in that continent. As we have seen, the second sentence does not contain any information relevant to the unknown word. The next sentence informs us that macropodidae hop and can be found on plains. In the fourth sentence, we learned that a macropodida is a marsupial, and in the fifth sentence, we find out something about what macropodidae eat. Finally, the last sentence informs us that mother macropodidae carry their young in openings on their front sides.

Normally, readers would not selectively encode all of the available information before proceeding to combine and compare the relevant facts. Usually, readers will shift from one process to another as they proceed through the paragraph. The listing of relevant data above is merely an attempt to show you the kinds of information that can be selectively encoded.

Box 5-2 contains a passage with a relatively low-frequency word embedded within it. Read the passage, and underline all portions of the text that seem to you to be relevant to figuring out the meaning of *sommelier*, the unknown word. Try to be conscious of how each underlined item relates to the target word. Then try to define sommelier before reading on.

As you may have noticed, there are many helpful pieces of information relating to the target word. The first thing we learn is that the sommelier serves some function at the biennial feast. Then, we are explicitly told that the sommelier is an elected position. In this same sentence, we learn that the

---

*Definitions of all unknown words in the boxes in this chapter are at the end of the chapter.

BOX 5-2

Once upon a time there was a kingdom famous for the wines produced from its vineyards. The wines were as sweet and delicious as any to be found in the world. Naturally, the wines were highly popular with the citizens of the kingdom, and the wine critics liked them, too.

In a feast held every two years, all in the kingdom met to celebrate past successes and to ask the gods for their continued blessings. The honor of being elected the *sommelier* was coveted by all. Invariably, an expert wine taster was chosen from among the ranks of the growers, producers, and merchants. Product knowledge, exquisite manners, and a touch of savoir faire were the desired characteristics. The tradition had existed for generations and had survived unchanged through countless kings, until King Klingo arrived on the scene. Klingo displayed a haughtiness and a brusqueness that offended everyone in the genial land. As the day of the celebration drew near, people wondered if Klingo would arbitrarily use his power to disrupt the wine feast. The people were not mistaken. Just as the elders were about to announce the newly elected *sommelier*, Klingo shouted, "The position of *sommelier* will be mine. As long as Klingo rules, Klingo will pour the wine."

position was coveted by all. From this statement we can infer that the position is desirable. In addition, the sommelier should be intimately familiar with the wines, so a grower, producer, or merchant has always been chosen. We learn that the position is a great honor, and that the chosen person should have exquisite manners. At the very end of the passage, we learn that Klingo plans to make himself sommelier and plans to pour the wine. It is reasonable to infer, therefore, that serving wine is one function of the sommelier. In fact, a sommelier is a wine steward. Were you able to use the cues to figure out the meaning of this word?

### Selective Combination

*Selective combination* involves combining selectively encoded information in such a way as to form an integrated, plausible definition of the previously unknown words. Simply sifting out the relevant cues is not enough to arrive at a tentative definition of a word: We must know how to combine these cues into an integrated representation of the word. When we encounter an unfamiliar word, we must selectively encode information about the meaning of the word before we can do anything else, but we usually do not selectively encode all of the relevant information before moving on to the selective combination of this information. The process of selective combination can begin just as soon as the second piece of information has been selectively encoded.

Typically, the available information can be combined in many ways, and inevitably, different persons will produce slightly different combinations. Usually, however, there is one optimal combination of information that exceeds any other possibilities in its usefulness. You can imagine an analogy to the job detectives do. First, they have to decide what the relevant clues are in figuring out who committed the crime (selective encoding). Once they have figured out some relevant clues, they begin to combine them selectively in such a way as to build a plausible case against the suspect. Combining the clues in an improper way can result in a false lead, and ultimately, the apprehension of the wrong suspect. Thus, just as the detective has to track down the individual who actually perpetrated the crime, you have to track down the meaning of the word that is appropriate in the given instance or instances.

Consider how the process of selective combination can be applied to the *macropodida* example in Box 5-1. From the first sentence, we selectively encoded the fact that macropodidae are something we can see, and that they are found in Australia. Thus, we know that they are something that we can see when we go to Australia. The third sentence provided us with the knowledge that macropodidae can be found on plains, and with the knowledge that they hop. We thus now know that macropodidae are something that we can see hopping on the plains of Australia. Later, we learned that they are marsupials, that they eat plants, and that they carry their young in front openings. In sum, we now know that macropodidae are plant-eating marsupials that can be seen hopping on the plains of Australia, and that may be carrying young in openings in front of them.

We now have a fairly extensive network of information about the word macropodida. Putting all the information together in a systematic manner yields a definition: A macropodida is a kangaroo.

Now read Box 5-3 and exercise your skills in selective combination. Locate the available cues in the passage (selective encoding), and then see if you can combine these cues into a meaningful definition or sentence describing the unknown word.

---

**BOX 5-3**

There is no question but that the *oont* is king of the Asian and African deserts. Despite its strong, unpleasant odor, its loud braying, and its obnoxious habits of viciously biting, spitting when irritated, and quitting on the job, the foul-tempered *oont* is widely used as a beast of burden by desert travelers. The brown, shaggy animal seems similar to a cow in its cud-chewing, and its long neck may remind one of a giraffe. Its large, cushioned feet could be of the canine family, and its humped back vaguely resembles that of some breeds of buffalo. But although its appearance is a hodgepodge of other animals' traits, the *oont* is a remarkable creature. Perfectly suited to desert conditions, it can store vast quantities of water in its body tissues.

---

This is an easy passage on which to practice your skills. Not only is there a wealth of helpful cues, but these cues are easily combined as well. The first sentence tells us where *oonts* are found, in the Asian and African deserts. In the second sentence, we learn that the oont is malodorous, and that it has a foul temper, bites viciously, spits when irritated, and quits on the job. Finally, we are told that the animal is used for portage in the desert. In the third sentence, we learned that oonts are brown, shaggy, and that they are long-necked. We also learned that they chew the cud. Later, we learn that oonts have padded feet, humped backs, and the ability to store vast quantities of water in their bodies. We also learn that they are suitable for desert conditions. One way of combining concrete information such as this is to attempt to form a visual image of what the object, in this case an animal, could look like. Before too long, the visual image that you form, as you combine into it more and more information, is quite likely to look like a camel, which is what an oont is.

### Selective Comparison

*Selective comparison* involves relating newly acquired information to information acquired in the past. As readers decide what information to encode and how to combine this information, what they already know about the topic can be quite useful as a guide. Any given bit of relevant information will probably be nearly useless if it cannot somehow be related to past knowledge. Without previous knowledge, the helpful hints that would normally lead readers to the definition of an unknown term will be meaningless, and the readers will probably not even recognize the hints as relevant information. New information can be related to old information, and vice versa, by the use of similes, metaphors, analogies, and models, but the goal is always the same: to give the new information meaning by connecting it to old information that is already known.

Look again at the passage in Box 5-1 to analyze how selective comparison operates. In selective comparison, we try to establish how the new word is similar to and different from old words that we already have stored in memory. We may end up deciding either that the new word is a synonym for an old word that we already know, or that a new concept has to be constructed that expands on our old concepts. In the case of the macropodida, the more information we have, the more restricted is the range of things that it might be. Initially, it might be anything that we might see in Australia—a very large list of things. Later, we are able to reduce our list as we learn that a macropodida is something seen on a plain, and something that hops. We can restrict our list of possibilities further when we learn that it is a herbivorous marsupial. If our original list of things indigenous to or particularly characteristic of Australia included such items as Aborigines, kangaroos, sheep, and eucalyptus trees, our developing list could no longer include all of these things. In fact, by the time we are done with the passage, the only item on this list that the passage could describe is the kangeroo. Thus, the process of selective comparison includes a whittling-down process whereby large numbers of possibilities are successively further reduced. Eventually, if only one possibility remains, that possibility is a likely synonym for the unknown word. If no possibilities remain, then we probably have to form a new concept that is related to, but is different from, all old concepts we have stored in memory.

Consider the sample passage in Box 5-4. The passage contains two unknown words. As you read the passage, try to be conscious of the background knowledge that you are bringing to bear on the passage. Create a list of possible meanings for each of the two unknown words, based on the selective comparisons that you make. As you progressively encode and combine more information, eliminate meanings from your lists that do not seem to fit the descriptions of each of the two words.

This passage has two target words, each of which must be analyzed sepa-

BOX 5-4

Two ill-dressed people, the one a haggard woman of middle years and the other a young man, sat around the fire where the common meal was almost ready. The mother, Tanith, peered at her son through the *oam* of the bubbling stew. It had been a long time since his last *ceilidh*, and Tobar had changed greatly. Where once he had seemed all legs and clumsy joints, he now was well formed and in control of his supple, young body. As they ate, Tobar told of his past year, recreating for Tanith how he had wandered long and far in his quest to gain the skills he would need to be permitted to rejoin the tribe. Then, all too soon, their brief *ceilidh* ended, Tobar walked over to touch his mother's arm and quickly left.

rately. Start with the word *oam*. The phrase "around the fire where the common meal was almost ready" contains much helpful information. There is a fire, and a meal is being prepared. Based on our previous experience, we can surmise that the stew is bubbling because it is being cooked over a fire. At this point, we can hypothesize that the word *oam* means "steam" or "aroma." We can choose between these two possibilities using the information supplied by the verb *peered*. Again, if we relate what we already know to the new information being supplied by the text, we will realize that aromas are not peered through, but steam could be. "Steam" is the best definition of *oam*, the first target word.

The word *ceilidh* is more difficult to define. The first clause of the first sentence in which the word appears tells us that it had been "a long time since his last *ceilidh*." From the context, we can infer that a ceilidh is something that takes place. We already know from the beginning of the paragraph that two people are preparing to eat. Selectively comparing what we know with what the passage tells us might result in the preliminary guess that a ceilidh is a meal. This guess is quickly proven wrong, however. The passage goes on to inform us that since his last ceilidh, Tobar has grown into a man. Tobar would be very hungry indeed if he had grown into a man between his last meal and the present time. Fortunately, we learn from the passage that the distance between ceilidhs is one year. This information may be ascertained on the basis of the phrase, "Tobar told of his past year." Now our long-term memory is again activated as we search for events that would take place annually. Perhaps a ceilidh is a holiday feast or a birthday. A holiday feast is quickly ruled out. From previous experience, we know that feasts have vast amounts of food and last for hours. This ceilidh is short and it is accompanied by a one-course meal. Birthday must also be eliminated as a possible meaning. It may fit the first use of the target word but it does not fit the second use. The last sentence of the text reads, "Then, all too soon, their brief ceilidh ended, Tobar walked over to touch his mother's arm and quickly left." Birthday cannot be the correct meaning because the word ceilidh relates to both mother and son. A ceilidh, then, is likely to be a visit. This is a difficult word to define on the basis of the passage, but if we selectively compare the available information to our store of previous information, the task is greatly facilitated.

Now, use what you have learned about selective encoding, selective combination, and selective comparison to try to define the two low-frequency words in Box 5-5.

According to legend, on the night of Francesco Louis-Philippe's birth, there streaked across the midnight sky a *bolide* more blindingly magnificent than any seen before. Indeed, under his rule, the kingdom of Montaldo flared to sudden, brilliant prominence, only to be extinguished when it was overrun by the barbarous Guntherians. The constant state of warfare was a fact of life in the reign of King Louis-Philippe, and although the *spaneria* was a high price to pay, the nation overflowed with riches and national pride. Religious and political leaders took measures to ease the effects of the *spaneria* by relaxing the strict marriage laws requiring monogamy. All in all, the period was marked by a meteoric rise and decline: the many deaths, the many victories, and ensuing collapse. The Montaldans ruled the region until the armies of Guntheria destroyed them.

**BOX 5-5**

Were you able to use selective encoding, selective combination, and selective comparison to figure out that a *bolide* is a shooting star (exploding meteor) and that a *spaneria* is a scarcity of men? Most people find *bolide* easier to figure out than *spaneria*.

## Context Cues

In learning about the three processes of knowledge acquisition, you may have noticed that the various kinds of textual cues that trigger selective encoding, selective combination, and selective comparison tend to be systematic. Various kinds of cues occur again and again from one passage to another. You will find these processes easier to apply if you have in your mind a classification (or *taxonomy*) of the kinds of cues that are useful for figuring out meanings of new words. Although different taxonomies are possible, a particularly useful one distinguishes among eight types of cues: (a) setting cues, (b) value/affect cues, (c) stative property cues, (d) active property cues, (e) causal/functional cues, (f) class membership cues, (g) antonymic cues, and (h) equivalence cues. The explanations below will help you to recognize and to use these eight kinds of cues.

### Setting Cues

*Setting cues* contain temporal, spatial, and situational information about the context in which the object or concept represented by an unknown word can be found. Examples of temporal setting cues are "in the afternoon," "every Monday," and "once upon a time." Examples of spatial setting cues are "at the intersection of Pine and Elm Streets," "on the roof," and "in Switzerland." Examples of situational cues are "at the Valentine's Day party," "during the last board meeting," and "while having dinner." In some cases, a single setting cue will provide information from two or more categories. For instance, "at dinner" implies a temporal frame of reference, evening, in a spatial frame of reference—at a table in a home or restaurant.

In judging a setting cue, as in judging any cue, you must first be sure that the cue relates information about the specific target word and not simply information about the general message conveyed by the context. In other words, you must be sure that the cue is relevant to defining the unknown word, rather than merely relevant to understanding the passage, in general.

Consider again the passage in Box 5-4. Consider how setting cues might help you in your use of selective encoding, combination, and comparison. This passage contains many setting cues. Start by analyzing the cues pertaining to the word *oam*. There are three setting cues in the first sentence, and the phrase, "around the fire where the common meal was almost ready," contains them all. "Around the fire" is a spatial cue because it tells where the action takes place. The words "common meal" provide a situational cue, and "almost ready" is a temporal cue. The trick now is to combine this information properly in order to arrive at the definition of oam.

*Ceilidh* is more difficult to define. The words "long time since" provide a temporal cue. Subsequently, the clause "where once he had seemed all legs and clumsy joints, he now was well formed and in control of his supple young body" provides us with a rather complicated temporal cue that brings us up to date about Tobar. This clause tells us that the "long time" refers to a much longer period than mere days or weeks. Therefore, a ceilidh cannot be a synonym for a meal. We get another temporal cue in the words "told of his past year": It has been one year since his last ceilidh. The context also provides a situational cue. Whatever a ceilidh is, this one takes place at a meal, in the midst of an amiable conversation. There are other types of cues present in the passage that help to isolate the correct meaning, yet it is evident that the setting cues have conveyed a large amount of information about the word.

Now go over the passage in Box 5-5. Identify each of the setting cues pertaining to the target words that appear in the passage. Write a "T," a "P," or an "S" in the margin near each setting cue to indicate whether it provides time, place, or situational information. If a cue contains two subcategories of information, consider the primary message carried by the cue, and classify it accordingly.

### Value/Affect Cues

*Value/affect cues* describe the evaluative connotations and the emotive content of the object or concept represented by an unknown word. They hint at the positive or negative qualities of the object or concept, its desirability, and the emotions that it might evoke. Value/affect cues also include syntactic information that conveys expectations, such as "despite" or "regardless of." Examples of value/affect cues include: "Jane was glad that. . . ."; "unfortunately"; ". . . is complex"; ". . . is simpleminded."

Now return to the passage in Box 5-2. Several value/affect cues appear in this passage, although the unknown word—*sommelier*—cannot easily be defined simply on the basis of these cues. Let us see what the cues do tell us about the unknown word. Obviously, the position of sommelier, whatever it is, is desirable. It is an honor "coveted by all" to be elected sommelier. Moreover, we know that the position is important to the tradition of the celebration. King Klingo himself values the distinction highly.

Now read the passage in Box 5-6 and mark any value/affect cues that you are able to find. Finally, define the unknown word. Remember at all times to apply the operations of selective encoding, selective combination, and selective comparison.

BOX 5-6

In our mobile society, where families are often spread across the states and neighbors are strangers, *eremophobia* is a constant complaint. Mental-health professionals treat the condition primarily through extended counseling sessions, but when anxiety and nervousness are pronounced, tranquilizers may be necessary. Often, not only the immediate sufferers but also those close to them may require counseling. Sufferers of *eremophobia* may exhibit intense dependency behavior, adversely affecting those close to them. For instance, an older couple, who lost all their children but one in a car accident, placed unreasonable demands for emotional support on the remaining child. He complained that his parents overfocused on him to the point where the quality of his life had declined drastically.

## Stative Property Cues

*Stative property cues* refer to descriptions of the state or condition implied by or associated with a word. They frequently include information that can be ascertained through the five senses—such as quantity, duration, and size—but they may also describe properties of the words that are not experienced directly through the senses. The cues are especially common in the form of adjectives. Examples of stative property cues include: "smelled atrocious," "could barely be seen," "has consciousness."

Now return to Box 5-3. This paragraph is practically a list of stative property cues. See how many can be identified. First, we are told that the *oont* is king of the desert. Then, we learn that the oont has a strong, unpleasant odor. The latter part of the passage contains several stative cues concerning the oont's physical appearance. The oont is brown and shaggy, it has a long neck and humped back, and its feet are padded.

Now read the passage in Box 5-7 and mark any stative property cues you are able to find. After you have done so, consider as well the setting cues and value/affect cues. See if you are able to define the unknown word. Remember at all times to apply the operations of selective encoding, selective combination, and selective comparison.

BOX 5-7

The *flitwite* was only one of the judicial remedies available to the justices of the Court of the King's Bench in the 11th century, but it was perhaps the most important. Its frequent use added enormously to the treasury's coffers, and new royal expenditures were often financed by the issuance of an increased number of *flitwites*. Even the most impartial of justices handed them down in multitudes, for the *flitwite* was as much a part of 11th-century society as the civil tort is of our own. Medieval men and women related in direct and personal ways; therefore, conflict was likely to take the form of actual fighting. In our litigious culture, the law must often deal with more subtle forms of conflict.

## Active Property Cues

*Active property cues* are the action-oriented counterparts of stative property cues. They describe the dynamic properties of a word. Active property cues may describe what a given person or thing does to other persons or things, what can be done to the person or thing, what the person or things can do to itself, or what or whom the thing can be done to. Some examples are "arose," "shines," "were burned by. . . ."

Consider the passage in Box 5-8. First read the passage, and then see what active property cues you are able to find.

---

**BOX 5-8**

The ultimate goal of those seriously involved in raising livestock is to produce animals with a high percentage of top quality meat and a low percentage of waste. Recently, livestock breeders have successfully developed a new breed of turkey whose market potential lies in its high proportion of white meat to dark. The most efficient way to improve stock, practiced by an increasing number of ranches, is to hire a *thremmatologist* to advise in the purchase and mating of different breeds. The *thremmatologist* carefully researches the characteristics of each breed involved and then examines the bloodlines of the specific animals under consideration. The encouraging results of scientific monitoring are now giving rise to predictions that the age of made-to-order livestock is just around the bend.

---

There are three groups of words in this passage that act as active property cues. A *thremmatologist* "advises in the purchase and mating of different breeds, researches the characteristics of the breeds, and examines the bloodlines of animals." These active property cues provide enough information to arrive at least at a tentative definition of the target word. In fact, a thremmatologist is a specialist in animal breeding.

Now read the passage in Box 5-9, marking any active property cues that occur. Also be aware of the other kinds of cues that have been discussed so far, and apply the processes of selective encoding, selective combination, and selective comparison to arrive at your best guess as to the meaning of the unknown word.

---

**BOX 5-9**

The students filed into the testing room, chattering nervously. When all were seated, the proctor began administering the dreaded Scholastic Aptitude Test. At exactly 9:00, the exam began. Not a whisper was heard as the students labored through the exam, deeply engaged in thought. Suddenly, a series of *rackarocks* shattered the silence, jolting everyone in the room. The proctor jumped to his feet and ran outside. He returned momentarily with two young pranksters, each subdued by the scruff of the neck. "Your parents are going to hear about this," he hollered above the laughter that now filled the air.

---

### Causal/Functional Cues

*Causal/functional cues* are a stronger form of active property cues. They focus more on the goal or end-state aspect of an unknown word. These cues describe causes, effects, functions, and purposes of the object or concept represented by the unknown word: what can cause the thing, what a thing can cause, what the thing is used for, and so on. These cues are related to active property cues in that they involve action, but the focus of the cue is more on the effect that the action can cause than on the action itself. Some examples are "can cause a flood," "caused by a villain," "resulted in a mishap."

Consider now the passage in Box 5-10. Mark each causal/functional cue, and see if you can define the unknown word.

---

**BOX 5-10**

Vocabulary skills are a crucial foundation of eloquent speech and concise prose. A good vocabulary is a powerful tool indeed, and the larger the fund of words people command, the richer will be their mode of expression. We must realize, however, that learning a new word does not entail simply the acquisition of the term's formal meaning. Moreover, dictionary definitions frequently are not sufficiently detailed to ensure proper usage. The goal must be to incorporate each new word into our active vocabularies. Words that lie gathering dust in the recesses of the mind serve no useful purpose, and a collection of half-learned words is bound to lead to *solecism*.

---

Although the target word, *solecism*, is difficult to define on the basis of the context, the causal/functional cue is clearly stated. It consists of the words "bound to lead to." The sentence in which the cue appears contains a cause-and-effect relation between half-learned words and solecism. The same sentence also contains a value/affect cue. We can infer that solecism is undesirable because half-learned words are undesirable. In this case, the causal/functional cues provide the connotational hints about the meaning of solecism—incorrect usage of words.

Now read the passage in Box 5-11, marking any causal/functional cues that may be present. Then define the two unknown words in the passage to the best of your ability. Be sure to use the other types of cues as well, and to apply to them selective encoding, selective combination, and selective comparison.

---

**BOX 5-11**

The drug C-37 was first discovered at Henish Laboratories by Dr. Alex Whichard in the early 1970s. When the lozenge form of the drug was first approved for public use as a cough remedy, some claimed that a new age of medicine had arrived. Since then, however, serious side effects of the *lambative* have been noted, resulting in a call for the restriction of its use. The chief drawback is the *oscitancy* that it induces. Whereas some *oscitancy* is expected with any drug that functions as a relaxant, the effects of C-37 may be sudden and profound. Doctors have suggested that patients use the *lambative* in the confines of their homes and completely avoid the use of alcohol, which exacerbates any *oscitancy* the patient may be feeling.

---

### Class Membership Cues

*Class membership cues* deal with the relations between the unknown object or concept and various kinds of classes. They may identify classes or groups to which the unknown belongs. Alternatively, the unknown object or concept may itself be a class, in which case examples of the class members are given. Class membership cues can be negative. For instance, they may contrast the unknown with members of a distinct group. Examples of class membership cues include: "lions and tigers and ———"; "he put his books, notes, and ——— into his satchel"; "——— is a typical mammal"; and "other ——— are bees, mosquitoes, and flies."

| BOX 5-12 | The time immediately following the Holy Revolution was one of strict government control of personal and public affairs. Records available from this period contain no overt criticism of the regime, but it is unclear whether this was because of censorship or overwhelming popular support. On the surface, the country appeared to be converting moral principles into law with little effort. Each Berhitian was required by statute to be *acapnotic*, and the tobacco industry was banned. The government also outlawed the use and production of alcohol, caffeine, marijuana, and dozens of other drugs. In addition, the new regime created a national department of *hamartiology* to advise on legislation concerning the prevailing morality. So successful was the new emphasis on righteous conduct that teenage delinquency virtually disappeared. |
|---|---|

Now read the passage in Box 5-12, noting the two unknown target words. Locate any class membership cues as you read the text.

Although there are no class membership cues for the second target word, *hamartiology*, there is one class membership cue for *acapnotic*. The sentence following the sentence containing the target word reads, "the government also outlawed the use and production of alcohol, caffeine, marijuana, and dozens of other drugs." You can infer that tobacco is a member of the class of substances including alcohol, caffeine, and marijuana. The sentence also suggests that the use and production of tobacco have been similarly banned. Dismantling the tobacco industry eliminates the production side and requiring everyone to be acapnotic eliminates the consumption side. Therefore, it seems reasonable to conclude that an acapnotic is a nonsmoker, which is in fact the meaning of the word. Hamartiology is the study of sin.

Now read the passage in Box 5-13 and mark any class membership cues you can discover. At the same time, be alert for the other kinds of cues we have discussed, and remember to use these cues in your processes of selective encoding, selective combination, and selective comparison. After you have spotted the cues, see which of the three unknown words in the passage you can define.

| BOX 5-13 | Having confidently entered the conference room expecting praise for a job well-done, the boy winced under the unexpected blasting *animadversion* of his teacher. Had the paper been full of misused words, or had it wandered off the main point, such a harsh response would have been more understandable, for the boy had learned well the importance of avoiding sentence fragments, run-ons, *catachreses*, and other breaches of grammatical and semantic etiquette. And his skill at *diaskeuasis* was not in such a state of disuse that he would allow egregious technical mistakes to occur. He was especially proud of his semantic prowess: Diction errors and *catachreses* rarely disgraced his papers. Unfortunately, the teacher was not attacking the written language, but rather the expressed idea itself, and the boy had trouble accepting that his work could be so utterly rejected. He slowly collected his books and left the room, knowing the class would never be as enjoyable for him again. |
|---|---|

### Antonymic Cues

*Antonymic cues* are opposites of the target word. The presence of an antonymic cue almost always leads the reader directly to the meaning of the target

**BOX 5-14**

Although the others were having a marvelous time at the party, the couple on the blind date was not enjoying the merrymaking in the least. A *pococurante*, he was dismayed by her earnestness. Meanwhile, she, who delighted in men with full heads of hair, eyed his substantial *phalacrosis* with disdain. When he failed to suppress an *eructation*, her disdain turned to disgust. He, in turn, was equally appalled by her noticeable *podobromhidrosis*. Although they both loved to dance, the disco beat of the music did not lessen either their ennui or their mutual discomfort. Both silently vowed that they would never again accept a blind date.

word. Such cues are easy to identify and they usually define the target word with ease. Some examples are "different as night and ————"; "I'll be there come rain or ————"; "Wildly happy yesterday, she was unbearably ———— today."

Now read the passage in Box 5-14, identifying all antonymic cues. See if you can figure out the meaning of each of the four unknown words.

The passage contains two antonymic cues. Both of them are quite useful in helping to define the target words. The meaning of the word *pococurante* is illuminated by the clause "he was dismayed by her earnestness." Evidently, pococurantes do not take life too seriously. The second antonymic cue is even more of a giveaway. She likes a full head of hair, and she views this fellow's head unfavorably. Apparently, he is balding noticeably.

The remaining target words in the passage are not associated with antonymic cues, but let us see if we can discover any other types of cues that would help to define these target words. The words "fail to suppress" serve as an active property cue for the meaning of the target word *eructation*. It seems as though an eructation is something one would normally attempt to suppress in public. Burps and the passing of wind come to mind. The word podobromhidrosis is not as easy to pin down. The value/effect cues contained in the phrase "He . . . was appalled by" tells us that podobromhidrosis is undesirable, but there are no further cues to aid us in figuring out its meaning. In fact, a pococurante is an indifferent person, one who is nonchalant about things. A phalacrosis is a bald spot. An eructation is a burp, and people suffering from podobromhidrosis have smelly feet.

Now read Box 5-15, marking any antonymic cues that you are able to find. Also be aware of other kinds of cues that may help you to define the unknown word.

**BOX 5-15**

The swampland is no place for the unprepared. The dangers are all too real. The insect-free life of the city is replaced by swarming clouds of poisonous mosquitoes; the warmth and dryness of the typical suburban dwelling is replaced by a perpetual musty dampness; and the firm, fertile land of meadows and pastures is replaced by wet, spongy soil and treacherous patches of *syrt*. It is as easy to sink in the stuff as it is to float in the sea. Of course, the reward for facing these dangers is the opportunity to learn about life conditions in the early years of the earth's existence.

### Equivalence Cues

*Equivalence cues* occur when a word is explicitly defined in context by the use of synonyms, restatements, appositives, or direct definitions. Equivalence cues are a type of class membership cue with the added feature that the "class" is identical to the meaning of the unknown word, so that no additional inferences need to be drawn concerning similarities and differences between the meaning of the unknown word and the cue. An equivalence cue may appear before or directly after the target word, or it may appear some distance away. In the latter case, the reader must infer that the target word and the cue relate to each other. Some examples of equivalence cues are "A dog is a domestic canine" and "The president, or head of state, is . . ."

Read Box 5-16 and mark any equivalence cues that you can identify.

---

**BOX 5-16**

A stroll through the private gallery of Luis Roberto will soon convince anyone with a taste for art that the 80-year-old master is a man to be watched. For fifty years, Don Luis painted only as a hobby, but at age 70, even in the face of impending *cecity*, Don Luis left the business world for a full-time career in art. His paintings glow with colors and forms that are alive, reaching off the canvas to pull the viewer into their play.

Healthy in every other respect, Don Luis is falling prey to *cecity*, an affliction he justifiably considers a demonic scourge. The onset of blindness marks the beginning of the end for the giant talent. Don Luis compensates for his darkening world by painting as boldly with texture as he does with color and form. Bodies are literally piled onto one another, forcing themselves into one's vision and begging one to reach out a hand to touch them.

---

The word *cecity* appears twice in this passage, but there is only one equivalence cue. In the sentence after the second appearance of the word, the phrase "the onset of blindness" occurs. As the previous sentence refers to *cecity* as an affliction, we have been on the lookout for diseases, terminal conditions, and other health problems. Blindness would certainly be considered an affliction—especially by an artist. *Cecity*, then, means blindness.

Notice that there are other kinds of cues in the context. The first use of the term cecity is accompanied by the adjective "impending." This cue not only provides us with temporal information, it is also a value/affect cue. We may infer from the meaning of the word "impending" that cecity is undesirable. We are later told, as related above, that cecity is an affliction. This is a stative property cue and also contains value/affect information. The use of the descriptive noun "affliction," informs us of the stative condition of cecity, and it reinforces the notion of undesirableness. Finally, Luis Roberto considers cecity a "demonic scourge." This is a value/affect cue par excellence.

Now read the passage in Box 5-17. See if you can use equivalence and other cues to figure out the meaning of the unknown word.

You have now completed the description of the eight types of contextual cues. To refresh your memory, they are setting cues, value/affect cues, stative property cues, active property cues, causal/functional cues, class membership cues, antonymic cues, and equivalence cues. You should be aware of the

BOX 5-17

A 4-year-old boy was found wandering around Center Park five days ago. Police reported that he seemed in good health despite being dazed, frightened, and hungry. An *ecchymosis* on his forehead suggested that he had fallen at some point. Fortunately, the rest of his body was free from other bruises or black and blue marks. The boy has brown hair, green eyes, and freckles. Any information leading to identification of his parents would be greatly appreciated by the Park Police.

characteristics of each kind of cue. Should you feel at all skeptical about the use of these cues in defining unknown words you encounter outside of this book, pick up a good novel and read until you come to an unfamiliar word. Then search for available cues. Almost invariably, you will find at least one. In the next section of the chapter, we will consider aspects of the unknown word and the surrounding text that make the knowledge-acquisition processes either easier or more difficult to apply to the recognition of the various kinds of contextual cues.

## Mediators

*Mediators* are variables that make application of the knowledge-acquisition processes to the contextual cues either easier or more difficult. Seven mediators that have been identified as particularly important in learning words from context are (a) the number of occurrences of the unknown word, (b) the variability of the contexts in which multiple occurrences of the unknown word appear, (c) the importance of the unknown word to understanding the context in which it is embedded, (d) the helpfulness of the surrounding context to understanding the meaning of the word, (e) the density of unknown words in the passage, (f) the concreteness of the unknown word and of the surrounding context, and (g) the usefulness of previously known information in understanding the passage or in understanding the meaning of the unknown word.

The following explanations are designed to teach you to recognize the mediators and to use them to your advantage when you encounter unfamiliar words. The explanations will draw on passages that you have previously analyzed, so that you will be better able to see how the mediators affect the application of the processes to the cues.

### Number of Occurrences of an Unknown Word

Frequent occurrences of an unknown word in a given passage affect the reader's ability to learn the word in several ways. First, the multiple occurrences are a signal that the word is important to the meaning of the context. Consequently, the reader is more likely to make a concerted effort to define the word. Second, each reappearance of the term provides additional information about its meaning. In both of these cases, multiple occurrences are desirable. They offer an incentive to learn the word, and they provide the reader with more contexts. Occasionally, however, multiple occurrences will hinder the ability to define an unfamiliar word. For instance, the reader may have difficulty selectively combining the information obtained from the cues surrounding the separate appearances of the word.

When a passage contains multiple occurrences of an unknown word, the best strategy is to treat each occurrence separately. What does each use of the word tell you about the word's meaning? If you think a single definition will suffice, try to form an integrated definition of the word, given what you know. If a single meaning does not appear to satisfy all of the occurrences of the term, if may be that different senses of the word are required.

Now return to the passage in Box 5-7. Use the strategy described above to verify that the definition of the unknown word is suitable for each appearance of the word. What do the multiple occurrences tell you about the word?

This passage is not a particularly easy one. We learn from the first sentence that the *flitwite* was an important judicial remedy in the 11th century. The context of the second occurrence tells us why the flitwite was important. Its "frequent use added enormously to the treasury's coffers." The context of the third use of the term informs us that regardless of the financial factors involved, flitwites were an important part of 11th-century culture. As we read on, we learn that the flitwite appears to be a penalty for fighting. Based on what we know from the first two occurrences of the term, we can surmise that a flitwite is a monetary fine for fighting. Notice how our use of selective encoding and selective combination is facilitated by the multiple occurrences of the unknown word. How do we know that a single definition is required? Notice that the first two uses of the term appear in consecutive sentences, the first and the second, and that the pronoun "its," which begins the second sentence, refers back to the word flitwite in the first sentence. Throughout the paragraph, the author always seems to be speaking about the same concept. Whatever else a flitwite may be, "a fine for fighting" is the only meaning required by this context.

In this passage, it is unlikely that *flitwite* is definable on the basis of only one appearance of the term. The reader probably needs all three occurrences to selectively encode, combine, and compare sufficient information to construct a definition. In the passage, the multiple occurrences fit together quite well, and each one adds a small bit of needed information.

Now return to the passage in Box 5-2. Decide whether the multiple manifestations of the target word do indeed fit with the single definition. Note how the multiple occurrences of the word help in its definition.

### Variability of Contexts

Different types of contexts—for example, different kinds of subject matter or different writing styles—are likely to supply different kinds of information about the unknown word. Variability of contexts increases the likelihood that a wide range of hints and cues will be supplied about the term in question, and thus increases the probability that the reader will get a full picture of the scope of a given word's meaning. On the other hand, mere repetition of a given term in essentially the same context as that in which it previously appeared is unlikely to be very helpful. Usually, variable contexts aid in the construction of a definition; sometimes, however, the multiple contexts may be hard to reconcile with each other. In this case, the additional information may be counterproductive.

Consider, for example, the passage in Box 5-16. In this passage, the target word *cecity* appears in two fairly divergent contexts. The first use of the word is surrounded by an only marginally helpful context. Based on the information contained in this context, we can infer because of a value/affect cue that *cecity*, whatever it is, is undesirable. At this point, we might guess that the term meant either "senility" or "death," but we would probably not feel very confident about the preliminary definition. It is not until the second context, and the equivalence cue, that we can gain confidence that *cecity* means "blindness." A quick check will verify that this definition fits the first occurrence of the word as well.

Now return to the passage in Box 5-4. Consider how variability of contexts and the different kinds of context cues provided help you to define the meaning of the word *ceilidh*.

### Importance of the Unknown Word to Its Context

If knowing the meaning of an unfamiliar word is judged to be necessary to understanding its surrounding material, the reader is much more likely to invest an effort in figuring out what the word means than if the unfamiliar word is judged to be irrelevant to understanding the passage. In your day-to-day reading, it is not realistic to expect that you will invariably look up every unfamiliar word that you encounter, or try to figure out the meaning of each new word. Therefore, it becomes important for you to be able to differentiate between those kinds that are more important to understanding the meaning of the passage and those that are less important.

Refer back to Box 5-9. First, briefly summarize the main idea of the passage. Would a lack of knowledge about the meaning of the target word hinder your ability to summarize the passage adequately? If so, it would seem that the word is important to understanding the meaning of the context as a whole. If not, then you could probably get by without figuring out or looking up the meaning of the unknown word.

As it turns out, this passage is fairly easy to summarize even without detailed information about the word *rackarocks*. A group of students is taking a standardized test that is suddenly disrupted by a ruckus created by a couple of jokesters. The meaning of rackarocks is relatively unimportant to the context in the passage because we do not need to know for sure that the word means firecrackers to understand that a disturbance is taking place. At the same time, understanding the meaning of the word helps us to understand the exact nature of the disturbance. Thus, the importance of the term to understanding the passage is probably best viewed as intermediate, relative to other words in other contexts.

Now consider the passage in Box 5-10. How important is understanding the meaning of the word *solecism* to understanding the meaning of this passage?

### Helpfulness of the Context

The helpfulness of the context to understanding the meaning of an unfamiliar word is an important mediator. If the context in which the word appears is laden with easily interpretable hints and cues, the construction of a definition is facilitated. On the other hand, the absence of contextual cues can make the task of defining an unknown word next to impossible. The helpfulness of contextual cues is affected by the position of the cues in the passage. If a given cue occurs in close proximity to the target word, then there is a higher likelihood that the cue will be recognized as relevant to inferring the unknown word's meaning. In contrast, a cue separated from the target word by a substantial portion of the text may go unrecognized. Yet such a cue may be useful for figuring out the meaning of the word. It is thus important to look not only at the contexts immediately surrounding the unknown word, but at contexts at a greater distance as well in order to see whether there are any helpful cues. Finally, it is important to understand that cues may occur both before and after the target word. If you stop reading as soon as you encounter an unfamiliar term, you will not give yourself a chance to find any cues that appear after the occurrence of that word. It is thus a good idea to continue reading somewhat beyond the word in order to discover any cue that may follow the occurrence of that word. By reading at least somewhat beyond the word, you will be less likely to overlook cues that appear after the word's occurrence.

Consider, for example, the unknown word in Box 5-3. Notice that there are many helpful cues in this passage, and that they occur both before and after each appearance of the word. Moreover, some of them occur at some distance from the presentation of the unknown word. Now look again at Box 5-17. Where do the context cues for defining *ecchymosis* appear? Which ones appear before the appearance of the word, and which appear after? Which are close in proximity to the word, and which are at some distance?

### Density of Unknown Words in a Passage

The density of unknown words in a passage can affect the ability to define unfamiliar words. If readers are confronted with a high density of previously unknown words, they may be unwilling or simply unable to use the available cues to best advantage. Moreover, when the density of unknown words is great, it can be difficult to discern which cues refer to which words. Some unknown words may actually get in the way of defining other unknown words.

When you are confronted by a passage containing several unfamiliar words, it is important not to panic or become discouraged. Often, if you crack the code and define even one of the difficult terms, the remaining terms will become much easier to understand. Resist the temptation to give up, and force yourself to read a substantial portion of a given paragraph or passage before trying to figure out the meaning of the unknown terms.

Consider again the passage in Box 5-13. There are three unknown words here, and only the first is relatively easy to define. The boy was expecting praise, but he received *animadversion* instead. Figuring out that *animadversion* is harsh criticism will make the task of defining the subsequent two unknown words easier. As you figure out the meaning of each word, even if tentatively, it will help you with the others. At times, if you figure out the later unknown words, you may have to go back and revise your tentative definition of the unknown words that occurred earlier in the passage. Now consider again the passage in Box 5-14. Notice that there are four unknown words in this passage, and that their occurrences in close proximity make defining each word relatively more difficult. Consider how selective encoding, selective combination, and selective comparison applied to the context cues in this passage can help in your definition of each of the unknown words.

### Concreteness of the Unknown Word and Its Context

The concreteness of the unknown word and of the context is another important mediator. Concrete words are words referring to concepts that can be perceived by the senses. Abstract words refer to those things that are not tangible, physical qualities or entities. Although it is convenient to refer to words as being either concrete or abstract, these attributes actually occur on a continuum. "Chair," "person," and "briefcase" are examples of concrete words. "Illness" and "warmth" are examples of words that straddle the line between concreteness and abstractness, and "freedom," "creativity," "communism," and "religion" are examples of abstract terms. It is usually easier to define concrete terms than abstract ones, because concrete terms have more straightforward definitions. Abstract terms are often difficult to define to the satisfaction of any large number of people. For example, what, exactly, does "freedom" mean?

As you read, it may be helpful to keep in mind whether you are grappling with a concrete or an abstract unknown word. First, the level of concreteness or abstractness of the concept the word represents may help you in deciding what information in the context is applicable to defining the word. Second, knowledge about the relative concreteness or abstractness of the term governs how "solid" a definition you may be able to give. The concreteness of the surrounding context also affects your ability to infer a word's meaning. In most cases, the greater the concreteness of the context, the easier it will be to define the word in question. If the passage is very abstract, you may have to compromise slightly in the quality of your definition.

Consider, for example, the word *thremmatologist* in Box 5-8. In this passage, we are dealing with a concrete context and a relatively concrete target word. Moreover, the context is relatively helpful. The cues are easily located and comprehended. In contrast, consider the meaning of the word *spaneria* and the surrounding context cues in Box 5-5. Here, the context that helps to define *spaneria* is more abstract, and the word itself has a more abstract meaning. As a result, it becomes more difficult to define this word.

### Usefulness of Previously Acquired Information

Whenever people read, they generally attempt to connect the ideas described in the text to things they already know about the subject of the text, using the process of selective comparison. Sometimes, background knowledge can be very helpful in illuminating the meaning of a text and of an unknown word. Inevitably, the usefulness of selective comparison hinges on the relevance of past knowledge to understanding the situation presented in a new passage. In some cases, you may have a considerable amount of knowledge to bring to bear on the passage, but it simply may not be very helpful in identifying the meanings of unknown words; in other cases, this knowledge may provide the critical information you need for defining one or more unknown words.

In using prior knowledge, ask yourself what sorts of situations you are familiar with that are relevant to the context in which the unknown word appears; also, ask yourself whether the target word seems similar to any other words or combinations of words that you have experienced before. This type of conscious brainstorming can often force you to retrieve relevant information from way down in your memory, and thus serve as a basis for unearthing the critical clue in defining a new word.

Consider again the passage in Box 5-11. This passage has two target words, *oscitancy* and *lambative*. *Lambative* is simply a synonym for the word "lozenge." You need only a moderate amount of previous knowledge to figure out the meaning of this word. Even if you did not realize that lambative referred to a lozenge, you probably guessed that a lambative was a medicine or a cough remedy. *Oscitancy* presents a different story, however. Previous knowledge is quite useful. We learn that oscitancy is a side effect of C-37. But what kind of side effect? We learned that it is a common problem with relaxants. Have you ever used relaxants? How did you feel when you were under their influence? We also learned that the oscitancy potentially created by C-37 is exacerbated by alcohol. Have you ever combined a cough remedy with a few glasses of wine? Did you then fall asleep? Defining this word will be easier for people with some experience with cough remedies and particularly for those people who have mixed alcohol and cough remedies. In this case, previous knowledge is almost a necessity for figuring out the meaning of the word. Consider also how previous knowledge can help you in defining the meaning of the word *syrt*, which appears in Box 5-15.

You have now learned about three kinds of entities that can assist you in figuring out the meanings of unknown words. When you encounter an unknown word in context, attempt to apply the processes of selective encoding, selective combination, and selective comparison to each of the eight kinds of contextual cues described in this chapter. Keep in mind, as you attempt to define the unknown word or words, that the mediators described above will make your job either easier or harder. Being aware of these mediators and attempting to use them to your advantage can facilitate your application of the processes to the context. If you are at all skeptical about the utility of the method described in this chapter, pick up a good novel and read until you come to an unfamiliar word. Use your knowledge about the processes, contextual cues, and mediating variables to aid you in defining the word. You may be pleasantly surprised with the result.

## Strategies for Memorizing

The emphasis in this chapter has been on learning meaningful material from context. Occasionally, however, you may need to memorize lists, facts, or basically unrelated strings of information, so it is useful to have a set of strategies for memorizing these kinds of materials. This section describes several such strategies.

### Categorical Clustering

Suppose you need to memorize a small shopping list. How can you increase the chances that when you get to the supermarket, you will actually remember what you wanted to buy?

One helpful technique that you may already use is *categorical clustering*. In this technique, you group things together by the category they are in. For example, suppose you need to buy apples, milk, Cheerios, grapes, yogurt, Wheaties, Swiss cheese, grapefruit, and lettuce. Rather than trying to memorize the list in unordered fashion, it helps to memorize by categories:

*Fruits*—apples, grapes, grapefruit

*Dairy Products*—milk, yogurt, Swiss cheese

*Cereals*—Cheerios, Wheaties

*Vegetables*—lettuce

Organizing the list by categories will help you remember the items when you get to the supermarket. Make sure you also know the number of categories you have memorized, so that if one is missing, you will know that you need to remember another category of things to buy.

Here is a list of things to buy at the hardware store. Use categorical clustering to help you learn the list: 1″ screws, hammer, mousetraps, box of nails, pliers, bug spray, saw, thumbtacks, light bulbs. Remember to count categories so that you know how many different kinds of things you will need to buy.

### Interactive Imagery

**INTERACTIONS WITHIN A LIST OF WORDS**   Sometimes the list you need to remember does not fit nicely into convenient categories. In such cases, you will need a more general method to help you remember the list. Suppose, for example, that you need to remember a list of basically unrelated words: cat, table, pencil, book, mirror, radio, Kansas, rain, electricity, stone. A useful technique for learning such lists is to generate *interactive images*. For example, you might imagine a *cat* sitting on a *table* holding a *pencil* in its paw and writing in a *book*, with *rain* pouring over *Kansas* (as pictured from a map) that lands on a *radio* that is sitting on a *stone*, which generates *electricity* reflected in a *mirror*. The number of items you wish to place in any one interactive image will depend on what you find comfortable when you have to remember the words. Generally, however, the interactive images will facilitate your recall of the list of words.

**PEGWORDS**   Sometimes it is easier to use a *pegword system* for remembering a list of words. In this system, each word is associated with a word on a previously memorized list, and an interactive image is created between the two words. The following list is frequently used:

| | |
|---|---|
| One is a bun. | Six is a stick. |
| Two is a shoe. | Seven is heaven. |
| Three is a tree. | Eight is a gate. |
| Four is a door. | Nine is a dime. |
| Five is a hive. | Ten is a hen. |

Once you memorize this list, you can use it over and over again as a basis for learning new lists.

Consider, for example, the previous list. The first word is *cat*: You might visualize a cat eating a delicious bun. The second word is *table*: You might imagine a shoe atop a tall table. The third word is *pencil*: You might visualize one large branch of a tree that ends with a sharp pencil point. The fourth word is *book*: You might imagine a door that is in fact the cover of a book with which you are familiar. The fifth word is *mirror*: You might imagine bees in a hive looking at themselves in a mirror. Then go on forming interactive images for each of the words in the list. When you need to remember the words, you first recall the numbered images and then recall the words when you visualize them in the interactive images. This technique has the advantage of facilitating recall of the order of the words as well as of the words themselves.

These techniques help facilitate recall because it is easier to remember interactive images than to remember words. Now, try applying each of the two techniques described above (interactive images within the list and pegwords) to the following two lists of words:

1.  *gorilla, dictionary, word, teacher, pear, sinister, air, lunch, red, tooth*

2.  *rock, ocean, tail, pretty, eraser, love, radiator, plug, television, rose*

**METHOD OF LOCI**   Yet another technique for memorizing words that makes use of interactive imagery is called the *method of loci*. This technique dates from ancient times, when it was used by orators who wished to remember key concepts for their speeches. The idea is simple: Visualize a walk around an area you know well. It might be your college campus, or the neighborhood in which you grew up. Along this walk there should be some major landmarks with which you are familiar—your own house, a neighborhood park, a stream, and so on. Decide in advance on the mental walk you will take and the landmarks you will visualize along the way.

Later, when you need to memorize a list of words, take the mental walk, depositing each word to be memorized along the walk at one of the distinctive landmarks. Visualize an interactive image between the new word and the landmark. For example, consider the following short list of words: *computer, ink, bird, heart, snow*. Suppose the first five landmarks on your mental walk are dormitory, a small stream, a clump of trees, a clock tower, and the building in which English classes are held. You might imagine a large *computer* in the lobby of your dormitory, *ink* (rather than water) flowing down the stream, a *bird* singing in the clump of trees, a *heart* beating the seconds where the clock normally is, and *snow* covering the English building. When you wish to remember the list, take your mental walk, and pick up the words you have learned from each of the landmarks along the walk.

Here is a new list of words. Use the method of loci with a familiar route to memorize and then recall the list of words: *rug, grave, blue, kangaroo, television, crate, briefcase, car, laugh, wheat.*

### Acronyms and Acrostics

These two techniques make use of verbal rather than imaginal encodings for words you wish to learn. An acronym is a word or expression each of whose letters stand for a certain other word or concept. For example, suppose you want to remember the list *Indian, roast, crater, hanger, pain*. You might form the acronym CHIRP, with the first letter of each word to be memorized represented by one of its letters: Crater, Hanger, Indian, Roast, Pain. This technique is useful if the first letters of the words to be memorized actually can be formed into a single word, or something close to one. It is less useful if the letters just don't happen to form into a word.

In an acrostic, one forms a sentence rather than a single word to help one remember the new words. For example, the list above might be remembered by the sentence "Children hop in roadsters punctually." Occasionally, it may be possible to use some of the words to be remembered in the sentence.

Use an acronym or acrostic to memorize the words in each of the following two lists:

1. *normal, baseball, story, intelligence, laundry, engine, gate, soap*

2. *terror, hotel, pavement, relish, curtain, seer, wood, lesson*

To summarize, a variety of methods—categorical clustering, interactive imagery between words in the list, pegwords, the method of loci, acronyms, and acrostics—can help you memorize lists of words. Using these methods is usually much easier than rote memorization.

---

### DEFINITIONS OF UNKNOWN WORDS IN BOXES

*acapnotic:* a nonsmoker.
*animadversion:* harsh, adverse criticism.
*bolide:* a shooting star; an exploding meteor.
*catachresis:* incorrect use of a word or phrase.
*cecity:* blindness.
*ceilidh:* a visit; a private conversation.
*diaskeuasis:* editorial revision.

*ecchymosis:* a bruise or contusion; a black and blue mark.

*eremophobia:* fear of loneliness.

*eructation:* a belch.

*flitwite:* a fine for fighting.

*hamartiology:* the study of sin.

*lambative:* medicine in lozenge form.

*macropodida:* kangaroo.

*oam:* steam.

*oont:* a camel.

*oscitancy:* drowsiness.

*phalacrosis:* baldness; a bald spot.

*pococurante:* a nonchalant or indifferent person.

*podobromhidrosis:* smelly feet.

*rackarock:* an explosive; a firecracker.

*solecism:* incorrect usage of words.

*sommelier:* a wine steward.

*spaneria:* a scarcity of men.

*syrt:* quicksand, bog.

*thremmatologist:* a specialist in animal breeding.

# 6
# Coping with Novelty

An important aspect of intelligence is the ability to cope with the unknown and the unexpected. Often, novel tasks and situations turn out to be those that most require us to exercise our intelligence. Coping with novelty can take different forms. Sometimes, the novelty is a function of understanding a new kind of task or situation; other times, the novelty is a function of knowing what to do in a new kind of task or situation. One of the most important mental skills for dealing with novelty is that of insight.

## Insight Skills

People have been interested in the nature of *insight* for many years. It is easy to see why: Insights such as Copernicus's, that the sun rather than the earth is the center of the solar system, and Galileo's, that two objects will fall from a height at the same rate of speed regardless of their weights, constitute some of the greatest discoveries in scientific history. It would be to the advantage of us all to understand the mental processes underlying insights of these kinds.

### The Nature of Insight

Conventional views of insight fall into two basic camps—the special-process views and the nothing-special views. According to *special-process* views, insight is a process that differs in kind from ordinary types of information processing. Among these views are the ideas that insight results from extended unconscious leaps in thinking, that it results from greatly accelerated mental processing, and that it results from a short-circuiting of normal reasoning processes. These views are intuitively appealing, but seem to carry with them at least three problematical aspects.

First, they do not really pin down what insight is. Calling insight an unconscious leap or a short-circuiting leaves insight pretty much a "black box" of unknown contents. Even if one of these theories was correct, just what insight is would remain to be identified. Second, virtually all the evidence in support of these views is anecdotal rather than experimental, and for each piece of anecdotal evidence to support one of these views, there is at least one corresponding piece of evidence to refute it. Finally, the positions are probably not pinned down sufficiently, as they stand, to permit experimental tests. As a result, it is not clear that the positions could even be proven right or wrong. It is this characteristic of provability that has probably been at least in part responsible for the scarcity of research on insight.

According to the *nothing-special* views, insight is merely an extension of ordinary perceiving, recognizing, learning, and conceiving. This view, most forcefully argued by David Perkins (1981), would view past failures to identify any special processes of insight as being due to the (alleged) fact that there is no special process of insight. Insights are merely significant products of ordinary processes. We can understand the kind of frustration that would lead Perkins and others to this view: After repeated failures to identify a construct empirically, the theorist can easily be tempted to ascribe the failure to the nonexistence of the construct. We cannot find what is not there! But it is not clear that we should yet be ready to abandon the notion that there is something special about insight. Arguments for the nothing-special views have been arguments by default—because we have not identified any of these processes, we are to believe that they have no independent existence—and such arguments would be unacceptable if we were able to make a positive case for the existence of insight processes.

### The Triarchic View of Insight

The view of insight that Janet Davidson and I have proposed (1984) is that insight consists of not one, but three separate but related psychological processes:

1. *Selective encoding.* Selective encoding involves sifting out relevant information from irrelevant information. Significant problems generally present us with large amounts of information, only some of which is relevant to problem solution. For example, the facts of a legal case are usually both numerous and confusing: An insightful lawyer must figure out which of the myriad facts are relevant to principles of law. Similarly, a doctor or psychotherapist must sift out those facts that are relevant for diagnosis or treatment. Perhaps the occupation that most directly must employ selective encoding is that of the detective: In trying to figure out who has perpetrated a crime, the detective must figure out what the relevant facts are. Failure to do so may result in the detective's following up on false leads, or in having no leads to follow up on at all.

2. *Selective combination.* Selective combination involves combining what might originally seem to be isolated pieces of information into a unified whole that may or may not resemble its parts. For example, the lawyer must

know how the relevant facts of a case fit together to make (or break) the case. A doctor or psychotherapist must be able to figure out how to combine information about various isolated symptoms to identify a given medical (or psychological) syndrome. A detective, having collected the facts that seem relevant to the case, must determine how they fit together to point at the guilty party rather than at anyone else.

   3. *Selective comparison.*   Selective comparison involves relating newly acquired information to information acquired in the past. Problem solving by analogy, for example, is an instance of selective comparison: The solver realizes that new information is similar to old information in certain ways (and dissimilar from it in other ways) and uses this information better to understand the new information. For example, an insightful lawyer will relate a current case to past legal precedents; choosing the right precedent is absolutely essential. A doctor or psychotherapist relates the current set of symptoms to previous case histories in his or her own or in others' past experiences; again, choosing the right precedents is essential. A detective may have been involved in or know about a similar case where the same modus operandi was used to perpetrate a crime. Drawing an analogy to the past case may be helpful to the detective both in understanding the nature of the crime and in figuring out who did it.

*insightful v/s insight ?*

   It should be evident that the processes of insight that are being proposed here are the same as the processes of knowledge acquisition proposed in the last chapter. Is insight, then, really nothing at all special, but merely a mundane extension of knowledge-acquisition skills? Davidson and I do not believe this to be the case. What seems to separate insightful use of selective encoding, selective combination, and selective comparison from ordinary use of these processes is the nonobviousness of how they are to be applied, or the non-obviousness of the appropriateness of their application. By contrast, the nature of the problem in learning vocabulary from context is very clear: The task is to define the unknown word. Moreover, the kinds of clues that are useful in defining an unknown word are circumscribed in scope. Thus, with practice, the finding and use of these clues can become fairly routine. In insightful selective encoding, selective combination, and selective comparison, it is not obvious how to apply these processes, and often it is not even obvious that they are appropriate in the first place.

   We therefore agree with Perkins that the processes of insight are the same as ordinary cognitive processes. However, the circumstances of their application are different. It is much more difficult to apply selective encoding, selective combination, and selective comparison in an insightful way than it is to apply them in a routine way. Thus, we do not agree with Perkins that insightful processing differs from noninsightful processing only in terms of the way the product is evaluated.

## Insight Problems
### *Selective Encoding*

Consider the following problem. As you do so, think about how selective encoding can help you to solve the problem.

Many scientists have offered explanations for the total extinction of dinosaurs and other creatures 65 million years ago. One of the facts agreed on by most geologists is that the earth was struck by a huge asteroid or comet approximately 10 kilometers in diameter. The data that support this theory rest on the fact that a thin layer of iridium, an element found mainly in meteors, is present in geological strata throughout the world. (Scientists know that the iridium itself did not cause the extinction of dinosaurs and plants, but it is simply proof that some catastrophic event involving meteors took place.)

The scientists explain that an asteroid crashed into the earth and caused huge amounts of dust and dirt to fly into the atmosphere. The dust blocked the sunlight, according to scientists, for approximately three months to a year, which caused the land to cool. Many animals died from starvation and from the cold.

One of the misunderstood things, until now, is the reason why the ocean ecology died. The ocean mass—which was then even larger than it is now—did not change temperature as drastically as did the earth. In view of the evidence, scientists have come up with an explanation. What might that explanation be?

In order to find relevant information, you might want to go through the following steps, at least mentally: First, restate the problem: A meteor crash killed many animals. What information in the above description of the event might show why a meteor crash would also kill ocean animals and plants?

Second, list all the information in the problem. In this problem, such information would include the following facts: (a) dinosaurs and other animals died suddenly 65 million years ago; (b) the earth was struck by a huge asteroid 10 kilometers in diameter; (c) a layer of iridium, mainly an element from meteors, is embedded throughout the earth; (d) when the meteor crashed, huge amounts of dust and dirt were thrown into the atmosphere; (e) dust blocked sunlight for three months to a year; (f) the land cooled; (g) the ocean mass was much larger than the land mass; (h) the temperature change was not important to the ocean.

Third, eliminate items of information that are probably or clearly irrelevant in solving the problem. In this case, information about the land dinosaurs and animals, the earth's being struck by the asteroid, and the layer of iridium is probably not directly relevant to this problem.

Fourth, consider the information that is relevant to solving the problem. In this problem, such information would include facts that might explain the results of the crash of the meteorite: that it threw large amounts of dust out into the atmosphere, that the dust blocked sunlight for three months to a year, that the land cooled in the darkness, and that the ocean temperature change was not important.

Fifth, think about whether or not you might be able to infer more information from the given relevant information. For example, the fact that large amounts of dust were thrown into the atmosphere would result in air pollution and blockage of sunlight. What effect might a blockage of sunlight have on the ocean ecology? What effect might pollution have on this ecology? What effect might the death of the plant life in the seas, due to lack of sunlight, have upon the total food chain upon which all animals in the sea depend?

**ARITHMETICAL AND LOGICAL WORD PROBLEMS**     Consider the following problem:

**You have black socks and blue socks in a drawer, mixed in a ratio of 4 to 5. Because it is dark, you are unable to see the colors of the socks that you take out of the drawer. How many socks do you have to take out of the drawer to be assured of having a pair of socks of the same color?**

This problem is a good example of the importance of selective encoding. People who answer the problem incorrectly tend to focus on information in the problem that is actually irrelevant—namely, that the sock colors are mixed in a ratio of 4 to 5. There are at least three reasons why this information might *seem* to be relevant, at first reading: First, people often assume that all the quantitative information given us in a mathematical problem will be relevant to solving that problem. This assumption, however, is incorrect. Second, there is so little quantitative information in this particular problem that people would assume that each bit given would be relevant, even if they did not always make this assumption. Third, people often start to solve problems of this kind by figuring out how to use the quantitative information in the problem before they even consider whether the information is relevant to the solution of the problem. Thus, people who answer the problem incorrectly often do so because they are misled by the irrelevant information in it.

The correct answer is "three." Consider the possibilities. If the first sock is blue and the second sock is blue, you immediately have a pair; similarly, if the first sock is black and the second sock is black, you also immediately have a pair. At worst, the first sock will be blue and the second sock black, or vice versa. In this case, it will take a third sock to create a pair of one color or the other.

In some cases, the use of selective encoding is on a fairly large scale, and the need for it may therefore suggest itself immediately, at least to some people. In other cases, selective encoding may need to be applied only on a very small scale, but its application may nevertheless determine the correct answer to a problem, as in the following:

**A teacher had 23 pupils in his class. All but 7 of them went on a museum trip and thus were away for the day. How many of them remained in class that day?**

This problem again requires selective encoding for its correct solution. People frequently read the problem and immediately subtract 7 from 23 to obtain 16 as their answer. But this answer is incorrect. The critical word in the problem is "but." It is not the case that seven students went on the museum trip but rather that "all but 7" went on the trip. Thus, the fact that there are a total of

23 students in the class actually becomes irrelevant, even though it is one of only two numbers in the problem. The correct answer to the problem is actually the single number in the problem that is relevant to the problem's solution, namely, 7.

A famous problem that is similar to the "museum" problem and similar in its selective encoding requirements is the following:

**An airplane crashes on the U.S.–Canadian border. In what country are the survivors buried?**

The correct solution to this problem requires careful reading and selective encoding of the word "survivors." Unless you read the problem very carefully, you will not come up with the correct answer that survivors are not buried.

Each of the following problems requires selective encoding for its solution. First list the relevant information for solving each problem (selective encoding). Then solve each problem. Answers appear after the problems.

1.  **According to the U.S. Constitution, if the vice-president of the United States should die, who would be the president?**

2.  **A man who lived in a small town married 20 different women in that same town. All of them are still living, and he never divorced any of them. Yet he broke no laws. How could he do this?**

3.  **A man was putting some finishing touches on his house and realized that he needed something that he did not have. He went to the hardware store and asked the clerk, "How much will 150 cost me?" The clerk in the hardware store answered, "They are 75 cents apiece, so 150 will cost you $2.25." What did the man buy?**

4.  **Fifteen percent of the people in a certain town have unlisted telephone numbers. You select 200 names at random from the local phone book. How many of these people can be expected to have unlisted telephone numbers?**

5.  **In the Thompson family, there are five brothers, and each brother has one sister. If you count Mrs. Thompson, how many females are there in the Thompson family?**

6.  **A taxi driver picked up a fare at the Hyatt Regency Hotel who wanted to go to the airport. The traffic was heavy, and the taxicab's average speed for the entire trip was just 40 miles per hour. The total time of the trip was 80 minutes, and the customer was charged accordingly. At the airport, the taxi driver picked up another customer who wanted to be taken to the same Hyatt Regency Hotel. The taxi driver returned to the hotel along the same route that he had used just before, and traveled with the same average speed. But this time the trip took an hour and 20 minutes. Can you explain why?**

7. A clothing store ordered 80 new dresses. Each dress cost the manager $40. The total bill was $3200. After he had placed the order, the store manager discovered that had he ordered 100 or more dresses, he would have received a 10% discount. If the manager had ordered five more dresses, how much more would he have had to pay?

8. One day, a woman hailed a passing taxicab. On the way to her destination, she chattered incessantly. The taxi driver got annoyed. In desperation, he finally said, "Lady, I can see in the mirror that you are trying to talk to me. I'm very sorry, but I cannot hear a single word you are saying. I am extremely hard of hearing, and my hearing aid has not worked all day." When the woman heard this, she stopped talking, feeling very sorry for the driver. But after she got out at her destination, paid her fare, and watched the cab drive away, she suddenly realized that the driver had lied to her. How did she know that the driver had lied?

9. Susan gets in her car in Boston and drives toward New York City, averaging 50 miles per hour. Twenty minutes later, Ellen gets in her car in New York City and starts driving toward Boston, averaging 60 miles per hour. Both women take the same route, which extends a total of 220 miles between the two cities. Which car is nearer to Boston when they meet?

10. On a certain house two halves of a roof are unequal: The right half slopes downward at an angle of 35 degrees, whereas the left half slopes downward at an angle of 75 degrees. Suppose a rooster lays an egg right on the peak of the roof. On which side of the roof can the egg be expected to fall?

---

## ANSWERS TO ARITHMETICAL AND LOGICAL WORD PROBLEMS

1. The president. The death of the vice-president has no effect upon who is the president.
2. The man is a minister. The critical word in this problem is "married." The man married the various women, but he did not himself become married to them.
3. The man was buying house numbers. His address is 150, so he needs three numbers for a total cost of $2.25.
4. None. Unlisted numbers do not appear in the phone book.
5. Two. The only females in the family are the mother and her one daughter, who is the sister to each of her brothers.
6. Eighty minutes and one hour and twenty minutes are the same amount of time.
7. $200.00. Because the store manager still was not buying 100 or more dresses, he received no discount.
8. The lady knew that the taxicab driver was lying because he had taken her to the destination that she had orally asked him to take her to.
9. Each car is at the same distance from Boston when they meet, as the cars are immediately next to each other.
10. Roosters don't lay eggs.

**INFORMATION–EVALUATION PROBLEMS**    In each of the following problems, you are presented with a question and a number of facts. Mark each fact as either relevant (R) or irrelevant (I) for answering the questions. In some cases, pieces of information may be relevant only when considered in conjunction with each other. In such cases, both pieces of information should be marked as relevant. You should therefore read all of the statements before marking any of them as relevant or irrelevant. Answers appear after the problems.

1. How do desert animals withstand the heat of the desert?
   a. Most desert animals cannot tolerate temperatures above 150 degrees Fahrenheit.
   b. Desert animals are often nocturnal, and live inside underground tunnels during the day.
   c. A typical burrow does not get any hotter than 80 degrees Fahrenheit.
   d. The burrows of desert animals have high relative humidity, which comes from the animals' own water vapor.
   e. The burrows prevent animals from becoming dehydrated.
2. How much work is performed in pulling on a stuck drawer?
   a. Many people think studying involves hard work.
   b. To the scientist, work is a measurable physical quantity in the same sense that length and height are measurable.
   c. Work can be accomplished in pushing a car up a hill.
   d. To qualify as a form of work, a force must push an object for a distance.
3. Why do television sets with cable connections get better reception than televisions with antennae?
   a. Televisions flash pictures on a screen at a rate of 30 pictures per second and so produce the effect of continuous motion.
   b. At the broadcast station, a television image must be analyzed into 200,000 electrical charges.
   c. Each of the 200,000 charges is discharged 30 times per second and transmitted to the viewers.
   d. The picture can be transmitted by a coaxial cable, which travels directly from the broadcast source to the viewer.
   e. Most television pictures are transmitted by waves (high-frequency short waves) similar to those used by radio stations.
   f. High-frequency short waves can travel only in straight lines; they cannot bend to follow the earth's surface. Their range is limited to the visual horizon.
4. Why are protective laboratory goggles made from Plexiglas?
   a. Ultraviolet rays and X rays pass through Plexiglas, but heat rays do not.
   b. Plexiglas is widely used in surgery for artificial limbs.
   c. Plexiglas has better transparency than ordinary glass.
   d. Plexiglas can withstand heat as high as 100 degrees Centigrade.

    e. Plexiglas resists water, caustic alkalies, dilute acids, gasoline, and mineral oil.
    f. Plexiglas can be used to replace defective heart valves.
5. Why is it necessary to add detergent to water in order to wash clothes?
    a. The combination of detergent and water allows the detergent to penetrate between the clothes and the dirt.
    b. One hundred pounds of domestic washing is soiled with between two and four pounds of dirt.
    c. Most dirt cannot be dissolved by water alone.
    d. One hundred pounds of domestic washing usually has 0.9 pounds of protein-free organic matter (waxes, alcohol), 0.3 pounds of protein (hair, skin), 0.15 pounds of grease and sweat, as well as sand and dust.
6. Why does only a fraction of an iceberg show above water?
    a. Icebergs are huge ice mountains that float.
    b. They are brilliantly lit and majestic.
    c. Icebergs may provide a source of fresh water.
    d. When water freezes into ice, it expands in size and becomes less dense. Ice is a little lighter than water.
    e. Icebergs have posed a great danger to ships in the past.
    f. Icebergs break off from the polar icecap.
7. Where do space satellites get the electricity to run their electronic equipment?
    a. Weather satellites, communication satellites, and probes are unmanned.
    b. The storage batteries of U.S. satellites are kept charged by current generated in solar cells.
    c. Satellites can alter their courses with control jets when they receive commands from earth monitoring stations.
    d. In 1965, the space probe Mariner 4 took 21 pictures of the planet Mars from a distance of 6,000 miles.
8. Are cameras limited to taking pictures only of things that can be seen by the human eye?
    a. Cameras can photograph heat waves.
    b. An infrared camera can take pictures in complete darkness.
    c. X rays can photograph the inside of the human body partly because X rays are only 100 angstroms in length.

---

## ANSWERS TO INFORMATION–EVALUATION PROBLEMS*

| 1. a. I | 2. a. I | 3. a. I | 4. a. R | 5. a. R | 6. a. R | 7. a. I | 8. a. R |
|---------|---------|---------|---------|---------|---------|---------|---------|
| b. R | b. I | b. I | b. I | b. I | b. I | b. R | b. R |
| c. R | c. I | c. I | c. R | c. R | c. I | c. I | c. R |
| d. R | d. R | d. R | d. R | d. I | d. R | d. I | |
| e. R | | e. R | e. R | | e. I | | |
| | | f. R | f. I | | f. I | | |

*Alternative answers are acceptable if you can provide a compelling justification.

**MYSTERY PROBLEMS**   It was said earlier that the prototypical situation for the application of insights is the situation faced by a detective trying to solve a crime. Selective encoding can be particularly important in detective work. Consider the following four mystery stories and solve them, using selective encoding as your primary basis for solution. Answers appear after the problems.

1.  Trying to fight his seasickness, Detective Ramirez went through the long corridor that led to the cabin of the late Mr. Saunders. Once he got to the cabin, Detective Ramirez saw Mr. Saunders's body slumped over the dresser. A small gun lay in one of his hands. Approaching the dresser, Ramirez could see some loose papers on it. Among them was a suicide note. In the suicide note, Mr. Saunders explained why he had suddenly decided to end his life. A pen without its cover was also on the dresser.

While reading the suicide note, Ramirez thought he would never understand how a famous writer such as Saunders could have committed suicide. Saunders was Detective Ramirez's favorite mystery writer, so Saunders's death upset him very much.

Ramirez shifted his eyes from the note to Saunders's body, which was lying on its left side. Saunders had been a tall man in his forties with fair complexion and blond hair that somehow masked a long scar on his right cheek. The body was dressed in a well-cut dark suit that showed the writer's taste for the good things in life. "What a loss," Ramirez thought.

A noise in the background reminded Ramirez that there were two more people in the cabin besides him: the ship's captain and Mr. Saunders's nephew, Mr. Prince, who was the one who had discovered the body. Detective Ramirez asked Prince to tell him everything he had heard or seen regarding the incident.

"We came back to Mr. Saunders's cabin shortly after the captain's reception was over," said Mr. Prince. "Mr. Saunders—my uncle—told me he wanted to be alone. He wanted to take some notes for his next book. So I left the cabin and went directly to my own cabin, which is next door."

"What happened after that?" asked Detective Ramirez.

"Shortly after I left, I heard a shot," Mr. Prince continued, "and when I came in, I saw my uncle's body slumped on the dresser. I called his name but I did not get any reply, so I went closer to see why he did not answer and then I noticed the bullet through his left temple."

"Did you touch anything?" asked Detective Ramirez.

"No, I did not. I left everything the way it was."

Ramirez was certain that the apparent suicide was in fact a murder. He said to Mr. Prince, "You'd better tell me the whole truth." How did Detective Ramirez know that Mr. Saunders's death was murder, not suicide?

2.  Detective Ramirez was about to go to bed after one of those very hot summer days in New York. He had already put his pajamas on when the clock struck nine and the phone rang. It was the police chief inspector, named Smith, who asked Ramirez to go immediately to a very old house

on the city outskirts. It was raining so it took Ramirez a while before he got to the house.

As soon as Detective Ramirez met Inspector Smith, he asked him what the problem was.

"This is Mr. Brown," said Smith, "he can explain everything better than I can."

"Well?" said Ramirez to a very nervous man who seemed to be in shock.

"We came back from the movies around 7:00 P.M. My wife went directly to our bedroom while I stayed in the library doing some work. One hour later I went upstairs to go to bed and I found our bedroom locked. I tried to get some response from my wife but I did not succeed. I thought she had forgotten to unlock the door and was taking a bath so I went back to the library and worked half an hour more. When I went back upstairs and again got no response, I started to worry and called the police," said Mr. Brown.

"Show us the room," said Ramirez.

Once upstairs Ramirez tried to force the door but he could not do it. He asked Brown if there was another way to enter the room. Mr. Brown called one of the servants and asked him to take Detective Ramirez outside the house and show him a window on the second floor. Once outside, Ramirez put a ladder up to the window and climbed up. When he finally entered the room, he could barely see enough to find the switch to turn on the light. He then opened the door to let Smith in. Mrs. Brown's body was slumped over a fine desk. There was a suicide note under the dead woman's hand. The handwriting was erratic and the lines sloped down to one side. The pen was still firmly grasped in the woman's hand. In a very unclear way, the woman explained why she had taken her life.

Just at that moment the oldest son arrived. When he saw the police there, he asked at once what was going on. The police officer told him there had been a death. His mother had committed suicide. When the young man heard this, he rushed up and found Detective Ramirez, Inspector Smith, and Mr. Brown reading the note. They were talking about the difficulty of reading the woman's handwriting.

"If only she had written a more legible note," said Inspector Smith. To which the young man replied: "Mother could never see very well in the dark."

Ramirez lit a cigar, looked at the young man, and asked him where he had been for the last three hours. Between sobs, the young man said to Ramirez, "I was in a nearby movie theater. I left home around 6:30 P.M. to get to the movie on time. Once the movie ended, I came home and found this terrible event."

Ramirez looked at the young man and said, "I would like you to come with me to police headquarters. I do not believe this was suicide; I think it was murder."

Why did Ramirez suspect Brown's son?

3.  Sitting in his office smoking a big cigar, Detective Ramirez was ready to question Mr. Haggerty about his friend's death. At that moment the

phone rang. It was the coroner. He called Detective Ramirez to report the cause of Mr. Lynch's death.

"The body has bruises everywhere, but Lynch died from a blow on the back of his head," said the coroner to Detective Ramirez. As soon as Ramirez hung up the phone, Mr. Haggerty started to tell in his very soft voice his version of what had happened to his friend, Mr. Lynch.

"Last night we were coming back from a party riding our motorcycles. It was raining very hard so we could hardly see where we were going. The only thing that prevented the rain from blinding us was our helmets. The streets were getting very slippery, so we had to ride very carefully if we wanted to avoid an accident. We had had a few drinks at the party and Lynch had had a few more than I did. He said he was getting tired of driving in the rain and getting all wet so he was going to go faster to get home sooner. I told him it was very dangerous to go faster; it was better to take it easy. But he did not listen to what I said and started to go faster and faster. I tried to make him listen to reason but he paid no attention. Suddenly we got on a steep downhill street and Lynch tried to slow down, but his motorcycle spun around and Lynch flew over the handlebars, hitting his head against a telephone pole. I got off my motorcycle and knelt down to help him, but he was already dead."

Detective Ramirez smiled as he booked Mr. Haggerty as a murder suspect.

Why did Detective Ramirez arrest Mr. Haggerty?

4. It was 4:00 in the afternoon when Detective Ramirez was on his way to a hotel located on Casanova Avenue. A few minutes before, somebody had phoned Ramirez to inform him of a death in the hotel. As soon as Ramirez arrived, he asked the hotel manager to tell him what he knew.

"This afternoon around 3:45 P.M. one of the maids told me about the incident."

"Could you tell me where to find this maid? I would like to ask her some questions," said Ramirez.

"Sure, I will send for her right away," the manager said.

As soon as Ramirez met the maid, he asked her to explain everything she knew about the incident. "Very well, sir! Usually, room 44 is one of the first rooms I clean after lunch, but today the 'Do not disturb' sign hung on the doorknob. I could hear the radio playing softly. So I went ahead and cleaned the other rooms. At 3:30 P.M., the sign was still there, so I started to wonder if maybe Ms. Rose was sick or had forgotten to remove the sign. I knocked on the door and there was no answer. Everything was quiet. I used my key to open the door and there I saw her, lying on her bed. She was very pale and her eyes were lifeless. I got scared and ran downstairs to tell the manager about it."

Ramirez asked the manager to tell him what he knew about the event.

"Well . . . when the maid came to inform me about the incident, both of us went upstairs to room 44 and there she was, lying on her bed, dead."

"Could you please take me to the room?" asked Ramirez.

"Sure I can! Follow me," said the hotel manager.

As soon as Detective Ramirez entered Ms. Rose's room he saw her lying on her bed, dead. Everything was quiet and there was no sign of any violent struggle or damage caused by somebody breaking into the room. Everything seemed to be in perfect order. Some details in the room showed Detective Ramirez some features of the dead woman's personality. There were flowers in a vase on a small table beside the window. There were some magazines and newspapers on a chair facing the small table. There was a big picture of the deceased on the bureau. In Ms. Rose's right hand there was a covered bottle of sleeping pills; only two were left. It looked like a typical suicide.

Touching the deceased's body, Detective Ramirez said, "This woman has been dead for hours." He asked the hotel manager, "Did you remove anything in this room?"

"No, we did not remove anything at all!"

"There is something odd here and I am going to find what it is," said Ramirez, looking at the maid. "I will need to talk with you a little longer."

Why does Detective Ramirez think there was something odd going on?

### ANSWERS TO MYSTERY PROBLEMS

1. Mr. Prince could not have known his uncle had a bullet through his left temple unless he had moved the body. Mr. Saunders fell on his left side and Ramirez noticed Saunders's right cheek, which has a scar on it.
2. How does Mr. Brown's son know that the lights were off in his parents' bedroom at the time his mother was writing the note?
3. It would be impossible to hold a conversation such as the one Haggerty described, while riding motorcycles with helmets on in a hard rain, especially since Haggerty has a soft voice.
4. Ms. Rose had been dead for hours, so someone must have turned off the radio that the maid heard after lunch but not at 3:30.

You have now completed various kinds of exercises on the process of selective encoding. The emphasis in these exercises was on your improving your ability to separate relevant from irrelevant information. In the next section, we will consider the problem of how to selectively combine information once you have decided it is relevant for problem solution.

### Selective Combination

**ARITHMETICAL AND LOGICAL WORD PROBLEMS**    Consider the following problem. As you do so, think about how selective combination—putting pieces of information together in new ways—can help you solve the problem. Consider some of the kinds of selective combination problems you might encounter.

There were 100 politicians at a meeting. Each politician was either honest or dishonest. We know the following two facts: First, at least 1 of the politicians was honest; second, for any 2 politicians at least 1 of the 2 was dishonest. How many of the politicians were honest and how many were dishonest, and what are the respective numbers of each?

In this particular problem, selective encoding of information is not particularly difficult. Indeed, the relevant clues—that at least 1 politician was honest and that for any 2 politicians, at least 1 was dishonest—are even emphasized. The problem is to figure out how to combine these clues.

The first clue tells you that there is at least 1 honest politician, and from this clue, you can infer that there are possibly 99 dishonest politicians. Of course, there may be fewer than 99 dishonest politicians. The second clue tells you that, if you take any two politicians, you are guaranteed that at least 1 of them (and possibly both of them) will be dishonest. Combining these 2 clues gives you an answer to the problem. The second clue tells you that if you take the honest politician in the first clue and match that politician with any other of the 99 politicians, at least 1 of the 2 politicians will be dishonest. Now, since you know that the politician from the first clue is honest, it follows that the other 99 must be dishonest. There is no other way of guaranteeing that at least 1 politician in each pair will be dishonest. You can conclude, then, that there is 1 honest politician and there are 99 dishonest politicians.

Now, consider another selective combination problem that many people find to be quite difficult, despite its deceptively simple appearance:

I bought 1 share in the Sure-Fire corporation for $70. I sold that share for $80. Eventually, I bought back the share for $90, but later sold it for $100. How much money did I make?

As in the preceding problem, the information that is relevant for solution is quite obvious. Indeed, all of the numerical information in this problem is relevant. The question is, how does one combine it? There are actually two ways to arrive at the answer. The first involves considering the first buying-selling sequence. When the share of stock is sold the first time, I make a profit of $10. When I sell the share the second time, I again make a profit of $10. My total profit, therefore, is $20. Another way to solve the problem involves simply adding up the amount of money I pay in purchasing shares—$70 + $90 = $160—and subtracting that sum from the total amount of money involved in my selling of the shares—$80 + $100 = $180. The difference, again, is $20, my profit on the transactions.

Each of the following problems requires selective combination for its solution. Although there may be other difficulties to each problem, the primary one is that of figuring out how to combine pieces of information in the problem (selective combination). See if you can solve each problem. Answers appear after the problems.

1. How many pets do I have if all of them are birds except 2, all of them are dogs except 2, and all of them are cats except 2?

2. Mr. Lester has a small outdoor grill that is just big enough to hold 2 T-bone steaks. Mr. Lester's wife and son are starved. Mr. Lester's problem, therefore, is to broil 3 steaks—one for each of the 3 members of the family—in the shortest possible amount of time. Mr. Lester says to his wife and son, "I know that it takes 30 minutes to broil both sides of one steak because each side takes 15 minutes. Since I can cook 2 steaks at the same time, 30 minutes will be enough time to get 2 steaks ready. Another 30 minutes will be needed to broil the third steak, so that I can finish the whole job in an hour." How can Mr. Lester complete the cooking of all 3 steaks in just 45 minutes?

3. Jeannie failed to show up for school time and again. Although she always came in with notes from her mother, the school's attendance officer became suspicious and called the mother. As the attendance officer had suspected, the notes were fakes. The attendance officer called Jeannie into his office for an explanation. Unfortunately for the attendance officer, Jeannie had an explanation for why she had no time for school.

"I sleep 8 hours a day. That makes 8 × 365 or 2,920 hours. There are 24 hours per day, so that's the same as 2,920 divided by 24 or about 122 days. Saturday and Sunday, of course, are not school days. That amounts to 104 days per year. As you know, we have 60 days of summer vacation. Now, I need 3 hours per day for meals—that's 3 × 365, or 1,095 hours per year. Now, if you divide 1,095 by 24, that gives you 45 days per year. Finally, I need at least 2 hours a day for recreation. That comes to 2 × 365 or 730 hours. If you divide 730 by 24, you come out with about 30 days per year." Jeannie jotted down these figures and added up the total:

| | |
|---|---|
| Sleep | 122 |
| Weekends | 104 |
| Summer | 60 |
| Meals | 45 |
| Recreation | 30 |
| Sum | 361 |

"As you can see," said Jeannie, "that leaves me with just four days to be sick, and I haven't even yet considered the school holidays we get per year! So you can scarcely fault me for having been out as many days as I have been."

The attendance officer didn't know how to respond to Jeannie, and was ready, in desperation, to let her go. Can you find the error in Jeannie's calculations, helping out yourself even if you are unwilling to help out the poor attendance officer?

4. You have three crates of china. One is labeled "cups," one is labeled "saucers," and one is labeled "cups and saucers." Unfortunately, each label is on a wrong box. By taking only one piece of china from one box, how can you label each box correctly?

5. You are at a party of truth-tellers and liars. The truth-tellers always tell the truth, and the liars always lie. You meet a new friend. He tells you that he just heard a conversation in which a girl said she was a liar. Is your new friend a liar or a truth-teller?

6. If a doctor gave you 30 pills and told you to take 1 every 30 minutes, how long would they last?

7. You have a new kind of bread dough that doubles in size every hour. When you first put the dough into a large bowl, it covers only the bottom of the bowl. It takes 12 hours to fill the bowl completely. How many hours does it take for the bowl to become half full?

8. A potted plant costs $15. The plant costs $10 more than the pot. How much is the pot worth?

9. A recipe calls for 4 cups of water. You have only a 3-cup container and a 5-cup container. How can you measure out exactly 4 cups of water using only these two containers?

10. You and I have the same amount of money. How much money must I give you so that you have $10 more than I have?

11. A boy and a girl are talking. "I'm a boy," said person A. "I'm a girl," said person B. If at least one of them is lying, which is the boy and which is the girl?

12. If you go to sleep at 8:00, having set your alarm so that you will wake up at 9:00, how many hours will you sleep?

---

### ANSWERS TO ARITHMETICAL AND LOGICAL WORD PROBLEMS

1. 3. The information that all of the pets except 2 are birds immediately tells you that the total number of pets is 2 plus the number of birds. The further information that all of the pets are dogs except 2 tells you that the total number of pets is equal to 2 plus the number of dogs. And finally, the information that all of the pets are cats except 2 tells you that the total number of pets is 2 plus the number of cats. Since you are told of 3 kinds of pets that the pet owner has, you have exhausted your "degrees of freedom." Aside from the birds, there must be 1 dog and 1 cat. Aside from the dogs, there must be 1 bird and 1 cat. Aside from the cat, there must be 1 dog and 1 bird. So, if there is 1 of each pet, the total number of pets is 3.

2. Suppose we label the steaks A, B, and C. In the first round of cooking, which takes 15 minutes, Mr. Lester can cook side 1 of steak A and side 1 of steak B. In a second round of cooking, which also takes 15 minutes, Mr. Lester can cook side 2 of steak A and side 1 of steak C, temporarily taking steak B off the flame. In a third round of cooking, which again takes 15 minutes, Mr. Lester can complete the job by putting back on the grill steak B and cooking side 2 of that steak, and also cooking side 2 of steak C. In this more efficient way of cooking the 3 steaks, there are always 2 steaks on the flame, so that the job can be completed in 45 minutes rather than in the full hour.

3. Jeannie is assuming, in her calculations, that the various partitions of her time are independent and therefore additive. Her additive logic would work only if time spent in sleep was distinct from time spent on weekends, if these two times were distinct from time spent during the summer, if these three times were distinct from time spent during meals, and if all these times were distinct from times spent during recreation. But clearly, the times spent on these various activities are overlapping. As a result, they cannot simply be added up.

4. The correct answer is to take a piece of china from the "cups and saucers" crate. Relabel the crate correctly (that is, if you pull out a cup, put the "cup" label on the crate, and if you pull out a saucer, put the "saucer" label on the crate). Then reverse the two labels that are left. A common mistake people make in this problem is to try taking the one piece of china from the crate labeled "cups" or the crate labeled "saucers." This procedure will not tell you what is in any of the crates. For example, if you happen to get a cup from the crate marked, "saucers," you would not know whether the crate contained only cups or whether it contained cups and saucers. However, because you know that every crate is mislabeled, you know that both cups and saucers cannot be in the crate labeled "cups and saucers." Whatever you draw from this crate is what the crate contains, and since *all* the boxes are mislabeled, you need simply switch the two remaining labels and the problem is solved.

5. Your new friend is clearly a liar. If the girl about whom the friend was talking were a truth-teller, she would have said that she was a truth-teller. If she were a liar, she would have said that she was a truth-teller also. Thus, regardless of whether the girl were a truth-teller or a liar, she would have said that she was a truth-teller. Since your friend has said that she said she was a liar, your friend must be lying, and hence must be a liar.

6. The pills would last 14 hours, 30 minutes. The thing to remember is that in the first hour, you take 3 pills, 1 at the start of the hour, 1 after the half hour, and 1 after an hour. Thus, you finish the complete set of 30 pills after 14 hours, 30 minutes, rather than after 15 hours. The pill you take at the start of the first hour is not available at the beginning of the 15th hour.

7. The correct answer is 11 hours. Since the dough doubles in size every hour, the bowl is half full the hour before it is completely full. The best way to solve this problem is to work backward from the last hour (hour 12) rather than forward from the first hour.

8. $2.50. This answer meets all of the conditions of the problem. If the pot is worth $2.50, the plant is worth $12.50. The plant is thus worth $10 more than the pot. (A common mistake people make in this problem is to assume that the plant costs $10. It does not: It costs $10 *more* than the pot. To find out how much the pot costs, first subtract $10 from $15. Then split the $5 in half. This gives you $2.50, what the pot is worth.)

9. Fill the 5-cup container with water. Pour as much of the contents as you can into the 3-cup container. Now spill out the contents that you just poured into the 3-cup container. You now have 2 cups in the 5-cup container. Pour the contents of the 5-cup container into the 3-cup container. Now fill the 5-cup container again. Pour as much of the contents in the 5-cup container as you can into the 3-cup container. This container will take only 1 cup. You now have 4 cups left in the 5-cup container.

10. $5 (as long as you both start out with a minimum of $5). If we both start out with $10, and I give you $5, then you will have $15, $10 more than the $5 I now have left.

11. Person A is the girl and Person B is the boy. If at least one of them is lying, then both of them must be lying. Suppose Person A is lying. Then Person A is actually a girl rather than a boy. Since we know that the situation involves a boy talking to a girl, then Person B must actually be a boy, and hence Person B must be lying. The identical logic applies if one starts off by assuming that Person B is lying.

12. 1. The alarm will go off in one hour.

**CONCEPTUAL PROJECTION PROBLEMS**    In these problems, you must predict states of the future from limited information. Consider first some "otherworldly" problems.

On the planet Kyron, in a faraway galaxy, there are four kinds of unisex humanoids:

A TWE is a Kyronian who is born a child and remains a child throughout its lifetime.

A NEL is a Kyronian who is born an adult and remains an adult throughout its lifetime.

A BIT is a Kyronian who is born a child and becomes an adult.

A DEK is a Kyronian who is born an adult and becomes a child.

Your task will be to analyze two pieces of information given to you about a particular Kyronian, and to decide whether these two pieces of information describe a TWE, NEL, BIT, or DEK. The two pieces of information will be a description of the Kyronian in the year of its birth, 1979, and a description of the Kyronian 21 years later, in the year 2000. The description of the Kyronian in the year 1979 will appear to the left, and the description in the year 2000 will appear to the right. Each description may take either of two forms. The description may be verbal, consisting of any of the words TWE, NEL, BIT, or DEK; or the description may be pictorial, consisting of either

the picture 🜊

or the picture 🜨

In order to make these judgments, you will need to know two additional facts. First, when a Kyronian is first born, it is not possible to distinguish a TWE from a BIT, or a NEL from a DEK. The reason for this is that at birth, both a TWE and a BIT appear to be children, and both a NEL and a DEK appear to be adults. It is only after one has an opportunity to see what effect, if any, the aging process has had, that one can distinguish a TWE from a BIT, or a NEL from a DEK. Second, after 21 years, it is possible to make these distinctions, because a BIT has changed from a child to an adult, and a DEK has changed from an adult to a child. A TWE and a NEL look exactly as they did at birth.

The kinds of judgments you will be making are of four types:

1.  The first category of judgment involves two pictures. You will be presented first with a picture of a Kyronian at birth in 1979, then a picture of the same Kyronian in the year 2000, and finally with three alternative verbal descriptions. Your task will be to judge which of the three verbal descriptions correctly identifies the kind of Kyronian depicted in the pictures. For example, you might be presented with the following problem:

                DEK          NEL          BIT

The correct answer to this problem is DEK, because the pictures depict a Kyronian who was born an adult and became a child.

2. The second category of judgments involves a verbal description of a Kyronian at birth in 1979, and a picture of the same Kyronian 21 years later in the year 2000. Your task is to judge which of three verbal descriptions correctly identifies the kind of Kyronian depicted in the verbal description and the picture. There is one important thing for you to realize in this kind of problem. Since it is not possible to tell at birth whether the individual is a TWE or a BIT, on the one hand (since both appear as children), or a NEL or a DEK, on the other (since both appear as adults), the verbal description for 1979 can be counted on only to identify correctly the physical appearance of the Kyronian; it may or may not correctly predict the appearance of the same Kyronian 21 years later. It is simply not possible, in 1979, to know what the Kyronian will look like 21 years later. Thus, if you are told that the Kyronian is a TWE, you can be assured that the Kyronian appears to be a child; you cannot be certain that 21 years later the Kyronian will still appear to be a child; if the Kyronian is actually a BIT, it will appear to be an adult. Similarly, if you are told the Kyronian is a BIT, you cannot be sure it is not actually a TWE. The same principle applies to NEL and DEK. If you are told that the Kyronian appears to be a NEL or a DEK in 1979, you can be sure only that the Kyronian appears to be an adult. You cannot be sure of what the Kyronian will look like in 2000. To summarize, the verbal description in 1979 will always cor-rectly describe the Kyronian's physical appearance in 1979, but it may or may not correctly predict the Kyronian's physical appearance in 2000. Consider two examples:

NEL                        NEL          BIT          DEK

The correct answer is NEL, since the Kyronian appears to be an adult in 1979, and appears to be an adult in 2000 as well. NEL thus correctly predicted the Kyronian's physical appearance in 2000.

DEK                        DEK          NEL          BIT

The correct answer is again NEL, since the Kyronian appears to be an adult in both 1979 and 2000. In this example, DEK failed to predict correctly the physical appearance of the Kyronian in 2000. As always, however, the description of physical appearance was correct for 1979.

3. The third category of judgment involves a picture of a Kyronian in the year 1979, followed by a verbal description of the same Kyronian in the year 2000. Your task is to indicate which of two pictures correctly describes the physical appearance of the Kyronian in the year 2000. Watch out for the case in which the verbal description of the Kyronian in the year 2000 is *inconsistent* with the picture of the Kyronian in the year 1979. In this event, you choose as your answer the letter "I." An inconsistency is different from a misprediction of physical appearance. An inconsistency represents an important situation—a contradiction in terms. Consider two example problems:

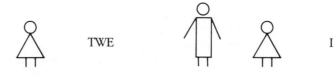

Here, the correct answer is 🔺, since the Kyronian was born as a child and remained a child throughout its lifetime. Note that the verbal description is consistent with the picture.

In this example, the correct answer is I. The picture depicts an adult Kyronian in 1979, but a BIT is born in 1979 as a child. Since this situation is impossible, the picture and verbal description are inconsistent.

4. The fourth category of judgments involves two verbal descriptions of a Kyronian, one in 1979 and the other in 2000. The verbal descriptions are followed by two alternative pictures and the letter I. Your task is to select the picture that correctly depicts in 2000 the Kyronian described in the two verbal descriptions, or else to indicate that the two verbal descriptions are inconsistent with each other (I). There are two important things for you to realize in this kind of problem. First, remember that verbal descriptions in 1979 always accurately represent the physical appearance of the Kyronian in 1979, but may or may not accurately predict the Kyronian's physical appearance in 2000. Second, it is possible for two verbal descriptions to be inconsistent. Two verbal descriptions are inconsistent if one describes a Kyronian being born as an adult, and the other describes the Kyronian being born as a child, or vice versa. This is not simply a case of misprediction; it is an impossibility. Consider some examples of this kind of problem:

In this case, the correct answer is obviously 🔺, since in 2000 a DEK appears to be a child.

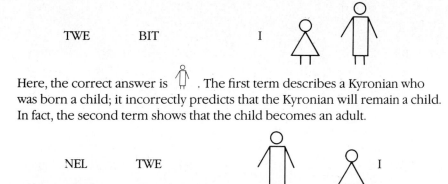

Here, the correct answer is 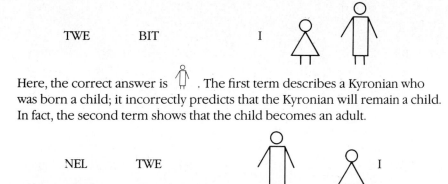. The first term describes a Kyronian who was born a child; it incorrectly predicts that the Kyronian will remain a child. In fact, the second term shows that the child becomes an adult.

Here, the correct answer is I, because the first term describes a Kyronian born as an adult, and the second term describes a Kyronian born as a child. This is impossible, and hence the two verbal descriptions are inconsistent.

Like the sample problems above, the problems that follow are in two parts. The left side contains the two pieces of information from 1979 and from 2000. The right side consists of three response choices. If the evidence from 2000 is a picture, the response choices are verbal descriptions. If the evidence from 2000 is a verbal description, the response choices will be pictures plus a letter "I" (representing a response of "Inconsistent"). Answers appear after the problems.

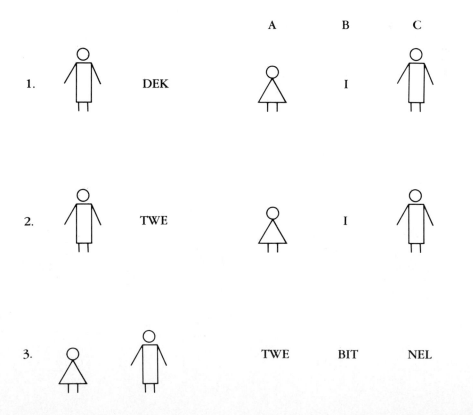

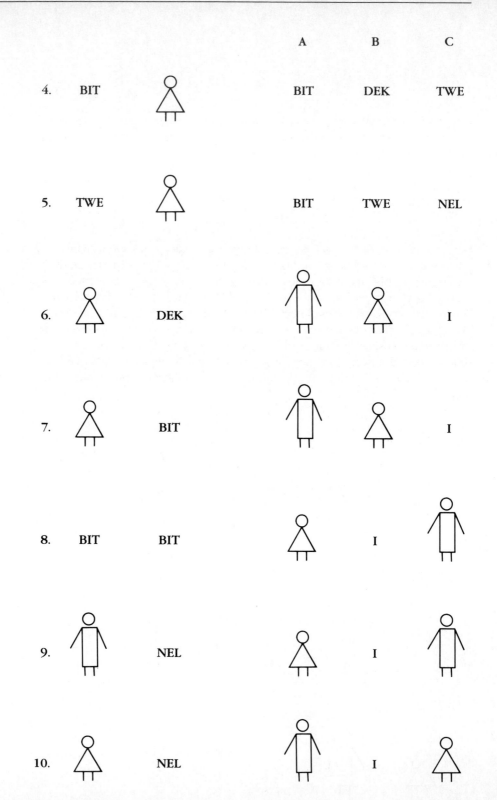

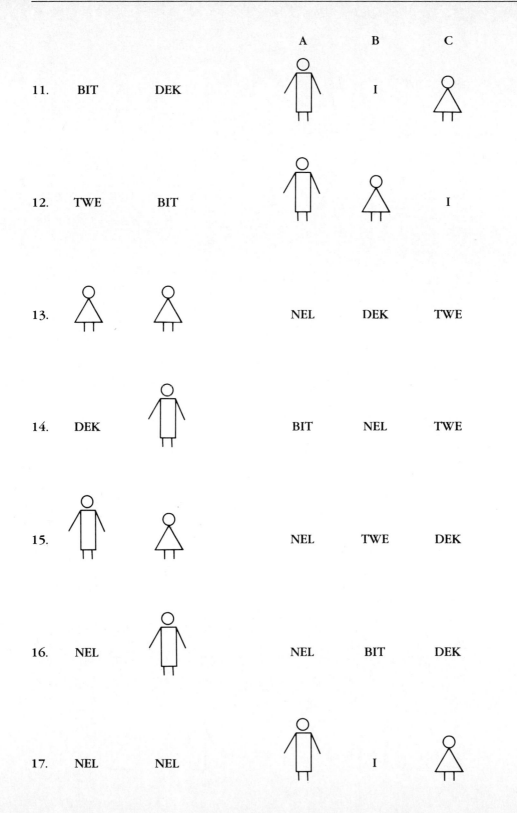

A        B        C

11.    BIT        DEK                                    I

12.    TWE        BIT

13.                                      NEL      DEK      TWE

14.    DEK                               BIT      NEL      TWE

15.                                      NEL      TWE      DEK

16.    NEL                               NEL      BIT      DEK

17.    NEL        NEL                             I

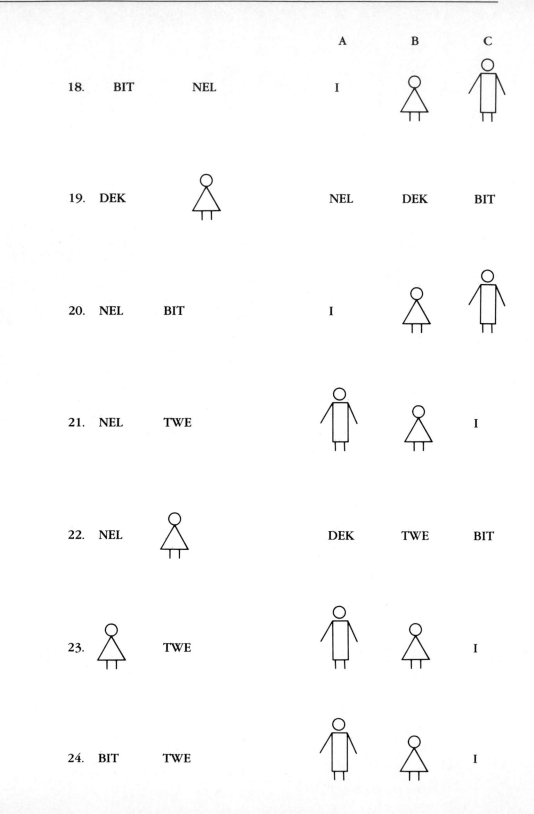

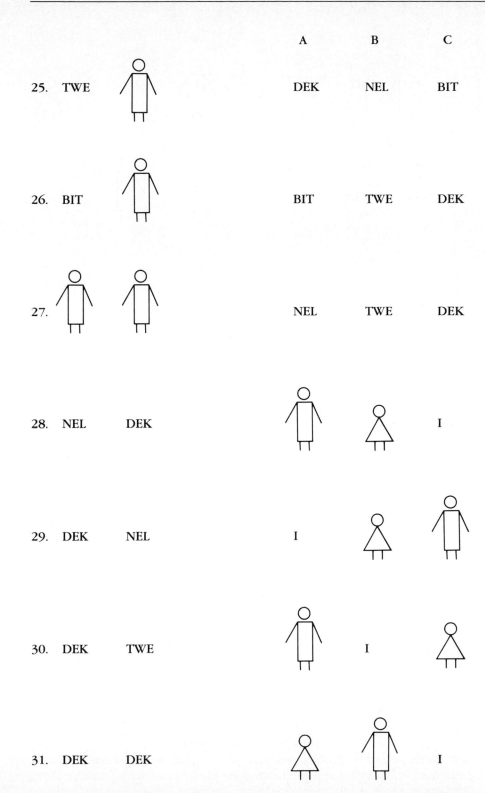

| | | | A | B | C |
|---|---|---|---|---|---|
| 25. | TWE | | DEK | NEL | BIT |
| 26. | BIT | | BIT | TWE | DEK |
| 27. | | | NEL | TWE | DEK |
| 28. | NEL | DEK | | | |
| 29. | DEK | NEL | | | |
| 30. | DEK | TWE | | | |
| 31. | DEK | DEK | | | |

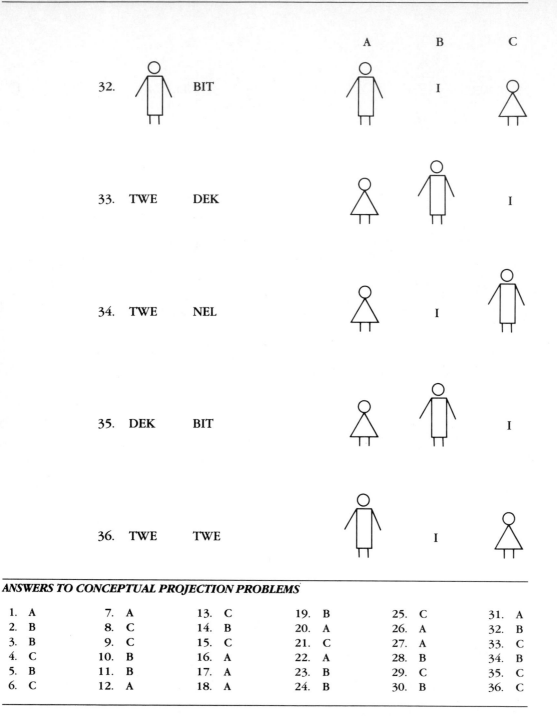

## ANSWERS TO CONCEPTUAL PROJECTION PROBLEMS

| | | | | | |
|---|---|---|---|---|---|
| 1. A | 7. A | 13. C | 19. B | 25. C | 31. A |
| 2. B | 8. C | 14. B | 20. A | 26. A | 32. B |
| 3. B | 9. C | 15. C | 21. C | 27. A | 33. C |
| 4. C | 10. B | 16. A | 22. A | 28. B | 34. B |
| 5. B | 11. B | 17. A | 23. B | 29. C | 35. C |
| 6. C | 12. A | 18. A | 24. B | 30. B | 36. C |

## *Selective Comparison*

Selective-comparison problems require you to relate new information to old information. Analogies are good examples of such problems, because they require you to draw on prior knowledge. Analogies also require you to infer a relation, and then use that relation to complete a new one. However, most analogies are not particularly novel.

   **NOVEL ANALOGIES**    It is possible to create novel analogies by selectively altering states of the world. Consider the analogies below. In solving these analogies, assume that the statement given before the analogy is true, whether or not it is actually true. Then solve the analogy taking this assumption into account. Sometimes the assumption will be true in the real world; other times it will be false. Sometimes the assumption will affect the solution you reach; other times it will not. The important thing is to assume the statement is true, regardless of its actual truth or falsity, and then to use the assumption, where needed, to solve the analogies. Answers appear after the problems.

1.  VILLAINS are lovable.

    HERO is to ADMIRATION as VILLAIN is to
    CONTEMPT          AFFECTION          CRUEL          KIND

2.  CHOWDER is sour.

    CLAM is to SHELLFISH as CHOWDER is to
    SOUP          STEAK          LIQUID          SOLID

3.  LAKES are dry.

    TRAIL is to HIKE as LAKE is to
    SWIM          DUST          WATER          WALK

4.  SPARROWS play hopscotch.

    TROUT is to SCALY as SPARROW is to
    FEATHERY          BUMPY          EAGLE          CANARY

5.  CHERRIES are fruits.

    EGG is to YOLK as CHERRY is to
    PASTURE          BONE          ORCHARD          PIT

6.  KITES are pretty.

    WAGON is to PULL as KITE is to
    PUSH          FLY          HANDLE          TAIL

7.  ELEPHANTS are enormous.

    MOUSE is to TINY as ELEPHANT is to
    TRAMPLE          LAZY          HUGE          SLEEP

8.  HUTS provide shelter.

    CASTLE is to LARGE as HUT is to
    IGLOO          POOR          SMALL          TENT

9. SOLDIERS wear boots.

GANGSTER is to REVOLVER as SOLDIER is to

UNIFORM          SWORD          RIFLE          SHIELD

10. DEER attack tigers.

LION is to COURAGEOUS as DEER is to

TIMID          AGGRESSIVE          COUGAR          ELK

11. BASEBALL is a game.

TENNIS is to RACKET as BASEBALL is to

CLUB          BAT          STRIKE          PUTT

12. CARPENTERS are people.

TAILOR is to CLOTH as CARPENTER is to

WALL          PAINT          CABINET          WOOD

13. COBRAS drink lemonade.

ROBIN is to BIRD as COBRA is to

DESERT          LIZARD          SNAKE          JUNGLE

14. NEEDLES are dull.

THIMBLE is to BLUNT as NEEDLE is to

SHARP          SMOOTH          STAB          BRUISE

15. PRESIDENTS give speeches.

CAPITOL is to PLACE as PRESIDENT is to

PERSON          DETECTIVE          AGENCY          GOVERNMENT

16. CLOCKS last forever.

CALENDAR is to DATE as CLOCK is to

TIME          PLACE          TICKING          HUMMING

17. PIGS climb fences.

GOLDFISH is to BOWL as PIG is to

PEN          CAGE          DIRTY          GRACEFUL

18. RADISHES are candies.

PRETZEL is to SALTY as RADISH is to

BITTER          CHOCOLATE          SALAD          SWEET

19.  MIDGETS wear armor.

GIANT is to TALL as MIDGET is to

SHORT          FAT          BOY          MAN

20.  RACCOONS eat meat.

MAN is to HANDS as RACCOON is to

COAT          TOES          PAWS          SHOE

21.  PADDLES are oars.

RUDDER is to STEER as PADDLE is to

PROPEL          MELT          WOOD          WAX

22.  BROOMSTICKS are machines.

JET is to PILOT as BROOMSTICK is to

HOUSE          HERMIT          WITCH          GARDEN

23.  GRANITE is fattening.

IRON is to METAL as GRANITE is to

SOLID          FOOD          TASTY          HARD

24.  WAITRESSES serve meals.

STEWARDESS is to PLANE as WAITRESS is to

BUS          RESTAURANT          MENU          SCHEDULE

25.  APACHES are humans.

PINTO is to PONY as APACHE is to

BARN          FARMER          RESERVATION          INDIAN

26.  DENIM is blue.

STEEL is to METAL as DENIM is to

FLIMSY          TILE          FABRIC          STURDY

27.  LAMBS are frisky.

CALF is to COW as LAMB is to

SHINY          DUCK          WOOLLY          SHEEP

28.  HAMSTERS are active.

DOLL is to TOY as HAMSTER is to

PET          PICTURE          LIVING          QUIET

29. DENTISTS wear coats.

   MECHANIC is to ENGINE as DENTIST is to
   PLEASANT          CAST          PAINFUL          TOOTH

30. MAPLES are purple.

   ROSE is to PETALS as MAPLE is to
   LEAVES          SYRUP          SUGAR          BARK

31. MOUNTAINS are invisible.

   CANYON is to LOW as MOUNTAIN is to
   FALL          STEEP          CLIMB          HIGH

32. TRAINS carry passengers.

   HOUSE is to BUILDING as TRAIN is to
   WAREHOUSE          BOX          STATION          VEHICLE

33. GOLF is a sport.

   WALTZ is to DANCE as GOLF is to
   BATTLE          GAME          CART          CADDY

34. SAINTS are demons.

   SINNER is to BAD as SAINT is to
   GOOD          HELL          HEAVEN          WICKED

35. LEMONS are animals.

   LIME is to GREEN as LEMON is to
   YELLOW          ORANGE          GROW          PICK

36. MILK is a liquid.

   CHEESE is to THICK as MILK is to
   JUICE          TASTY          THIN          CEREAL

37. SHAMPOO is black.

   SOAP is to BODY as SHAMPOO is to
   HAIR          RUG          WASHED          STAINED

38. CATS scratch things.

   PERSON is to FINGERNAIL as CAT is to
   BRUSH          FUR          KNIFE          CLAW

39. THUNDER is silent.

LIGHTNING is to VISIBLE as THUNDER is to
QUIET              FEEL            INAUDIBLE         NOISY

40. DIAMONDS are fruits.

PEARL is to OYSTER as DIAMOND is to
MINE            TREE           RING           PIE

41. MOTHS kill people.

HORNET is to DANGEROUS as MOTH is to
HARMLESS        ·     SCORPION         DEADLY         BUTTERFLY

42. LOVE is wonderful.

KISS is to ACTION as LOVE is to
IMAGINARY        DEGREE         FEELING        REAL

43. CANTALOUPES are fruits.

ZUCCHINI is to SQUASH as CANTALOUPE is to
NUT            MELON         EAT          CRACK

44. OVENS produce heat.

REFRIGERATOR is to COLD as OVEN is to
STOVE          COOL          SINK         HOT

45. OXYGEN is pink.

BLOOD is to HEART as OXYGEN is to
LIVER          LUNG          DRY         DAMP

46. SAPPHIRES are junk.

CARNATION is to FLOWER as SAPPHIRE is to
JEWEL         SPARKLING       MINERAL       DULL

47. SHARKS chase foxes.

BEE is to INSECT as SHARK is to
AMPHIBIAN       WATER        MAMMAL       LAND

48. LIFE JACKETS prevent drowning.

PARACHUTE is to SKY as LIFE JACKET is to
SEA         DITCH        FLOATING       COVERING

49. GOATS are robots.

    CHICKEN is to HATCHED as GOAT is to
    BORN          FARM          BUILT          FACTORY

50. CHINESE drink tea.

    GERMAN is to EUROPEAN as CHINESE is to
    ENGLISH          ASIAN          CHINA          JAPAN

51. ZEBRAS are wildlife.

    LEOPARD is to SPOT as ZEBRA is to
    STRIPE          STAR          SHOOT          HOLD

52. KIDNAPPERS are acrobats.

    HOSTAGE is to VICTIM as KIDNAPPER is to
    POLICEMAN          CRIMINAL          RANSOM          JAIL

53. GHOSTS are athletes.

    WEREWOLF is to MONSTER as GHOST is to
    DRAMA          SPIRIT          HAUNT          ACT

54. GUITARS are instruments.

    BUGLE is to BLOW as GUITAR is to
    TYPE          STRUM          OFFICE          CONCERT

55. PIANOS make music.

    HAMMER is to TOOL as PIANO is to
    BENCH          INSTRUMENT          KEYS          LEGS

56. GREYHOUNDS are fast.

    FOXHOUND is to HUNT as GREYHOUND is to
    SPEEDY          CRAWL          RACE          SLOW

57. BALLS are flat.

    POLE is to CYLINDER as BALL is to
    SPHERE          CIRCLE          BOUNCE          THROW

58. APPLES are vegetables.

    CARAMEL is to CHEWY as APPLE is to
    SOFT          CRISP          SAUCE          STEW

59. TOASTERS write cookbooks.

SPATULA is to UTENSIL as TOASTER is to
WRITER            APPLIANCE            BREAD            BOOK

60. EARTH is hollow.

SUN is to STAR as EARTH is to
PLANET            MOON            SPINNING            FALLING

---

## ANSWERS TO NOVEL ANALOGIES

| | | | |
|---|---|---|---|
| 1. AFFECTION | 16. TIME | 31. HIGH | 46. MINERAL |
| 2. SOUP | 17. CAGE | 32. VEHICLE | 47. MAMMAL |
| 3. WALK | 18. SWEET | 33. GAME | 48. SEA |
| 4. FEATHERY | 19. SHORT | 34. WICKED | 49. BUILT |
| 5. PIT | 20. PAWS | 35. YELLOW | 50. ASIAN |
| 6. FLY | 21. PROPEL | 36. THIN | 51. STRIPE |
| 7. HUGE | 22. WITCH | 37. HAIR | 52. CRIMINAL |
| 8. SMALL | 23. FOOD | 38. CLAW | 53. SPIRIT |
| 9. RIFLE | 24. RESTAURANT | 39. INAUDIBLE | 54. STRUM |
| 10. AGGRESSIVE | 25. INDIAN | 40. TREE | 55. INSTRUMENT |
| 11. BAT | 26. FABRIC | 41. DEADLY | 56. RACE |
| 12. WOOD | 27. SHEEP | 42. FEELING | 57. CIRCLE |
| 13. SNAKE | 28. PET | 43. MELON | 58. CRISP |
| 14. SMOOTH | 29. TOOTH | 44. HOT | 59. WRITER |
| 15. PERSON | 30. LEAVES | 45. LUNG | 60. PLANET |

---

## Selective Encoding, Combination, and Comparison

**SCIENTIFIC INSIGHT PROBLEMS**    Now combine the use of the three insight skills—selective encoding, selective combination, and selective comparison—in solving the scientific insight problems that follow. Answers appear after the problems.

1.  A scientist is doing a study for the Department of Energy to see if some clothes keep people warmer than other clothes. This is his description of the experiment: Two women are walking along a road. The sun is shining brightly overhead, throwing shadows behind the women. The women are the same height and weight. One wears a white dress and the other wears a black dress. The dresses are identical except for color: They are both cotton and are the same style and length. The woman in the black dress is comfortable, and the woman in the white dress is cold. The scientist concluded, based on these facts, that dark-colored clothes help

a person to keep body heat, whereas light-colored clothes let the body heat disappear. The Department of Energy fired the scientist. What did he do wrong?

2. Dr. Smith was reading the newspaper when she saw an article called "Plants Have Feelings, Too." It reported that a scientist had conducted an experiment to see if plants had feelings. The scientist decided that plants conveyed their feelings not by smiles or frowns, but by electromagnetic waves. To test this theory, she connected the plants to machines that measured the waves, and had different people approach the plants and talk to them. The scientist was pleased to discover that Person A, who spoke kindly to the plants, registered one way on the machine, whereas Person B, who abused the plants, registered in a different way. She concluded that plants responded to different human actions in different ways.

Dr. Smith wanted to test this theory. She repeated the experiment, but this time she attached the machines to plants and to empty Styrofoam cups. At the end of the experiment, she was surprised. Sure enough, the plants responded to different people in different ways. But so did the Styrofoam cups!

Dr. Smith was mystified; but slowly, an incredible idea began to form in her mind. "I can't believe this discovery," she said. "I've . . . I've learned that Styrofoam cups have feelings!"

Unfortunately, Dr. Smith had made the wrong conclusion. What conclusion would you draw?

3. Christopher Wood, a doctor at the Bowman Gray School of Medicine, was hiking along a riverbank. In the middle of the river were some boulders that blocked the water. Looking down, Dr. Wood saw that when the current hit the boulders, it split. In the process of breaking, a couple of things happened—some water actually went rippling upstream a little way, and some eddies went wandering off downstream, but most of it went rushing downstream. As the water eddies moved out from main current, the water slowed down, and dropped whatever rocks and dirt it was carrying. Along the banks, these deposited particles began to build up the riverbank.

On Monday, Dr. Wood went into the laboratory. He was studying atherosclerosis, a condition in which the arteries (especially those carrying blood to the brain) grow thicker, decreasing the flow of blood. He decided to look at the carotid arteries, where atherosclerosis usually takes places.

Using special sonar equipment, he looked at the vessels in a patient. Focusing in on the point where the two carotid arteries split off from one artery, he noticed a strange thing. At the fork, the blood started to move in a funny way. And it was just beyond this point that he saw the unusual but deadly thickening of the artery walls.

Suddenly he said, "Aha!"

What do you think he realized?

4.  When a jet airliner is flying at a cruising altitude of 35,000 feet, it leaves behind it a white wake—a white trail that traces its path. High in the sky where the jets travel, conditions are very cold. Jet aircraft derive the energy that keeps them flying from the combustion of fuel (petroleum). In chemical terms, petroleum is a hydrocarbon, that is, for the most part, a combination of carbon and hydrogen. When the fuel is burned, the oxygen from the air combines with the carbon and the hydrogen, releasing energy and leaving a gas that is a combination of carbon and oxygen (carbon dioxide) and water. When a jet flies, streaming out carbon dioxide and water vapor behind it, the carbon dioxide is as invisible as the oxygen and nitrogen of which the air itself is composed. What is the white trail?

5.  Every morning, millions of microscopic crustaceans in the world's lakes and oceans migrate to water many fathoms deep. And late each afternoon, they surface again. For them, this is an expensive round trip to commute, requiring enormous amounts of energy and time, and students of migration have wondered for years what such zooplankton gain by spending their days in cold, dark waters, where food is scarce, and where they cannot reproduce quickly.

To find out, two scientists spent a year observing two species, *Daphnia hyalina* and *Daphnia galeata*. Both species spend the night near the surface, but in the morning, *D. hyalina* departs for the depths, rejoining *D. galeata* only when shadows lengthen in early evening.

All day long, *D. galeata* enjoys the benefits of warmth and abundant food near the lake's surface, while, far below, *D. hyalina* is deprived. Under such conditions, one would expect *D. galeata* to thrive and multiply until it drove its neighbor out.

Not so, the scientists report. Even though *D. galeata* grows and reproduces faster, its population is equaled—and often outnumbered—by *D. hyalina*.

Can you think why?

6.  Dr. Smith learned from a friend that he could grow living creatures by boiling the seeds of pumpkins. He was surprised, because he had been taught that living creatures reproduced themselves; now, if this friend was right, he could grow microorganisms and animals and birds from scratch. The doctor was excited, because he knew he would be famous if the discovery was true. He decided to test it. He took a flask and carefully cleaned it so no organisms were left alive. Next, he added water and the pumpkin seeds, and boiled them to make sure he killed the germs. Finally, he put a plastic stopper in the bottle and sealed it so no organisms could get in. Suddenly, he realized he'd made a mistake. If he wanted something to grow, he had to give it air! So he took out the plastic stopper and put in a cork, which let air through. Two days later there were lots of microorganisms swimming in the water. Dr. Smith knew he had successfully

grown them from pumpkin seeds, and rushed out to tell his friends of his great discovery.

Unfortunately, Dr. Smith made a big mistake. What was it?

7.  There is at least one known instance of a jet fighter pilot shooting his own plane out of the air, using his own guns. Amazing as it seems, aeronautical engineers have made it possible for a supersonic jet fighter to catch up with the fire from its own guns with sufficient speed to shoot itself down. If a plane, flying at 1,000 miles per hour, fires a burst from 20-millimeter guns, the shells leave the plane with an airspeed of about 3,000 miles per hour.

Why won't a plane which continues to fly straight ahead fly into its own bullets?

8.  Scientists have noticed that on rainy days following hot, dry summer days, the air takes on a fresh, clean, spring smell. What causes that? To some extent, the falling rain washes pollutants out of the air. But that is not the main reason. Think about the following facts from the reports of two Australian scientists, Dr. Bear and Dr. Thomas, and see if you can get the answer.

a.  Air is full of plant vapor in the form of invisible oils and essences.

b.  These substances—pinene, myrcene, isoprene, and linalool—are the substances you smell when you get close to living plants.

c.  Clay is a major component of toothpastes and antacids (Maalox, DiGel, and so on) and one of its primary characteristics is its ability to act as a sponge, absorbing many times its weight in liquids.

d.  On hot days, the clay is baked dry of any water. What it does then is to absorb the scents of plants from the air, so the scents are trapped and pulled out of the air.

What do you think happens when it starts to rain that makes the air smell so fresh?

9.  Napoleon surrendered to the British in 1815. The British sent him in exile to the island of St. Helena because they wanted to eliminate any possibility that he would rebuild his army. Napoleon and a few attendants were sent to Longwood House, a moldy, damp place which, as their only concession to the once-powerful emperor, the British repapered in green and gold wallpaper.

Over the past few years, Dr. Stan Forshufrud has studied the medical accounts of Napoleon's last months at St. Helena. The scientist developed a theory that Napoleon was deliberately and systematically poisoned by his enemies with arsenic. Napoleon's symptoms were classic for arsenic poisoning: shivering, swelling of the limbs, and repeated gastric upsets. Napoleon's companions in exile also suffered from these symptoms.

Another scientist, Dr. David Jones, has been studying the uses of arsenic over the years. This is his report:

By 1800, a popular and cheap dye, "Scheele green," was used in paints, fabrics, and wallpapers. The dye contained arsenic. As long as the wallpaper, fabric, or paint was dry, it was quite harmless. But once it got wet—from condensation, rising damp, or whatever—it could go moldy. To survive on the wallpaper, the mold must somehow get rid of the arsenic. Many molds convert it to a vapor.

What do you think might have caused Napoleon's death?

10.  In 1960, Dr. Wooton, a doctor and professor of medicine at the University of Tennessee, was surprised to see a young man walk into his office. The young man was orange.

Dr. Wooton was even more surprised when the man said that his problem was a stomach pain, but made no mention of his color. Quickly, Dr. Wooton recalled various medical disorders that could cause skin color to change: liver damage turned a victim yellow, heart disease turned a victim blue, pituitary disease turned a victim paper-white. But he couldn't imagine what turned a person orange.

After examining the patient, Dr. Wooton discovered that he had an abnormal pancreas, which could mean cancer. He scheduled the young man for tests at the hospital, and took a detailed history. One of the doctor's questions was, "When did you turn orange?" The man said he hadn't realized he was turning orange, because it happened so gradually. The doctor found nothing else unusual in the man's background, except for his diet. He ate lots of vegetables—carrots, rutabaga, squash, beans, spinach— as well as oranges and eggs, and he drank gallons of tomato juice each day.

The man went to the hospital and had tests performed. They showed that his stomach pain was not cancer, but a simple cyst that could be easily removed. It was not responsible for the strange color of his skin.

Dr. Wooton did more research into the problem of the man's skin color, and finally found documented proof that food could change a person's color. Foods like carrots, oranges, and eggs contain carotene, which turn a person yellow, but not orange. Then he found reports that tomatoes contain lycopene, a red dye. But tomatoes were not known to turn a person orange. What do you think caused the man to turn orange?

11.  Copernicus was standing on the beach, watching the sailing ships come in and leave. He noticed a strange thing about the ships that were coming in from the sea. As a ship moved closer, he could see the very tip of it. Then he could see the masts, and finally, the body. "How odd," he thought. "It looks as if the ship is actually rising from the ocean. But I know it isn't—it simply confirms my suspicions that the earth is round, and not flat." How did Copernicus reach this conclusion?

12.  Many lepidopterists (people who study butterflies) believe that male butterflies are brightly colored and vividly patterned in order to appeal to the female. Robert Silberglied tested this belief by changing the colors of a

male butterfly's wings. He found that females did not discriminate against the males with incorrectly colored wings.

Instead, he has proposed another theory. It is based on the fact that, because butterflies are so fragile and easily injured, they have developed characteristics that allow them to avoid physical fights. In addition, to support his theory, Silberglied reported the well-known fact that territorial birds can intimidate their enemies without ever touching them.

What do you suppose Silberglied's theory is?

13. Heat pumps, air conditioners, and refrigerators are very similar machines. What each of them does is to pump heat from one place to another. Heat pumps move heat from air that is outside a house into the inside of a house (even when it is cold outside, the air still has some heat). Air conditioners move heat from inside a house to the outside of a house. Refrigerators take heat from inside a refrigerator and move it outside of the refrigerator.

On a hot afternoon, if you opened the door of your refrigerator, do you think it would significantly cool off your kitchen? Why?

14. Dr. Eureka and his fellow scientists suspected that germs caused diseases and that they could live and travel on the air or in living creatures. But they had a problem: They thought that each kind of germ caused a different kind of disease, but they could never grow one kind of germ by itself without a lot of other kinds of disease germs appearing.

Still, Dr. Eureka wanted to try the experiment again. He took a test tube and cleaned it carefully. Then he prepared a soup that the germs liked to eat and put it in the test tube. Finally, he took a germ and put it in the liquid. He placed the test tube in a warm place so the germ could grow.

A week later he came back and discovered that some other germs had somehow gotten in, and now all the germs were swimming together, completely mixed. Oh, well, he thought, I guess my samples will always be contaminated.

Then, while he was sadly walking around his lab, he found half a baked potato he'd left lying on his desk after lunch the previous week. On it were little dots, each a different color. Looking at the potato closely, he realized that the little dots were germs—but they hadn't gotten mixed in together: Each kind sat on its own part of the solid potato surface. He had perfect samples of individual kinds of germs.

Suddenly, he slapped his forehead and said, "How stupid can we be? It's easy to keep germs from mixing together: This potato tells us what's wrong with our soups!" What's the difference between the potato and the soup?

15. According to Pasteur's account, he once placed under the microscope a drop of sugar solution that was in the process of changing into butyric acid. The drop contained bacteria, which were at first rapidly mobile. Then he observed the odd fact that, while the bacteria at the center

of the drop continued to move, those at the edge that were more exposed to air came to a standstill. From this simple observation, Pasteur made an important discovery. What was it?

## ANSWERS TO SCIENTIFIC INSIGHT PROBLEMS

1. The scientist did not take into account the effect of solar radiation. Sunshine made the woman in dark clothes warm because dark colors tend to absorb heat. The woman in white was cooler because light colors tend to reflect heat.

2. When Dr. Smith's Styrofoam cups registered on the machine, she should have known that something else other than the plants was causing the vibrations. Instead, she misinterpreted the evidence offered by the "control" condition. The machine registered for irrelevant reasons.

3. Dr. Wood realized that what was happening in the blood vessel was probably similar to what happened to the river: The fork or branching of the artery acted like the boulder in the river.

4. The white trail is the water vapor, which begins to condense once it hits the cold upper atmosphere.

5. Fish feed during the day and since *D. galeata* remains near the surface during the day, it is much more visible and convenient prey than *D. hyalina*, which departs to the depths during the same time.

6. Dr. Smith allowed microbes that travel in the air to get into the flask when he opened it and when he continued to allow air to move in and out.

7. Gravity pulls the bullets down; thus, unless a pilot consciously dives to run into the bullets, they will not hit the plane.

8. When it rains, the clay begins to absorb the water. Much like a soapy sponge that has water falling on it, the clay begins to release some of what it has absorbed (the scents). Then the falling rain actually washes the scents out of the clay and releases them into the air.

9. Napoleon's death was caused by arsenic poisoning from the arsenic that was present in the wallpaper. Because of the dampness of the house, the wallpaper became wet and moldy. The mold's exudation, which contained arsenic, was mixed with the air that Napoleon was breathing constantly.

10. Carotene, which is yellow and which is present in carrots, oranges, and eggs, and lycopene, a red dye present in tomatoes, combined in the patient's blood to produce the orange color.

11. Copernicus's reasoning was that if the earth were flat, he would have seen the entire ship appear at once, instead of watching it appear bit by bit, as it did.

12. Silberglied's theory is that bright colors tend to intimidate the predators of butterflies, and therefore serve as a defense.

13. No, it would not cool off the kitchen to open the refrigerator. Heat from the room would move inside it, only to be pumped back into the room.

14. The potato is solid. Therefore, when germs land on it, they remain in the same place. The soup is liquid, and when germs land in it they can move around without difficulty.

15. Pasteur's important discovery was that air can affect certain bacteria, either immobilizing or killing them.

# 7

# Automatizing Information Processing

## What Is Automatization?

Think about what happens when you read a newspaper or a magazine article. Unless the article is unusually technical or poorly written, the chances are that you can comprehend it with little or no difficulty. You are probably scarcely aware of the mental processing you are doing while you are reading, despite the enormous complexity of the reading process. Because you are a skilled reader (at least, in comparison to young children), you can concentrate on absorbing the new facts and ideas in the article without having to pay attention to things such as what the individual letters of each word are, how the words are pronounced, how the words fit together to form sentences, what the words mean, and so on. If you were in early elementary school, however, you would not be able to devote as much attention to absorbing the main facts and ideas of the newspaper or magazine article. Rather, you would have to concentrate on some of the basic processes—such as letter and word encoding, figuring out meanings of words, and so on—that are required for comprehending the gist of a text.

Stated in another way, as an adult reader, you have *automatized*—or made automatic—the lower-level information processing involved in reading, and hence you are able to devote most of your mental resources to deciphering the higher-level information contained in a text. Young children have not fully automatized the processes of reading and hence must devote relatively more of their attention to lower-level processing at the expense of higher-level processing. Young children do not have the mental resources left over to comprehend fully the article that can easily and effortlessly be comprehended by an adult.

Consider another example of automatization. When you drive, you are very likely able to listen to the radio and even carry on a conversation as well. If you are driving by yourself, you may find yourself listening to the radio and even thinking about your activities for the day as you both drive and listen to the radio. You are able to devote so many mental resources to listening, talking, and thinking about matters other than road conditions and the state of your automobile because, for you, driving has long ago become automatic. But try to remember back to when you were first learning to drive. You probably had to devote your full attention to studying the road and to the readiness of you and your automobile to respond to it. If you learned how to drive standard shift, you may have found that just paying attention to shifting seemed to require more attention than you could possibly spare, given the necessity of watching out for where you were going and what was getting in your way. When you were first learning to drive, you would scarcely have been in a position to carry on a serious conversation about driving-irrelevant matters as you watched the road. As in the case of reading, your automatizing of information processing, in this case about how to drive, has freed the mental resources you once needed to devote fully to driving for other mental tasks, such as carrying on a conversation or thinking about your activities for the day.

If you are a touch typist, you will have observed the same course of development. When you first learned to type without looking at the keys, you may well have thought seriously about each keystroke, trying to ensure that you hit the right key. Your typing when you first learned was probably slow and effortful. If you have since become an efficient touch typist, however, you no longer need to devote much attention to individual keystrokes. To the contrary, you may be practically unaware of them. As an efficient touch typist myself, I find that when I see a string of words, I automatically type the correct letters, with hardly any realization at all of what my fingers are doing. The process of typing has become so automatized that I am not even fully aware, at a conscious level, of which keys are where on the typewriter keyboard. In fact, if someone were to ask me the letter that corresponds to a key in a certain position, I would probably have great difficulty in telling them. I seriously doubt that I could fill in the letters on a blank keyboard. Yet I can rapidly type a paper without the least bit of thought as to which keys are where. Again, the process that was once highly conscious, effortful, and controlled has become effortless, subconscious, and automatic.

These examples show that performance in almost any kind of cognitive or motor skill can become more rapid and accurate with practice. Practice seems to bring about a qualitative change in the kind of processing a person does on a given task. Several investigators have actually proposed that there are two distinct forms of information processing. Walter Schneider and Richard Shiffrin (1977) refer to these two types of processing as *controlled* and *automatic* processing. Controlled processing is (a) comparatively slow, (b) sequential in nature (executed one step after another), (c) effortful, (d) under conscious control, (e) limited by short-term memory, and (f) requires little or no training to develop. Automatic processing is (a) relatively fast, (b) executed in parallel (multiple operations done at once), (c) almost effortless, (d) not limited by short-term memory capacity, (e) for the most part subconscious, and (f) requires extensive practice to develop. Tasks such as reading, playing the piano, and driving require largely controlled processing when they are first learned, but later require primarily automatic processing.

Reading, driving, and typing illustrate the transition of three kinds of information processing from controlled to automatic. They also serve to illustrate the trade-offs between novelty (Chapter 6) and automatization. People who are able to automatize information processing efficiently have more mental resources left over to devote to novel stimulus inputs. In contrast, people who have difficulty automatizing information processing may find themselves simply lacking the mental resources to deal with novelty. Even if they have the mental powers needed to deal with novelty, they will be so busy dealing with the basic aspects of a given task or situation that they will be unable to find the attentional resources to cope with the novel aspects of the task or situation.

This view of the trade-off between dealing with novelty and automatizing information processing has important implications for distinguishing between facile learners, on the one hand, and slow learners, on the other. Fast learners are often those who can automatize information processing with relatively little effort. Their efficient automatization leaves them with plenty of mental resources left over to process the new in a given task or situation. Slow learners may have difficulty with the automatization of information processing. As a result, they may have few resources left over to deal with novelty.

Note that, according to this view, slow learners are often *not* people who are intrinsically lacking in mental power. To the contrary, they may even be superior in the kinds of knowledge-acquisition and other processes discussed earlier in this book. Some slow learners may thus be in a paradoxical situation of being highly intelligent, according to conventional intelligence tests, and yet being slow learners. Such people are referred to as being "learning disabled." Learning disabilities, therefore, often (but not always) result from inefficiency in the automatization of information processing. Fortunately, difficulties in automatization are often limited to specific media or symbol systems. For example, individuals who are reading disabled are often quite effective in other areas, such as numerical computation or reasoning. Mathematically disabled individuals are often highly effective readers, and may be astute reasoners in domains other than that of mathematics. In short, inefficiency of automatization is often limited to only certain domains of information processing, rather than being general to all of them.

### *Implications of Automatization*
### *for Intelligence Theory and Testing*

The view presented above has important implications both for understanding and measuring intelligence. Consider, for example, some of the findings about intelligence that have emerged from laboratory studies of intellectual functioning (as discussed in Chapter 1).

One finding that consistently emerges is that speed of performing elementary cognitive tasks is often correlated with psychometrically measured intelligence. To many, these correlations have seemed surprising. Why should the rate at which an individual responds to a choice reaction-time task (in which a light goes on and the individual must rapidly press a button corresponding to that light, which turns it off) correlate with performance on an intelligence test? The choice reaction-time problems are about as simple as problems can get, whereas the problems on intelligence tests are far along the road of task complexity. The present view suggests that such a correlation is derived from the importance of automatization in intelligent performance, overall, and from the degree to which the choice reaction-time test measures automatization. Why should the speed with which an individual can name a single letter of the alphabet, or compare whether two letters have the same name, correlate with psychometrically measured intelligence? Again, the present theory would suggest that the two tasks correlate because of the role of automatization in intelligence.

Theorists such as Arthur Jensen (1982) and Earl Hunt (1980) have suggested that such tasks correlate with measured intelligence because of the importance of sheer speed of mental functioning in intellectual ability. They may be correct, in part. But efficiency of automatization seems to play at least as much of a role in these statistical correlations as does sheer speed. In tasks such as choice reaction time, letter identification, and letter comparison, subjects are usually given large numbers of test trials, for which their reaction time is measured. Some may rapidly automatize performance on tasks such as these, whereas others may not. The rate and amount of automatization that eventually takes place may tell us more about intelligence than the sheer speed with which simple tasks such as choice reaction time are processed.

The point of view expressed above has certain implications for fully understanding the nature of bias in mental testing. Traditional forms of analysis of test bias may insufficiently take into account the roles of novelty and automatization. Suppose that the exact same test items are given to two groups of people. One group of people is highly familiar with the kinds of items that appear on the test. Indeed, they may scarcely have to read the directions in order to get started solving the test items. For them, performance on the given type of task is probably at least somewhat automatized before the test even begins, so that the individuals in this group will have ample mental resources left over to deal with the novelty in the test items in the test situation. For another group of people, however, the test items may be quite unfamiliar. These people may have to read the instructions quite carefully, and even then may need substantial practice before they reach the level of automatization that members of the other group started off with. Members of this group will begin with relatively few mental resources left over to deal with the novelty in the test items and stimuli. As a result, the test will be measuring performance that is at quite different levels on the experiential continuum for the two groups of tested individuals. Even though the two groups of individuals may have the same mental structures and process the test items using the same mental processes and strategies, the members of the second group will be at a clear disadvantage. They will be hampered by their previous unfamiliarity with the kinds of items appearing on tests, or even with the kinds of past experiences that would enable them rapidly to automatize performance on these items. As a result, the test will not really be measuring the same thing for the two groups of people.

In sum, understanding intelligence requires more than understanding the various kinds of components discussed in the previous part of the book: metacomponents, performance components, and knowledge-acquisition components. We also need to consider the level of experience people have with the tasks and situations that require these components. A full theory of intelligence must therefore take into account not only mental processing, but people's level of experience with the tasks and situations that require this mental processing. Dealing with novelty and automatizing information processing along the continuum of experience with tasks and situations constitute two important aspects of intellectual skills.

## Increasing the Efficacy of Automatization

We can conclude from the above analysis that the ability to automatize information processing rapidly and to a high level is an important, if not obvious, part of intelligence. As we have seen, people who are able to automatize well have more resources available for other new things in their lives. In general, automatization lets people take in more of the world, and learn more.

How can people increase the efficacy with which they automatize information processing and the level to which processes are automatized? Suprisingly, there has been relatively little research on this topic. Fortunately, however, one researcher, Walter Schneider (1977, 1982), has devoted a major portion of his career to discovering the principles that lead to rapid automatization. The discussion in this section is based largely on his work, in which he has subjects perform relatively simple tasks over thousands of test trials, and observes the course of automatization. Here are some of the main findings from his research.

First, Schneider has found that consistency in information processing is a necessary condition for the development of automatization. In other words, when we practice a task that we wish to automatize, it is necessary to develop a strategy that can be used consistently throughout the task. At least in initial learning, it is also important that the task be fairly homogeneous. Schneider has found that performance on the task improves as a multiplicative function of the number of trials of past performance and the degree of consistency in that performance (number of trials × degree of consistency).

Second, Schneider has found that improvement in performance appears to be primarily a function of correct execution of the process or processes to be automatized. In many kinds of learning, we learn from our mistakes. In essence, errors teach us what *not* to do next time. However, if our goal is to make a given process automatic, then it is correct rather than incorrect performances that contribute to this goal. Note that, in automatization, your goal is not to learn what to do (as in learning from your mistakes), but rather to learn how to do it (as efficiently as possible).

Third, although the development of a full level of automatization can take anywhere from 200 to 2,000 (or even more) trials of performance on a task, automatization can begin to set in at as few as 10 trials, so long as those trials involve consistency in strategic performance. In other words, although you could not expect to automatize a task fully without a great deal of experience with that task, you can expect to see at least some results fairly rapidly if you follow the principles discussed in this chapter and if you are able to develop a consistent strategy for task performance.

Fourth, there may be some degree of "consolidation time" in our automatization of information processing. You have probably often noticed that when you are learning how to do something new, whether it be typing, playing the piano, or performing arithmetic computations, you reach a point where you are just not improving any more. You may even notice that you start to make a number of mistakes. The best thing to do at such a point is often to stop for a while, or at least to slow yourself down for a short period of time. Often, learning has taken place and is continuing to take place, but it needs time to consolidate. In other words, your performance may not fully reflect your learning. So take a break, and then go back to the task.

Fifth, it helps to learn the task that we wish to automatize under moderate speed stress. Schneider has found that people learning a task show little speedup if they are not pushed, at least a bit, to perform faster. In other words, it is not enough that you merely perform the task again and again. You also have to push yourself to speed up. So, for example, if you wish to increase your typing speed, you have to work at it consciously and not just expect that typing lots and lots of papers will result in the speedup you desire.

Sixth, automatization is likely to be more rapid if we are able to devote our full attentional resources to the task at hand. The more distraction we encounter, and the less attention we can devote to the task as a result, the less we are likely to be able to efficaciously to automatize our performance. So, when you decide that you would like to increase your automatization of performance on a given task, try to devote as much of your attention as you can to that task, at least during the periods when you are trying to improve your performance on it.

Seventh, automatization of performance can be substantially influenced by the context in which that performance occurs. Consider, for example, typing. We may learn to type quite rapidly on our own typewriter in our own room under the normal conditions under which we typically type. However, if we find ourselves using a different typewriter in a different room under different circumstances, we may find ourselves typing considerably more slowly, more effortfully, and with more mistakes. So, you need to realize that automatization does not necessarily generalize right away. If you wish to perform a certain task automatically under a variety of circumstances, then at some point you will have to practice that task under a variety of circumstances. Automatization can be expected to generalize only if you help it along in this way.

Eighth, automatization and generalization of that automatization require that learning be done at the appropriate level of the task being learned. Consider, for example, that you are learning to play the piano. Initially, you will learn with easy pieces, and you may actually become quite adept with them. But eventually, you must move on to harder material. Similarly, in learning to drive, you would probably be at a disadvantage if your initial learning were on a busy rush-hour street in New York or Caracas or Rome. Eventually, though, if you will have to negotiate such traffic, it will be important for your training to include it. For almost any task that will eventually be automatized, it is necessary to start with easy subtasks and to move on to more difficult ones. The difficulty of the subtask has to be graded in an appropriate way for one's level of expertise.

Ninth, motivation is often more important to automatizing information processing than is any other single variable. The automatization of processing often requires many, many trials of repeated practice. It is very easy for motivation to flag under these circumstances. After a certain point, the task can become repetitive and boring. It is therefore important to build in ways of motivating yourself. Such ways might include considering the future benefits of automatized processing (such as being able to type papers quickly, or to play the piano in concerts), evaluating your progress (by plotting a graph of the speed at which you are performing the task at different points in time), or considering how much more enjoyable it is and will be to you to perform the task rapidly and effortlessly rather than slowly and effortfully. Many people never automatize task performance simply because they have lost the motivation to do so.

Tenth and finally, it may help you more to think of yourself as your own "coach" rather than as your own "teacher." The practice required to automatize performance is more like that required for sports or music or dance than for the kind of academic learning required in school. Relatively few scholastic activities require repeated performance on a single type of task, whereas a number of extracurricular activities do. Viewing yourself as a coach rather than as a teacher may put yourself more in the correct frame of mind for the task at hand.

## Automatization: Some Practice Problems

As you can see from the above discussion, there is no one general skill of automatized information processing. Automatization occurs at different rates in different domains. It may be present to a high degree in one kind of performance, but entirely absent in another. Thus, any practice in task automatization must necessarily be limited in scope and domain.

The following practice exercises are intended to help you automatize performance on four tasks in the domain of letter and symbol recognition. As you perform these tasks, keep in mind the findings of Walter Schneider as described above. You will need a clock or watch with a second hand.

### *Letter Comparison*

In the letter-comparison task, you will be presented with four sets of letter pairs. Each set contains 80 pairs of letters. Your task is to scan these pairs of letters rapidly and in order, and to indicate whether each pair of letters has the same name or a different name. For example, the following pairs are

composed of letters with the same name: AA, Dd, fF, nn. The following pairs
are composed of letters with different names: BK, Nb, gF, hz. For each pair,
indicate as quickly as you can whether the letters are the same (S) or different
(D). Time yourself as you work through each set of these letter pairs. See if
you can improve your speed. Try not to make mistakes. Answers appear after
the last set.

## LETTER-COMPARISON TASK

### SET 1

| | | | | | | | | | | | | | |
|---|---|---|---|---|---|---|---|---|---|---|---|---|---|
| 1. | j | o | 17. | O | S | 33. | O | T | 49. | Q | Q | 65. | y | s |
| 2. | i | n | 18. | w | W | 34. | r | R | 50. | N | n | 66. | L | E |
| 3. | k | k | 19. | L | i | 35. | b | c | 51. | E | z | 67. | C | C |
| 4. | l | v | 20. | R | r | 36. | U | u | 52. | m | i | 68. | E | F |
| 5. | q | x | 21. | T | t | 37. | Q | r | 53. | F | F | 69. | d | d |
| 6. | D | D | 22. | F | W | 38. | x | g | 54. | V | v | 70. | A | P |
| 7. | v | Y | 23. | B | b | 39. | a | a | 55. | K | H | 71. | E | E |
| 8. | P | P | 24. | R | u | 40. | Z | Z | 56. | S | s | 72. | c | W |
| 9. | x | X | 25. | i | P | 41. | R | R | 57. | T | T | 73. | A | A |
| 10. | f | F | 26. | s | k | 42. | V | r | 58. | o | g | 74. | F | o |
| 11. | N | N | 27. | e | e | 43. | E | J | 59. | C | y | 75. | z | Z |
| 12. | r | t | 28. | T | t | 44. | N | n | 60. | h | h | 76. | t | F |
| 13. | K | I | 29. | r | s | 45. | G | G | 61. | l | u | 77. | k | k |
| 14. | c | C | 30. | V | E | 46. | f | u | 62. | i | n | 78. | d | D |
| 15. | L | I | 31. | h | h | 47. | J | g | 63. | o | o | 79. | N | N |
| 16. | h | h | 32. | s | S | 48. | a | c | 64. | f | f | 80. | x | B |

### SET 2

| | | | | | | | | | | | | | |
|---|---|---|---|---|---|---|---|---|---|---|---|---|---|
| 1. | u | R | 17. | A | A | 33. | I | K | 49. | c | b | 65. | a | C |
| 2. | f | f | 18. | f | E | 34. | D | D | 50. | Z | z | 66. | X | x |
| 3. | P | i | 19. | Y | y | 35. | e | r | 51. | D | d | 67. | B | B |
| 4. | s | Y | 20. | k | k | 36. | t | F | 52. | E | L | 68. | j | o |
| 5. | W | e | 21. | l | v | 37. | N | n | 53. | c | c | 69. | L | l |
| 6. | h | h | 22. | n | N | 38. | r | V | 54. | H | c | 70. | H | K |
| 7. | M | E | 23. | q | x | 39. | m | m | 55. | T | t | 71. | c | C |
| 8. | q | Q | 24. | G | G | 40. | J | E | 56. | l | u | 72. | u | m |
| 9. | E | E | 25. | s | i | 41. | Q | r | 57. | i | n | 73. | t | T |
| 10. | x | B | 26. | N | N | 42. | k | k | 58. | O | O | 74. | G | m |
| 11. | a | a | 27. | E | z | 43. | S | s | 59. | g | x | 75. | P | P |
| 12. | O | F | 28. | i | I | 44. | t | F | 60. | e | E | 76. | R | P |
| 13. | T | O | 29. | W | w | 45. | F | E | 61. | S | O | 77. | F | F |
| 14. | I | I | 30. | a | y | 46. | r | S | 62. | T | T | 78. | y | C |
| 15. | s | S | 31. | J | j | 47. | d | d | 63. | r | h | 79. | W | w |
| 16. | V | E | 32. | V | v | 48. | T | t | 64. | u | u | 80. | i | g |

## SET 3

| | | | | | | | | | | |
|---|---|---|---|---|---|---|---|---|---|---|
| 1. | f | O | 17. | c | c | 33. | x | q | 49. | c | b |
| 2. | I | I | 18. | A | n | 34. | y | Y | 50. | O | d |
| 3. | s | i | 19. | B | B | 35. | a | q | 51. | n | n |
| 4. | E | E | 20. | R | P | 36. | u | m | 52. | u | R |
| 5. | f | T | 21. | v | V | 37. | g | G | 53. | f | f |
| 6. | E | E | 22. | D | D | 38. | E | F | 54. | M | w |
| 7. | i | g | 23. | e | w | 39. | c | c | 55. | a | a |
| 8. | k | k | 24. | z | E | 40. | l | l | 56. | T | t |
| 9. | f | t | 25. | V | I | 41. | T | O | 57. | F | K |
| 10. | z | Z | 26. | c | C | 42. | s | S | 58. | s | S |
| 11. | F | f | 27. | R | r | 43. | h | j | 59. | U | u |
| 12. | s | s | 28. | T | T | 44. | Q | q | 60. | i | n |
| 13. | p | I | 29. | u | u | 45. | P | P | 61. | I | K |
| 14. | G | G | 30. | K | H | 46. | g | x | 62. | e | r |
| 15. | x | b | 31. | r | V | 47. | Q | r | 63. | N | N |
| 16. | E | L | 32. | J | J | 48. | s | S | 64. | I | i |

| | | |
|---|---|---|
| 65. | n | X |
| 66. | W | w |
| 67. | O | S |
| 68. | h | r |
| 69. | r | R |
| 70. | C | c |
| 71. | Z | j |
| 72. | v | l |
| 73. | Z | z |
| 74. | E | V |
| 75. | O | o |
| 76. | H | C |
| 77. | v | V |
| 78. | X | x |
| 79. | j | o |
| 80. | F | F |

## SET 4

| | | | | | | | | | | |
|---|---|---|---|---|---|---|---|---|---|---|
| 1. | N | n | 17. | Q | Q | 33. | f | f | 49. | w | W |
| 2. | E | z | 18. | a | c | 34. | o | o | 50. | L | l |
| 3. | m | i | 19. | J | j | 35. | f | E | 51. | O | o |
| 4. | D | D | 20. | u | f | 36. | l | u | 52. | q | x |
| 5. | V | v | 21. | P | A | 37. | d | d | 53. | l | v |
| 6. | H | K | 22. | E | E | 38. | F | E | 54. | k | k |
| 7. | u | u | 23. | e | W | 39. | C | C | 55. | i | n |
| 8. | T | T | 24. | I | I | 40. | Ė | L | 56. | j | o |
| 9. | g | i | 25. | O | f | 41. | f | F | 57. | x | X |
| 10. | C | y | 26. | Z | z | 42. | N | N | 58. | P | P |
| 11. | a | y | 27. | t | F | 43. | r | t | 59. | Y | q |
| 12. | G | G | 28. | k | k | 44. | K | I | 60. | D | D |
| 13. | n | N | 29. | E | e | 45. | c | C | 61. | V | E |
| 14. | E | J | 30. | x | B | 46. | L | I | 62. | h | h |
| 15. | V | v | 31. | N | N | 47. | r | r | 63. | s | S |
| 16. | R | P | 32. | s | y | 48. | S | O | 64. | T | O |

| | | |
|---|---|---|
| 65. | e | E |
| 66. | c | b |
| 67. | S | s |
| 68. | r | Q |
| 69. | x | g |
| 70. | a | a |
| 71. | E | E |
| 72. | P | i |
| 73. | u | R |
| 74. | B | b |
| 75. | G | F |
| 76. | T | t |
| 77. | r | s |
| 78. | T | t |
| 79. | c | c |
| 80. | k | s |

## ANSWERS TO LETTER-COMPARISON TASK

### SET 1

| | | | | | | | | | | |
|---|---|---|---|---|---|---|---|---|---|
| 1. | D | 5. | D | 9. | S | 13. | D | 17. | D |
| 2. | D | 6. | S | 10. | S | 14. | S | 18. | S |
| 3. | S | 7. | D | 11. | S | 15. | D | 19. | D |
| 4. | D | 8. | S | 12. | D | 16. | S | 20. | S |

| | | | | |
|---|---|---|---|---|
| 21. S | 33. D | 45. S | 57. S | 69. S |
| 22. D | 34. S | 46. D | 58. D | 70. D |
| 23. S | 35. D | 47. D | 59. D | 71. S |
| 24. D | 36. S | 48. D | 60. S | 72. D |
| 25. D | 37. D | 49. S | 61. D | 73. S |
| 26. D | 38. D | 50. S | 62. D | 74. D |
| 27. S | 39. S | 51. D | 63. S | 75. S |
| 28. S | 40. S | 52. D | 64. S | 76. D |
| 29. D | 41. S | 53. S | 65. D | 77. S |
| 30. D | 42. D | 54. S | 66. D | 78. S |
| 31. S | 43. D | 55. D | 67. S | 79. S |
| 32. S | 44. S | 56. S | 68. D | 80. D |

## SET 2

| | | | | |
|---|---|---|---|---|
| 1. D | 17. S | 33. D | 49. D | 65. D |
| 2. S | 18. D | 34. S | 50. S | 66. S |
| 3. D | 19. S | 35. D | 51. S | 67. S |
| 4. D | 20. S | 36. D | 52. D | 68. D |
| 5. D | 21. D | 37. S | 53. S | 69. S |
| 6. S | 22. S | 38. D | 54. D | 70. D |
| 7. D | 23. D | 39. S | 55. S | 71. S |
| 8. S | 24. S | 40. D | 56. D | 72. D |
| 9. S | 25. D | 41. D | 57. D | 73. S |
| 10. D | 26. S | 42. S | 58. S | 74. D |
| 11. S | 27. D | 43. S | 59. D | 75. S |
| 12. D | 28. S | 44. D | 60. S | 76. D |
| 13. D | 29. S | 45. D | 61. D | 77. S |
| 14. S | 30. D | 46. D | 62. S | 78. D |
| 15. S | 31. S | 47. S | 63. D | 79. S |
| 16. D | 32. S | 48. S | 64. S | 80. D |

## SET 3

| | | | | |
|---|---|---|---|---|
| 1. D | 17. S | 33. D | 49. D | 65. D |
| 2. S | 18. D | 34. S | 50. D | 66. S |
| 3. D | 19. S | 35. D | 51. S | 67. D |
| 4. S | 20. D | 36. D | 52. D | 68. D |
| 5. D | 21. S | 37. S | 53. S | 69. S |
| 6. S | 22. S | 38. D | 54. D | 70. S |
| 7. D | 23. D | 39. S | 55. S | 71. D |
| 8. S | 24. D | 40. S | 56. S | 72. D |
| 9. D | 25. D | 41. D | 57. D | 73. S |
| 10. S | 26. S | 42. S | 58. S | 74. D |
| 11. S | 27. S | 43. D | 59. S | 75. D |
| 12. S | 28. S | 44. S | 60. D | 76. D |
| 13. D | 29. S | 45. S | 61. D | 77. S |
| 14. S | 30. D | 46. D | 62. D | 78. S |
| 15. D | 31. D | 47. D | 63. S | 79. D |
| 16. D | 32. S | 48. S | 64. S | 80. S |

**SET 4**

| | | | | | | | | | |
|---|---|---|---|---|---|---|---|---|---|
| 1. | S | 17. | S | 33. | S | 49. | S | 65. | S |
| 2. | D | 18. | D | 34. | S | 50. | S | 66. | D |
| 3. | D | 19. | S | 35. | D | 51. | S | 67. | S |
| 4. | S | 20. | D | 36. | D | 52. | D | 68. | D |
| 5. | S | 21. | D | 37. | S | 53. | D | 69. | D |
| 6. | D | 22. | S | 38. | D | 54. | S | 70. | S |
| 7. | S | 23. | D | 39. | S | 55. | D | 71. | S |
| 8. | S | 24. | S | 40. | D | 56. | D | 72. | D |
| 9. | D | 25. | D | 41. | S | 57. | S | 73. | D |
| 10. | D | 26. | S | 42. | S | 58. | S | 74. | S |
| 11. | D | 27. | D | 43. | D | 59. | D | 75. | D |
| 12. | S | 28. | S | 44. | D | 60. | S | 76. | S |
| 13. | S | 29. | S | 45. | S | 61. | D | 77. | D |
| 14. | D | 30. | D | 46. | D | 62. | S | 78. | S |
| 15. | S | 31. | S | 47. | S | 63. | S | 79. | S |
| 16. | D | 32. | D | 48. | D | 64. | D | 80. | D |

## *Visual Search*

This task, which has been studied by William Estes and others, requires you to search a string of letters for a target letter. If you find the target letter in the string of letters, you indicate this with a "Y" (Yes). If you do not find the target letter in the string of letters, you indicate this with an "N" (No). In this task, unlike the previous task, the case of the letter does matter. In other words, the case of the letter (capital or lower) in the target must match the case of the letter in the subsequent letter string. For example, if you see the target letter *K* followed by the letter string *g  H  N  p  K*, you should indicate "Y." But if you see the target letter *z* followed by the letter string *g  A  Z  P  u*, you should indicate "N."

Eight sets of visual-search items follow. Each set contains 40 items. The items become progressively more difficult in terms of the number of letters in the letter string following the target. Try to increase the speed with which you scan the letter strings as you progress through the successive sets of exercises. Answers appear after the last set.

## VISUAL SEARCH TASK

### SET 1

| | | | | | | | | | | |
|---|---|---|---|---|---|---|---|---|---|---|
| 1. | f | K | n | p | C | 21. | P | B | P | I | N |
| 2. | B | L | x | B | r | 22. | T | m | v | E | Y |
| 3. | n | e | p | b | n | 23. | J | K | o | b | J |
| 4. | V | R | S | T | O | 24. | e | r | e | x | c |
| 5. | t | b | t | n | q | 25. | g | m | T | S | u |
| 6. | I | Y | o | M | p | 26. | N | C | S | Q | W |
| 7. | c | m | W | c | l | 27. | f | i | h | n | f |
| 8. | P | S | K | P | Y | 28. | A | F | C | v | p |
| 9. | v | t | L | N | v | 29. | y | h | y | e | a |
| 10. | m | f | r | e | p | 30. | A | K | D | L | G |
| 11. | g | S | g | L | u | 31. | p | O | F | v | M |
| 12. | S | L | R | Y | M | 32. | F | W | c | F | k |
| 13. | l | n | c | l | x | 33. | G | l | C | P | O |
| 14. | O | E | s | F | R | 34. | h | i | j | e | h |
| 15. | x | v | T | I | d | 35. | M | c | g | M | F |
| 16. | B | N | E | B | V | 36. | d | u | r | m | w |
| 17. | J | t | O | J | f | 37. | v | g | U | s | n |
| 18. | n | l | f | c | d | 38. | R | M | R | G | T |
| 19. | K | A | r | G | n | 39. | t | C | h | t | M |
| 20. | E | A | F | H | E | 40. | F | v | R | N | o |

### SET 2

| | | | | | | | | | | |
|---|---|---|---|---|---|---|---|---|---|---|
| 1. | P | J | m | A | h | 21. | w | b | t | w | k |
| 2. | c | o | m | c | y | 22. | Y | D | Y | O | E |
| 3. | E | M | C | G | E | 23. | R | E | u | M | k |
| 4. | x | b | O | m | P | 24. | i | m | j | d | i |
| 5. | l | w | l | c | k | 25. | Q | C | A | F | N |
| 6. | H | K | E | D | Z | 26. | c | h | U | s | c |
| 7. | V | P | o | V | y | 27. | b | i | T | H | d |
| 8. | f | m | k | z | v | 28. | K | M | U | l | k |
| 9. | A | f | V | A | r | 29. | r | Y | o | M | q |
| 10. | C | T | L | J | E | 30. | s | o | l | f | p |
| 11. | k | a | R | f | M | 31. | C | T | P | O | C |
| 12. | H | M | r | T | z | 32. | B | i | G | H | q |
| 13. | s | a | F | s | N | 33. | T | N | A | J | D |
| 14. | L | M | e | L | x | 34. | d | s | t | c | r |
| 15. | f | r | m | c | k | 35. | E | p | E | F | k |
| 16. | g | n | Z | g | d | 36. | o | T | S | u | r |
| 17. | S | R | o | E | j | 37. | L | O | M | T | Y |
| 18. | c | m | i | c | g | 38. | P | r | W | P | u |
| 19. | R | Z | D | R | F | 39. | y | k | b | o | t |
| 20. | f | R | m | k | D | 40. | a | J | d | a | M |

**SET 3**

| | | | | | | | | | | |
|---|---|---|---|---|---|---|---|---|---|---|
| 1. | M | L | q | M | g | 21. | p | s | O | N | b |
| 2. | S | T | N | T | W | 22. | F | h | e | F | W |
| 3. | O | C | n | k | O | 23. | Q | N | I | W | Q |
| 4. | c | T | m | A | I | 24. | h | z | h | i | o |
| 5. | r | p | Y | m | F | 25. | M | Z | b | M | s |
| 6. | B | S | G | B | I | 26. | d | u | r | m | w |
| 7. | j | d | R | k | j | 27. | e | v | A | W | d |
| 8. | n | e | f | l | c | 28. | M | G | T | M | Z |
| 9. | K | e | R | G | n | 29. | t | b | t | E | R |
| 10. | F | S | F | T | O | 30. | R | f | A | o | V |
| 11. | e | l | I | A | n | 31. | W | T | G | W | D |
| 12. | B | m | k | B | H | 32. | q | v | S | M | u |
| 13. | m | q | l | m | e | 33. | J | y | m | J | O |
| 14. | V | O | T | R | D | 34. | u | c | p | u | l |
| 15. | t | r | x | u | t | 35. | g | o | m | T | S |
| 16. | M | Q | i | T | d | 36. | E | A | R | S | W |
| 17. | c | m | c | S | t | 37. | f | p | f | i | v |
| 18. | L | S | W | B | O | 38. | A | F | r | M | k |
| 19. | v | t | L | v | N | 39. | s | m | s | p | i |
| 20. | k | x | m | o | r | 40. | B | H | Y | T | D |

**SET 4**

| | | | | | | | | | | | | | | |
|---|---|---|---|---|---|---|---|---|---|---|---|---|---|---|
| 1. | M | L | R | q | T | u | c | 21. | U | M | T | U | S | O | L |
| 2. | p | c | a | x | t | m | y | 22. | C | t | M | a | f | C | i |
| 3. | i | v | O | S | x | b | l | 23. | n | i | c | d | s | e | m |
| 4. | T | S | N | E | T | M | G | 24. | v | t | L | o | v | Q | r |
| 5. | B | G | S | n | d | r | m | 25. | F | T | I | D | F | S | A |
| 6. | a | u | F | v | M | s | P | 26. | Y | l | u | Y | k | C | E |
| 7. | f | r | u | t | f | m | z | 27. | A | I | C | L | O | N | R |
| 8. | N | B | c | G | d | s | j | 28. | g | m | p | g | t | e | n |
| 9. | J | E | B | G | J | N | A | 29. | e | S | n | T | l | o | R |
| 10. | t | h | U | m | B | t | p | 30. | P | u | R | n | O | p | A |
| 11. | n | b | p | e | n | i | z | 31. | G | C | T | W | G | Q | R |
| 12. | a | o | M | S | v | l | B | 32. | e | u | K | l | A | r | C |
| 13. | K | R | O | x | K | g | l | 33. | A | m | Q | s | R | i | e |
| 14. | J | O | T | M | I | S | B | 34. | R | K | o | B | G | f | q |
| 15. | v | l | u | v | r | x | m | 35. | b | y | e | r | b | s | u |
| 16. | d | m | T | s | U | O | q | 36. | M | Q | D | M | E | J | G |
| 17. | X | A | r | S | i | T | m | 37. | h | m | l | q | v | s | h |
| 18. | L | B | W | U | L | F | R | 38. | f | k | B | v | q | P | R |
| 19. | s | p | l | w | b | h | m | 39. | q | L | N | q | a | r | F |
| 20. | P | M | A | H | P | T | X | 40. | g | i | t | s | o | m | x |

## SET 5

| | | | | | | | | | | | | | | | |
|---|---|---|---|---|---|---|---|---|---|---|---|---|---|---|---|
| 1. | P | | V | R | n | y | f | z | 21. | S | | T | I | D | S | F | M |
| 2. | t | | m | b | E | U | t | n | 22. | B | | g | n | S | d | R | q |
| 3. | M | | E | T | M | V | G | H | 23. | f | | i | c | d | s | m | b |
| 4. | e | | r | L | O | s | Q | p | 24. | r | | M | a | z | O | T | r |
| 5. | g | | m | g | p | t | d | h | 25. | T | | N | G | W | T | P | Y |
| 6. | N | | J | O | d | F | m | v | 26. | x | | r | Y | l | S | m | a |
| 7. | f | | p | l | t | f | v | r | 27. | A | | C | s | F | r | A | T |
| 8. | A | | L | U | M | C | N | J | 28. | o | | r | e | n | s | y | t |
| 9. | Y | | w | D | i | Y | k | E | 29. | M | | T | U | A | R | M | W |
| 10. | a | | U | x | r | M | C | s | 30. | Q | | r | M | T | o | W | a |
| 11. | P | | O | R | V | F | P | K | 31. | e | | f | x | m | t | i | r |
| 12. | s | | w | m | i | l | h | u | 32. | c | | n | L | e | P | c | z |
| 13. | q | | K | c | e | P | r | n | 33. | P | | F | S | W | R | O | L |
| 14. | h | | v | s | h | l | a | f | 34. | f | | S | M | f | E | n | q |
| 15. | D | | R | S | M | U | D | H | 35. | Y | | h | U | o | n | G | A |
| 16. | u | | d | m | T | S | i | p | 36. | b | | x | u | g | b | i | l |
| 17. | l | | v | r | x | m | l | b | 37. | J | | O | T | V | I | R | F |
| 18. | R | | G | o | B | U | h | p | 38. | n | | e | b | p | n | t | i |
| 19. | A | | v | S | M | u | y | B | 39. | K | | R | o | X | g | K | h |
| 20. | W | | T | C | R | l | W | S | 40. | a | | G | c | P | n | E | w |

## SET 6

| | | | | | | | | | | | | | | | |
|---|---|---|---|---|---|---|---|---|---|---|---|---|---|---|---|
| 1. T | v | p | M | A | j | q | p | h | 21. r | h | w | s | q | t | b | r | o |
| 2. c | s | f | p | r | c | y | o | m | 22. M | Y | U | R | F | D | O | A | G |
| 3. B | E | M | C | B | A | R | W | Z | 23. I | R | e | Z | j | a | T | I | u |
| 4. h | t | b | O | m | P | s | Q | y | 24. s | m | i | r | l | a | o | g | d |
| 5. m | l | a | w | g | k | r | m | o | 25. Q | J | U | R | C | F | T | B | Q |
| 6. Z | H | O | D | U | C | Y | K | E | 26. d | C | h | U | s | n | O | r | t |
| 7. V | y | P | o | N | r | X | f | e | 27. g | b | l | T | H | s | g | D | r |
| 8. l | f | r | m | k | z | s | q | t | 28. K | s | M | u | L | P | r | E | i |
| 9. F | A | e | R | I | m | F | V | l | 29. y | h | g | E | r | V | O | s | X |
| 10. J | C | T | L | J | E | B | O | H | 30. s | t | o | l | d | i | r | m | a |
| 11. k | a | R | f | M | i | T | Y | l | 31. P | R | O | T | C | P | A | X | Y |
| 12. E | h | A | m | C | O | R | t | d | 32. R | h | i | G | R | o | v | A | C |
| 13. a | S | l | Q | R | m | c | a | B | 33. T | S | W | J | A | D | M | R | N |
| 14. I | T | I | L | M | R | E | C | D | 34. c | d | n | e | s | t | c | r | z |
| 15. e | f | r | m | k | c | p | t | l | 35. H | E | S | p | N | m | a | T | I |
| 16. z | G | n | z | D | r | M | Q | k | 36. f | o | m | T | S | u | r | A | c |
| 17. W | g | E | R | l | s | i | h | p | 37. Y | L | C | O | M | T | Y | B | U |
| 18. n | c | m | a | e | g | n | f | j | 38. R | p | z | I | W | s | U | L | B |
| 19. S | L | I | R | M | Z | S | K | D | 39. q | y | m | k | o | b | u | q | r |
| 20. o | f | R | m | K | d | A | s | L | 40. m | A | l | J | d | m | K | s | P |

**SET 7**

| | | | | | | | | |
|---|---|---|---|---|---|---|---|---|
| 1. | a | w | E | n | P | c | G | S | h |
| 2. | K | H | K | g | X | O | R | b | y |
| 3. | n | i | t | n | p | b | e | f | z |
| 4. | R | p | h | U | B | o | G | s | M |
| 5. | b | l | i | x | u | b | g | q | r |
| 6. | Y | A | G | n | o | U | h | d | t |
| 7. | f | q | n | E | f | S | K | X | o |
| 8. | P | L | O | R | W | S | F | A | X |
| 9. | c | z | P | L | c | e | N | v | a |
| 10. | e | r | z | t | m | x | f | g | i |
| 11. | q | A | w | O | t | M | r | g | n |
| 12. | M | W | R | M | A | O | T | Y | U |
| 13. | o | t | y | s | n | e | r | h | g |
| 14. | B | T | A | f | r | B | c | S | O |
| 15. | x | a | m | S | D | i | K | g | E |
| 16. | T | G | W | Y | T | P | N | Q | V |
| 17. | r | M | a | X | u | t | r | C | N |
| 18. | f | b | m | s | k | d | u | h | z |
| 19. | b | Q | r | D | s | N | G | i | p |
| 20. | S | M | F | T | D | I | S | W | Q |
| 21. | W | S | T | C | W | R | I | G | O |
| 22. | A | S | M | y | V | g | k | e | J |
| 23. | J | F | R | I | V | O | T | Z | N |
| 24. | l | b | m | x | l | r | v | h | k |
| 25. | u | p | I | S | t | m | d | o | v |
| 26. | D | H | D | U | M | R | S | L | E |
| 27. | h | f | a | l | h | s | v | r | p |
| 28. | q | n | R | p | E | C | k | y | L |
| 29. | s | u | h | l | i | m | w | e | j |
| 30. | P | K | F | V | P | O | R | U | N |
| 31. | a | s | C | M | r | x | U | l | V |
| 32. | Y | E | k | i | D | Y | w | h | S |
| 33. | A | J | N | C | M | U | L | R | P |
| 34. | f | r | v | f | t | l | p | o | y |
| 35. | N | v | M | F | d | o | J | s | U |
| 36. | g | h | d | g | m | o | w | f | r |
| 37. | e | p | r | O | L | s | Q | z | K |
| 38. | M | H | G | V | M | E | X | L | R |
| 39. | t | n | t | U | E | b | K | f | O |
| 40. | P | z | f | N | Y | o | g | i | r |

**SET 8**

| | | | | | | | | | | |
|---|---|---|---|---|---|---|---|---|---|---|
| 1. | e | K | l | A | n | P | u | r | c | G | o |
| 2. | K | g | m | q | R | O | x | K | d | i | l |
| 3. | n | m | q | l | e | p | b | n | i | a | r |
| 4. | J | B | X | H | V | I | M | O | R | S | T |
| 5. | b | m | e | v | x | u | s | b | r | h | y |
| 6. | X | Y | o | M | P | q | i | l | S | r | A |
| 7. | o | M | s | t | p | C | F | o | X | E | n |
| 8. | L | P | I | M | R | O | F | U | S | W | B |
| 9. | s | c | t | L | N | e | B | o | R | s | A |
| 10. | g | p | e | r | f | x | m | o | s | t | i |
| 11. | M | S | L | q | r | H | t | O | u | B | C |
| 12. | U | A | E | R | Y | M | T | U | S | O | L |
| 13. | p | o | r | e | n | c | a | x | t | m | y |
| 14. | C | T | m | A | l | C | s | f | R | i | p |
| 15. | i | r | P | Y | l | v | o | S | t | X | B |
| 16. | T | V | Z | S | E | N | T | M | G | Y | P |
| 17. | v | t | O | L | d | R | m | A | x | v | Q |
| 18. | n | f | l | e | i | c | d | s | b | o | m |
| 19. | B | s | A | r | G | N | h | d | R | m | T |
| 20. | F | N | O | M | E | F | A | S | T | I | D |
| 21. | G | P | S | l | W | G | B | Q | C | R | T |
| 22. | A | e | b | l | Q | i | O | u | M | S | v |
| 23. | R | y | m | K | o | B | U | g | f | q | p |
| 24. | v | c | l | u | v | r | x | a | q | i | m |
| 25. | d | o | m | T | S | u | I | l | p | R | a |
| 26. | M | A | R | M | Q | E | D | B | X | I | J |
| 27. | h | r | p | i | h | m | t | v | s | l | q |
| 28. | q | F | r | m | k | C | B | v | e | o | p |
| 29. | f | s | w | i | m | p | l | u | y | b | h |
| 30. | P | B | L | T | H | A | M | C | O | R | P |
| 31. | a | l | P | u | s | O | F | q | M | T | v |
| 32. | Y | h | o | W | D | l | u | C | Y | k | e |
| 33. | A | R | N | I | C | O | P | L | U | M | S |
| 34. | f | e | z | p | l | t | i | v | r | u | f |
| 35. | N | Z | s | M | B | c | g | D | F | j | O |
| 36. | g | j | u | r | m | g | p | t | d | e | n |
| 37. | e | A | g | U | s | n | t | L | O | p | r |
| 38. | J | M | R | V | T | E | B | J | A | N | G |
| 39. | t | C | h | U | m | b | t | E | R | n | p |
| 40. | P | c | f | A | z | V | R | n | O | H | Y |

## ANSWERS TO VISUAL SEARCH TASK

### SET 1

| | | | | | | | | | | | |
|---|---|---|---|---|---|---|---|---|---|---|---|
| 1. | N | 8. | Y | 15. | N | 22. | N | 29. | Y | 36. | N |
| 2. | Y | 9. | Y | 16. | Y | 23. | Y | 30. | N | 37. | N |
| 3. | Y | 10. | N | 17. | Y | 24. | Y | 31. | N | 38. | Y |
| 4. | N | 11. | Y | 18. | N | 25. | N | 32. | Y | 39. | Y |
| 5. | Y | 12. | N | 19. | N | 26. | N | 33. | N | 40. | N |
| 6. | N | 13. | Y | 20. | Y | 27. | Y | 34. | Y | | |
| 7. | Y | 14. | N | 21. | Y | 28. | N | 35. | Y | | |

### SET 2

| | | | | | | | | | | | |
|---|---|---|---|---|---|---|---|---|---|---|---|
| 1. | N | 8. | N | 15. | N | 22. | Y | 29. | N | 36. | N |
| 2. | Y | 9. | Y | 16. | Y | 23. | N | 30. | N | 37. | N |
| 3. | Y | 10. | N | 17. | N | 24. | Y | 31. | Y | 38. | Y |
| 4. | N | 11. | N | 18. | Y | 25. | N | 32. | N | 39. | N |
| 5. | Y | 12. | N | 19. | Y | 26. | Y | 33. | N | 40. | Y |
| 6. | N | 13. | Y | 20. | N | 27. | N | 34. | N | | |
| 7. | Y | 14. | Y | 21. | Y | 28. | N | 35. | Y | | |

### SET 3

| | | | | | | | | | | | |
|---|---|---|---|---|---|---|---|---|---|---|---|
| 1. | Y | 8. | N | 15. | Y | 22. | Y | 29. | Y | 36. | N |
| 2. | N | 9. | N | 16. | N | 23. | Y | 30. | N | 37. | Y |
| 3. | Y | 10. | Y | 17. | Y | 24. | Y | 31. | Y | 38. | N |
| 4. | N | 11. | N | 18. | N | 25. | Y | 32. | N | 39. | Y |
| 5. | N | 12. | Y | 19. | Y | 26. | N | 33. | Y | 40. | N |
| 6. | Y | 13. | Y | 20. | N | 27. | N | 34. | Y | | |
| 7. | Y | 14. | N | 21. | N | 28. | Y | 35. | N | | |

### SET 4

| | | | | | | | | | | | |
|---|---|---|---|---|---|---|---|---|---|---|---|
| 1. | N | 8. | N | 15. | Y | 22. | Y | 29. | N | 36. | Y |
| 2. | N | 9. | Y | 16. | N | 23. | N | 30. | N | 37. | Y |
| 3. | N | 10. | Y | 17. | N | 24. | Y | 31. | Y | 38. | N |
| 4. | Y | 11. | Y | 18. | Y | 25. | Y | 32. | N | 39. | Y |
| 5. | N | 12. | N | 19. | N | 26. | Y | 33. | N | 40. | N |
| 6. | N | 13. | Y | 20. | Y | 27. | N | 34. | N | | |
| 7. | Y | 14. | N | 21. | Y | 28. | Y | 35. | Y | | |

### SET 5

| | | | | | | | | | | | |
|---|---|---|---|---|---|---|---|---|---|---|---|
| 1. | N | 8. | N | 15. | Y | 22. | N | 29. | Y | 36. | Y |
| 2. | Y | 9. | Y | 16. | N | 23. | N | 30. | N | 37. | N |
| 3. | Y | 10. | N | 17. | Y | 24. | Y | 31. | N | 38. | Y |
| 4. | N | 11. | Y | 18. | N | 25. | Y | 32. | Y | 39. | Y |
| 5. | Y | 12. | N | 19. | N | 26. | N | 33. | N | 40. | N |
| 6. | N | 13. | N | 20. | Y | 27. | Y | 34. | Y | | |
| 7. | Y | 14. | Y | 21. | Y | 28. | N | 35. | N | | |

**SET 6**

| | | | | | | | | | | |
|---|---|---|---|---|---|---|---|---|---|---|
| 1. N | 8. N | 15. N | 22. N | 29. N | 36. N |
| 2. Y | 9. Y | 16. Y | 23. Y | 30. N | 37. Y |
| 3. Y | 10. Y | 17. N | 24. N | 31. Y | 38. N |
| 4. N | 11. N | 18. Y | 25. Y | 32. Y | 39. Y |
| 5. Y | 12. N | 19. Y | 26. N | 33. N | 40. Y |
| 6. N | 13. Y | 20. N | 27. Y | 34. Y | |
| 7. N | 14. Y | 21. Y | 28. N | 35. N | |

**SET 7**

| | | | | | | | | | | |
|---|---|---|---|---|---|---|---|---|---|---|
| 1. N | 8. N | 15. N | 22. N | 29. N | 36. Y |
| 2. Y | 9. Y | 16. Y | 23. N | 30. Y | 37. N |
| 3. Y | 10. N | 17. Y | 24. Y | 31. N | 38. Y |
| 4. N | 11. N | 18. N | 25. N | 32. Y | 39. Y |
| 5. Y | 12. Y | 19. N | 26. Y | 33. N | 40. N |
| 6. N | 13. N | 20. Y | 27. Y | 34. Y | |
| 7. Y | 14. Y | 21. Y | 28. N | 35. N | |

**SET 8**

| | | | | | | | | | | |
|---|---|---|---|---|---|---|---|---|---|---|
| 1. N | 8. N | 15. N | 22. N | 29. N | 36. Y |
| 2. Y | 9. Y | 16. Y | 23. N | 30. Y | 37. N |
| 3. Y | 10. N | 17. Y | 24. Y | 31. N | 38. Y |
| 4. N | 11. N | 18. N | 25. N | 32. Y | 39. Y |
| 5. Y | 12. Y | 19. N | 26. Y | 33. N | 40. N |
| 6. N | 13. N | 20. Y | 27. Y | 34. Y | |
| 7. Y | 14. Y | 21. Y | 28. N | 35. N | |

### Digit-Symbol Pairing

This task presents you with a key that pairs a set of symbols with a set of digits. Following this key, you will find 120 symbols. Your task is to indicate the appropriate digit for each symbol. For example, you might see the following pairings:

| + | − | × | \ |
|---|---|---|---|
| 1 | 2 | 3 | 4 |

Following this set of pairings, you would see 120 of those four symbols, which you are to match as quickly as possible with the appropriate digit.

What follow are eight sets of different pairings of digits with symbols. Each set of items contains from four to eight pairings followed by 120 symbols. As you work through these sets, try to increase your speed while maintaining perfect or near-perfect accuracy. Answers appear after the last set.

## DIGIT-SYMBOL PAIRING TASK

**SET 1**   KEY:

| ^ | ( | + | " |
|---|---|---|---|
| 1 | 2 | 3 | 4 |

| | | | | | |
|---|---|---|---|---|---|
| 1. ( | 21. + | 41. + | 61. + | 81. + | 101. + |
| 2. ^ | 22. " | 42. " | 62. " | 82. " | 102. " |
| 3. " | 23. ^ | 43. ^ | 63. ^ | 83. ^ | 103. ^ |
| 4. + | 24. " | 44. ( | 64. " | 84. " | 104. ( |
| 5. ^ | 25. + | 45. + | 65. + | 85. + | 105. " |
| 6. + | 26. " | 46. ( | 66. " | 86. ^ | 106. + |
| 7. " | 27. ^ | 47. " | 67. ^ | 87. ( | 107. ( |
| 8. ^ | 28. " | 48. + | 68. + | 88. + | 108. ^ |
| 9. ( | 29. + | 49. " | 69. ( | 89. " | 109. " |
| 10. " | 30. ^ | 50. ^ | 70. " | 90. ^ | 110. + |
| 11. ^ | 31. ( | 51. ( | 71. + | 91. ( | 111. " |
| 12. + | 32. ( | 52. " | 72. " | 92. + | 112. ^ |
| 13. " | 33. + | 53. + | 73. ( | 93. " | 113. ( |
| 14. ( | 34. " | 54. ^ | 74. ^ | 94. ^ | 114. + |
| 15. ^ | 35. ^ | 55. ( | 75. " | 95. + | 115. " |
| 16. " | 36. + | 56. + | 76. ( | 96. " | 116. ^ |
| 17. ( | 37. " | 57. " | 77. " | 97. ( | 117. + |
| 18. ^ | 38. ^ | 58. ^ | 78. + | 98. ^ | 118. ( |
| 19. + | 39. " | 59. ( | 79. " | 99. " | 119. " |
| 20. ^ | 40. ( | 60. + | 80. ^ | 100. + | 120. ^ |

**SET 2**   KEY:

| [ | \ | ; | – |
|---|---|---|---|
| 1 | 2 | 3 | 4 |

| | | | | | |
|---|---|---|---|---|---|
| 1. ; | 21. \ | 41. \ | 61. \ | 81. \ | 101. \ |
| 2. \ | 22. – | 42. [ | 62. ; | 82. – | 102. ; |
| 3. – | 23. [ | 43. ; | 63. [ | 83. ; | 103. – |
| 4. \ | 24. ; | 44. – | 64. – | 84. [ | 104. ; |
| 5. ; | 25. \ | 45. ; | 65. \ | 85. \ | 105. – |
| 6. [ | 26. [ | 46. \ | 66. ; | 86. [ | 106. \ |
| 7. ; | 27. – | 47. – | 67. [ | 87. – | 107. ; |
| 8. – | 28. ; | 48. [ | 68. – | 88. ; | 108. [ |
| 9. \ | 29. [ | 49. ; | 69. ; | 89. [ | 109. – |
| 10. – | 30. ; | 50. \ | 70. [ | 90. \ | 110. ; |
| 11. ; | 31. \ | 51. ; | 71. \ | 91. ; | 111. [ |
| 12. [ | 32. [ | 52. [ | 72. – | 92. [ | 112. \ |
| 13. ; | 33. \ | 53. – | 73. \ | 93. – | 113. [ |
| 14. \ | 34. ; | 54. ; | 74. ; | 94. ; | 114. – |
| 15. [ | 35. [ | 55. – | 75. [ | 95. \ | 115. \ |
| 16. – | 36. – | 56. \ | 76. – | 96. [ | 116. – |
| 17. \ | 37. ; | 57. [ | 77. \ | 97. \ | 117. \ |
| 18. ; | 38. \ | 58. ; | 78. ; | 98. – | 118. [ |
| 19. – | 39. – | 59. \ | 79. [ | 99. \ | 119. \ |
| 20. \ | 40. ; | 60. – | 80. ; | 100. ; | 120. [ |

**SET 3**    KEY:

| # | $ | \| | } |
|---|---|---|---|
| 1 | 2 | 3 | 4 |

| | | | | | |
|---|---|---|---|---|---|
| 1.  } | 21.  } | 41.  } | 61.  # | 81.  } | 101.  $ |
| 2.  \| | 22.  $ | 42.  # | 62.  } | 82.  # | 102.  # |
| 3.  # | 23.  \| | 43.  \| | 63.  $ | 83.  # | 103.  } |
| 4.  $ | 24.  } | 44.  } | 64.  \| | 84.  \| | 104.  \| |
| 5.  \| | 25.  # | 45.  # | 65.  } | 85.  } | 105.  # |
| 6.  } | 26.  \| | 46.  } | 66.  # | 86.  # | 106.  $ |
| 7.  # | 27.  } | 47.  $ | 67.  \| | 87.  $ | 107.  } |
| 8.  $ | 28.  # | 48.  # | 68.  $ | 88.  # | 108.  \| |
| 9.  } | 29.  $ | 49.  \| | 69.  } | 89.  } | 109.  $ |
| 10.  \| | 30.  \| | 50.  } | 70.  \| | 90.  # | 110.  # |
| 11.  # | 31.  } | 51.  \| | 71.  $ | 91.  $ | 111.  } |
| 12.  $ | 32.  $ | 52.  $ | 72.  # | 92.  \| | 112.  # |
| 13.  \| | 33.  \| | 53.  } | 73.  } | 93.  } | 113.  $ |
| 14.  # | 34.  # | 54.  # | 74.  \| | 94.  # | 114.  } |
| 15.  $ | 35.  } | 55.  $ | 75.  } | 95.  $ | 115.  # |
| 16.  } | 36.  \| | 56.  \| | 76.  \| | 96.  } | 116.  $ |
| 17.  # | 37.  # | 57.  } | 77.  $ | 97.  # | 117.  } |
| 18.  } | 38.  $ | 58.  # | 78.  # | 98.  $ | 118.  \| |
| 19.  $ | 39.  } | 59.  \| | 79.  } | 99.  \| | 119.  # |
| 20.  \| | 40.  \| | 60.  $ | 80.  \| | 100.  } | 120.  $ |

**SET 4**    KEY:

| { | & | @ | * | ~ |
|---|---|---|---|---|
| 1 | 2 | 3 | 4 | 5 |

| | | | | | |
|---|---|---|---|---|---|
| 1.  * | 21.  * | 41.  * | 61.  & | 81.  * | 101.  * |
| 2.  @ | 22.  { | 42.  @ | 62.  ~ | 82.  @ | 102.  & |
| 3.  ~ | 23.  @ | 43.  ~ | 63.  @ | 83.  ~ | 103.  { |
| 4.  & | 24.  & | 44.  { | 64.  { | 84.  @ | 104.  ~ |
| 5.  { | 25.  @ | 45.  * | 65.  @ | 85.  ~ | 105.  * |
| 6.  * | 26.  * | 46.  & | 66.  ~ | 86.  @ | 106.  @ |
| 7.  & | 27.  ~ | 47.  * | 67.  * | 87.  { | 107.  ~ |
| 8.  * | 28.  { | 48.  @ | 68.  { | 88.  * | 108.  & |
| 9.  @ | 29.  @ | 49.  ~ | 69.  ~ | 89.  & | 109.  ~ |
| 10.  ~ | 30.  * | 50.  @ | 70.  @ | 90.  @ | 110.  * |
| 11.  * | 31.  ~ | 51.  * | 71.  & | 91.  * | 111.  { |
| 12.  { | 32.  & | 52.  { | 72.  ~ | 92.  ~ | 112.  & |
| 13.  & | 33.  { | 53.  & | 73.  * | 93.  & | 113.  ~ |
| 14.  ~ | 34.  * | 54.  ~ | 74.  ~ | 94.  ~ | 114.  * |
| 15.  @ | 35.  ~ | 55.  * | 75.  { | 95.  { | 115.  @ |
| 16.  * | 36.  @ | 56.  ~ | 76.  * | 96.  * | 116.  & |
| 17.  & | 37.  & | 57.  @ | 77.  ~ | 97.  @ | 117.  { |
| 18.  ~ | 38.  * | 58.  & | 78.  @ | 98.  * | 118.  & |
| 19.  { | 39.  ~ | 59.  { | 79.  * | 99.  ~ | 119.  ~ |
| 20.  * | 40.  { | 60.  & | 80.  @ | 100.  @ | 120.  { |

**SET 5**    KEY:

| = | ? | % | ! | < |
|---|---|---|---|---|
| 1 | 2 | 3 | 4 | 5 |

| | | | | | |
|---|---|---|---|---|---|
| 1. % | 21. ! | 41. % | 61. % | 81. % | 101. = |
| 2. < | 22. ? | 42. ? | 62. < | 82. ! | 102. % |
| 3. ? | 23. < | 43. = | 63. ! | 83. < | 103. ? |
| 4. ! | 24. % | 44. ! | 64. ? | 84. = | 104. = |
| 5. = | 25. = | 45. < | 65. = | 85. < | 105. % |
| 6. ! | 26. % | 46. = | 66. < | 86. % | 106. ? |
| 7. % | 27. ? | 47. % | 67. ! | 87. ? | 107. = |
| 8. ? | 28. ! | 48. ? | 68. ? | 88. ! | 108. % |
| 9. < | 29. = | 49. % | 69. = | 89. < | 109. ! |
| 10. % | 30. < | 50. ! | 70. ! | 90. % | 110. ? |
| 11. < | 31. ? | 51. = | 71. < | 91. = | 111. < |
| 12. ? | 32. % | 52. < | 72. ? | 92. ! | 112. % |
| 13. % | 33. = | 53. = | 73. % | 93. ? | 113. = |
| 14. ! | 34. ? | 54. % | 74. ? | 94. % | 114. < |
| 15. < | 35. % | 55. ! | 75. ! | 95. < | 115. ! |
| 16. = | 36. ? | 56. ? | 76. = | 96. = | 116. = |
| 17. ! | 37. ! | 57. = | 77. < | 97. ! | 117. ? |
| 18. % | 38. % | 58. % | 78. % | 98. % | 118. ! |
| 19. < | 39. < | 59. ? | 79. < | 99. ! | 119. % |
| 20. ! | 40. = | 60. ! | 80. ! | 100. < | 120. < |

**SET 6**    KEY:

| \ | [ | , | = | x | o |
|---|---|---|---|---|---|
| 1 | 2 | 3 | 4 | 5 | 6 |

| | | | | | |
|---|---|---|---|---|---|
| 1. o | 21. , | 41. x | 61. o | 81. = | 101. \ |
| 2. x | 22. \ | 42. o | 62. x | 82. , | 102. , |
| 3. = | 23. x | 43. = | 63. = | 83. \ | 103. = |
| 4. , | 24. o | 44. [ | 64. x | 84. x | 104. [ |
| 5. [ | 25. = | 45. , | 65. o | 85. = | 105. x |
| 6. \ | 26. [ | 46. \ | 66. = | 86. [ | 106. = |
| 7. [ | 27. , | 47. x | 67. [ | 87. x | 107. o |
| 8. , | 28. \ | 48. o | 68. , | 88. [ | 108. , |
| 9. o | 29. , | 49. = | 69. [ | 89. , | 109. [ |
| 10. x | 30. [ | 50. [ | 70. = | 90. = | 110. x |
| 11. [ | 31. = | 51. = | 71. o | 91. \ | 111. \ |
| 12. = | 32. \ | 52. \ | 72. \ | 92. x | 112. o |
| 13. o | 33. o | 53. = | 73. x | 93. [ | 113. = |
| 14. x | 34. x | 54. , | 74. = | 94. o | 114. \ |
| 15. \ | 35. , | 55. o | 75. , | 95. = | 115. o |
| 16. o | 36. [ | 56. x | 76. \ | 96. \ | 116. x |
| 17. = | 37. = | 57. \ | 77. o | 97. x | 117. , |
| 18. , | 38. \ | 58. o | 78. , | 98. = | 118. [ |
| 19. \ | 39. , | 59. [ | 79. x | 99. , | 119. = |
| 20. x | 40. [ | 60. , | 80. [ | 100. x | 120. \ |

**SET 7**    KEY:

| | − | 8 | / | = | v | ] |
|---|---|---|---|---|---|---|
| | 1 | 2 | 3 | 4 | 5 | 6 |

| | | | | | | |
|---|---|---|---|---|---|---|
| 1. − | 21. − | 41. v | 61. − | 81. = | 101. / |
| 2. / | 22. v | 42. 8 | 62. = | 82. / | 102. = |
| 3. = | 23. / | 43. − | 63. v | 83. = | 103. ] |
| 4. v | 24. 8 | 44. = | 64. 8 | 84. − | 104. − |
| 5. ] | 25. ] | 45. − | 65. ] | 85. v | 105. / |
| 6. / | 26. = | 46. / | 66. = | 86. = | 106. v |
| 7. v | 27. v | 47. v | 67. / | 87. − | 107. 8 |
| 8. = | 28. ] | 48. 8 | 68. v | 88. ] | 108. = |
| 9. − | 29. − | 49. − | 69. = | 89. v | 109. − |
| 10. / | 30. v | 50. / | 70. − | 90. 8 | 110. / |
| 11. 8 | 31. 8 | 51. = | 71. / | 91. / | 111. ] |
| 12. v | 32. ] | 52. v | 72. 8 | 92. 8 | 112. v |
| 13. / | 33. v | 53. / | 73. / | 93. ] | 113. ] |
| 14. ] | 34. ] | 54. ] | 74. v | 94. = | 114. 8 |
| 15. / | 35. = | 55. − | 75. / | 95. / | 115. / |
| 16. − | 36. v | 56. 8 | 76. = | 96. − | 116. 8 |
| 17. 8 | 37. − | 57. v | 77. ] | 97. v | 117. = |
| 18. v | 38. / | 58. / | 78. − | 98. / | 118. − |
| 19. − | 39. = | 59. ] | 79. ] | 99. − | 119. ] |
| 20. v | 40. [ | 60. − | 80. 8 | 100. − | 120. / |

**SET 8**    KEY:

| | / | t | [ | ; | z | \ | = | ] |
|---|---|---|---|---|---|---|---|---|
| | 1 | 2 | 3 | 4 | 5 | 6 | 7 | 8 |

| | | | | | | |
|---|---|---|---|---|---|---|
| 1. \ | 21. = | 41. \ | 61. = | 81. = | 101. / |
| 2. / | 22. [ | 42. ; | 62. ] | 82. / | 102. = |
| 3. = | 23. / | 43. ] | 63. / | 83. ; | 103. ] |
| 4. z | 24. ; | 44. [ | 64. t | 84. = | 104. z |
| 5. t | 25. z | 45. = | 65. / | 85. z | 105. ; |
| 6. ] | 26. ] | 46. ] | 66. ; | 86. ; | 106. [ |
| 7. / | 27. t | 47. ; | 67. z | 87. t | 107. \ |
| 8. ; | 28. ] | 48. t | 68. t | 88. ] | 108. t |
| 9. = | 29. [ | 49. = | 69. = | 89. / | 109. = |
| 10. \ | 30. / | 50. ] | 70. [ | 90. t | 110. / |
| 11. z | 31. z | 51. / | 71. ; | 91. ; | 111. ] |
| 12. ] | 32. = | 52. \ | 72. = | 92. z | 112. z |
| 13. t | 33. t | 53. z | 73. t | 93. ] | 113. ; |
| 14. / | 34. ; | 54. ; | 74. / | 94. [ | 114. t |
| 15. \ | 35. / | 55. t | 75. ] | 95. / | 115. ; |
| 16. = | 36. z | 56. ] | 76. = | 96. \ | 116. / |
| 17. ] | 37. ] | 57. = | 77. ; | 97. t | 117. \ |
| 18. z | 38. = | 58. / | 78. t | 98. = | 118. ] |
| 19. t | 39. \ | 59. z | 79. = | 99. z | 119. [ |
| 20. / | 40. t | 60. ] | 80. \ | 100. = | 120. \ |

## ANSWERS TO DIGIT-SYMBOL PAIRING TASK

### SET 1

| | | | | | | | | | | | |
|---|---|---|---|---|---|---|---|---|---|---|---|
| 1. | 2 | 21. | 3 | 41. | 3 | 61. | 3 | 81. | 3 | 101. | 3 |
| 2. | 1 | 22. | 4 | 42. | 4 | 62. | 4 | 82. | 4 | 102. | 4 |
| 3. | 4 | 23. | 1 | 43. | 1 | 63. | 1 | 83. | 1 | 103. | 1 |
| 4. | 3 | 24. | 4 | 44. | 2 | 64. | 4 | 84. | 4 | 104. | 2 |
| 5. | 1 | 25. | 3 | 45. | 3 | 65. | 3 | 85. | 3 | 105. | 4 |
| 6. | 3 | 26. | 4 | 46. | 2 | 66. | 4 | 86. | 1 | 106. | 3 |
| 7. | 4 | 27. | 1 | 47. | 4 | 67. | 1 | 87. | 2 | 107. | 2 |
| 8. | 1 | 28. | 4 | 48. | 3 | 68. | 3 | 88. | 3 | 108. | 1 |
| 9. | 2 | 29. | 3 | 49. | 4 | 69. | 2 | 89. | 4 | 109. | 4 |
| 10. | 4 | 30. | 1 | 50. | 1 | 70. | 4 | 90. | 1 | 110. | 3 |
| 11. | 1 | 31. | 2 | 51. | 2 | 71. | 3 | 91. | 2 | 111. | 4 |
| 12. | 3 | 32. | 2 | 52. | 4 | 72. | 4 | 92. | 3 | 112. | 1 |
| 13. | 4 | 33. | 3 | 53. | 3 | 73. | 2 | 93. | 4 | 113. | 2 |
| 14. | 2 | 34. | 4 | 54. | 1 | 74. | 1 | 94. | 1 | 114. | 3 |
| 15. | 1 | 35. | 1 | 55. | 2 | 75. | 4 | 95. | 3 | 115. | 4 |
| 16. | 4 | 36. | 3 | 56. | 3 | 76. | 2 | 96. | 4 | 116. | 1 |
| 17. | 2 | 37. | 4 | 57. | 4 | 77. | 4 | 97. | 2 | 117. | 3 |
| 18. | 1 | 38. | 1 | 58. | 1 | 78. | 3 | 98. | 1 | 118. | 2 |
| 19. | 3 | 39. | 4 | 59. | 2 | 79. | 4 | 99. | 4 | 119. | 4 |
| 20. | 1 | 40. | 2 | 60. | 3 | 80. | 1 | 100. | 3 | 120. | 1 |

### SET 2

| | | | | | | | | | | | |
|---|---|---|---|---|---|---|---|---|---|---|---|
| 1. | 3 | 21. | 2 | 41. | 2 | 61. | 2 | 81. | 2 | 101. | 2 |
| 2. | 2 | 22. | 4 | 42. | 1 | 62. | 3 | 82. | 4 | 102. | 3 |
| 3. | 4 | 23. | 1 | 43. | 3 | 63. | 1 | 83. | 3 | 103. | 4 |
| 4. | 2 | 24. | 3 | 44. | 4 | 64. | 4 | 84. | 1 | 104. | 3 |
| 5. | 3 | 25. | 2 | 45. | 3 | 65. | 2 | 85. | 2 | 105. | 4 |
| 6. | 1 | 26. | 1 | 46. | 2 | 66. | 3 | 86. | 1 | 106. | 2 |
| 7. | 3 | 27. | 4 | 47. | 4 | 67. | 1 | 87. | 4 | 107. | 3 |
| 8. | 4 | 28. | 3 | 48. | 1 | 68. | 4 | 88. | 3 | 108. | 1 |
| 9. | 2 | 29. | 1 | 49. | 3 | 69. | 3 | 89. | 1 | 109. | 4 |
| 10. | 4 | 30. | 3 | 50. | 2 | 70. | 1 | 90. | 2 | 110. | 3 |
| 11. | 3 | 31. | 2 | 51. | 3 | 71. | 2 | 91. | 3 | 111. | 1 |
| 12. | 1 | 32. | 1 | 52. | 1 | 72. | 4 | 92. | 1 | 112. | 2 |
| 13. | 3 | 33. | 2 | 53. | 4 | 73. | 2 | 93. | 4 | 113. | 1 |
| 14. | 2 | 34. | 3 | 54. | 3 | 74. | 3 | 94. | 3 | 114. | 4 |
| 15. | 1 | 35. | 1 | 55. | 4 | 75. | 1 | 95. | 2 | 115. | 2 |
| 16. | 4 | 36. | 4 | 56. | 2 | 76. | 4 | 96. | 1 | 116. | 4 |
| 17. | 2 | 37. | 3 | 57. | 1 | 77. | 2 | 97. | 2 | 117. | 2 |
| 18. | 3 | 38. | 2 | 58. | 3 | 78. | 3 | 98. | 4 | 118. | 1 |
| 19. | 4 | 39. | 4 | 59. | 2 | 79. | 1 | 99. | 2 | 119. | 2 |
| 20. | 2 | 40. | 3 | 60. | 4 | 80. | 3 | 100. | 3 | 120. | 1 |

## SET 3

| | | | | | | | | | | |
|---|---|---|---|---|---|---|---|---|---|---|---|
| 1. | 4 | 21. | 4 | 41. | 4 | 61. | 1 | 81. | 4 | 101. | 2 |
| 2. | 3 | 22. | 2 | 42. | 1 | 62. | 4 | 82. | 1 | 102. | 1 |
| 3. | 1 | 23. | 3 | 43. | 3 | 63. | 2 | 83. | 1 | 103. | 4 |
| 4. | 2 | 24. | 4 | 44. | 4 | 64. | 3 | 84. | 3 | 104. | 3 |
| 5. | 3 | 25. | 1 | 45. | 1 | 65. | 4 | 85. | 4 | 105. | 1 |
| 6. | 4 | 26. | 3 | 46. | 4 | 66. | 1 | 86. | 1 | 106. | 2 |
| 7. | 1 | 27. | 4 | 47. | 2 | 67. | 3 | 87. | 2 | 107. | 4 |
| 8. | 2 | 28. | 1 | 48. | 1 | 68. | 2 | 88. | 1 | 108. | 3 |
| 9. | 4 | 29. | 2 | 49. | 3 | 69. | 4 | 89. | 4 | 109. | 2 |
| 10. | 3 | 30. | 3 | 50. | 4 | 70. | 3 | 90. | 1 | 110. | 1 |
| 11. | 1 | 31. | 4 | 51. | 3 | 71. | 2 | 91. | 2 | 111. | 4 |
| 12. | 2 | 32. | 2 | 52. | 2 | 72. | 1 | 92. | 3 | 112. | 1 |
| 13. | 3 | 33. | 3 | 53. | 4 | 73. | 4 | 93. | 4 | 113. | 2 |
| 14. | 1 | 34. | 1 | 54. | 1 | 74. | 3 | 94. | 1 | 114. | 4 |
| 15. | 2 | 35. | 4 | 55. | 2 | 75. | 4 | 95. | 2 | 115. | 1 |
| 16. | 4 | 36. | 3 | 56. | 3 | 76. | 3 | 96. | 4 | 116. | 2 |
| 17. | 1 | 37. | 1 | 57. | 4 | 77. | 2 | 97. | 1 | 117. | 4 |
| 18. | 4 | 38. | 2 | 58. | 1 | 78. | 1 | 98. | 2 | 118. | 3 |
| 19. | 2 | 39. | 4 | 59. | 3 | 79. | 4 | 99. | 3 | 119. | 1 |
| 20. | 3 | 40. | 3 | 60. | 2 | 80. | 3 | 100. | 4 | 120. | 2 |

## SET 4

| | | | | | | | | | | |
|---|---|---|---|---|---|---|---|---|---|---|---|
| 1. | 4 | 21. | 4 | 41. | 4 | 61. | 2 | 81. | 4 | 101. | 4 |
| 2. | 3 | 22. | 1 | 42. | 3 | 62. | 5 | 82. | 3 | 102. | 2 |
| 3. | 5 | 23. | 3 | 43. | 5 | 63. | 3 | 83. | 5 | 103. | 1 |
| 4. | 2 | 24. | 2 | 44. | 1 | 64. | 1 | 84. | 3 | 104. | 5 |
| 5. | 1 | 25. | 3 | 45. | 4 | 65. | 3 | 85. | 5 | 105. | 4 |
| 6. | 4 | 26. | 4 | 46. | 2 | 66. | 5 | 86. | 3 | 106. | 3 |
| 7. | 2 | 27. | 5 | 47. | 4 | 67. | 4 | 87. | 1 | 107. | 5 |
| 8. | 4 | 28. | 1 | 48. | 3 | 68. | 1 | 88. | 4 | 108. | 2 |
| 9. | 3 | 29. | 3 | 49. | 5 | 69. | 5 | 89. | 2 | 109. | 5 |
| 10. | 5 | 30. | 4 | 50. | 3 | 70. | 3 | 90. | 3 | 110. | 4 |
| 11. | 4 | 31. | 5 | 51. | 4 | 71. | 2 | 91. | 4 | 111. | 1 |
| 12. | 1 | 32. | 2 | 52. | 1 | 72. | 5 | 92. | 5 | 112. | 2 |
| 13. | 2 | 33. | 1 | 53. | 2 | 73. | 4 | 93. | 2 | 113. | 5 |
| 14. | 5 | 34. | 4 | 54. | 5 | 74. | 5 | 94. | 5 | 114. | 4 |
| 15. | 3 | 35. | 5 | 55. | 4 | 75. | 1 | 95. | 1 | 115. | 3 |
| 16. | 4 | 36. | 3 | 56. | 5 | 76. | 4 | 96. | 4 | 116. | 2 |
| 17. | 2 | 37. | 2 | 57. | 3 | 77. | 5 | 97. | 3 | 117. | 1 |
| 18. | 5 | 38. | 4 | 58. | 2 | 78. | 3 | 98. | 4 | 118. | 2 |
| 19. | 1 | 39. | 5 | 59. | 1 | 79. | 4 | 99. | 5 | 119. | 5 |
| 20. | 4 | 40. | 1 | 60. | 2 | 80. | 3 | 100. | 3 | 120. | 1 |

## SET 5

| | | | | | |
|---|---|---|---|---|---|
| 1. 3 | 21. 4 | 41. 3 | 61. 3 | 81. 3 | 101. 1 |
| 2. 5 | 22. 2 | 42. 2 | 62. 5 | 82. 4 | 102. 3 |
| 3. 2 | 23. 5 | 43. 1 | 63. 4 | 83. 5 | 103. 2 |
| 4. 4 | 24. 3 | 44. 4 | 64. 2 | 84. 1 | 104. 1 |
| 5. 1 | 25. 1 | 45. 5 | 65. 1 | 85. 5 | 105. 3 |
| 6. 4 | 26. 3 | 46. 1 | 66. 5 | 86. 3 | 106. 2 |
| 7. 3 | 27. 2 | 47. 3 | 67. 4 | 87. 2 | 107. 1 |
| 8. 2 | 28. 4 | 48. 2 | 68. 2 | 88. 4 | 108. 3 |
| 9. 5 | 29. 1 | 49. 3 | 69. 1 | 89. 5 | 109. 4 |
| 10. 3 | 30. 5 | 50. 4 | 70. 4 | 90. 3 | 110. 2 |
| 11. 5 | 31. 2 | 51. 1 | 71. 5 | 91. 1 | 111. 5 |
| 12. 2 | 32. 3 | 52. 5 | 72. 2 | 92. 4 | 112. 3 |
| 13. 3 | 33. 1 | 53. 1 | 73. 3 | 93. 2 | 113. 1 |
| 14. 4 | 34. 2 | 54. 3 | 74. 2 | 94. 3 | 114. 5 |
| 15. 5 | 35. 3 | 55. 4 | 75. 4 | 95. 5 | 115. 4 |
| 16. 1 | 36. 2 | 56. 2 | 76. 1 | 96. 1 | 116. 1 |
| 17. 4 | 37. 4 | 57. 1 | 77. 5 | 97. 4 | 117. 2 |
| 18. 3 | 38. 3 | 58. 3 | 78. 3 | 98. 3 | 118. 4 |
| 19. 5 | 39. 5 | 59. 2 | 79. 5 | 99. 4 | 119. 3 |
| 20. 4 | 40. 1 | 60. 4 | 80. 4 | 100. 5 | 120. 5 |

## SET 6

| | | | | | |
|---|---|---|---|---|---|
| 1. 6 | 21. 3 | 41. 5 | 61. 6 | 81. 4 | 101. 1 |
| 2. 5 | 22. 1 | 42. 6 | 62. 5 | 82. 3 | 102. 3 |
| 3. 4 | 23. 5 | 43. 4 | 63. 4 | 83. 1 | 103. 4 |
| 4. 3 | 24. 6 | 44. 2 | 64. 5 | 84. 5 | 104. 2 |
| 5. 2 | 25. 4 | 45. 3 | 65. 6 | 85. 4 | 105. 5 |
| 6. 1 | 26. 2 | 46. 1 | 66. 4 | 86. 2 | 106. 4 |
| 7. 2 | 27. 3 | 47. 5 | 67. 2 | 87. 5 | 107. 6 |
| 8. 3 | 28. 1 | 48. 6 | 68. 3 | 88. 2 | 108. 3 |
| 9. 6 | 29. 3 | 49. 4 | 69. 2 | 89. 3 | 109. 2 |
| 10. 5 | 30. 2 | 50. 2 | 70. 4 | 90. 4 | 110. 5 |
| 11. 2 | 31. 4 | 51. 4 | 71. 6 | 91. 1 | 111. 1 |
| 12. 4 | 32. 1 | 52. 1 | 72. 1 | 92. 5 | 112. 6 |
| 13. 6 | 33. 6 | 53. 4 | 73. 5 | 93. 2 | 113. 4 |
| 14. 5 | 34. 5 | 54. 3 | 74. 4 | 94. 6 | 114. 1 |
| 15. 1 | 35. 3 | 55. 5 | 75. 3 | 95. 4 | 115. 6 |
| 16. 6 | 36. 2 | 56. 5 | 76. 1 | 96. 1 | 116. 5 |
| 17. 4 | 37. 4 | 57. 1 | 77. 6 | 97. 5 | 117. 3 |
| 18. 3 | 38. 1 | 58. 6 | 78. 3 | 98. 4 | 118. 2 |
| 19. 1 | 39. 3 | 59. 2 | 79. 5 | 99. 3 | 119. 4 |
| 20. 5 | 40. 2 | 60. 3 | 80. 2 | 100. 5 | 120. 1 |

## SET 7

| | | | | | | | | | |
|---|---|---|---|---|---|---|---|---|---|
| 1. | 1 | 21. | 1 | 41. | 5 | 61. | 1 | 81. | 4 |
| 2. | 3 | 22. | 5 | 42. | 2 | 62. | 4 | 82. | 3 |
| 3. | 4 | 23. | 3 | 43. | 1 | 63. | 5 | 83. | 4 |
| 4. | 5 | 24. | 2 | 44. | 4 | 64. | 2 | 84. | 1 |
| 5. | 6 | 25. | 6 | 45. | 1 | 65. | 6 | 85. | 5 |
| 6. | 3 | 26. | 4 | 46. | 3 | 66. | 4 | 86. | 4 |
| 7. | 5 | 27. | 5 | 47. | 5 | 67. | 3 | 87. | 1 |
| 8. | 4 | 28. | 6 | 48. | 2 | 68. | 5 | 88. | 6 |
| 9. | 1 | 29. | 1 | 49. | 1 | 69. | 4 | 89. | 5 |
| 10. | 3 | 30. | 5 | 50. | 3 | 70. | 1 | 90. | 2 |
| 11. | 2 | 31. | 2 | 51. | 4 | 71. | 3 | 91. | 3 |
| 12. | 5 | 32. | 6 | 52. | 5 | 72. | 2 | 92. | 2 |
| 13. | 3 | 33. | 5 | 53. | 3 | 73. | 3 | 93. | 6 |
| 14. | 6 | 34. | 6 | 54. | 6 | 74. | 5 | 94. | 4 |
| 15. | 3 | 35. | 4 | 55. | 1 | 75. | 3 | 95. | 3 |
| 16. | 1 | 36. | 5 | 56. | 2 | 76. | 4 | 96. | 1 |
| 17. | 2 | 37. | 1 | 57. | 5 | 77. | 6 | 97. | 5 |
| 18. | 5 | 38. | 3 | 58. | 3 | 78. | 1 | 98. | 3 |
| 19. | 1 | 39. | 4 | 59. | 6 | 79. | 6 | 99. | 4 |
| 20. | 5 | 40. | 6 | 60. | 1 | 80. | 2 | 100. | 1 |

| | | | |
|---|---|---|---|
| 101. | 3 |
| 102. | 4 |
| 103. | 6 |
| 104. | 1 |
| 105. | 3 |
| 106. | 5 |
| 107. | 2 |
| 108. | 4 |
| 109. | 1 |
| 110. | 3 |
| 111. | 6 |
| 112. | 5 |
| 113. | 6 |
| 114. | 2 |
| 115. | 3 |
| 116. | 2 |
| 117. | 4 |
| 118. | 1 |
| 119. | 6 |
| 120. | 3 |

## SET 8

| | | | | | | | | | | | |
|---|---|---|---|---|---|---|---|---|---|---|---|
| 1. | 6 | 21. | 7 | 41. | 6 | 61. | 7 | 81. | 7 | 101. | 1 |
| 2. | 1 | 22. | 3 | 42. | 4 | 62. | 8 | 82. | 1 | 102. | 7 |
| 3. | 7 | 23. | 1 | 43. | 8 | 63. | 1 | 83. | 4 | 103. | 8 |
| 4. | 5 | 24. | 4 | 44. | 3 | 64. | 2 | 84. | 7 | 104. | 5 |
| 5. | 2 | 25. | 5 | 45. | 7 | 65. | 1 | 85. | 5 | 105. | 4 |
| 6. | 8 | 26. | 8 | 46. | 8 | 66. | 4 | 86. | 4 | 106. | 3 |
| 7. | 1 | 27. | 2 | 47. | 4 | 67. | 5 | 87. | 2 | 107. | 6 |
| 8. | 4 | 28. | 8 | 48. | 2 | 68. | 2 | 88. | 8 | 108. | 2 |
| 9. | 7 | 29. | 3 | 49. | 7 | 69. | 7 | 89. | 1 | 109. | 7 |
| 10. | 6 | 30. | 1 | 50. | 8 | 70. | 3 | 90. | 2 | 110. | 1 |
| 11. | 5 | 31. | 5 | 51. | 1 | 71. | 4 | 91. | 4 | 111. | 8 |
| 12. | 8 | 32. | 7 | 52. | 6 | 72. | 7 | 92. | 5 | 112. | 5 |
| 13. | 2 | 33. | 2 | 53. | 5 | 73. | 2 | 93. | 8 | 113. | 4 |
| 14. | 1 | 34. | 4 | 54. | 4 | 74. | 1 | 94. | 3 | 114. | 2 |
| 15. | 6 | 35. | 1 | 55. | 2 | 75. | 8 | 95. | 1 | 115. | 4 |
| 16. | 7 | 36. | 5 | 56. | 8 | 76. | 7 | 96. | 6 | 116. | 1 |
| 17. | 8 | 37. | 8 | 57. | 7 | 77. | 4 | 97. | 2 | 117. | 6 |
| 18. | 5 | 38. | 7 | 58. | 1 | 78. | 2 | 98. | 7 | 118. | 8 |
| 19. | 2 | 39. | 6 | 59. | 5 | 79. | 7 | 99. | 5 | 119. | 3 |
| 20. | 1 | 40. | 2 | 60. | 8 | 80. | 6 | 100. | 7 | 120. | 6 |

## Complex Visual Search

This task resembles the earlier visual-search task except that it is more difficult and challenging. A task very similar to this one was used by Schneider and Shiffrin (1977) in their original studies of controlled and automatic information processing. In this task, you will find a set of two to four target letters followed by 40 items arrayed in a variety of physical patterns. Your task is to indicate for each of the 40 items whether *any* of the target letters appears in the visual array. If one or more of the target letters do appear, you should indicate this with a "Y" (Yes). If none of the letters appear, you should indicate this with an "N" (No). If, for example, the target letter string is (a b c) and the following array is

you should indicate a "Y." If, on the other hand, the target letters are h and q, and you see the visual array

a       d<br>
c<br>
e f

you should indicate an N.

Note that this task is more challenging than the previous task because of two variations: First, the number of targets is greater; second, the letters to be compared to the targets are arrayed in two dimensions rather than just one. As you work through the twelve sets of items, try to increase your speed while maintaining perfect or near-perfect accuracy. Answers appear after the last set.

### COMPLEX VISUAL SEARCH

**SET 1**
TARGET LETTERS: ( r   j )

1.  q      p
      s
      d

2.  n  o
        j
    v

3.    b  r
    z      z

4.  m
     y
      e
       f

5.  o
    p
    x
    r

6.  u  q
     b  o

7.                    a      8.            v     b        9.            x
              o                                                 n    i    o
        u                                  j
    r                                      g

10.   b        c          11.   u    p           12.   k    k    d
      t        w                l                                        g
                                     p

13.            v          14.            r    s        15.   z    u
     f              m                         v                   o
        p                                                         f
                                g

16.   b   q              17.      a    b    c         18.            w
          d                                                    w
          n                       e                              u  u

19.   h              o    20.            g           21.            r        p
         r    v                      v                      s    z
                                 b
                                 d

22.   t        b          23.   k    w               24.            j
      j        p                     u    s                k
                                                                       z   q

25.        p    o         26.   w                     27.            y
     d              l            x                           o
                                 y                                        u
                                   i                         v

28.        e     p        29.   y                     30.   w    w    d
    r   e                            z    x    q                          r

31.    f    a              32.              h    g        33.    t
   j         v                s    r                   r
                                                          d
                                                             b


34.    t    y    j          35.    o    u              36.    x    w
   l                           r    z                        z         e


37.                   q      38.                   y    39.        w    o        p
   w         p                 d    s    r              r
      j


40.    p    p
   g    h

---

## SET 2
TARGET LETTERS: ( u    e )

1.         o    s          2.    i              p        3.    v    e    a
      c                             z    u                                  c
   n


4.    m    v    s          5.         p              6.    o    n    d
   x                          d                                      p
                                     g
                             u


7.    b         x          8.    i              9.    m         c
      r         t                o    r    n          x         v


10.         f         f    11.    o    r    b    12.    i    o    u
   s                             c                           q
   c


13.         g              14.         a    z    15.    b              b
   z    w         p           n    e                        e    d

16.  y
          o
            a
              u

17.                    s
              a
                    e
         b

18.  p    q
     u    e

19.  o    k
     u        k

20.       z
          y
          p
     r

21.              r    t
         r
         m

22.         w    w
     v b

23.  t    y    i
                    e

24.                        q
                        r
              u
          w

25.              r
     t    e    y

26.       h    j    l
              u

27.  u
              z
                    g
          d

28.            p
     g        e
         b

29.       p    q    s
     h

30.  c        d
     d
     g

31.       w
     x        y
         b

32.       s    d
     g
              e

33.            q        c
     w
     m

34.  c    b    a
     e

35.            f    f
              j
     u

36.  n    m
     v    h

37.            p
     g    v
     r

38.  m    m
     b    z

39.                        i
         q        h
              k

40.     e        o
     d        f

**SET 3**
TARGET LETTERS: (t   l)

1.         m                     2.   r        l                     3.                    u      y      t
  w                                    v      x                              c


                    z
            t



4.    a                          5.              i                     6.          q      s
        s                                   o                                   u
  s                                                      p                              k
        a                                   t



7.  m   x    z                   8.                        o         9.                    r      z
        l                             l        d      f                     k
                                                                                          t



10.  q                           11.         d      c                  12.         b      x
        s                              w                                     l              f
    l                                                        m
  m



13.  v                  l        14.                  u                15.         b      a      s
            d      s                   p          o        t                 r



16.  w            e              17.                  l                18.         m
        c              k                g          h                                     b
                                             v                                  d      w



19.              i               20.         m      b                  21.              n
  a       d                            n      t                              m                  o
              n                                                                    p



22.  z                           23.                  p                24.                    d
  j                                          o                               w      e
  r                                               a                                        l
  v                                     f

25.  j  
　　　　l  
　r  
　　　r  

26.　　　o  
　　　i  
　　　　d  
　　　　b  

27.　　　　a　　v　a  
　　　s  

28.  q　r  
　　　　a　　d  

29.  h　　f  
　　　x　　i  

30.  w　　　c  
　　　　s　　　t  

31.  b　s  
　i　　　t  

32.　　f　　u　　c  
　　　l  

33.　　　n  
　　　d  
　　　　b  
　　　x  

34.　　　s　　g  
　　　　b  
　d  

35.　　　　w  
　　　f  
　　　　l　m  

36.　　　w  
　　　　　c  
　　　w  
　　a  

37.　　　　p  
　　　　f  
　e  
　　　m  

38.　　　i  
　　　　e  
　　t　　r  

39.  q　　w  
　　　d  
　　　　e  

40.  w  
　　e  
　g  
　d  

---

**SET 4**
TARGET LETTERS: ( h   z )

1.  w  e  r  
　　s　　　　y  
　　h　　　w  

2.　　t　　a  
　s　　　j  
　　e　　b  

3.　　　　i  
　z　d  
　d　f　u  

4.　　w  
　s  
　　g  
a  
　　a　q  

5.  d　z　x  
　　　s v b  

6.　u　　　y  
　w  
　　b v a

7.    s         n
         x         w
   q         d

8.         v    m    j
                    c
      i         o

9.                        p
         d    h
         s    n    m

10.  a    b    c    d
      z    k

11.  e         e
      f         f
      g         h

12.                t         y
         w         n    q
                r

13.         b    n
   q              r
         c x

14.         i    f    g
         h    t
            v

15.                        u
         e   g  f
                  j   a

16.  z    b              p
         d    n
      s

17.  m    x
         c
      w         z
         c

18.  i         e
            c    v
      k         a

19.   s
   w
         w
               z
   q

20.              w   t   y
         f  g  h

21.  i    n    s    a
            n
            e

22.         r         y
   b    s    e
            h

23.         w    z    x
      w              v
            j

24.         e
      v
                     f
         e
                  t  y

25.      t         o
      r      r
   z
         b

26.              p
      p    u
         w         n  m

27.      a
      s         s
      s              h
            o

28.         s
         r      w
   s    z    l

29.         v    c
      x    z
               m
            v

30.      d    f    g
         a
      c
            h

31.        a      p     32.        x   c   v    33.        i   v  q

```
31.          a       p      32.          x   c   v      33.              i   v  q
       l    v                            p                        a   f  z
   z  e                               m n

34.             j          35.          w e          36.  c    b    n
       d   m                    s    n                              e  a  l
   p    l   u                   z    c

37.  s        m          38.      b    v          39.        w           i
       b                     f               n                          m
   r        k                   k   j                        m
       e                                                          y
                                                           a

40.          r    t
   k
     l
       q
          c
```

SET 5

TARGET LETTERS: ( o    k )

```
1.   l    m    n      2.  p     n                3.          c    a
        n                  s     k                           s    z
     w          z          b     x                        b     o

4.    a            5.       l          q      6.        v    b
   d                              s  o               v c
   e                          l       r                    i    d
 k
     f    g

7.  s        v    h      8.     m   v       b      9.       b    x
       q        o                        k                 h    n
          r                       g   b                    x  z

10.  o          p   b      11.       s                12.    s         y
      s                              d         h                  m
      d                              u                       c  n  v
              a                  k        b
```

13.  b    m    v    c          14.    d         f          15.         n    h  b
         x                                 u                        c                o
     t                                  g    f    x                          z

16.  s       c       n          17.  s    d    s          18.         c       n
         a    v       n                    g                      f    s    b
                                          f                           o
                                          k

19.         c       o          20.         w    r  a       21.         s       f
     a    d                            y    v  c                   a
              f  g                                             o            r
                                                                  t

22.       w                     23.  z    z               24.              f  d
     p            t                           g               a  o
         n        d                      h                              v  x
     a        d                          k    p

25.  e       y                  26.              o         27.       s    s
     v       u                                   b            a       k        p
     k       r                                   l                    r
                                                 m
                                    q    e                                 v

28.       b    j                29.              l         30.  z
     f                              g    h                           d    f
         k    l                                  k  l            a    g    h
     c                                  v

31.       w  i                  32.              j         33.       c  v
     x    b  v                                   l            a       o  g        p
                                           h
         f                          e    w    t

34.        d          35.  p     q             36.  u     i

      f                l         j                 s     t

    s                                              d  g

  l       a                 o     y

      c

37.           w    r     38.          e    t    u    39.      s     f

        j     l                      k              a     g           m

                b                                           x

  v    x                  m

40.  p    w

    m

      b

      d

      v

---

## SET 6
TARGET LETTERS: ( a   b )

1.  q             u      2.  p     t     y      3.                d    f

    r           t                  u                     l    k

    f        r                a     l                     b    d

        b                  z     m                     i

                                            q

4.    f     h    j     5.  g    y         6.  w    s    g    h

  d         k            v    n                 x    c    b    k

    s  x  c               x    z

                        m    n

7.    s    f    v     8.  f     g         9.  r    q    v    z

  d             p        p     d            s

    a    i    o          g     r            d

                       k     d            l

                                         u

10.                     p        11.  b    n    m        12.  q    w
              r                           c    v n              d    s
         i                                u                 d    b
      j                                   x                 x    z
   n   f   h   g

13.  q                 s        14.  e    r        n        15.        o    e
        m         g                      f                      u  y
      b       l                      w         p                g  h
      x                                  s    h                w k
         a

16.      e    v    k        17.                 e   r        18.          p   i
   a         c    x                  q    w                     k
         n    m                               m                        m
                                     s    z                     c  x
                                     l  p                           n    b

19.        q            20.              f  g    h        21.        f    r t
   s       z     x s          i  o  p                     q      s      g j
      d    m                              l               c
   r         s                            z
      n

22.        e    y        23.              t        24.        r  y    i
      a    g                      f    e                      j          k
      l  k                    u         d                          u
   w o                        y              i                o              w
                          i

25.  q    a        26.        c    x        27.              r  u  f
      w                      f    g              z  h  l
   d    p                   d    t                          l
      h                     l    o
   i    y                                                   b

28.      t    i        29.          t    i        30.  k              v
   f    g                      p  u              t          u
      d                          m n        g          q    g
                                        g              s  s
      k                                                     m
   a   k

31.                c v b        32.          e          i        33.  e w y u
                                              o    u                        s x a n
           w    s    v    c                         m    n
                        n
                                         r    w


34.              o    i        35.          s        f        36.              z    c b
                        j            d        a        l             q                r
        d s                              z  x      n                          n m    k
           x    z    n


37.       r  t                 38.          s d f        39.    s    x    c    n
        c i  l                       j              k             x      a    m p
           v b  n                          n m
                                                     l


40.              u
        i
                    i
        d
                    y
        k
                    r
           j


---

**SET 7**
TARGET LETTERS: $(g \quad m)$

1.       w    d    f        2.                n        3.        e    q
        w    c                        f              g             t      l
                v b                      s    j                   n
                                      a    z    x                s d    z


4.    q                     5.                    r        6.       r v
     a    y    w    s                        d                   e          k
        c    b                            k                         n b
           z                           a e    y    u    i        n    m


7. y e r t y                 8. j    r                9. q w q
     s                          d    l                      k
     d                          d    m                      a e
     x                          e    n                      v    z

10.  u    i    o  
  s    h    g  
    b  
  b  

11.          f    l  
          k  
    r    t  
    x  z    m  

12.          j    k  
      g    f  
  s  w  r    y  

13.  r    v    p    w  
      a  
  z    v    m  

14.        j    l  
    m    s  
      v  
  f    c    n    h  

15.        f    x    q  
  j    e        m  
      v    c  

16.      d  x      n  
      x  
  m  
  f  
  z    b  

17.        t  u  i  
    s    c  
  d  s    l  

18.        w    a  
        m  
      d    a  
  x c s  

19.        e    y  u  
  a    s    c  
  x  
  g  

20.      q    i  z  
  v  b  x  
      d  s  

21.        w  
      f    g  
    s      l  
  a      c  
      w  

22.      w    o  
  q    j  
    d  s  
  z    z  

23.    a    d    f  
  s    x    z  
      m  
  b  

24.    c    b  
  a  s  k  
    c    n    f  

25.      y  u  
  d  g  
  n  h  
  z  x  

26.    a    d  
  n      z.  
    b  
  c  v    m  

27.          a  
  c      d  
      v  
  z  
      n  
    b  
  z  

28.    q  p  
  s    j  
    b  
  x    n    g  

29.    f    h    q  
  h  
      m  
  v  c    s  

30.    s    q  
  s    h  
    m    l  
  x    v

31.    a         z        32.        z      c      33.        a    f    h

        j                     l  k                      

        n                              m  b      s    n    g

        v                     n                            v d

  c    b    l                          v

34.  o    p          35.      u      i     36.  t    b      l    p

      n    c         y t  r

  j    l                   b  n    f            c    d      a

      c    s                                        m

37.  u    i    p      38.    p    t    w    39.        z  n  m

      n                       b              a    s    d

  b        v                   v                        l

      b  c              s  x    z    q             p

40.                  o

                u

            y

          v

        c

      m

    q  a

---

## SET 8
TARGET LETTERS: ( a   x   t )

1.  w             r    2.      y    i      3.    r    y

          e           m                 b    x

      a                      n

4.  c                5.      x      u    6.  w    t

    n                                    g

      m                        g          c

        t              s

7.  v      b        8.  d                9.        c      h

      x                g                    v      x

      c                j

                      k

10.              n
        m

        a
    p

11.    g        t

        b        o

12.    t

                r

                        p s

13.              s f
    x        c

14.          w    r
        v
            c

15.          q
        e        r
        g

16.    c
        f
            h        f

17.    w    p
        b
            a

18.          s    p
        k
                x

19.    z        n    m

        c

20.    n    o

        x

        u

21.          e        t
        s        b

22.      q
    f    n
        a

23.    w    t

        r    e

24.    q        a z

        v

25.    d        b
    b
    f

26.              q
        e    t    h

27.              u
            c
            m
    n

28.    a        p
        m
    j

29.    m    x
            k l

30.              u p
        r    t

31.      l        z

    d    f

32.      n
        r        l
        v

33.    y
        n
            x
            p

34.              u
    m    n
        c

35.        i
        a    d
            j

36.    q              g
            b v

37.           n           38.          t    y        39.  s  v  n

      p                      f

           m                     v                          n

      k

40.          o

        u

      c

    r

---

## SET 9
TARGET LETTERS: (u   c   p)

1.     e     d          2.        w          3.      v    p

                          j

                                    k             l

     z       x               v                    o

4.     a     c       5.        o        6.    q    a

    n                        d

    m                  x                f       u

                              f

7.       n    v     8.        p       9.        i

    s                 l    k             u

    b                      j             m

                                        v

10.    w            11.       i    p    12.        r

    d     i                l                u    t

      n                    y                      m

13.   e     g     h   14.       q     15.   q       y

                     g                   i

      b                   f                p

                      d

16.       d       17.        u     18.      r

     z                    k                    l  w

        n                  b

   w                    f                  s

19.  a      x          20.          w   o          21.          z       b
       c                             p                            f           c
       v                                         m

22.        y    i       23.   g                      24.                       u
      h                        r                              m
    s                          l                           r
                               f                                          j

25.              g       26.          e               27.              g
    f            i             i                                           p
                                      p                         a
         j                                 o              s

28.        y  u         29.          l   p             30.          u   o
    j                          k                                a
         m                      j                                         k

31.          a       p   32.          i   t           33.          i  y  e
    l                          f
         i                     g                              r

34.      t       w       35.   a                      36.   q  w
    d                          c
         b                          d                        f              j
                                    f

37.  e        f          38.          a               39.          r       t
      l                         s                                    c
    d                               l                        s
                                g

40.      q
         g
    j
             m

**SET 10**
TARGET LETTERS: (r   b   a)

```
1.        q       i          2.              u          3.            o   u
          u                                t   e                    b       n
      q           o                          c                    f  g
          b                              g     r

4.                    d      5.            g              6.            i
      q           d                a  v                              g       k
          f       r                   n                           p           u
              n                       z                                       a
                                      c

7.  e      w      e          8.      q       s          9.          y   e  w
          m                                k                      k       d   y
      w                              c           b
          z                              m

10.         f                11.              z  x         12.          r
        t       o                        l                          l    k
      e               y                          r                  v
            p                          n  m                         c
                                                                            o

13.             y            14.             u            15.        t       e
            o                        h  l       o   w                b   v
          u                                                                  p
          x                                                                  w

        i                                    e
      d

16.  a        d              17.           j            18.      q    l
        s                                m                        r    l
        d                                   v                              p
        j                                 l                            o
        x                              y    o
```

19. z   c   x
    s   g   h

20.              o
         r   t   u  p
                 j

21. w      s      n
                o
                    i
             r

22.      q      a
    k  l
           d      z

23.       i  o
    j  h  g
          m
          l

24.       i  u
              s      l
          z          d

25.           x      b
    s             n
         l
                  f

26.      p    o  e
    w  a      s

27. u        q
             j
        z       x
        v

28.              w
          m
    z             v
       b  c

29.    i       t
       k    d
       h
             x

30. a       z
              f      l
                         d  s

31. i      n
    k
    c
        b
        g

32.           o  r
        e    l
          e  s

33.        v   c
                 f
           g
           d   n

34.       q  w
          c
    d  s
       h

35.            w  e
            g
               j
         a

36.                    y
                   n    q
             c
                   z  x

37.           s    c
        f
            j    k
    s

38.         q
                    l
                    l
        l
        l        a

39. z    x  v
       z
         x
         v

40. l    t
    e    w
         r

         m

## SET 11
TARGET LETTERS: ( i    o    u )

1.        w        s    c        2.                p        3.                        i

    e                            z                        f  g
  a                                    j                        m        n
        o                            d    s                            d
                                r


4.   t    y            5.                    w    6.                    w
  g    h                            e        h  j
  s    a                        d            f  d
                    g                    o
                u
                f


7.        q        t    8.        s    a    9.        w    r        y
    u                    c    c
  f        v    z            n                            t
                    a                    d        u


10.    d        g    z    11.  e    n    m    12.                q

                        r                    l    p
  f                        k            n  b        x
        v    b            i


13.  w                14.            r    e    15.            i    p
    c                    f  d                    m
        o                            m                            l
        n                        n        l            k        m
            s


16.        g  h        17.            e    k    18.            y  t  w
    v    b                m  b  s    a                    m
  s            u                            d
                        a

19.       q
         v
 x
    s  x  z

20.       h  b
      m
      n
        b  c

21.   d
    s
    a
    u
    d
    n

22.       p   l
    n  b
 k
 c

23.  y  t
  k  j
  n  b

24.      b   c
        v
    z    x
        d

25. y h g
   m
   i
   b

26.   h   d
      l
    o      c
        p

27.   a        q
         n  b
  c        x

28.    g   f
 m        l
   b  x

29.     p   r
   k  d
     v   t

30.      d  s  z
       f
     d
    l

31.    q
     i
      e   y
 w     t

32.       y   r
        h
  x   c   n

33.     a   v
     o   m
  c    n

34.    v  k
 b g
   j
   t

35.      h   t
     u   s
   p   b

36. a   c
  f
      j
      v
      i

37.     e
     p
 r  t
    n  m

38. y  w q   u
      m
      v

39. t   r  q
   g
    d      o

40.    a  q
    m
  i
 d  e

**SET 12**
TARGET LETTERS: (t   g   i   f)

1.     s     a
         h
         c
   z   s

2.       i   h
     p  o
     b       m

3.                 b  d
               l  w g
           n

4.   a               h
             i
       d       j
         l

5.               e   w
     s             a
             m v

6.   t     y
           l
           k     r
           w

7.           i
       e       o
     u
   z             z

8.       o   x
     o u   y
           b

9.           y
           j     k
           f     m
           v

10.               d
     s  a  e
           f
         c

11.                 o
     v n x p r

12.         y
     h d     o
         k
         e

13.           v
     b         t
       c       p
         x

14.   i     d
     l p u w

15.   s  a
     o  p
     f  a

16.         n
     m
   c
       z
         a
           q

17.               u
     m n
             p
             k
             j

18.   y   r
         s
         o
         w
         y

19.       u
     c
         g
   r     a   s

20.           h
     k   l
         y e w

21.         w     t
         r  e
         a           o
         k

22.           h
   d   h  k
        o  p
    j

23.     y       j
          h      p
           o
   d

24.      n    m
     v   b
    c   d

25.        m  e
    n
  v   c  x  d

26.        i
     m      u  r
      s       v

27.     y  m
   f      k
   n  m

28.     u
  j  g  h
    x  z

29.      p  u  y
   l  x  e

30.    u
    s     d
  x   z
  g

31.     p
  k    h
   n    n
    l

32.  i    e
   l   s
      m  n

33.     g  d
  b  v
  m
    l

34.    j
  m  b  i
    z
  c

35.    u   y
  k  s  a
     l

36.    p
  h
    v
  j
    c
  z

37.    j  e
   m  b
   d
  c

38.    k  x
   l    d
    m    f

39.     v  l
  a  z
    b  n
       n  g

40.    u
  j    l
   m   b
   n

## ANSWERS TO COMPLEX VISUAL SEARCH

### SET 1

| | | | | | |
|---|---|---|---|---|---|
| 1. N | 2. Y | 3. Y | 4. Y | 5. Y | 6. N |
| 7. Y | 8. Y | 9. N | 10. N | 11. N | 12. N |
| 13. N | 14. Y | 15. N | 16. N | 17. N | 18. N |
| 19. Y | 20. N | 21. Y | 22. Y | 23. N | 24. Y |
| 25. N | 26. N | 27. N | 28. Y | 29. N | 30. Y |
| 31. Y | 32. Y | 33. Y | 34. Y | 35. Y | 36. N |
| 37. Y | 38. Y | 39. Y | 40. N | | |

### SET 2

| | | | | | |
|---|---|---|---|---|---|
| 1. N | 2. Y | 3. Y | 4. N | 5. Y | 6. N |
| 7. N | 8. N | 9. N | 10. N | 11. N | 12. Y |
| 13. N | 14. Y | 15. Y | 16. Y | 17. Y | 18. Y |
| 19. Y | 20. N | 21. N | 22. N | 23. Y | 24. Y |
| 25. Y | 26. Y | 27. Y | 28. Y | 29. N | 30. N |
| 31. N | 32. Y | 33. N | 34. Y | 35. Y | 36. N |
| 37. N | 38. N | 39. N | 40. Y | | |

### SET 3

| | | | | | |
|---|---|---|---|---|---|
| 1. Y | 2. Y | 3. Y | 4. N | 5. Y | 6. N |
| 7. Y | 8. Y | 9. Y | 10. Y | 11. N | 12. Y |
| 13. Y | 14. Y | 15. N | 16. N | 17. Y | 18. N |
| 19. N | 20. Y | 21. N | 22. N | 23. N | 24. Y |
| 25. Y | 26. N | 27. N | 28. N | 29. N | 30. Y |
| 31. N | 32. Y | 33. N | 34. N | 35. Y | 36. N |
| 37. N | 38. Y | 39. N | 40. N | | |

### SET 4

| | | | | | |
|---|---|---|---|---|---|
| 1. Y | 2. N | 3. Y | 4. N | 5. Y | 6. N |
| 7. N | 8. N | 9. Y | 10. Y | 11. Y | 12. N |
| 13. N | 14. Y | 15. N | 16. Y | 17. Y | 18. N |
| 19. Y | 20. Y | 21. N | 22. Y | 23. Y | 24. N |
| 25. Y | 26. N | 27. Y | 28. Y | 29. Y | 30. Y |
| 31. Y | 32. N | 33. Y | 34. N | 35. Y | 36. N |
| 37. N | 38. N | 39. N | 40. N | | |

### SET 5

| | | | | | |
|---|---|---|---|---|---|
| 1. N | 2. Y | 3. Y | 4. Y | 5. Y | 6. N |
| 7. Y | 8. Y | 9. N | 10. Y | 11. N | 12. Y |
| 13. N | 14. N | 15. Y | 16. Y | 17. Y | 18. Y |
| 19. N | 20. Y | 21. N | 22. Y | 23. Y | 24. N |
| 25. Y | 26. N | 27. N | 28. Y | 29. N | 30. N |
| 31. Y | 32. Y | 33. Y | 34. Y | 35. N | 36. N |
| 37. Y | 38. N | 39. Y | 40. N | | |

## SET 6

| | | | | | | | | | | | |
|---|---|---|---|---|---|---|---|---|---|---|---|
| 1. | Y | 2. | N | 3. | Y | 4. | Y | 5. | Y | 6. | N |
| 7. | N | 8. | Y | 9. | Y | 10. | Y | 11. | Y | 12. | N |
| 13. | N | 14. | Y | 15. | N | 16. | N | 17. | N | 18. | Y |
| 19. | Y | 20. | Y | 21. | N | 22. | N | 23. | N | 24. | N |
| 25. | N | 26. | Y | 27. | N | 28. | N | 29. | Y | 30. | Y |
| 31. | N | 32. | N | 33. | N | 34. | Y | 35. | Y | 36. | N |
| 37. | Y | 38. | N | 39. | Y | 40. | Y | | | | |

## SET 7

| | | | | | | | | | | | |
|---|---|---|---|---|---|---|---|---|---|---|---|
| 1. | N | 2. | Y | 3. | N | 4. | N | 5. | N | 6. | Y |
| 7. | N | 8. | Y | 9. | N | 10. | Y | 11. | Y | 12. | Y |
| 13. | Y | 14. | Y | 15. | Y | 16. | Y | 17. | N | 18. | Y |
| 19. | Y | 20. | N | 21. | Y | 22. | N | 23. | Y | 24. | N |
| 25. | Y | 26. | Y | 27. | N | 28. | Y | 29. | Y | 30. | Y |
| 31. | N | 32. | Y | 33. | Y | 34. | N | 35. | N | 36. | Y |
| 37. | N | 38. | N | 39. | Y | 40. | Y | | | | |

## SET 8

| | | | | | | | | | | | |
|---|---|---|---|---|---|---|---|---|---|---|---|
| 1. | Y | 2. | N | 3. | Y | 4. | Y | 5. | Y | 6. | Y |
| 7. | Y | 8. | N | 9. | Y | 10. | Y | 11. | Y | 12. | Y |
| 13. | Y | 14. | N | 15. | N | 16. | N | 17. | Y | 18. | Y |
| 19. | N | 20. | Y | 21. | Y | 22. | Y | 23. | Y | 24. | Y |
| 25. | N | 26. | Y | 27. | N | 28. | Y | 29. | Y | 30. | Y |
| 31. | N | 32. | N | 33. | Y | 34. | N | 35. | Y | 36. | N |
| 37. | N | 38. | Y | 39. | N | 40. | N | | | | |

## SET 9

| | | | | | | | | | | | |
|---|---|---|---|---|---|---|---|---|---|---|---|
| 1. | N | 2. | N | 3. | Y | 4. | Y | 5. | N | 6. | Y |
| 7. | N | 8. | Y | 9. | Y | 10. | N | 11. | Y | 12. | Y |
| 13. | N | 14. | N | 15. | Y | 16. | N | 17. | Y | 18. | N |
| 19. | Y | 20. | Y | 21. | Y | 22. | N | 23. | N | 24. | Y |
| 25. | N | 26. | Y | 27. | Y | 28. | Y | 29. | Y | 30. | Y |
| 31. | Y | 32. | N | 33. | N | 34. | N | 35. | Y | 36. | N |
| 37. | N | 38. | N | 39. | Y | 40. | N | | | | |

## SET 10

| | | | | | | | | | | | |
|---|---|---|---|---|---|---|---|---|---|---|---|
| 1. | Y | 2. | Y | 3. | Y | 4. | Y | 5. | Y | 6. | Y |
| 7. | N | 8. | Y | 9. | N | 10. | N | 11. | Y | 12. | Y |
| 13. | N | 14. | N | 15. | Y | 16. | Y | 17. | N | 18. | Y |
| 19. | N | 20. | Y | 21. | Y | 22. | Y | 23. | N | 24. | N |
| 25. | Y | 26. | Y | 27. | N | 28. | Y | 29. | N | 30. | Y |
| 31. | Y | 32. | Y | 33. | N | 34. | N | 35. | Y | 36. | N |
| 37. | N | 38. | Y | 39. | N | 40. | Y | | | | |

## SET 11

| | | | | | |
|---|---|---|---|---|---|
| 1. Y | 2. N | 3. Y | 4. N | 5. Y | 6. Y |
| 7. Y | 8. N | 9. Y | 10. N | 11. Y | 12. N |
| 13. Y | 14. N | 15. Y | 16. Y | 17. N | 18. N |
| 19. N | 20. N | 21. Y | 22. N | 23. N | 24. N |
| 25. Y | 26. Y | 27. N | 28. N | 29. N | 30. N |
| 31. Y | 32. N | 33. Y | 34. N | 35. Y | 36. Y |
| 37. N | 38. Y | 39. Y | 40. Y | | |

## SET 12

| | | | | | |
|---|---|---|---|---|---|
| 1. N | 2. Y | 3. Y | 4. Y | 5. N | 6. Y |
| 7. Y | 8. N | 9. Y | 10. Y | 11. N | 12. N |
| 13. Y | 14. Y | 15. Y | 16. N | 17. N | 18. N |
| 19. Y | 20. N | 21. Y | 22. N | 23. N | 24. N |
| 25. N | 26. Y | 27. Y | 28. Y | 29. N | 30. Y |
| 31. N | 32. Y | 33. Y | 34. Y | 35. N | 36. N |
| 37. N | 38. Y | 39. Y | 40. N | | |

# 8

# Practical
# Intelligence

By her fourth year in college, Mary C. had managed to antagonize
practically all of the faculty in the philosophy department, which
was the department of her major subject. Her course papers were certainly
acceptable, and there was nothing wrong with her senior thesis, but it was
clear that no one liked to have her around. When she applied to the graduate
program, members of the department were dismayed. They finally decided
that she did not have the right "values" for a career as a philosopher. No one
overtly admitted the true reason for the negative decision on her application
to graduate school: No one liked Mary.

Tom J. went to his literature class after a long night spent doing the reading
for the class. The topic of discussion was Dostoevsky's *Crime and Punishment*.
The class discussion started with an analysis of the protagonist, Raskolnikov.
John, a classmate, repeatedly made remarks that obviously impressed the
professor. Tom was frustrated: He knew not only that John had not read the
book, but also that John had spent the previous night at a party. John always
seemed to have a way of saying the things people wanted to hear, whether or
not those things had any substance.

Dr. W. was tired after a long day seeing patients, and upon arriving at her
home, turned on the television. As soon as the screen lit up, a look of conster-
nation and then exasperation crossed her face: There, on the screen, was Dr.
J., being interviewed on yet another talk show. Dr. W. and her professional
colleagues were convinced that Dr. J.'s diet plan was useless in the long run
for taking off weight, and also that it had harmful side effects on the health of
its users. Despite this fact, Dr. J. seemed repeatedly to manage to obtain
favorable media publicity both for his diet and for himself.

The department chairman thumbed through the course evaluations of his teaching staff. The pattern of ratings depressed him. As usual, Mr. A. had received highly favorable ratings from the students in his classes. The chairman had attended a number of Mr. A.'s lectures: They were extremely entertaining, but, in the chairman's opinion, devoid of substance. Mrs. N.'s lectures, on the other hand, were rather dry, but very carefully organized and full of both substance and informed comment on the substance. Mrs. N., however, had once again received only mediocre ratings for her teaching. Despite her solidity as a teacher, she simply failed to kindle the enthusiasm of the students, and it showed in her ratings.

## What Is Practical Intelligence?

Each of these anecdotes illustrates a pervasive but little-understood aspect of our daily lives: intelligence as it operates in real-world contexts, or *practical intelligence*. In school, there is tremendous interest in and concentration on the teaching of academic knowledge and skills: Students are taught academic knowledge; they are tested on it; they are graded on it; their admission to further educational programs depends on it; and ultimately, their salability in the marketplace for jobs will be largely determined by it, at least for many higher-level jobs. Despite the overwhelming emphasis we place on academic knowledge and skills, we all know the inestimable importance of practical knowledge and skills in our daily lives, even in academic settings. However useful academic intelligence may be, most of us know people whose professional or personal life has been drastically affected, for better or for worse, by their practical intelligence. The anecdotes above are just a few examples of how high or low practical intelligence can affect real-world outcomes.

Although there is no universally accepted definition, practical intelligence can be defined as intelligence that operates on real-world contexts through efforts to achieve adaptation to, shaping of, and selection of environments. In adaptation, people seek to accommodate themselves to the environment so as to obtain an optimal fit between the self and the environment. For example, one seeks to fit oneself to the requirements of a job. In shaping, people seek to accommodate the environment to themselves, also to obtain an optimal fit between the self and the environment. For example, one seeks to modify the requirements of a job to suit oneself. In selection, people seek a new environment to which they would be a better fit, usually after having decided that their present environment is unsuitable and probably cannot be changed so as to be suitable. For example, one decides one is best off finding a new job. In everyday life, we often call practical intelligence "common sense," although what constitutes common sense may vary from one society or culture to another, and may vary even within societies and cultures.

## Developing Your Practical Intelligence

The above discussion should indicate that there are many forms of practical intelligence. Indeed, an entire book could be devoted to exercises designed to test or improve a person's functioning in the various domains that constitute the "practical." The exercises in this chapter represent only a small portion of the possible skills that might be assessed and developed. For the most part, these exercises are taken from my own investigations of practical intelligence.

### Adaptive Behavior Checklist

Sternberg, Conway, Ketron, and Bernstein (1981) conducted a survey in which they asked people to list behaviors that they believed to be distinctively characteristic of either particularly intelligent persons or of particularly unintelligent ones. Analysis of these behaviors revealed that they fell into three general classes: practical problem-solving skills, verbal skills, and social competence. They then refined the checklist of behaviors so that it could be used as an instrument for self-evaluation. A person can rate the extent to which each of a set of behaviors characterizes himself or herself, and then compare this self-characterization to the characterization people have given for a highly intelligent person. Berg and Sternberg (1984) have conducted a similar survey for adults of systematically varying ages from 30 to 70 years old, and Sternberg and Rodriguez-Lansberg (1984) have conducted a similar study in a Venezuelan population.

Below you will find a listing of some of the behaviors that have emerged from this research: Rate on a 1 (low) to 9 (high) scale the extent to which each of these behaviors characterizes your typical performance. In general, higher ratings are associated with better performance.

**BEHAVIORAL CHECKLIST**

I. Practical problem-solving ability

Reasons logically and well

Identifies connections among ideas

Sees all aspects of a problem

Keeps an open mind

Responds thoughtfully to others' ideas

Sizes up situations well

Gets to the heart of problems

Interprets information accurately

Makes good decisions

Goes to original sources for basic information

Poses problems in an optimal way

Is a good source of ideas

Perceives implied assumptions and conclusions

Listens to all sides of an argument

Deals with problems resourcefully

II. Verbal ability

Speaks clearly and articulately

Is verbally fluent

Converses well

Is knowledgeable about a particular area of subject matter

Studies hard

Reads with high comprehension

Reads widely

Writes without difficulty

Sets aside time for reading

Displays good vocabulary

III.  Social competence

Accepts others for what they are

Admits mistakes

Displays interest in the world at large

Is on time for appointments

Has social conscience

Thinks before speaking and doing

Displays curiosity

Does not make snap judgments

Makes fair judgments

Assesses well the relevance of information to a problem at hand

Is sensitive to other people's needs and desires

Is frank and honest with self and others

Displays interest in the immediate environment

### *Decoding Nonverbal Cues*

One important aspect of your everyday life is the ability to decode the nonverbal messages that people send to you. Such messages, transmitted during the course of a conversation, may in some cases correspond to what a person is saying, but in other cases, they may not. Often, the nonverbal messages are a better indication of a person's true feelings than the verbal messages that they accompany. It is therefore quite important to be able to decode such messages.

On the following pages, you will find 30 pictures of pairs of individuals. The first 20 pairs are of heterosexual couples. Ten of the couples are genuinely involved in romantic relationships; the other 10 are not. Your task is to guess which couples are involved in relationships, and which are not. In the second set of pictures, you will see sets of two individuals, one of whom is the other's supervisor. Your task is to guess who is the supervisor of the other individual.

You may want to do these tasks without first being told what kinds of nonverbal cues are indicative of the true situation. If so, you should proceed right now to do the problems. If you would rather first have some guidance as to what cues are diagnostic of the relations between each of the pairs, you should now skip to page 315 and read on. Answers appear after the pictures.

## FIGURE 8-1

## Couples

## FIGURE 8-1 continued

**FIGURE 8-1 continued**

# FIGURE 8-1 continued

## FIGURE 8-1 continued

## FIGURE 8-1 continued

## FIGURE 8-1 continued

19

20

## FIGURE 8-2

### Supervisor/Supervisee

## FIGURE 8-2 continued

**FIGURE 8-2 continued**

**FIGURE 8-2 continued**

*ANSWERS: COUPLES (FIGURE 8-1)*

**R = Real couple; F = Fake couple**

| | | | | | | | | |
|---|---|---|---|---|---|---|---|---|
| 1. | F | 5. | R | 9. | R | 13. | F | 17. | R |
| 2. | R | 6. | R | 10. | R | 14. | F | 18. | F |
| 3. | F | 7. | F | 11. | R | 15. | F | 19. | F |
| 4. | F | 8. | R | 12. | F | 16. | R | 20. | R |

---

**ANSWERS: SUPERVISOR/SUPERVISEE (FIGURE 8-2)**

**L = Supervisor on the left; R = Supervisor on the right**

| 1. | L | 3. | R | 5. | R | 7. | R | 9. | R |
|----|---|----|---|----|---|----|---|----|---|
| 2. | L | 4. | R | 6. | R | 8. | L | 10. | L |

---

Consider first the heterosexual couples task. What kinds of things should you look for in deciding whether each pair of individuals is a genuine or a fake couple? Sternberg and Smith found several nonverbal clues to be diagnostic. The things to look for are these:

1. *Relaxation.* The individuals constituting the genuine couples look, on the average, more relaxed with each other.

2. *Angle of bodies.* Individuals constituting genuine couples tend to lean toward each other more than do individuals who constitute fake couples.

3. *Positioning of arms and legs.* Individuals in genuine couples tend to position their arms and legs more naturally than do individuals who are just posing.

4. *Tenseness of the hands.* Individuals in fake couples tend to have hands showing tenseness and discomfort, whereas individuals in real couples do not show these symptoms.

5. *Match in socioeconomic class.* Individuals in genuine couples appear to be a better match in socioeconomic class than do individuals in fake couples. One generally guesses socioeconomic class from clothes and physical appearance.

6. *Distance between bodies.* The individuals in fake couples are generally at a greater physical distance from each other than are the individuals in real couples.

7. *Amount of physical contact.* Individuals in real couples generally show more physical contact with each other than do individuals in fake couples.

8. *General similarity.* Individuals in real couples generally tend to be more similar in appearance, including such factors as dress, age, race, and ethnic group.

In the supervisors task, the variables that predict which individual is the supervisor (and which the supervisee) are these:

1. *Direction of eye gaze.* The supervisor tends more to gaze directly at the supervisee, whereas the supervisee tends more to look away.

2. *Formality of dress.* The supervisor tends to be more formally dressed.

3. *Age.* The supervisor tends to be the older of the two individuals.

4. *Tenseness of hands.* The supervisor tends to have less tense hands than does the supervisee.

5. *Socioeconomic class.* The supervisor tends to be the individual who appears to be of the higher socioeconomic class.

## Everyday Situations

Below are 20 everyday situations. After each situation, you are presented with three options that represent alternative ways of handling the situation. One of these options represents a solution of adaptation—you try to accommodate yourself to the environment. A second option represents a solution of shaping—you attempt to accommodate the environment to yourself. The third option represents a solution of selection—you decide to leave that environment altogether. You should consider the available information, and decide which of these kinds of solutions is best. Questions to ask yourself include:

1. Given the person you are, could you behave in ways that are adaptive to the situation as it is presented, or could you change yourself so as to make your behavioral pattern more adaptive?
2. If not, could the environment be shaped so as to conform better to the behaviorial repertoire you have available? In other words, can you see ways of changing the situation so as to make it more suitable for yourself?
3. If you do not see ways of adapting yourself or of shaping the situation, might it be better to find a new environment altogether? If so, what kinds of alternative environments might be available to you?

Note that in problems such as these, there is no one right or wrong answer. To the contrary, the "right" answer will depend upon the individual, the situation, and the interaction between the two. Your goal, therefore, ought to be to find the course of action that is right for you. Thinking about the options of adaptation, selection, and shaping, about the constraints that exist in your own personality and abilities, and about the way your personality and abilities interact with the situation will help you to make a more practically intelligent decision in situations such as those presented here. A key to the answers appears after the problems.

### REAL-WORLD PROBLEMS

1. **The nation of Dragonia is characterized by its authoritarian structure, elitist culture, brutal repression of dissent, and general intolerance. Life in this undeveloped third-world nation is predictable, monotonous, and gray. The small class of elites holds the bureaucratic and military positions while an army of second-class citizens wrest a living working in urban factories and on collectivized farms.**

**You are a young person of high birth who has just completed your education at a prestigious institution of higher learning in Europe. Upon returning to Dragonia, do you:**
   a) **accept the calling of your birth, resolving to perform your duties to the best of your ability?**
   b) **renounce the culture of elitism and seek to build a more just order?**
   c) **decide you cannot live amid such hypocrisy and moral depravity, and move to a large cultural metropolis elsewhere, where you can live in relative freedom and obscurity?**

2.  Your 1969 Plymouth station wagon is about to give up the ghost. To avoid the inevitable breakdown, you decide to purchase a new car, a Ford Thunderbird, no less. The dealership in your town is well stocked with the new model, and it has a good reputation. After describing to the salesman just what you have in mind, you find out that the price is much higher than you expected. Do you:

    a)  decide to haggle and bargain for the absolute lowest price possible?

    b)  resign yourself to the purchase of a different type of auto?

    c)  buy the car of your dreams, knowing that you will have to acquire a second job to supplement your income?

3.  Television reception in your area is hampered by a nearby mountain range. The reruns of *Bonanza*, your favorite show, are hardly worth watching, given all the double images and static interference. Given that you value your leisure time highly, do you:

    a)  continue watching your favorite show in its crippled form?

    b)  buy a deep-dish antenna to improve the reception?

    c)  take up bridge?

4.  As you are putting on your brand-new suit from Brooks Brothers, you notice that there is a large stain on the inside lining of the jacket. Since you are proud of your appearance, do you:

    a)  wear another suit and take the spotted one to the cleaners?

    b)  realize that the stain cannot be seen with the jacket on, and therefore, decide the stain is harmless?

    c)  return the suit to Brooks Brothers and select a new one?

5.  Your 16-year-old son arrives home four hours after curfew (that is, at 4:00 A.M.) in an inebriated state. As a concerned parent, do you:

    a)  grab him as soon as he wakes up the next day in order to discuss the meaning of responsibility, impressing on him the importance of punctuality and moderation?

    b)  take your son out of public school, and send him to private school where he will find a more mature peer group than his old friends?

    c)  say to yourself that boys will be boys, and a 16-year-old can take care of himself?

6.  All semester long your class in cognitive psychology has been your arch-nemesis. Two weeks before the final, you contract a severe case of the flu. The illness robs you of a week of valuable study time, forcing you to cram for several exams in one week. Faced with the prospect of ruining your 4.0 GPA, do you:

    a)  pull off a superhuman series of all-nighters?

    b)  ask the professor to reschedule your exam?

    c)  drop some courses as the pressure is just too great?

7. Aunt Gertrude gives you a shirt for Christmas that is not quite your style. Poor Aunt Gertrude is always giving the most hideous gifts, and this one is no exception: an ugly, red plaid, 100 percent polyester, Nehru-collared nightmare. In this delicate situation, do you:

    a) exchange the shirt for a nice Oxford cloth button-down?

    b) take Aunt Gertrude aside to discuss in private the nature of the gifts that in the future you would like to receive?

    c) hang the shirt in the back of the closet and resolve to wear it at the next Halloween party you attend?

8. Your best friend, Jill, always cheats when the two of you play tennis. She reflexively calls any ball out that falls even remotely near a line. In the face of this inexplicable ridiculousness, do you:

    a) refuse to play tennis with her? After all, you have plenty of other tennis partners who do not cheat.

    b) decide that tennis is only a game to be enjoyed, and knowing in your heart that you are a better player, elect to tolerate her foolishness?

    c) take Jill aside, tell her with all the tact you can muster that this type of behavior is abominable, and make her promise to play squarely?

9. You are having dinner at an expensive restaurant. After a marvelous series of the most exquisite preliminary courses, the chateaubriand for two arrives quite overdone. Do you and your partner:

    a) eat the dish, although it is obviously way below par?

    b) demand that the waiter take it back?

    c) leave the dish essentially untouched, and vow never to return to the establishment?

10. Your assigned seat on Flight 114 from New York to Paris is next to a very addicted smoker. The area around your seat is shrouded in a cloud of blue smoke, and your allergies are stifling you. To remedy the situation, do you:

    a) go to the bathroom every time he lights up?

    b) ask him not to smoke?

    c) call for the stewardess and demand a new seat?

11. The cafeteria at your place of work serves virtually inedible food. Everyone in the company agrees that the food is horrible, but nobody can agree on a solution. Do you:

    a) buy their fruit and yogurt, which are rather difficult to ruin?

    b) petition for a new, improved food service?

    c) eat at the diner down the street?

12.  You are a construction worker on a large project in the city. Your foreman is a cantankerous, ill-mannered, arbitrary martinet. No one likes him, but what is a laborer to do? Do you:
  a)  look for another place to work?
  b)  do your best to tolerate the unfortunate aspects of the job?
  c)  take the foreman out for a beer (or three), and when he loosens up, explain the nature of your grievance?

13.  The beautiful house you just bought needs a fresh coat of paint. Unfortunately, all the companies that submit bids are very high-priced. In light of the fact that the house really needs painting, do you:
  a)  call the companies back, and attempt to bargain down the price?
  b)  accept the fact that the job is going to be expensive, bite the bullet, and hire the most reputable of the companies?
  c)  have your two 15-year-old sons paint the house? The job will be second-rate, but nevertheless adequate.

14.  Imagine you are a high school math teacher. One morning, you discover that the eraser for the blackboard is missing. In light of this calamity, do you:
  a)  send one of the students to hunt for another one?
  b)  wipe the board with your hand?
  c)  decide to use the opaque projector instead?

15.  You are the president of a large, democratic country. Suddenly, your pacific nation is rocked by a scandal involving one of your most trusted ministers. Do you:
  a)  understand that an occasional impropriety is bound to occur, and resolve to support your beleaguered minister to the fullest?
  b)  call the man in question to your office, chastise him severely, warn him that any further breach of etiquette will result in his dismissal, and inform him that you plan to rebuke him publicly for his unfortunate activities?
  c)  issue an immediate dismissal, as your administration must not be associated with even the slightest degree of corruption?

16.  Your son gets his birthday wish: a cute cocker spaniel puppy. Eight months later, the dog is untrained, unruly, and a general nuisance. Do you:
  a)  tell your son he had better do something about the dog, and fast?
  b)  proceed to train the dog yourself?
  c)  sell the dog?

17.  You are considering flying to Florida for a winter vacation. Unfortunately, the plane fare is more than you expected. Do you:
  a)  shop around for the lowest fare?
  b)  decide to drive?
  c)  spend the extra money? After all, you are going on vacation.

18. With three kids and New York City prices, you are having trouble making ends meet in your current job. Do you:
   a) make do as well as you can?
   b) ask the boss for a raise?
   c) look for a new position?

19. You are currently in the midst of a midlife crisis. Your children disappoint you, your spouse is a bore, and your job is depressing. In order to improve the quality of your life, do you:
   a) seek psychiatric counseling?
   b) explain to your family what you are going through, and tell them they must do their share to remedy the situation?
   c) leave home for a younger woman or man?

20. Since there is virtually no free parking near your place of work, you are gradually building a collection of parking tickets. In view of this situation, do you:
   a) let the tickets accumulate—you will pay them at some point?
   b) start parking in one of the overpriced garages?
   c) go to court, and try to convince the judge that you should not have to pay the fines?

---

### ANSWERS TO REAL-WORLD PROBLEMS

| | | |
|---|---|---|
| 1. a) adaptation<br>   b) shaping<br>   c) selection | 8. a) selection<br>   b) adaptation<br>   c) shaping | 15. a) adaptation<br>   b) shaping<br>   c) selection |
| 2. a) shaping<br>   b) selection<br>   c) adaptation | 9. a) adaptation<br>   b) shaping<br>   c) selection | 16. a) shaping<br>   b) adaptation<br>   c) selection |
| 3. a) adaptation<br>   b) shaping<br>   c) selection | 10. a) adaptation<br>   b) shaping<br>   c) selection | 17. a) shaping<br>   b) selection<br>   c) adaptation |
| 4. a) shaping<br>   b) adaptation<br>   c) selection | 11. a) adaptation<br>   b) shaping<br>   c) selection | 18. a) adaptation<br>   b) shaping<br>   c) selection |
| 5. a) shaping<br>   b) selection<br>   c) adaptation | 12. a) selection<br>   b) adaptation<br>   c) shaping | 19. a) adaptation<br>   b) shaping<br>   c) selection |
| 6. a) adaptation<br>   b) shaping<br>   c) selection | 13. a) shaping<br>   b) adaptation<br>   c) selection | 20. a) adaptation<br>   b) selection<br>   c) shaping |
| 7. a) selection<br>   b) shaping<br>   c) adaptation | 14. a) shaping<br>   b) adaptation<br>   c) selection | |

---

### Tacit Knowledge

*Tacit knowledge* is knowledge we pick up by osmosis from our experience. It is usually not explicitly taught. Although the tacit knowledge needed for success varies from one occupation or life course to another, practically intelligent people tend to be those who are good at putting themselves in others' shoes. In other words, they tend to know how to use the knowledge they have to make right decisions, and to be able to apply this knowledge to a broad range of types of tasks. The tacit-knowledge tests below (from Wagner & Sternberg, 1985) require you to play two roles—business executive in the first set of questions and professor in a university psychology department in the second set. Draw upon your full knowledge of the world in order to answer these questions. The questions assess quite general abilities—the ability to manage yourself, to manage others, and to manage tasks. After you have answered the questions, the answer key will tell you the kind of responses that successful people in these fields give.

**QUESTIONNAIRE FOR BUSINESS MANAGEMENT**    This task asks you about your views on matters pertaining to the work of a manager. The questions ask you to rate the importance you would assign to various items in making work-related decisions and judgments. Use a 1 to 7 rating scale, with 1 signifying "not important," 4 signifying "moderately important," and 7 signifying "extremely important."

| 1 | 2 | 3 | 4 | 5 | 6 | 7 |
|---|---|---|---|---|---|---|
| not important | | | moderately important | | | extremely important |

Try to use the entire scale when responding, although not necessarily for each question. For example, you may decide that none of the items listed for a particular question are important, or that they all are. There are, of course, no "correct" answers. You are encouraged to scan briefly the items of a given question before responding to get some idea of the range of importance for the items. Remember, you are being asked to rate the importance you *personally* would assign each item in making the judgment or decision mentioned in the question stem.

   1.  **It is your second year as a mid-level manager in a company in the communications industry. You head a department of about 30 people. The evaluation of your first year on the job has been generally favorable. Performance ratings for your department are at least as good as they were before you took over, and perhaps even a little better. You have two assistants. One is quite capable, but the other just seems to go through the motions without being of much real help.**
   **You believe that, although you are well-liked, there is little that would distinguish you in the eyes of your superiors from the nine other managers at a comparable level in the company.**
   **Your goal is rapid promotion to the top of the company. The following is a list of things you are considering doing in the next two months. You obviously cannot do them all. Rate the importance of each as a means of reaching your goal.**

_____ a.   Participate in a series of panel discussions to be shown on the local public television station.

_____ b.   Find ways to make sure your superiors are aware of your important accomplishments.

_____ c.   As a means of being noticed, propose a solution to a problem outside the scope of your immediate department that you would be willing to take charge of.

_____ d.   When making decisions, give a great deal of weight to the way your superior likes things to be done.

_____ e.   Accept a friend's invitation to join the exclusive country club that many higher-level executives belong to.

2.  Your company has sent you to a university to recruit and interview potential trainees for management positions. You have been considering characteristics of students that are important to later success in business. Rate the importance of the following student characteristics by the extent to which they lead to later success in business:

_____ a.   ability to set priorities according to the importance of the task

_____ b.   motivation

_____ c.   ability to follow through and complete tasks

_____ d.   ability to promote one's ideas; to convince others of the worth of one's work

_____ e.   the need to win at everything no matter what the cost

3.  A number of factors enter into the establishment of a good reputation in a company as a manager. Consider the following factors and rate their importance:

_____ a.   critical thinking ability

_____ b.   speaking ability

_____ c.   extent of college education and the prestige of the school attended

_____ d.   no hesitancy to take extraordinarily risky courses of action

_____ e.   a keen sense of what superiors can be sold on

4.  Rate the following strategies of working according to how important you believe them to be for doing well at the day-to-day work of a business manager:

_____ a.   Think in terms of tasks accomplished rather than hours spent working.

_____ b.   Be in charge of all phases of every task or project you are involved with.

_____ c.   Use a daily list of goals arranged according to your priorities.

_____ d.  Carefully consider the optimal strategy before beginning a task.

_____ e.  Reward yourself upon completion of important tasks.

5.  You are looking for several new projects to tackle. You have a list of possible projects and desire to pick the best two or three. Rate the importance of the following considerations when selecting projects:

_____ a.  Doing the project should prove to be fun.

_____ b.  The project should attract the attention of the local media.

_____ c.  The project is of special importance to me personally.

_____ d.  The risk of making a mistake is virtually nonexistent.

_____ e.  The project will require working directly with several senior executives.

**QUESTIONNAIRE FOR ACADEMIC PSYCHOLOGY**   This questionnaire asks you about your views on matters pertaining to the work of an academic psychologist. The directions are identical to those in the preceding questionnaire.

1.  It is your second year as an assistant professor in a prestigious psychology department. This past year you published two unrelated empirical articles in established journals. You don't, however, believe there is yet a research area that can be identified as your own. You believe yourself to be about as productive as others. The feedback about your first year of teaching has been generally good. You have as yet to serve on a university committee. There is one graduate student who has chosen to work with you. You have no external source of funding, nor have you applied for funding.

Your goals are to become one of the top people in your field and to get tenure in your department. The following is a list of things you are considering doing in the next two months. You obviously cannot do them all. Rate the importance of each as a means of reaching your goals.

_____ a.  Improve the quality of your teaching.

_____ b.  Write a grant proposal.

_____ c.  Begin long-term research that may lead to a major theoretical article.

_____ d.  Serve on a committee studying university–community relations.

_____ e.  Participate in a series of panel discussions to be shown on the local public television station.

_____ f.  Write a paper for presentation to an upcoming American Psychological Association convention.

_____ g.  Adjust your work habits to increase your productivity.

_____ h.  Write an integrative literature review chapter for a soon to be published book (due in six weeks).

_____ i.   Accept an invitation to be on an American Psychological Association task force on ethics in psychological experiments.

_____ j.   Ask for comments from senior members of the department on future papers.

_____ k.   Write a paper for possible publication in a general circulation magazine.

_____ l.   Become more involved in local public-service organizations.

_____ m.   Volunteer to be chairperson of the undergraduate curriculum committee.

2.  You have been asked to serve on an admissions committee that will select students to be admitted to your psychology department. You have been thinking about what leads to later success in the field of psychology. Rate the importance of the following graduate student characteristics to later success in the field of academic psychology:

_____ a.   scholastic aptitude

_____ b.   ability to set priorities according to the importance of the task

_____ c.   interpersonal skills

_____ d.   tendency to try to do everything perfectly

_____ e.   broad-ranging interests and hobbies

_____ f.   knowledge of the relevant literature

3.  A number of factors enter into the establishment of a good reputation among scholars in one's field. Consider the following factors and rate their importance:

_____ a.   teaching ability

_____ b.   judged quality of research

_____ c.   quantity of research published

_____ d.   involvement in public service and charitable organizations

_____ e.   a tendency usually to be the initiator of research projects

_____ f.   having written popular books on psychology for the general public

_____ g.   visibility (being well known to the scientific community)

4.  An undergraduate student has asked for your advice in deciding to which graduate programs in psychology to apply. Consider the following dimensions for rating the overall quality of a graduate program in psychology and rate their importance:

_____ a.   teaching ability of the faculty

_____ b.   job placement of recent graduates of the program

_____ c.   number of required courses

_____ d.   number of graduate students in the program

_____ e.   percentage of faculty time spent on formal teaching
_____ f.   extracurricular and athletic facilities
_____ g.   flexibility of program
_____ h.   equipment and facilities (computers, labs, and so on)
_____ i.   amount of research currently being conducted by faculty

5.  You have been asked to edit a new journal. You would like to have guidelines available to those who will review submitted manuscripts for the purpose of deciding whether to accept or reject them. Rate the importance of the following criteria for evaluating the quality of research articles:

_____ a.   an abundance of tables and figures
_____ b.   importance of questions addressed
_____ c.   number of entries in reference list
_____ d.   infrequent grammatical errors or misused words
_____ e.   cleverness of the research design

---

## "ANSWERS" TO TACIT-KNOWLEDGE QUESTIONNAIRES

In these solutions, a + indicates a relatively higher rating by individuals more advanced in the field relative to individuals less advanced in the field. A − indicates a relatively lower rating by individuals more advanced in the field. Keep in mind, then, that the +'s and −'s are *relative*. There are no correct answers, per se, only trends distinguishing more from less experienced individuals. As you will see, in some cases the "answers" are counterintuitive.

### Business Management

| 1. a. | − | 5. a. | − |
|---|---|---|---|
| b. | − | b. | − |
| c. | − | c. | − |
| d. | + | d. | − |
| e. | − | e. | − |
| 2. a. | + | | |
| b. | − | | |
| c. | + | | |
| d. | − | | |
| e. | + | | |
| 3. a. | − | | |
| b. | − | | |
| c. | − | | |
| d. | + | | |
| e. | − | | |
| 4. a. | + | | |
| b. | + | | |
| c. | + | | |
| d. | − | | |
| e. | − | | |

### Academic Psychology

| 1. a. | − | 3. a. | − | 5. a. | − |
|---|---|---|---|---|---|
| b. | + | b. | + | b. | + |
| c. | + | c. | + | c. | − |
| d. | − | d. | − | d. | − |
| e. | − | e. | + | e. | − |
| f. | − | f. | − | | |
| g. | + | g. | + | | |
| h. | + | 4. a. | − | | |
| i. | − | b. | − | | |
| j. | − | c. | − | | |
| k. | − | d. | − | | |
| l. | − | e. | − | | |
| m. | − | f. | − | | |
| 2. a. | + | g. | − | | |
| b. | + | h. | − | | |
| c. | − | i. | + | | |
| d. | − | | | | |
| e. | + | | | | |
| f. | + | | | | |

## Conflict Resolution

Presented below are six stories involving three different kinds of conflicts: between individuals in personal relationships, between individuals in organizations, and between countries. Read each story, then read the seven styles of conflict resolution that follow the story. Rate the desirability of each style of conflict resolution from 1 (poor) to 10 (excellent). In other words, how desirable is each of the proposed strategies for resolving the conflict presented in the story? In general, these conflict-resolution situations have no one "correct" solution. It is worth remembering, however, that more intelligent people tend to try to defuse rather than to exacerbate the conflicts in which they find themselves. A key that lists styles of conflict resolution appears after the problems.

**CONFLICT-RESOLUTION PROBLEMS**

1.  A recent acquisition of the University of Colego economics department, instead of being a benefit to the department, has turned out to be a source of conflict among the faculty, students, and staff. The controversy centers on the new multipurpose computer. The department obtained the new computer with hopes that the machine would expedite the various functions of the economics department. Unfortunately, this purpose has not been realized. If anything, the computer has been a source of hard feelings, departmental division, and reduced efficiency in the department's workload.

Part of the problem revolves around the dual function of the university's economics department, which prides itself on being both "a foremost research institution" and "a high quality place of teaching and learning." The department has been divided into two subdivisions, one research-oriented, the other teaching-oriented, to meet its various commitments and interests. Consequently, there has been intense competition between the two factions for use of the new computer.

The research subdivision has extensive use of the computer for its various research projects in the private sector for different large corporations, and in the public sector for governmental contracts dealing with the development of economic policy. All of these projects take up large amounts of time on the computer. The research subdivision justifies this use of the computer as "necessary if the department is to maintain its reputation as a major research institution." Furthermore, the various research contracts bring in a major portion of the operating budget for the economic department. Without the research contracts, the department would have to make drastic cutbacks in its existing program.

The faculty and students of the economics department's teaching subdivision also have extensive need for the computer. This group uses the computer for different class projects, for a variety of student projects, and for grading large standardized tests, which would take hours to correct without the computer. The education group sees its work as no less important than that of the research group. In fact, many of the faculty feel the teaching function of the department should receive first priority. Without at least equal use of the computer, the education group knows it could not continue to attract high-quality teachers and students. Also, without the tuition students pay to the university, the department would find it impossible to carry on either education or research.

In other words, both subdivisions of the department need each other to carry on the work each wishes to accomplish. At a recent department meeting, it was determined to be impossible to obtain another computer until at least next year because of the prohibitive cost of a new computer.

At the meeting of the research group, the following different options were considered:

\_\_\_\_\_ a. The research group could try to get the education group's budget reduced if the education group does not comply with the needs of the research group.

\_\_\_\_\_ b. The research group could decide to take no action at this time and wait to see what the education group will do.

\_\_\_\_\_ c. The research group could prohibit the education group from using the computer by using a strategy of signing up to use the computer well in advance, even if the research group does not have an immediate use for the machine.

\_\_\_\_\_ d. The research group could bring in a third party, like a university decision-making board, and plead the group's case before the board.

\_\_\_\_\_ e. The research group could be openly critical of the function of the education group to the other members of the economics department, hoping to receive support for the research group's position.

\_\_\_\_\_ f. The research group could accept the fact that there is a scarcity of resources and try to make the best of the situation.

\_\_\_\_\_ g. The research group could voluntarily reduce its own use of the computer, only using the machine for its most essential projects, or agree to use the computer only during odd hours at night or on the weekend.

2. Bill and Sue Martin have been married for the past 14 years and have two children, a boy, 13, and a daughter, 12. For the past five years Bill has been working as a car salesman in town. Although his income has thus far been steady, because of a drop-off in auto sales he has been unable to increase his earnings despite working longer hours. Sue works as a sales clerk in a local department store to help supplement the family's income.

The Martin family lives in what was originally a two-bedroom house. During the early years, the boy and the girl shared the same bedroom while the parents had the other bedroom. As the children grew older, the Martins realized that they either would need a larger home, or they would need to add another bedroom to their present home. Since it was clear the family could not afford a new home, the Martins spent a moderate amount to build an extra bedroom in the basement for their son. This way, each of the children could have a separate room and some privacy. This seemed like the most workable solution to the family's space problem.

Then, about six months ago, Mrs. Martin's father died, leaving Mrs. Martin's mother, Mrs. Jones, all alone with little financial support. The elderly Mrs. Jones had severe difficulty adjusting to her husband's death. She totally isolated herself from family and friends and preferred to spend her days alone in her small apartment. The elderly woman's physical and mental health rapidly began to deteriorate. Mrs. Martin tried to help her mother as much as possible, but as the months passed, it became increasingly clear that Mrs. Jones could no longer manage living alone.

Naturally quite concerned, Mrs. Martin approached her husband about the possibility of her mother moving in with the family. Mr. Martin, who had never gotten along with the mother, was totally against the idea. Mr. Martin pointed out the family's space problem. If the mother moved in, the now teenage children would again have to share a room. Moreover, someone would always have to be at home to supervise Mrs. Jones to make sure she was all right. Since both Mr. and Mrs. Martin work full-time, this necessity would pose difficulties for the family. Finally, the added friction between Mr. Martin and the mother-in-law might make the situation intolerable.

Mr. Martin suggested the family look into the possibility of a nursing home for Mrs. Jones. The family could afford only a limited-care facility, but at least Mrs. Jones would have a safe place to stay and someone to look after her. Mrs. Martin was especially against putting her mother in a nursing home. She had heard the horror stories about the poor care provided in such homes and vowed she would never put any of her family in a nursing home if she could possibly avoid it. Furthermore, Mrs. Martin had always been dependent on her mother for emotional support and she wanted her mother close by.

The Martins further considered hiring a full-time nurse to look after the mother, but this option was quickly ruled out for financial reasons. Since Mrs. Martin is the only child in the family, and there are no other relatives to take care of Mrs. Jones, the only likely possibilities are for Mrs. Jones to move into the Martins' home, or to have Mrs. Jones move into a nursing home. Since Mr. Martin is set against the mother moving in, and Mrs. Martin is set against her mother moving into a nursing home, what should Mr. Martin do?

_____ a.   Mr. Martin might seek an outside counselor to help the family solve its dilemma.

_____ b.   Mr. Martin could be openly critical of both the wife and mother-in-law for forcing him to have the mother-in-law stay in the house.

_____ c.   Mr. Martin could just accept the mother-in-law's moving into the house and try to make the best of a difficult situation.

_____ d.  Mr. Martin could refuse to pay anything in support of the mother-in-law while she stays in the house.

_____ e.  Mr. Martin could decide to take no action and wait to see what would happen.

_____ f.  Mr. Martin could physically bar the mother-in-law from entering the house against his wishes.

_____ g.  Mr. Martin might agree to a trial period with the mother-in-law in the house and try to be as kind and positive as possible.

3.  The two nations of Uvolo and Mboka share a common border in the northeast corner of Africa. Although the two nations have had cordial relations for a number of years, recently a source of great conflict has arisen having to do with the utilization of the area's major natural resource, the Kilo River. Both Uvolo and Mboka depend heavily on the Kilo for crop irrigation, hydroelectric power generation, transportation, and a sustained water supply for the two countries' ever-growing populations.

The problem centers on Mboka, which is upriver from Uvolo and controls the source of the Kilo River. Mboka has experienced an immense population increase within the last 10 years. To support this large increase, Mboka has found it necessary to utilize ever increasing amounts of water from the Kilo. Rich farmlands have been planted where there was once only barren desert. Huge dams have been built for hydroelectric power generation and flood control. Large factories that use millions of gallons of water per day have been constructed near the border with Uvolo, and have greatly increased the amount of pollutants flowing into the river. Subsequently, the amount of water flowing into Uvolo has decreased by at least 50 percent and the water that does flow is so polluted that without a very expensive water treatment process, it is almost unusable for human consumption and crop irrigation.

Recently, Uvolo's health ministry published a report noting a significant increase in illnesses from people drinking the polluted water. In addition, the agricultural ministry in Uvolo has gleaned some preliminary findings that indicate vast crop damage and drought will ensue without some significant change in the present situation.

Upon hearing the evidence presented by the two ministries, the Uvolon government filed a formal protest to the government of Mboka demanding a change in that government's present water policies. The Mbokan government, although concerned about the plight of the Uvolons, maintains that where the Kilo flows within their borders, it is their property to be used as the people of Mboka best see fit. Thus, there will be no change in their policies.

The Mbokans maintain that they are not the cause of Uvolo's problem, but cite Uvolo's inefficient farming methods as the cause of their agricultural dilemmas. Mboka also maintains that Uvolo's health conditions were poor long before Mboka's present water management policies. Mboka also claims that it must be Uvolon factories causing the pollution problem along the Kilo because Mbokan factories use the most technologically advanced pollution control devices in their factories. Given Mboka's unwillingness to share responsibility for the water problems along the Kilo, what should Uvolo do?

_____ a.  Uvolo could take action to destroy Mboka's dams and factories along the border.

_____ b.  Uvolo could accept the situation as it is even though the situation is not perfect.

_____ c.  Uvolo could try to take its case to the World Court or another international body to gain a change in Mboka's policies or some compensation.

_____ d.  Uvolo could decide to take no action at this time and to wait and see what Mboka will do.

_____ e.  Uvolo could try to find a solution without the help of Mboka by searching for another source of water other than the Kilo River.

_____ f.  Uvolo could break off diplomatic ties and denounce Mboka before the world community in order to persuade Mboka to change.

_____ g.  Uvolo could cease all trade with Mboka and try to convince other nations to do the same until Mboka changes its water management policies.

4.  Tom and Kathy Clark just recently celebrated their tenth wedding anniversary. Unfortunately, what should have been a happy occasion was marred by a bitter disagreement between the couple. Within the last year, Kathy has become increasingly unhappy about the amount of time Tom spends away from home.

From the beginning, Tom has worked long hours, often several nights a week, running his own accounting firm in New Haven. Especially during tax time between December and April, Tom finds that he must spend long hours at his office. In addition to his regular hours at work, Tom is involved in extra commitments which keep him away from home several nights a week. On Tuesday evenings, Tom attends meetings of the local school board, a position to which Tom was appointed two years ago, and which he enjoys very much. Another important activity for Tom is his Thursday evening Bible study at the local church. Several times, Tom has invited Kathy to attend his various activities and has offered to pay for a sitter for the children. Each time, Kathy has declined.

Consequently, with such a full and active schedule, Tom feels that it is imperative that he allow himself some leisure time on Wednesday night to play racketball at the local YMCA with his colleagues. This is Tom's only opportunity for exercise during the week. And unlike his friends, Tom does not go out drinking after the games, but goes right home to Kathy and the children. He often arrives home only after the family has already gone to bed.

The couple has three children, all in school. Kathy is worried that the children will be grown up before long and will never have a chance to spend much time with their father.

Tom feels that he cannot cut anything out of his present schedule if he is to provide adequately for his wife and children, engage in community service, practice his religious faith, and allow himself some leisure time for his physical health. Tom loves his family and hopes they understand this. He tries to spend as much quality time as possible with the family during the weekends. Moreover, because Tom offers to have Kathy accompany him to the various activities, he feels he has taken the initiative to spend time with her. Each time Kathy declines because she has her own friends and activities she would rather pursue during the evenings.

Although Kathy has tried to be understanding of her husband's needs, she is starting to get resentful of the amount of time Tom spends away from home. To supplement the family's income, Kathy is working part-time as a library assistant at the high school while the children are in school. Kathy also feels pressured for time, but she has the children to take care of before she can pursue her own interests. Kathy is tired of nagging Tom about his schedule, but nothing seems to change his habits. Kathy has come to the end of her patience and realizes that something has to change if she is to be happy. Kathy considered the following solutions:

_____ a.  Kathy might try criticizing Tom's behavior with family, friends, and Tom's professional colleagues to get him to spend more time at home.

_____ b.  Kathy could spend the money she makes at the high school on herself and the children only and not let Tom benefit from her extra income.

_____ c.  Kathy might try to find some counseling for the couple to work out an agreement which is satisfying to both.

_____ d.  Kathy could decide to take no action at this time and wait to see what Tom will do.

_____ e.  Kathy could accept the situation with Tom as it is even though the situation is far from perfect.

_____ f.  Kathy might try being "supergood" to Tom, hoping this would convince him to spend more time with the family.

_____ g.  If Tom continues to spend most of his evenings away from home, Kathy might consider a separation and possible divorce from Tom to show him she is serious about his being with the family.

5. The nations of Omat and Qarah are two small countries sharing a common border along the Persian Gulf. A geological survey conducted in the late 1960s indicated the existence of a rich field of petroleum deposits right along the border between the two countries. From the early 1970s, the nation of Omat has aggressively exploited the oil field by building hundreds of oil wells along the common border with Qarah. Sales from the

oil brought Omat huge sums of capital, which has been used to develop local industry and thereby upgrade that standard of living for the people of Omat. The government of Qarah, on the other hand, decided not to use any of their oil reserves, but instead wanted to let the oil lie in reserve at least until the year 2000, when the oil could be sold for a higher price and also be used to assure domestic supplies to local industrial development. Qarah felt it would not need the oil money until then. In the meantime, Qarah, unlike Omat, planned to depend on its long established tradition of an agriculturally based economy for the improved livelihood of its people.

Late in 1980, Qarah commissioned another survey to determine just how vast their oil reserves were, in order to begin planning for their use around the year 2000. Much to the shock of the people of Qarah, the commission reported that the oil reserves were rapidly diminishing each year and that within five to ten years, there would be no oil left at all. The commission attributed this rapid depletion of Qarah's oil reserves to the aggressive oil exploitation of neighboring Omat. Although Omat was only drilling for oil on their side of the border, apparently, the oil field was subterraneanly connected and drilling on one side of the border was depleting reserves on the other side. Upon receiving the commission's report, the government of Qarah sent an immediate protest to the government of Omat and demanded an immediate cessation of drilling until some sort of solution could be mutually agreed upon. Omat responded that "although our people are sympathetic to the plight of Qarah, a cessation of drilling would be impossible because of longstanding oil contracts with the United States and Western Europe. Moreover, our own economic health depends on the continued flow of oil from our land." Furthermore, Omat stated, "because we have been scrupulous in making sure our drilling has been conducted only within our territory, we can in no way be held responsible for your regrettable situation. But out of respect for your present plight, our nation is willing to reduce slightly our oil production on a temporary basis." Given Omat's reply, what should Qarah do?

_____ a.   Qarah could try to get other nations on its side by openly criticizing Omat's practices.

_____ b.   Qarah could just accept the present situation and try to make the best of it.

_____ c.   Qarah could take action to destroy Omat's oil fields unless Omat immediately stops its oil production.

_____ d.   Qarah could decide to take no action at this time and wait to see what Omat will do.

_____ e.   Qarah could stop all trade with Omat and try to convince other nations to do the same.

_____ f.   Qarah could go to the World Court or some other international body and state its case against Omat.

_____ g.   Qarah could try to build up its other resources and try to buy its oil from Omat.

6. Since its establishment in 1945, World Press International (WPI) has been the leading wire news service in the Western world. WPI has continued to enhance its reputation as an accurate, reliable, expeditious source of world and national news stories for newspapers, radio, and television. For years, no other news wire service could compare with WPI's news gathering and reporting network, at least until recently, when formidable competition appeared on the scene.

World Press International's competition has come from a newly established news wire company called National Wire Service (NWS), which was founded in 1972 by wealthy Chicago newspaper owner R. William Hastings. With the new company's substantial financial backing, it was, in a short time, able to gather a reporting, writing, and transmitting network rivaling the longer established WPI news wire service.

Because of the two company's similar functions, they immediately found they were sharing a variety of news sources and lines of communication over the telephone and telegraph lines throughout the world. More heated than their competition for news stories was the competition between the two companies in their search for customers among the various newspapers, television, and radio stations.

The board of directors of World Press became alarmed at the increasing number of customers NWS was attracting. Even some of WPI's long-established customers were switching over to the new service. Since the companies charged the same amount of money for their services, a possible reason for the turnover was NWS's aggressive sales and promotional practice. WPI's directors knew something had to be done to meet their competition from NWS, or their company would soon be out of business.

The WPI board met to consider its options. Because of the magnitude of the problems facing the company, it was determined that even drastic measures had to be considered. Here are some of the possibilities the board considered:

_____ a.   WPI could just accept the present situation even though it is not perfect.

_____ b.   WPI might try secretly sabotaging NWS's news transmission lines and news reporting networks.

_____ c.   WPI might temporarily reduce its prices to bring some of its old customers back from NWS.

_____ d.   WPI could try to find flaws in the NWS news reporting network and begin to make those flaws known to NWS customers.

_____ e.   WPI might consider offering to merge with NWS.

_____ f.   WPI could try to find a third party to mediate some of the disagreements between NWS and WPI.

_____ g.   WPI could decide to take no action at this time and wait to see what NWS will do.

## "ANSWERS" TO CONFLICT-RESOLUTION PROBLEMS

The seven suggested modes of conflict resolution were the same in each of the six stories, although of course specifics of each proposed solution were tailored to the individual parties and conflict situations. The seven modes of conflict resolution were

(a) *physical action*, in which the target party attempts to get its way through physical force or coercion directed at the other party;

(b) *economic action*, in which the target party attempts to get its way through economic pressure directed at the other party;

(c) *wait and see*, in which the target party decides to wait things out and see if the situation improves;

(d) *accept the situation*, in which the target party decides to accept the situation as it is and make the best of it;

(e) *step-down*, in which the target party attempts to defuse the conflict by reducing or negating its demands on the other party;

(f) *third-party intervention*, in which the target party seeks some outside third party to mediate the conflict;

(g) *undermine esteem*, in which the target party seeks to undermine the esteem in which the opposing party is held by other parties outside the conflict situation.

Options (c), (d), (e), and (f) tend to defuse conflicts; (a), (b), and (g) tend to exacerbate them.

1. a.  economic
   b.  wait and see
   c.  physical
   d.  third-party
   e.  undermine esteem
   f.  accept situation
   g.  step-down
2. a.  third-party
   b.  undermine esteem
   c.  accept situation
   d.  economic
   e.  wait and see
   f.  physical
   g.  step-down
3. a.  physical
   b.  accept situation
   c.  third-party
   d.  wait and see
   e.  step-down
   f.  undermine esteem
   g.  economic

4. a.  undermine esteem
   b.  economic
   c.  third-party
   d.  wait and see
   e.  accept situation
   f.  step-down
   g.  physical
5. a.  undermine esteem
   b.  accept situation
   c.  physical
   d.  wait and see
   e.  economic
   f.  third-party
   g.  step-down
6. a.  accept situation
   b.  physical
   c.  economic
   d.  undermine esteem
   e.  step-down
   f.  third-party
   g.  wait and see

# Improving Your Response to Practical Situations

This chapter has reviewed some of the literature on the assessment of practical intelligence, and has also presented four kinds of exercises intended to develop your skills in exercising practical intelligence. Practical problems, unlike academic ones, often have no single right or wrong answer. Indeed, the mistake people often make is looking for the certainty that just does not exist in practical situations. Practical situations of any importance almost always involve some elements of risk, uncertainty, and ambiguity. You are probably often aware that you are not sure whether you made the right decision or took the right course of action, even after you executed the decision or course of action. What, then, can you do to maximize the effectiveness of your responses to practical situations? The following guidelines may be helpful:

1. Consider the possibility, in real-life decision-making situations, of employing what Irving Janis calls a decisional balance sheet. In the decisional balance sheet, you write out each possible course of action. For each course of action, you then list each possible outcome, both positive and negative. You also list the possible effects the courses of action will have on yourself and others. The object is to determine which course of action has the highest number of potentially favorable outcomes associated with it—which course of action maximizes the favorable consequences for oneself and others. Sometimes, it may be useful to estimate the desirability of the favorable outcomes and the undesirability of the unfavorable outcomes on some kind of rating scale. The reason for this is that although one possible course of action may appear to yield more potentially favorable outcomes, these outcomes may not be as highly favorable as the smaller number of favorable outcomes associated with an alternative course of action. You can calculate the overall perceived favorability of an outcome by summing the products of the favorability of each consideration (say, on a 9-point scale) by the weight given to that consideration (say, on a 5-point scale). Thus, suppose that one reason you want to buy a given automobile is its attractive price. On a 9-point scale ($1$ = low favorability, $9$ = high favorability), you might rate the car 7. If you weigh the price on the 5-point scale ($1$ = low weight, $5$ = high weight) as 4, then the product of $7 \times 4 = 28$. You sum all the products to get an overall score, and you can do the same for the unfavorable aspects of a given choice. The best choice is then that choice for which the overall favorable score minus the overall unfavorable score is *highest*. For example, if your overall favorability score for a given car is 355 and the overall unfavorability score is 240, then the difference of $355 - 240$ is 115. If the overall difference score for another car is 60, then the first car is your preferred choice. A format for a decisional balance sheet is shown in Figure 8-3.

2. Be sure to consider as much information as possible, and fully to weigh the consequences of this information. A common mistake that people make is to act impulsively on the basis of incomplete information, when more nearly complete information would be fairly readily accessible. A key

## FIGURE 8-3

## A Decisional Balance Sheet

Decision to be made: _____

| Favorable Outcomes | | | | Unfavorable Outcomes | | | |
|---|---|---|---|---|---|---|---|
| For Myself | **a**<br>How favor-able? | **b**<br>Importance of consideration | **a** × **b** | For Myself | **a**<br>How unfavor-able? | **b**<br>Importance of consideration | **a** × **b** |
| | | | | | | | |
| For Others | | | | For Others | | | |
| | | | | | | | |
| Sum of **a** × **b** _____<br>( = total "favorable" score) | | | | Sum of **a** × **b** _____<br>( = total "unfavorable" score) | | | |

element of intelligence is the ability to withhold an impulsive response and to substitute for it a delayed, reflective response. Of course, there are times to act impulsively and times to act reflectively. But when the stakes are high, and the time for thought is available, be sure to use the full information at your disposal in making a decision, and also to seek as much information as you can from available sources.

3. Consider the relative efficacies of the three basic strategies for coping with real-world problems: adaptation, shaping, and selection. Very often, you will believe your options in a situation to be more limited than they really are. For example, many times people assume that they have to adapt to a situation, when actually they have open to them the option of shaping it. At other times, people may assume that their only options are either to adapt to the situation or to try to shape it, but they do not realize the real possibility of getting out of it altogether. The practically intelligent person knows when to persevere, but he or she also knows when to quit. When considering how to solve an everyday problem, consider solutions that involve courses of action that involve adaptation, shaping, or selection.

4. Most important, choose solutions to problems that take into account in a realistic way the person you are and the situation you are in, drawing on the experience of others and your own past experience in attempting to solve the problems that confront you on a day-to-day basis. But in drawing on past solutions, both your own and others', remember to take into account the person you are at a given time and place. Solutions that work for others may not work for you, and solutions that may have worked for you in the past may not work for you in the present. You must thus adopt the present time and place as your frame of reference, drawing upon, but not being confined by, past experience. By doing so, you will find that you are best able to utilize your practical intelligence.

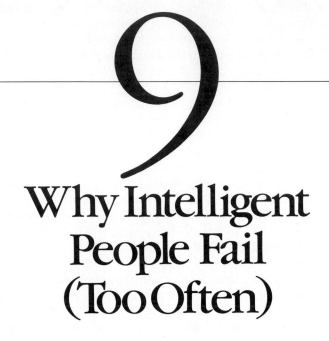

# 9

# Why Intelligent People Fail (Too Often)

Everyone fails sometimes. Indeed, it is doubtful that we could ever learn if we never failed at anything. The sign of intelligence is not never making mistakes, but rather learning from those mistakes so that they are not made again and again. An intelligent person can be forgiven for making mistakes, but perhaps not for making the same ones repeatedly.

Almost all of us know seemingly intelligent people who make mistakes too often and who fail at what they do too often. It is as though their intelligence is for naught when they confront the problems of the real world. Clearly, intelligence is not enough for successful performance in the everyday world, no matter how broadly intelligence is defined. People can come into the world with some of the best intellectual gifts heredity has to offer, or they can be brought up in a highly advanced environment, or they can read a book such as this and practice their intellectual skills, and they can still routinely make a mess of their lives. Unless they can circumvent or otherwise bypass the stumbling blocks that get in the way of optimal intellectual performance, they may find that most, if not all, of their intellectual gifts are of little value.

This chapter discusses 20 stumbling blocks that can get in the way of even the most intelligent individuals. For the most part, these stumbling blocks are not strictly intellectual ones, but if people can keep these sorts of problems under control, then they can truly concentrate upon developing their intellects, knowing that this development will reflect itself in improved task performance. As you read the 20 impediments to the full realization of intelligence, it may become increasingly obvious to you why conventional intelligence tests, and perhaps even more broadly defined ones, can account for only relatively small proportions of variance in real-world performance.

*1. Lack of motivation.*    It scarcely matters what talents people have if they are not motivated to use them. In many if not most environments, motivation counts at least as much as intellectual skills in the attainment of success. The reason motivation is so important is that individuals within a given environment—for example, a classroom—tend to represent a relatively narrow range of ability, but a much broader range of motivation. Motivation thus becomes a key source of individual differences in success. For some people, motivation will come from external sources—approval of peers, attainment of recognition, attainment of money, or whatever. For others, motivation will be internal, deriving from their own satisfaction in a job well-done. Most people will be both internally and externally motivated in different proportions. Whatever the source of the motivation, it is critical to the expression of intelligence and to success. On the whole, it is probably preferable for motivation to be internally—rather than externally— generated for the reason that external sources of motivation tend to be transient. As a result, people who are primarily externally motivated are likely to lose their motivation when the external sources of reward diminish or disappear. Internally motivated individuals are able to maintain their motivation over the rises and falls of external rewards.

*2. Lack of impulse control.*    There are times in life when people need to act impulsively, but impulsive behavior tends to detract from rather than enhance intellectual work. In one of his earliest books, L. L. Thurstone (1924) claimed that a key feature of intelligent persons is their ability to control impulsive responses. Many years later a comparative psychologist, D. Stenhouse (1974), independently came to the same conclusion. Habitual impulsiveness gets in the way of optimal intellectual performance by not allowing people to bring their full intellectual resources to bear on a problem. While endless reflection is also clearly undesirable, people should not let themselves get carried away by the first solution that occurs to them in attempting to solve a problem. Better solutions may arise after further thought.

*3. Lack of perseverance and perseveration.*    Some people, despite all their intelligence, give up too easily. If things do not immediately go their way, or if their initial attempts at something are unsuccessful, they drop whatever they are doing. They thereby lose the opportunity to complete, possibly in a highly suitable way, the tasks they undertake. It is as though the least frustration of any kind is enough to keep them from persevering. At the other extreme are people who continue working on a problem long after they should have quit. They perseverate even after it should have become clear to them that they are going to be unable to solve the problem, at least at that time. Alternatively, they may basically have solved the problem, but they then go on to solve it again and again. One can see in certain scholarly careers the existence of this tendency toward perseveration. The scholar conducts an important piece of work, perhaps as his or her Ph.D. thesis, then follows up the work with some subsequent studies that address what are usually the more minor problems that evolve out of that initial work. At some point, people in the field generally expect that scholar to move on to another problem, or at least to a different approach to the same problem. Instead, the scholar continues to do what to most people appears to be the same research, over and over again. There may be minor changes in or additions to the research, but from the point of view of practically anyone but the scholar, the scholarly contribution essentially ceased long ago. Perseveration occurs in other areas of life as well. Almost everyone knows someone who, having been rejected repeatedly by a potential romantic partner, nevertheless keeps trying again and again, despite the persistence of negative signals from that potential partner. It is as though the person is unable to stop in a fruitless quest. He or she perseverates long after it has become obvious to everyone else, and sometimes even to the person, that he or she is making no headway.

*4. Using the wrong abilities.*    Many people become aware, at some time during their lives, that they are either in the wrong occupation, or that they are going about the occupation they are in incorrectly. It is as though the work they are doing requires one set of abilities, and they are attempting to do it with a different set of abilities. This phenomenon, of course, can occur during their schooling as well as in later life. They may find themselves in law school and realize that their cognitive abilities would have been much more suitable for an academic career. Or they may find themselves in medical school and come to the conclusion that their real abilities lie in sales. Their discovery, basically, is that they do have strong abilities, but not for the kinds of tasks in which they are engaged. At such points, the intelligent thing to do may be to select another course of schooling or career, or at least to switch study or career strategies.

*5. Inability to translate thought into action.*    Some people are very adept at coming up with solutions to their problems, and may actually seem to have a solution for everything in their lives as well as in the lives of other people, but they seem unable to translate their thought into action. In the words of the psychologist E. R. Guthrie (1935), they become "buried in thought." No matter how good their ideas, they rarely seem to be able to do anything about them. In order fully to capitalize on our intelligence, we must have not only good ideas, but the ability to do something about these ideas—to translate thought into action. Almost everyone knows of people who have made an important decision for their lives, but seem unable to act on it. Having decided to get married, for example, they cannot set a date. When it comes to action, paralysis sets in. Whatever their level of intelligence, such people are unable to benefit from it. At times, we are all like this. The problem we face is to do something about it and to act when appropriate rather than remaining buried in thought.

*6. Lack of product orientation.*    Some people seem very concerned about the process by which things are done, but not nearly as concerned about the resulting products. Yet it is primarily on the basis of what we produce that our accomplishments are judged, whether in school or in later life. I have had students who have done really classy research that will have an important impact on the field, but when it comes to writing up their research, they do a clearly second- or third-rate job. They were very involved in the process of the research, but they lost their involvement and enthusiasm once it was time to turn that process into a final product. As a result, their contributions are not seen as being as important as they potentially could be, and their full level of intelligence does not manifest itself.

7. *Inability to complete tasks and to follow through.*   The one certain prediction about "noncompleters" is that whatever they begin they will not finish. Nothing in their lives ever seems to draw quite to a close. Perhaps they are afraid to finish things for fear that they will not know what to do with themselves next. Or they may overwhelm themselves with the details of a project, becoming so hopelessly enmeshed that they are unable to progress. The lives of these people often seem to embody Zeno's paradox. In this paradox, a man wishes to get from point A to point B. In order to traverse this distance, he has to traverse half the distance. In order to traverse the remaining half of the distance, he has first to traverse half of that distance, leaving one quarter of the total distance remaining to be traversed. But in order to traverse that distance, he first has to traverse half of that. In the paradox, the man always goes half the remaining distance without ever arriving. Similarly, in the situations life presents, some people seem unable to reach the end.

8. *Failure to initiate.*   Other people seem unwilling or unable to initiate projects; they are always trying to decide what to do. Often, this inability to initiate results from fear of commitment. These people are afraid to become too committed to anything, and as a result they are unwilling to undertake anything. Consider, for example, the problem of a student trying to decide on a dissertation topic. Some students fail to complete graduate school because they can never commit themselves to a topic. A dissertation requires a substantial investment of time and energy, and some students are simply unwilling to make this commitment. Many people act this way in interpersonal relationships. They never seem to want to go beyond just meeting other people, for fear of becoming committed to the relationship. As a result, they go through life in a series of superficial relationships, unable to initiate anything more substantial that runs the risk of leading to a commitment.

9. *Fear of failure.*   Fear of failure seems to start early in life. To some extent, I can see it at work in my own son. He is very able, but sometimes seems unwilling to undertake things for fear of failing at them. Many people fail to realize their full intellectual potential because of their fear that they will fail at what they do. In college, they may not take the difficult courses that they need because they do not expect to do well in them. As a result, they may do well in the courses they take, but later have no use for those courses. Later on, as lawyers or doctors or scientists or business executives, they may

not undertake the projects that could really make a difference to their careers because of their fear that the projects will not succeed. Indeed, they may not even enter the occupation of their choice because of their fear that they will not succeed in it, or they may not continue with a personal relationship, not because of the way it is going, but because of their fear of the way it might go.

In some cases, fear of failure may be realistic. If the consequences of failure are high enough, fear of failure can be quite adaptive. For example, the whole strategy of nuclear deterrence depends on fear of failure—the theory being that no country will start a nuclear war because of the fear that it will be a disaster for them as well as for their opponents. Thus, there are times at which it is quite reasonable not to take risks. But there are other times when we must take risks, and the unwillingness or inability to do so results in loss of life opportunities that may never return.

*10. Procrastination.*    Procrastination seems to be a universal fact of life. We all, at some time or another, procrastinate, putting off for later the things we know should be done now. Procrastination becomes a serious problem only when it is a uniform style in our way of doing things. Some students tend always to be looking for little things to do so as to put off the big things. They always manage to get their daily reading and assignments done, but seem to procrastinate forever in undertaking the large-scale projects that can really make a difference to their careers. In any career or stage of life, it is easy to become immersed in the daily trivia that can gobble up all of one's time. The tendency to become so immersed may actually result in short-term success, but often results in long-term failure. Those with a tendency toward procrastination often have to force themselves to undertake the big things, because they are simply unable to do them without pressure, whether self-imposed or imposed from the outside.

*11. Misattribution of blame.*    Some people feel they can do no wrong, and are always looking for others to blame for even the slightest mishap. Others are always blaming themselves for everything, regardless of their role in the event or events that led to mishap. Misattribution of blame can seriously hinder one's intellectual self-realization. For example, I had a graduate student working with me who was very able and competent in research. The faculty thought the world of her, and yet she always blamed herself for anything that went wrong. It reached the point where she felt that she could do nothing right, and she seemed traumatized much of the time. Eventually, she left our program. Another graduate student was exactly the opposite. She managed always to blame others for things that went wrong in her graduate career. Although it was clear to practically everyone surrounding her that she was just not working very hard, she always had an excuse for why things were not getting done, and the excuse tended to involve the machinations of others that prevented her from working and reaching her goals. If there is blame to be placed, it is important to know where to place it. Misattributions of blame close the door to self-improvement, and prevent us from exploiting our talents to the fullest.

*12. Excessive self-pity.*    We all pity ourselves sometimes. When things do not go just right, it is difficult not to do so. But constant self-pity is highly maladaptive. When one of my graduate students entered our program, he had certain clear disadvantages in terms of preparation, and obviously felt sorry for himself. At that point, others felt sorry for him, too. But after a while, people became annoyed and even angry at his continual self-pity. After a point, everyone expected him to pull himself up by his bootstraps and make a go of things. But the self-pity never seemed to end. A vicious circle ensued in which as he became sorrier and sorrier for himself, others became less and less sorry, until finally they wanted to have little to do with him. He seemed to spend more time feeling sorry for himself than making the effort that would be required so that he no longer would have any cause to feel sorry. Self-pity is not only useless for getting work done, but after a certain point, it tends to put off those who might otherwise be most helpful.

*13. Excessive dependency.*    In most of the tasks people face, they are expected to acquire a certain degree of independence. Often, people's home lives may ill prepare them for the independence that will later be expected of them, for once they enter a career, they are expected to fend for themselves, and to rely upon others only to the minimally necessary degree. Many students seem not to learn this, and expect others either to do things for them or constantly to show them how to get things done. Without such aid, they are at a total loss. The result is that they often have to seek less responsible jobs, or never do as well as they otherwise might in the job that they have. In school, as well as in work, do not expect either your professors or your fellow students to get things done for you. If you want to get them done, the best way to do so is either to do them yourself or to take responsibility for having someone else get them done. Don't expect others to take the responsibility that you yourself must take.

*14. Wallowing in personal difficulties.*    Everyone has personal difficulties, but their extent differs widely from one person to another. Some people have repeated tragedies in their lives, others seem to lead charmed existences and almost never encounter difficulties. During the course of your life, you can expect some real joys, but also some real sorrows. The important thing is to try to keep both the joys and the sorrows in perspective. Some people let their personal difficulties interfere grossly with their work; others seem to be unaffected in their work. Major life crises will almost always have some effect on your work, whether you like it or not. The best thing is to accept that this will happen and take it in stride. It is equally important that you not wallow in your personal difficulties and let them drag down your work and you with it. Indeed, in times of personal hardship, your work, as well as other people, may provide you with some of the solace you need. It is a mistake to avoid the personal difficulties that you must often face; it is equally a mistake to allow yourself to be consumed by them.

*15. Distractibility and lack of concentration.*    There are any number of very intelligent people who, despite their high intelligence, never seem to be able to concentrate on anything for very long. They are highly distractible, and tend to have short attention spans. As a result, they tend not to get much done. To some extent, distractibility is an attentional variable over which we do not have total control. If you tend not to be distractible and to have good concentration, then it is not something you have to worry about particularly. If you tend to be distractible, however, and to have difficulty concentrating, then you should do your best to arrange your working environment so as to minimize distractions. In effect, you have to create an environment in which you can achieve your goals. If you do not, you will have difficulty in reaching them.

16. *Spreading oneself too thin or too thick.*    People with the tendency to spread themselves too thin need to recognize this tendency within themselves and to counteract it as necessary. People who spread themselves too thin sometimes find that they can get nothing done not because they don't work hard enough, but because they are making only little degrees of progress on each of the large number of projects they are pursuing. If you undertake multiple projects, it is important to stagger or otherwise arrange them so that you have a reasonable probability of finishing each of them in an acceptable amount of time.

Other people find themselves unable to undertake more than one or at most two things at a given time. This disposition is fine, so long as they can progress through the things they undertake with reasonable dispatch, and not miss opportunities that may present themselves. But undertaking too little at one time can result in missed opportunities and reduced levels of accomplishment. The important thing is to find the right distribution of activities for yourself, and then to maximize your performance within that distribution. Avoid undertaking either more or less than you can handle at a single time.

17. *Inability to delay gratification.*    Mentioned earlier are the people who always seem to be doing little things at the expense of big things. Some of these are people who simply procrastinate on big things, but others are people who are unable to delay gratification. They reward themselves and others reward them for finishing the little things, but they pass up the larger rewards that they could receive from doing bigger things. Any number of scientists and other scholars fail to undertake the really big projects that could make the critical difference in their careers or repeatedly write short articles instead of books because of their inability to delay the gratification that would come from the completion of a longer but more substantial project. Serious intellectual work occasionally requires one to delay gratification, sometimes for relatively long periods of time. Without the ability to achieve this delay, you may find yourself passing up the larger rewards that might otherwise await you at the end of the bigger projects.

18. *Inability or unwillingness to see the forest for the trees.*    I have worked with several students who have been intellectually very capable but who have been relatively unsuccessful in their careers as students because of their inability to see the forest for the trees: They obsess over small details, and are unwilling or unable to see or deal with the larger picture in the projects they undertake. They become so absorbed with the microstructure of whatever they undertake that they ignore or pay only the most minimal attention to the macrostructure. There are times and places where minutiae can become important. In designing computers or spacecraft or cars, for

example, even the most minor slips can become major when the product malfunctions. But in many aspects of life, it is necessary to concentrate on the big picture, or at least never to lose sight of it. It is very easy for students to become so bogged down in the day-to-day details of student life that they lose sight of the big picture. If this is happening to you, deliberately set aside time for thinking about large issues. Decide that during those times you will think about the meaning of what you are doing and where you wish it to lead you. Without such time, you may find yourself not only losing track of what your goals originally were but losing track as well of how what you are doing will help you reach those goals.

*19. Lack of balance between critical, analytic thinking and creative, synthetic thinking.*    There are times in life when we need to be critical and analytic; there are other times when we should be creative and synthetic. It is important to know which times are which. Some students seem frequently to make the wrong judgments on this matter. They complain bitterly that their teachers fail to recognize their creativity on objective, multiple-choice tests, or they complain that their teachers do not give them credit for how well organized, if uninspired, their papers are. Although these students may have good analytic and synthetic abilities, they don't know when to apply which ones. It is important to learn what kind of thinking is expected of you in different kinds of situations, and then to try to do the kind of thinking that is appropriate for the given situations. For example, standardized multiple-choice mental ability tests do not usually provide good opportunities in which to demonstrate creativity, unless they are explicitly designed to measure creativity. Research projects, on the other hand, are excellent opportunities to show your creativity. The point is that it is important not only to have both analytic and synthetic abilities, but to know when to use them.

*20. Too little or too much self-confidence.*    Everyone needs a hefty measure of self-confidence to get through life. There can be so many blows to our self-esteem and view of ourselves that without self-confidence, we are at the mercy of all the minor and major setbacks that continually will confront us. Lack of self-confidence seems to gnaw away at some people's ability to get things done well because they actually seem to realize in their work their own self-doubt: These self-doubts become self-fulfilling prophecies. Self-confidence is often essential for success. After all, if you do not have confidence in yourself, how can you expect others to?

At the same time, it is important not to have too much or misplaced self-confidence. As many students fail through too much self-confidence as through too little. Individuals with too much self-confidence do not know when to admit they are wrong or in need of self-improvement. As a result, they rarely improve as rapidly as they could.

To little or too much self-confidence can be especially damaging in job interviews. Applicants with too little self-confidence fail to inspire the confidence of those who might employ them. Their lack of self-confidence transfers to the potential employer, who also ends up not having confidence in them. Too much self-confidence can put people off, and lead to resentment and the desire to strike back—to tell the individual in some way that he or she is not so great as he or she thinks. Unfortunately, this striking back can occur in the form of a decision not to hire that person. It is important, here as elsewhere, to strike just the right balance between too little or too much of a good thing.

This chapter has described 20 potential stumbling blocks to the realization of your intellectual potential. The material in this chapter may seem only vaguely related to the topic of the book—understanding and increasing your intelligence—or may even seem moralistic. I gave serious thought as to whether to include such a chapter, but I decided to do so because I have seen so many people falter in the realization of their intellectual prowess. They have failed fully to adapt to, shape, or select their environments because of self-imposed obstacles that got in their way. It is easy, indeed, for those who wish to understand and develop the intellect to become "buried in thought." We must never lose sight of the fact that what really matters in the world is not the level of our intelligence, but what we achieve with this intelligence. Our ultimate goal in understanding and increasing our intelligence should be the full realization in our lives of the intellectual potential we each have within us.

# References

**Archer, D.** (1980). *How to expand your social intelligence quotient.* New York: M. Evans.

**Beck, A.** (1976). *Cognitive therapy and the emotional disorders.* New York: International Universities Press.

**Berg, C., & Sternberg, R. J.** (in press). A triarchic theory of adult intellectual development. *Developmental Review.*

**Binet, A., & Simon, T.** (1973). *Classics in psychology: The development of intelligence in children.* New York: Arno Press.

**Boring, E. G.** (1923, June 6). Intelligence as the tests test it. *New Republic,* 35–37.

**Brown, W., & Thomson, G. H.** (1921). *The essentials of mental measurement.* Cambridge, England: Cambridge University Press.

**Burt, C.** (1940). *The factors of the mind.* London: University of London Press.

**Butterfield, E. C., & Belmont, J. M.** (1977). Assessing and improving the cognition of mentally retarded people. In I. Bialer & M. Sternlicht (Eds.), *Psychology of mental retardation: Issues and approaches.* New York: Psychological Dimensions.

**Cattell, J. M.** (1890). Mental tests and measurements. *Mind, 15,* 373–380.

**Cattell, R. B.** (1971). *Abilities: Their structure, growth, and action.* Boston: Houghton Mifflin.

**Chapin, F. S.** (1967). *The social insight test.* Palo Alto, CA: Consulting Psychologists Press.

**Chase, W. G., & Simon, H. A.** (1973). The mind's eye in chess. In W. G. Chase (Ed.), *Visual information processing.* New York: Academic Press.

**Chi, M. T.** (1978). Knowledge structures and memory development. In R. S. Siegler (Ed.), *Children's thinking: What develops?* Hillsdale, NJ: Erlbaum.

**Cole, M., Gay, J., Glick, J., & Sharp, D. W.** (1971). *The cultural context of learning and thinking.* New York: Basic Books.

**Copi, I.** (1978). *Introduction to logic* (5th ed.). New York: Macmillan.

**Darwin, C.** (1872). *Origin of species* (6th ed.). London: Murray.

**Davidson, J. E. & Sternberg, R. J.** (1984). The role of insight in intellectual giftedness. *Gifted Child Quarterly, 28,* 58–64.

**Donders, F. C.** (1868–1869). Over de snelheid van psychische processen. Onderzoekingen gedaan in het Physiologisch Laboratorium der Utrechtsche Hoogeschool. *Tweede Reeks, 2.*

**Dweck, C., & Elliot, E.** (1983). Achievement motivation. In P. Mussen (Series Ed.) & M. Hetherington (Volume Ed.), *Handbook of child psychology* (Vol. 4). New York: Wiley.

**Edgerton, R.** (1967). *The cloak of competence.* Berkeley: University of California Press.

**Estes, W. K.** (1982). Learning, memory, and intelligence. In R. J. Sternberg (Ed.), *Handbook of human intelligence.* New York: Cambridge University Press.

**Feldman, R. D.** (1982). *Whatever happened to the quiz kids?* Chicago: Chicago Review Press.

**Ferguson, G. A.** (1956). On transfer and the abilities of man. *Canadian Journal of Psychology, 10,* 121–131.

**Feuerstein. R.** (1980). *Instrumental enrichment: An intervention program for cognitive modifiability.* Baltimore: University Park Press.

**Frederiksen, N.** (1962). Factors in in-basket performance. *Psychological Monographs, 71,* (9, Whole No. 438).

**Galton, F.** (1883). *Inquiry into human faculty and its development.* London: Macmillan.

**Ghiselli, E. E.** (1966). *The validity of occupational aptitude tests.* New York: Wiley.

**Goldin, S. E., & Hayes-Roth, B.** (1980, June). *Individual differences in planning processes.* (Rand Technical Report No. N-1488-ONR).

**Guilford, J. P.** (1967). *The nature of human intelligence.* New York: McGraw-Hill.

**Guthrie, E. R.** (1935). *The psychology of learning.* New York: Harper & Row.

**Hayes, J. R., & Simon, H. A.** (1976). The understanding process: Problem isomorphs. *Cognitive Psychology, 8,* 165–190.

**Heath, S.** (1983). *Ways with words.* New York: Cambridge University Press.

**Horn, J. L.** (1968). Organization of abilities and the development of intelligence. *Psychological Review, 75*, 242–259.

**Hunt, E. B.** (1980). Intelligence as an information-processing concept. *British Journal of Psychology, 71*, 449–474.

**Hunt, E. B., & Davidson, J. E.** (1981). *Age effects on sentence verification strategies.* Paper presented at the annual meeting of the Psychonomic Society, Philadelphia.

**Hunt, E. B., & Lansman, M.** (1982). Individual differences in attention. In R. J. Sternberg (Ed.), *Advances in the psychology of human intelligence* (Vol. 1). Hillsdale, NJ: Erlbaum.

**Hunt, E. B., Lunneborg, C., & Lewis, J.** (1975). What does it mean to be high verbal? *Cognitive Psychology, 7*, 194–227.

Intelligence and its measurement: A symposium. (1921). *Journal of Educational Psychology, 12*, 123–147, 195–216, 271–275.

**Jackson, M. D., & McClelland, J. L.** (1979). Processing determinants of reading speed. *Journal of Experimental Psychology: General, 108*, 151–181.

**Janis, I. L., & Mann, L.** (1977). *Decision making: A psychological analysis of conflict, choice, and commitment.* New York: Free Press.

**Jensen, A. R.** (1969). How much can we boost IQ and scholastic achievement? *Harvard Educational Review, 39*, 1–123.

**Jensen, A. R.** (1982). Reaction time and psychometric g. In H. J. Eysenck (Ed.), *A model for intelligence.* Heidelberg: Springer-Verlag.

**Keating, D.** (1982). The emperor's new clothes: The "new look" in intelligence research. In R. J. Sternberg (Ed.), *Advances in the psychology of human intelligence* (Vol 2). Hillsdale, NJ: Erlbaum.

**Langer, E.** (1978). Rethinking the role of thought in social interaction. In J. Harvey, W. Ickes, & R. Kidd (Eds.), *New directions in attribution research.* Hillsdale, NJ: Erlbaum.

**Lemmon, V. W.** (1927). The relation of reaction time to measures of intelligence, memory, and learning. *Archives of Psychology, 15*, 5–38.

**Linville, P. W.** (1982). The complexity-extremity effect and age-based stereotyping. *Journal of Personality and Social Psychology, 42*, 198–211.

**Lipman, M., Sharp, A. M., & Oscanyan, F. S.** (1980). *Philosophy in the classroom* (2nd ed.). Philadelphia: Temple University Press.

**Lunneborg, C.** (1977). Choice reaction time: What role in ability measurement? *Applied Psychological Measurement, 1*, 309–330.

**MacLeod, C. M., Hunt, E. B., & Mathews, N. N.** (1978). Individual differences in the verification of sentence-picture relationships. *Journal of Verbal Learning and Verbal Behavior, 17*, 493–507.

**Markman, E. M.** (1979). Realizing that you don't understand: Elementary school children's awareness of inconsistencies. *Child Development, 50*, 643–655.

**Miller, G. A., Galanter, E., & Pribram, K.** (1960). *Plans and the structure of behavior.* New York: Holt.

**Moss, F. A., Hunt, T., Omwake, K. T., & Woodward, L. G.** (1949). *Social intelligence test, George Washington University Series.* Washington, DC: Center for Psychological Service.

**Neisser, U.** (1979). The concept of intelligence. *Intelligence, 3*, 217–227.

**Newell, A., Shaw, J. C., & Simon, H. A.** (1958). Elements of a theory of human problem solving. *Psychological Review, 65*, 151–166.

**Nolen-Hoeksema, S., & Sternberg, R. J.** (1983). *Test of informal reasoning.* Unpublished document.

**Pellegrino, J. W., & Glaser, R.** (1982). Analyzing aptitudes for learning: Inductive reasoning. In R. Glaser (Ed.), *Advances in instructional psychology* (Vol 2). Hillsdale, NJ: Erlbaum.

**Perfetti, C. A., & Lesgold, A. M.** (1977). Discourse comprehension and individual differences. In P. Carpenter & M. Just (Eds.), *Cognitive processes in comprehension: The 12th annual Carnegie symposium on cognition.* Hillsdale, NJ: Erlbaum.

**Perkins, D. N.** (1981). *The mind's best work.* Cambridge, MA: Harvard University Press.

**Piaget, J.** (1972). *The psychology of intelligence.* Totowa, NJ: Littlefield, Adams.

**Posner, M. I., & Mitchell, R. F.** (1967). Chronometric analysis of classification. *Psychological Review, 74*, 392–409.

**Raaheim, K.** (1974). *Problem solving and intelligence*. Oslo: Universitetsforlaget.

**Robinson, R.** (1950. *Definition*. Oxford: Oxford University Press.

**Rosenthal, R., Hall, J. A., DiMatteo, M. R., Rogers, P. L., & Archer, D.** (1979) *Sensitivity to nonverbal communication: The PONS test*. Baltimore: Johns Hopkins University Press.

**Schneider, W.** (1982). *Automatic/control processing concepts and their implications for the training of skills* (Final Report HARL-ONR-8101). Champaign, IL: University of Illinois, Department of Psychology.

**Schneider, W., & Shiffrin, R.** (1977). Controlled and automated human information processing I. Detection, search, and attention. *Psychological Review, 84*, 1–66.

**Siegler, R. S., & Richards, D. D.** (1982). The development of intelligence. In R. J. Sternberg (Ed.), *Handbook of human intelligence*. New York: Cambridge University Press.

**Simon, H. A.** (1957). *Administrative behavior*. New York: Free Press.

**Simon, H. A., & Reed, S. K.** (1976). Modeling strategy shifts in a problem-solving task. *Cognitive Psychology, 8*, 86–97.

**Snow, R. E.** (1979). Theory and method for research on aptitude processes. In R. J. Sternberg & D. K. Detterman (Eds.), *Human intelligence: Perspectives on its theory and measurement*. Norwood, NJ: Ablex.

**Spearman, C.** (1904). General intelligence, objectively determined and measured. *American Journal of Psychology, 15*, 201–293.

**Spearman, C.** (1923). *The nature of 'intelligence' and the principles of cognition*. London: Macmillan.

**Stenhouse, D.** (1973). *The evolution of intelligence: A general theory and some of its implications*. New York: Harper & Row.

**Sternberg, R. J.** (1981). Intelligence and nonentrenchment. *Journal of Educational Psychology, 73*, 1–16.

**Sternberg, R. J.** (1985). *Beyond IQ: A triarchic theory of human intelligence*. New York: Cambridge University Press.

**Sternberg, R. J., Conway, B. E., Ketron, J. L., & Bernstein, M.** (1981). People's conceptions of intelligence. *Journal of Personality and Social Psychology, 41*, 37–55.

**Sternberg, R. J., & Gardner, M. K.** (1983). Unities in inductive reasoning. *Journal of Experimental Psychology: General, 112*, 80–116.

**Sternberg, R. J., & Rifkin, B.** (1979). The development of analogical reasoning processes. *Journal of Experimental Child Psychology, 27*, 195–232.

**Sternberg, R. J., & Rodriguez-Lansberg, M.** (1984). *Venezuelan conceptions of intelligence*. Manuscript in preparation.

**Sternberg, R. J., & Smith, C.** (1985). Social intelligence and decoding skills in nonverbal communication. *Social Cognition, 2*, 168–192.

**Sternberg, R. J., & Soriano, L. J.** (1984). Styles of conflict resolution. *Journal of Personality and Social Psychology, 47*, 115–126.

**Sternberg, R. J., & Weil, E. M.** (1980). An aptitude-strategy interaction in linear syllogistic reasoning. *Journal of Educational Psychology, 72*, 226–234.

**Sternberg, S.** (1969). Memory-scanning: Mental processes revealed by reaction-time experiments. *American Scientist, 4*, 421–457.

**Thomson, G. H.** (1939). *The factorial analysis of human ability*. London: University of London Press.

**Thorndike, E. L.** (1924). The measurement of intelligence. Present status. *Psychological Review, 31*, 219–252.

**Thorndike, E. L., Bregman, E. O., Cobb, M. V., & Woodyard, E. I.** (1926). *The measurement of intelligence*. New York: Harcourt Brace Jovanovich.

**Thurstone, L. L.** (1924). *The nature of intelligence*. New York: Harcourt Brace Jovanovich.

**Thurstone, L. L.** (1938). *Primary mental abilities*. Chicago: University of Chicago Press.

**Thurstone, L. L.** (1947). *Multiple factor analysis*. Chicago: University of Chicago Press.

**Tversky, A., & Kahneman, D.** (1974). Judgment under uncertainty: Heuristics and biases. *Science, 185*, 1124–1131.

**Vernon, P. E.** (1971). *The structure of human abilities*. London: Methuen.

**Wagner, R. K., & Sternberg, R. J.** (in press). Executive processes in reading. In B. Britton (Ed.), *Executive control processes in reading*. Hillsdale, NJ: Erlbaum.

**Wagner, R. K., & Sternberg, R. J.** (1985). Practical intelligence in real-world pursuits: The role of tacit knowledge. *Journal of Personality and Social Psychology, 49*, 436–458.

**Watson, J. B.** (1930). *Behaviorism* (rev. ed.). New York: Norton.

**Wechsler, D.** (1958). *The measurement and appraisal of adult intelligence.* Baltimore: Williams & Wilkins.

**Willis, S., Schaie, K. W., & Lueers, N.** (1982). *Fluid-crystallized correlates of real-life tasks.* Unpublished manuscript.

**Wissler, C.** (1901). The correlation of mental and physical tests. *Psychological Review, Monograph Supplement, 3*, (6).

**Wober, M.** (1974). Towards an understanding of the Kiganda concept of intelligence. In J. W. Berry & P. R. Dasen (Eds.), *Culture and cognition: Readings in cross-cultural psychology.* London: Methuen.

**Yussen, S. R., & Kane P.** (in press). Children's concept of intelligence. In S. R. Yussen (Ed.), *The growth of reflection in children.* New York: Academic Press.

# Annotated Bibliography

**Adams, J. L.** (1974). *Conceptual blockbusting: A guide to better ideas.* San Francisco: Freeman.
  A useful guide for solving the complex problems one faces in everyday life.

**Baron, J.** (1985). *Rationality and intelligence.* New York: Cambridge University Press.
  A new view of intelligence based on rational thinking.

**Berry, J. W.** (1974). Radical cultural relativism and the concept of intelligence. In J. W. Berry & P. R. Dasen (Eds.), *Culture and cognition: Readings in cross-cultural psychology.* London: Methuen.
  A classic paper on the radical contextualist view of intelligence, which presents intelligence as a completely relativistic concept.

**Binet, A., & Simon, T.** (1973). *Classics in psychology: The development of intelligence in children.* New York: Arno Press.
  The best introduction to Alfred Binet's theory of intelligence, which served as the basis for the Stanford-Binet Intelligence Scale.

**Boring, E. G.** (1923, June 6). Intelligence as the tests test it. *New Republic,* 35–37.
  The original statement of the view that intelligence is what intelligence tests test.

**Campione, J. C., & Brown, A. L.** (1979). Toward a theory of intelligence: Contributions from research with retarded children. In R. J. Sternberg & D. K. Detterman (Eds.), *Human intelligence: Perspectives on its theory and measurement.* Norwood, NJ: Ablex.
  An introduction to Campione and Brown's information-processing theory of intelligence based on research with retarded children.

**Carroll, J. B.** (1976). Psychometric tests as cognitive tasks: A new "structure of intellect." In L. B. Resnick (Ed.), *The nature of intelligence.* Hillsdale, NJ: Erlbaum.
  A classic paper on the foundations of the information-processing approach to intelligence.

**Cattell, R. B.** (1971). *Abilities: Their structure, growth, and action.* Boston: Houghton Mifflin.
  This most comprehensive single presentation of Cattell's psychometric theory of intelligence defines two major subfactors of general intelligence: fluid and crystallized abilities.

**Charlesworth, W. R.** (1979). An ethological approach to studying intelligence. *Human Development, 22,* 212–216.
  A lucid and useful primer to a contextual view of intelligence deriving from ethology (the study of animal behavior and how it compares across species).

**Chipman, S., Segal, J., & Glaser, R.** (Eds.). (1984). *Thinking and learning skills: Current research and open questions* (2 vols.). Hillsdale, NJ: Erlbaum.
  A large collection of papers that describes and evaluates the strengths and weaknesses of current programs for training intelligence.

**Covington, M. V., Crutchfield, R. S., Davies, L., & Olton, R. M.** (1974). *The productive thinking program: A course in learning to think.* Columbus, OH: Merrill.
  A description of the Productive Thinking Program, widely used for the training of thinking skills.

**Cronbach, L. J.** (1984). *Essentials of psychological testing* (4th ed.). New York: Harper & Row.
  An excellent introduction to the principles and practices of intelligence and testing methods.

**Cronbach, L. J.** (1957). The two disciplines of scientific psychology. *American Psychologist, 12,* 671–684.
  In this classic paper Cronbach becomes the first to call for an integration of the correlational and experimental methodologies used in studying, among other things, intelligence.

**Cronbach, L. J., & Snow, R. E.** (1977). *Aptitudes and instructional methods.* New York: Irvington.
  The best and most comprehensive single account of the relations between patterns of aptitude and optimal instructional methods.

**DeBono, E.** (1983). The direct teaching of thinking as a skill. *Phi Delta Kappan, 64,* 703–708.
  An introduction to DeBono's views regarding the training of thinking skills.

**Detterman, D. K., & Sternberg, R. J.** (Eds.). (1982). *How and how much can intelligence be increased?* Norwood, NJ: Ablex.
  A collection of papers on programs for increasing intelligence.

**Eysenck, H. J.** (Ed.). (1982). *A model for intelligence.* Heidelberg: Springer-Verlag.
This collection of papers examines the nature of intelligence and emphasizes the importance of mental speed in intelligence.

**Feuerstein, R.** (1980). *Instrumental enrichment: An intervention program for cognitive modifiability.* Baltimore: University Park Press.
A thorough description of Feuerstein's important Instrumental Enrichment program for training intellectual skills.

**Gardner, H.** (1983). *Frames of mind: The theory of multiple intelligence.* New York: Basic Books.
Howard Gardner describes his theory of multiple intelligences.

**Guilford, J. P.** (1967). *The nature of human intelligence.* New York: McGraw-Hill.
Guilford presents the structure-of-intellect model, a widely cited psychometric theory of intelligence.

**Hayes, J. R.** (1981). *The complete problem solver.* Philadelphia: Franklin Institute Press.
A useful course covering a wide range of problem-solving skills.

**Horn, J. L.** (1968). Organization of abilities and the development of intelligence. *Psychological Review, 75,* 242–259.
Horn discusses the life-span development of fluid and crystallized abilities.

**Hunt, E. B.** (1980). Intelligence as an information-processing concept. *British Journal of Psychology, 71,* 449–474.
An exposition of Hunt's important information-processing theory of intelligence.

Intelligence and its measurement: A symposium. (1921). *Journal of Educational Psychology, 12,* 123–147, 195–216, 271–275.
The first major collection of papers seeking to define intelligence.

**Jacobs, P. I.** (1977). *Up the IQ!* New York: Wyden Press.
A series of exercises designed to improve matrix problem-solving skills.

**Jensen, A. R.** (1969). How much can we boost IQ and scholastic achievement? *Harvard Educational Review, 39,* 1–123.
A famous paper in which Jensen discusses why he is pessimistic about the possibility of increasing intelligence through training.

**Jensen, A. R.** (1980). *Bias in mental testing.* New York: Free Press.
In this well-known treatment of test bias, Jensen claims that intelligence tests in general are not biased against subgroups, and he presents his information-processing theory of intelligence.

**Jones, B. F.** (1982). *Chicago mastery learning: Reading* (2nd ed.). Watertown, MA: Mastery Education Corporation.
The Chicago program for the training of reading and learning skills.

**Lipman, M., Sharp, A. M., & Oscanyan, F. S.** (1980). *Philosophy in the classroom* (2nd ed.). Philadelphia: Temple University Press.
An introduction to the principles behind Lipman's Philosophy for Children program, designed to train thinking skills.

**Matarazzo, J. D.** (1972). *Wechsler's measurement and appraisal of adult intelligence* (5th ed.). Baltimore: Williams & Wilkins.
An exposition of David Wechsler's theory of intelligence and the basic nature of the Wechsler Adult Intelligence Scale.

**McClelland, D. C.** (1973). Testing for competence rather than for "intelligence." *American Psychologist, 28,* 1–14.
McClelland's classic paper in which he argues that conventional intelligence tests define intelligence and competence too narrowly.

**Meirovitz, M., & Jacobs, P. I.** (1983). *Brain muscle builders: Games to increase your natural intelligence.* Englewood Cliffs, NJ: Prentice-Hall.
A set of games to improve thinking skills.

**Neisser, U.** (1979). The concept of intelligence. *Intelligence, 3,* 217–227.
The presentation of a view that intelligence is a "prototype" or family-resemblance concept that we create for ourselves.

**Nickerson, R. S., Perkins, D. N., & Smith, E. E.** (1985). *Teaching thinking.* Hillsdale, NJ: Erlbaum.
The most thorough available review of programs for training thinking skills.

**Pellegrino, J. W., & Glaser, R.** (1980). Components of inductive reasoning. In R. E. Snow, P. A. Federico, W. Montague (Eds.), *Aptitude, learning, and instruction: Cognitive process analyses of aptitude* (Vol. 1). Hillsdale, NJ: Erlbaum.
> An introduction to Pellegrino and Glaser's information-processing view of inductive reasoning, an important aspect of intelligence.

**Perkins, D. N.** (1981). *The mind's best work.* Cambridge, MA: Harvard University Press.
> A fascinating description of research on creativity and giftedness.

**Piaget, J.** (1972). *The psychology of intelligence.* Totowa, NJ: Littlefield, Adams.
> Piaget presents his theory of intelligence.

**Resnick, L. B.** (Ed.). (1976). *The nature of intelligence.* Hillsdale, NJ: Erlbaum.
> The first major collection of papers on the information-processing approach to intelligence.

**Snow, R. E.** (1980). Aptitude processes. In R. E. Snow, P. A. Federico, & W. Montague (Eds.), *Aptitude, learning, and instruction: Cognitive process analyses of aptitude* (Vol. 1). Hillsdale, NJ: Erlbaum.
> Snow's information-processing view of intelligence is presented.

**Spearman, C.** (1927). *The abilities of man.* New York: Macmillan.
> A classic book on Spearman's "two-factor" psychometric theory of intelligence.

**Sternberg, R. J.** (1977). *Intelligence, information processing, and analogical reasoning: The componential analysis of human abilities.* Hillsdale, NJ: Erlbaum.
> A description of Sternberg's componential theory of intelligence.

**Sternberg, R. J.** (Ed.). (1982, 1984). *Advances in the psychology of human intelligence* (Vols. 1 & 2). Hillsdale, NJ: Erlbaum.
> Two collections of papers that examine contemporary views of human intelligence and research programs for studying it.

**Sternberg, R. J.** (Ed.). (1982). *Handbook of human intelligence.* New York: Cambridge University Press.
> A comprehensive collection of papers on human intelligence.

**Sternberg, R. J.** (1985). *Beyond IQ: A triarchic theory of human intelligence.* New York: Cambridge University Press.
> Sternberg presents his triarchic theory of intelligence.

**Sternberg, R. J.** (Ed.) (1984). *Human abilities: An information-processing approach.* New York: Freeman.
> An introduction to the information-processing approach to human abilities.

**Sternberg, R. J., & Detterman, D. K.** (Eds.) (1979). *Human intelligence: Perspectives on its theory and measurement.* Norwood, NJ: Ablex.
> A collection of papers on information-processing approaches to intelligence and intelligence testing.

**Thurstone, L. L.** (1938). *Primary mental abilities.* Chicago: University of Chicago Press.
> Thurstone's theory of primary mental abilities is presented.

**Vernon, P. E.** (1971). *The structure of human abilities.* London: Methuen.
> Vernon describes a hierarchical theory of intelligence.

**Wagner, R. K., & Sternberg, R. J.** (1984). Alternative conceptions of intelligence and their implications for education. *Review of Educational Research, 54,* 197–224.
> A review of theories of and programs for training intelligence.

**Whimbey, A., & Lochhead, J.** (1979). *Problem solving and comprehension: A short course in analytic reasoning.* Philadelphia: Franklin Institute Press.
> A course in analytical reasoning, emphasizing logical-mathematical skills.

**Whimbey, A., with Whimbey, L. S.** (1975). *Intelligence can be taught.* New York: E. P. Dutton.
> An early and well-known book that argues that intelligence can be improved through training and provides some training of intellectual skills.

**Wickelgren, W.** (1974). *How to solve problems: Elements of a theory of problems and problem solving.* San Francisco: Freeman.
> A course in how to solve complex problems.

# Index